GURŪ NĀNAK
AND THE
SIKH RELIGION

GURŪ NĀNAK
AND THE
SIKH RELIGION

W. H. McLEOD

OXFORD
AT THE CLARENDON PRESS
1968

Oxford University Press, Ely House, London W. 1

GLASGOW NEW YORK TORONTO MELBOURNE WELLINGTON
CAPE TOWN SALISBURY IBADAN NAIROBI LUSAKA ADDIS ABABA
BOMBAY CALCUTTA MADRAS KARACHI LAHORE DACCA
KUALA LUMPUR HONG KONG TOKYO

PRINTED IN GREAT BRITAIN

To

PROFESSOR A. L. BASHAM

in gratitude

ਤਿਨ ਬੇਦੀਅਨ ਕੇ ਕੁਲ ਬਿਖੇ ਪ੍ਰਗਟੇ ਨਾਨਕ ਰਾਇ ॥
ਸਭ ਸਿੱਖਨ ਕੋ ਸੁਖ ਦਏ ਜੱਹ ਤੱਹ ਭਏ ਸਹਾਇ ॥
ਤਿਨ ਇਹ ਕਲ ਮੋ ਧਰਮੁ ਚਲਾਇਓ ॥
ਸਭ ਸਾਧਨ ਕੋ ਰਾਹੁ ਬਤਾਇਓ ॥
ਜੇ ਤਾਕੇ ਮਾਰਗਿ ਮਹਿ ਆਏ ॥
ਤੇ ਕਬਹੂੰ ਨਹੀ ਪਾਪ ਸੰਤਾਏ ॥
ਜੇ ਜੇ ਪੰਥ ਤਵਨ ਕੇ ਪਰੇ ॥
ਪਾਪ ਤਾਪ ਤਿਨ ਕੇ ਪ੍ਰਭ ਹਰੇ ॥
ਦੂਖ ਭੂਖ ਕਬਹੂੰ ਨ ਸੰਤਾਏ ॥
ਜਾਲ ਕਾਲ ਕੇ ਬੀਚ ਨ ਆਏ ॥

—ਬਚਿੱਤਰ ਨਾਟਕ, ੫ : ੪–੬

PREFACE

For no one is the injunction to tread softly more relevant than for the historian whose study carries him into regions beyond his own society. Should his study extend to what other men hold sacred the injunction becomes a compelling necessity. For this reason the westerner who ventures upon a study of Sikh history must do so with caution and almost inevitably with a measure of trepidation. In such a field the risk of giving offence is only too obvious.

This risk may perhaps be minimized if we state at the outset the meaning which the title of the book is intended to communicate and the methodology upon which this study is based. It should not be assumed that this book is intended to be, in any direct sense, a study of the faith of modern Sikhs. The book is a study of the man Gurū Nānak. A reference to the Sikh religion has been included in the title because the adherents of that religion quite rightly regard Gurū Nānak as a determinative formulator of the beliefs which have ever since constituted the primary basis of the Sikh religion. For this reason a study of Gurū Nānak must inevitably involve a study of the Sikh religion in its primitive form. The emphasis has, however, been laid upon the man Gurū Nānak. This study is intended to discharge a three-fold task. In the first place it seeks to apply rigorous historical methodology to the traditions concerning the life of Gurū Nānak; secondly, it attempts to provide a systematic statement of his teachings; and thirdly, it endeavours to fuse the glimpses provided by the traditional biographies with the personality emerging from the teachings.

The sources which have been used for the first of these tasks are the hagiographic accounts called 'janam-sākhīs'. A cursory reading at once reveals the unreliable nature of these works as records of the actual life of the Gurū, but they constitute our only source of any importance and we are accordingly compelled to use them as best we can. In order to do so a number of criteria have been posited. These criteria are applied to individual *sākhīs*, or 'incidents', and in this manner a decision is reached concerning the extent to which any such *sākhī* can be accepted. It should be noted that the rejection of much contained in the janam-sākhīs should not imply that these works lack significance and that having rejected many of their traditions in the context of a study of Gurū Nānak we can afford to ignore them altogether. For an understanding of later Sikh history they retain a vital importance which has been obscured by the failure to detach them from the person of the historical Nānak. If, however, our subject is

Gurū Nānak, and if our method is historical, much that they contain must inevitably be rejected.

For the section dealing with the teachings of Gurū Nānak the methodology adopted is much simpler. The works attributed to Gurū Nānak in the *Ādi Granth* have been accepted as authentic and an effort has been made to gather into a systematic form the various beliefs which we find dispersed through his works. This can be done with relative ease, for it is clear that such a pattern was present in the mind of their author.

If we are to indicate a more general purpose beyond the three-fold task pursued in this study it could perhaps be expressed in terms of a quest for creative understanding. We are now beyond the stage where an understanding of one's own society can be accepted as sufficient. This study accordingly represents an initial attempt to know a people of unusual interest and ability. It is no more than a beginning, but it is a necessary beginning. An understanding of later Sikh history or of contemporary Sikh society requires a prior understanding of the man whom Sikhs own as their first Gurū.

As this study is largely based upon Pañjābī sources, words which are common to Pañjābī and other north Indian languages have almost all been transliterated in their Pañjābī forms (*śabad* instead of *śabda*, *gurū* instead of *guru*, etc.). The only exceptions to this rule are a few instances in which a Sanskrit or Hindī form has secured an established place in English usage (e.g. bhakti, *karma*). Transliterated forms have presented the usual problem of when to retain diacritics and when to dispense with them. In almost all cases the diacritics have been retained, the only exceptions being the names of modern authors and a few words which have acquired a standardized form in English usage. Except in quotations from other works the forms *ch* and *chh* have been used in preference to *c* and *ch* (*chitta*, not *citta*).

Almost all passages quoted from the *Ādi Granth* have been given in English translation only, and this pattern has also been followed in the case of quotations from other works in Pañjābī or Hindī. Many of the extracts from the *Ādi Granth* have been translated with some freedom in an effort to bring out their meanings with greater clarity. Bracketed portions indicate words which do not occur in the original but which have been inserted in order to give continuity to a translation. The translations are my own, but in the case of passages from the *Ādi Granth* extensive use has been made of the modern Pañjābī paraphrases provided in a number of vernacular commentaries. One of my great regrets will ever be that when dealing with the compositions of Gurū Nānak I can in no measure reproduce in English translation the beauty of the original utterance. My primary concern in such cases has been to produce an accurate translation and in numerous instances I have felt compelled to sacrifice felicity of style in the interests of exactness.

Except where otherwise indicated dates are all A.D. For all quotations from the *Ādi Granth* I have used the text printed in *Śabadārath Srī Gurū Granth Sāhib Jī*, a work which follows the standard *Ādi Granth* pagination. Attention is drawn to the three indexes. In addition to the General Index a Biographical Index and a Doctrinal Index have been provided.

This book represents a revised version of my thesis *The Life and Doctrine of Gurū Nānak* submitted for the degree of Doctor of Philosophy in the University of London, 1965. To my supervisor, Professor A. L. Basham, I owe a particular debt of gratitude and I take this opportunity of acknowledging it with warmest thanks. For assistance and encouragement I should also like to thank Dr. F. R. Allchin, Dr. John Carman, Dr. Ganda Singh, Dr. J. S. Grewal, Dr. Norvin Hein, Dr. Jodh Singh, Dr. R. S. McGregor, Dr. Maqbul Ahmad, Dr. V. L. Ménage, Dr. Niharranjan Ray, Professor Parkash Singh, Dr. Geoffrey Parrinder, Professor Pritam Singh, Dr. R. H. L. Slater, Dr. Wilfred Cantwell Smith, Dr. Charlotte Vaudeville, and Mr. John C. B. Webster. In fairness to them I must add that for opinions expressed in this book I alone am to be held responsible. I also acknowledge with thanks help received from the Principal and staff of Baring College, Batala; from various people associated with Punjabi University, Patiala; from the office staff of the Shiromani Gurdwara Prabandhak Committee, Amritsar; and from Messrs. Singh Brothers of Bazar Mai Sewan, Amritsar. Finally I should like to thank my wife for her sympathetic endurance.

Batala, 1967 W. H. McLEOD

CONTENTS

ABBREVIATIONS

AG	The *Ādi Granth*.
Aṣṭ	*aṣṭapadī*
Bālā JS	The *Bālā* janam-sākhī lithographed by Hāfaz Qutub Dīn of Lahore in A.D. 1871.
BG	The *Vārs* of Bhāī Gurdās.
BM	British Museum.
GR	The edition of the *Gyān-ratanāvalī* lithographed by Charāg Dīn and Sarāj Dīn, Lahore, A.D. 1891.
IOL	India Office Library
KG	*Kabīr-granthāvalī* (Pāras-nāth Tivārī edition).
Mih JS	*Miharbān Janam-sākhī* (*Pothī Sach-khaṇḍ*), edited by Kirpāl Siṅgh and Shamsher Siṅgh Ashok and published under the title *Janam-sākhī Srī Gurū Nānak Dev Jī*, Amritsar, 1962.
MK	Kāhn Siṅgh Nābhā, *Guruśabad Ratanākar Mahān Koś* (commonly referred to as the *Mahān Koś*), 2nd edition revised with Addendum, Patiala, 1960.
Pur JS	Vīr Siṅgh (ed.), *Purātan Janam-sākhī*, 5th edition, Amritsar, 1959.
S	Samvat, dating according to the Vikrama era.
SOAS	Library of the School of Oriental and African Studies, London.

With references from the *Ādi Granth* a number in brackets indicates the number of a stanza (*aṅk* or *pauṛī*). The designation (1R) indicates a reference from the *rahāu*, or refrain, of a hymn.

1

THE SETTING

SIKHISM is now almost five hundred years old. Gurū Nānak, acknowledged by Sikhs as the founder of their faith, was born in 1469 and the quincentenary of his birth is accordingly very near. The period is a comparatively brief one in the context of the history of religions, but it has been an eventful period and the product is a significant one. During the five centuries of its existence Sikhism has known persecution and triumph, decadence and reform. The result is a community with a high degree of ethnic homogeneity, a strong sense of loyalty to the Pañjāb, and above all a common allegiance to a religion of refined and noble quality.

In a strict sense there can be no such thing as a perceptible beginning to Sikh history, for like all religious systems Sikhism has antecedents which defy ultimate scrutiny. This should not, however, suggest that the Sikh people are necessarily mistaken in tracing their beginnings as a religious community to Gurū Nānak. In another sense it is entirely permissible to claim that Sikh history begins with Gurū Nānak. He did indeed receive an inheritance and its influence is abundantly evident in all his works, but it would be altogether mistaken to regard him as a mere mediator of other men's ideas. In his hands the inheritance was transformed. Moreover the pattern which was produced by this transformation has endured. There have been subsequent developments of considerable significance, but this same pattern has remained the core and essence of the continuing Sikh faith.

In this latter sense Sikh history begins with Gurū Nānak and continues for two centuries through a line of nine successors. This initial period, terminating with the death of Gurū Gobind Singh in 1708, is of fundamental importance, for it was during these first two centuries that most of the distinctive features of Sikhism as a religion took shape. Three key events took place during this period, each of them representing a decision made by a Gurū. The first was the formal appointment by Gurū Nānak of a successor to the leadership of the community which had gathered around him. The second was the compilation of a canonical scripture by Gurū Arjan, the fifth Gurū, in 1603–4. The third was the founding of the Khālsā by Gurū Gobind Singh in 1699. The first of these events established a regular, recognized succession within the new community and so provided an effective apostolic continuity in its leadership. The second enshrined in permanent form the teachings of the first five Gurūs soon after the original delivery of those teachings.[1] The third event provided a visible insignia and an explicit discipline which members of the community could renounce only at the cost of virtual excommunication.

The measure of cohesion and stability conferred upon the Sikh community by these three key events was further strengthened by a development which took place during the eighteenth century. Tradition records that Gurū Gobind Singh, immediately before his death, declared that with his departure the line of personal Gurūs would end and that thenceforth the function and authority of the Gurū would vest in the scripture (the *Ādi Granth*) and in the corporate community (the *Panth*, or K͟hālsā). The tradition that this came as a dying declaration from the tenth Gurū himself must be regarded with some doubt,[2] but the distinctive doctrine of the Gurū which it expresses certainly evolved in some manner and has been a concept of fundamental importance in subsequent Sikh history. It is clear that before the eighteenth century had run its course the Sikh community had come to accept the *Ādi Granth* as 'the manifest body of the Gurū', and to accord, at least in theory, a religious sanction to the corporate decisions of the K͟hālsā. It is the first aspect of this doctrine which has been of particular significance. A unique authority was thereby conferred upon the scripture compiled by Gurū Arjan and as a result the inner strength of the community was further consolidated.

The period of almost one hundred years which intervenes between the death of Gurū Gobind Singh and the emergence of Rañjīt Singh is an obscure one. The broad outline of Sikh military and political activity is known and has been recorded many times, but surprisingly little is known about the religious development of the period, and much remains to be done in terms of analysis of the military and political activity. After the death of Gurū Gobind Singh and the succeeding seven years of turmoil associated with the enigmatic figure of Bandā there followed a period of persecution during which the Mughal authorities in the Pañjāb sought to suppress the Sikhs and their religion. It was, however, Mughal authority which met destruction. Out of the confusion of this period, much of it wrought by the successive invasions of Ahmad Shāh Abdālī, there emerged the Sikh *misls*, groups of irregular troops owing primary allegiance to the chieftain of the group but united in a loose confederacy. Eventually one such chieftain, Rañjīt Singh of the Śukerchakīā *misl*, secured an indisputable ascendancy and with his success came the Sikhs' period of political and military triumph. The triumph was qualified by the activities of the British

[1] A number of compositions by the ninth Gurū, Tegh Bahādur, were subsequently added.

[2] J. S. Grewal and S. S. Bal, *Guru Gobind Singh*, Chandigarh, 1967, pp. 188–9. J. S. Grewal, 'The *Prem Sumarg*: a Theory of Sikh Social Order', in the *Proceedings of the First Session of the Punjab History Conference*, Patiala, 1966, p. 110.

on Rañjīt Singh's eastern frontier, but it was a considerable triumph nonetheless and one which still evokes an evident nostalgia.

The political and military successes were, however, accompanied by developments which a later revived Sikhism was to regard as serious deviations from the teachings of the Gurūs.[1] Rañjīt Singh himself provided an illustration in the deference which he showed towards brāhmaṇs, and at his death the rite of *satī* was performed by four queens and seven maidservants. It was this kind of custom which the Gurūs had sought to destroy.[2] During the years which followed the annexation of the Pañjāb by the British in 1849 these developments became even more pronounced.

> The Sikh religion was losing its characteristic vigour and its votaries were relapsing into beliefs and dogmas from which their new faith had extricated them. Absorption into ceremonial Hinduism seemed the course inevitably set for them.[3]

Sikhism was saved from this absorption by two of its distinctive features. The immutable scripture and the recognizable insignia, particularly the uncut hair, preserved it from irrevocable dissolution. When the reformers of the Singh Sabhā Movement began their activities towards the end of the century they had an objective standard to which they could appeal and they knew precisely to whom they should address the appeal. A religious revival followed and although much of the original religious impulse has run out into political sands the effects of the revival were nevertheless considerable and are in appreciable measure still evident today.

The present study takes us back to the very beginning of this period in the history of the Pañjāb and the history of religions. It concerns Gurū Nānak, the acknowledged founder of the Sikh religion and incomparably the greatest of the Gurūs in the shaping of that religion. The sixth Gurū, Hargobind, gave the community a new direction when he assumed military and quasi-political functions, and the conferring of the function of Gurū jointly upon the scripture and the community introduced a highly significant supplement, but the religious content of Sikhism remained, and still remains, the content given it by Gurū Nānak. For this reason the primary and by far the most important part of a study of the Sikh religion must be a study of the life and teachings of its first Gurū.

Gurū Nānak was born on the threshold of a momentous period in Indian history. In the course of his lifetime he witnessed the dominance and the decline of the Lodī Sultanate, and its final extinction by Bābur in 1526. It was not as a casual witness that he observed the events which brought the downfall of the Lodīs and its replacement by Mughal rule. In four of his compositions he comments on the Mughal invasions, interpreting the fall

[1] Teja Singh, *Sikhism: Its Ideals and Institutions*, pp. 86–87.

[2] Cf. Gurū Arjan, *Gauṛī Guārerī* 99, *AG*, p. 185. Gurū Gobind Siṅgh, *Akāl Ustati*, 84.

[3] Harbans Singh, *The Heritage of the Sikhs*, p. 129.

of the Sultanate as the due reward of Lodī unrighteousness.[1] The last eight years of his life were spent in a Pañjāb ruled by Kāmrān, the rebellious brother of Humāyūn. Little is known of this interlude in Pañjāb history and Gurū Nānak himself makes no apparent reference to it.

The birth of Gurū Nānak took place during the reign of Sultan Bahlūl Lodī (1451–89) and the formative years of his life accordingly coincided with the period of Lodī ascendancy under Bahlūl and his son Sikandar. This is a point of some significance in the context of a study of Gurū Nānak's life, for it means that he grew to maturity in a period of comparative peace and prosperity. It is true that the half-century preceding the accession of Sultan Bahlūl had been, for the Pañjāb, a time of political instability accompanied by widespread violence and suffering. The invasion of Tīmūr in 1398–9 brought much damage to the Pañjāb, and the years between 1421 and 1434 brought considerably more. These were the years of Jasrat Khokhar of Siālkoṭ, Faulād Turkbachchā of Bhaṭiṇḍā, and Sheikh 'Alī of Kābul, three agents of havoc and destruction who brought extensive disorder and suffering to the Pañjāb. The effect of their operations would have been even more serious had it not been for the energy and ability of Mubārak Shāh, the second of the Sayyid sultans of Delhi. The activities of these three adventurers have attracted much less attention than the spectacular career of Tīmūr, but in the Pañjāb they were responsible for far more suffering than their celebrated predecessor, for their depredations were spread over a much wider area and over a lengthier period of time.[2]

All this, however, would have been but an unpleasant memory during the years following the birth of Gurū Nānak. By 1469, the year of Gurū Nānak's birth, Bahlūl Lodī had established his authority, and the relative stability which he introduced was further strengthened by his son Sikandar. The praises heaped upon Sikandar Lodī by the Persian chroniclers of the period must be treated with considerable caution, but there is no apparent reason to doubt that his reign provided a period of comparative peace and prosperity. In the circumstances of the time a measure of prosperity would have been a natural development and Bābur seems to imply that it had in fact taken place.[3] A fertile soil, a favourable climate, a relatively limited population, and an appreciable measure of security would all have combined to produce this favourable economic condition. The district around Lahore was, and still is, particularly fertile.[4] Food and other necessities appear to have been readily available, manufactures were developing,

[1] See *infra*, pp. 135–8.

[2] Yāḥyā bin Aḥmad, *Tārīkh-i-Mubārak Shāhī* (trans. K. K. Basu), pp. 200–40. Nizāmuddīn Aḥmad, *Tabaqāt-i-Akbarī* (trans. B. De), vol. i, pp. 300–21. See also K. S. Lal, *Twilight of the Sultanate*, pp. 84–113, 121.

[3] A. S. Beveridge, *The Bābur-nāma in English*, vol. ii, p. 480.

[4] *Āīn-i-Akbarī* (trans. H. S. Jarrett), vol. ii, p. 312.

and there was a satisfactory trade balance.[1] Even during the period of Lodī decline under Sultan Ibrāhīm (1517–26) the stability of the Pañjāb appears to have been maintained by the governor, Daulat Khān Lodī, until the last three years of the Sultanate's existence.[2] It seems clear that Gurū Nānak was born into a favoured period, at least as far as security and economic conditions were concerned.

Our sources for the life of Gurū Nānak are, as we shall see, generally unreliable, but it is possible to set out with some assurance a brief outline of his life. He was born in 1469 and grew up in his father's village of Talvaṇḍī.[3] At some point in early manhood he moved to the town of Sultānpur[4] where he probably secured employment in the service of Daulat Khān Lodī. From Sultānpur he began a period of travels within and perhaps beyond India. At the conclusion of this period he settled in the village of Kartārpur on the right bank of the Rāvī river,[5] and it was there that he died, probably in the year 1539.

By the time he died Gurū Nānak had obviously gathered many disciples and within this following his numerous compositions were preserved. The point at which these compositions were committed to writing is not positively known, but it cannot have been long after his death and may well have been during his lifetime. A collection which included the works of Gurū Nānak was prepared at the instance of the third Gurū, Amar Dās, who occupied the office from 1552 until 1574, and this collection was subsequently used by Gurū Arjan when compiling the *Ādi Granth*.[6] The compositions attributed to Gurū Nānak which have been incorporated in the *Ādi Granth* are in an entirely different category from the material offered by the works which purport to record the events of his life. The *Ādi Granth* collection may be unhesitatingly accepted as authentic and consequently we have, in contrast with the paucity of reliable biographical material, ample access to his teachings.

The teachings of Gurū Nānak are dispersed throughout his numerous works, but from these dispersed elements it is possible to reconstruct a coherent theology. The basis of the theology is a belief in a personal God, the omnipotent Creator of the universe, a Being beyond time and human

[1] I. H. Qureshi, *The Administration of the Delhi Sultanate*, pp. 225–6.

[2] Daulat Khān Lodī was appointed governor of Lahore by Sultan Sikandar Lodī sometime between 1500 and 1504. The stability of the Pañjāb during his lengthy term as governor may be safely assumed from the almost total neglect of the Pañjāb by the Persian chroniclers. Serious disorders would have drawn action from the sultan and comment from the chroniclers. Daulat Khān remained governor of Lahore until Bābur's 1524 invasion.

[3] Rāi Bhoi dī Talvaṇḍī, approximately forty miles south-west of Lahore.

[4] Kapūrthalā District.

[5] Opposite the town of Dehrā Bābā Nānak.

[6] The collection commissioned by Gurū Amar Dās was prepared by his grandson Sahansrām. It consisted of two volumes and included the works of the first three Gurūs and of the *bhagats* (*MK*, p. 320 and Addendum, p. 44).

comprehending yet seeking by His grace the salvation of man and for this purpose revealing Himself in His own creation. To the offer of salvation man is called to respond by a life of meditation on the divine self-revelation and of conformity to it. If man responds he progressively grows into the likeness of God and ultimately into an ineffable union with the Timeless One. If he refuses he follows the path of spiritual death and remains firmly bound to the wheel of transmigration.

It is the author of this theology whom we seek, the greatest of the sons of the Pañjāb and the founder of the religion which continues to dominate the attitudes and beliefs of contemporary Pañjāb. We are here engaged in a quest for the historical Nānak, for there is a Nānak of both legend and faith as well as a Nānak of history. It is a quest which must take us to the traditional biographies and to the collection of his works preserved in the *Ādi Granth*. In many places, and indeed in practically all that we find in the traditional biographies, the search must yield disappointing results, but it is a search which should nevertheless be made. Gurū Nānak is too important to be ignored. Without some understanding of him and of his teachings one can understand neither the Sikh religion nor the Pañjāb of today.

2

THE SOURCES

The Ādi Granth

THE obvious place to seek information concerning the life of Gurū Nānak is the *Ādi Granth*, or *Gurū Granth Sāhib*, the scripture compiled by Gurū Arjan in 1603–4. It is the obvious place as it contains numerous works by Gurū Nānak which can safely be accepted as authentic. In this respect, however, the *Ādi Granth* offers an initial disappointment, for it provides us with surprisingly little information concerning the actual events of his life. It contains more than nine hundred of his compositions and yet the biographical details which may be extracted from them are negligible. Indeed, there is no explicit reference at all to any incident in his life, no *śabad* or *ślok*[1] which points unmistakably to an event in which he was directly involved. Even the famous references to Bābur, the so-called *Bābar-vāṇī*, are not exceptions to this rule. They do indicate that Gurū Nānak witnessed something of Bābur's depredations, but if read apart from the traditional biographies (the janam-sākhīs) they do not necessarily point to his presence at the sack of Saidpur.

As far as biographical detail is concerned the most we can do is draw some limited conclusions from the more obvious hints which Gurū Nānak's writings contain. In the case of the *Bābar-vāṇī* we may confidently assume that he witnessed something of the devastation caused by Bābur's army and that accordingly he was in the Pañjāb during at least one of Bābur's incursions into North India. In the same manner we may deduce with confidence that he had frequent contact with Nāth yogīs. The extensive use of their terminology and the frequent instances in which a yogī appears to be addressed makes this aspect of his life perfectly plain. None of these conclusions can, however, take us far in our effort to reconstruct the actual events of Gurū Nānak's life. They are certainly of value, but their scope is obviously very limited.

[1] *śabad* or *śabda*: literary 'word'. In Sikh usage it designates both the divine 'Word' received from God, and the expression of that Word in a hymn or song of praise. In the latter sense it corresponds to the Hindi word *pad*.

ślok: couplet or stanza. Most of Gurū Nānak's *śloks* are incorporated in the composite *vārs* of the *Ādi Granth*. These *vārs* consist of a series of stanzas (*pauṛīs*) each of which is preceded by two or more *śloks*. Some of Gurū Nānak's *śloks* are couplets, but most are stanzas in their own right.

Gurū Nānak himself tells us very little and his four successors, whose works are also recorded in the *Ādi Granth*, add nothing of any importance. Gurū Aṅgad and Gurū Arjan both refer to him,[1] but their references are eulogistic comments, entirely appropriate in their contexts but telling us nothing about Gurū Nānak himself. The same applies to the *savayyās* of the *bhaṭṭs*.[2] Gurū Nānak is mentioned several times,[3] but as one would expect from the nature of the *savayyās* the references are of the same kind as those provided by Gurū Aṅgad and Gurū Arjan. The only work which offers any detail at all is the *Vār* in Rāg Rāmakalī by the *bhaṭṭs* Rāi Balvaṇḍ and Sattā the Ḍūm. In the first four stanzas the authors repeat a single fact, namely that Gurū Nānak appointed Aṅgad as his successor.[4]

As we shall see, the *Ādi Granth* does offer much that is relevant to our biographical concern, but its contribution to our knowledge of the actual events of Gurū Nānak's life is slight. For these we are compelled to resort to our only other available source, the traditional biographies called 'janam-sākhīs'.

The janam-sākhīs

The janam-sākhīs[5] are hagiographic accounts of the life of Gurū Nānak, each consisting of a series of separate incidents, or chapters, entitled *sākhīs* or *goṣṭs*. Although these incidents are normally linked in a chronological sequence the order is frequently erratic and in a few cases it is totally absent. The script used for all the important janam-sākhīs is Gurmukhī, but the language may be either Pañjābī or the composite dialect called *Sādhukkaṛī* or *Sant Bhāṣā*.[6]

These janam-sākhīs are also highly unsatisfactory sources, but for an entirely different reason. Here there is no question of material being in short supply, for the janam-sākhīs provide it in abundance. The problem as far as the janam-sākhīs are concerned is to determine how much of their material can be accepted as historical. A very substantial proportion of it is obviously legend and much of what cannot be summarily dismissed in this way is open to grave suspicion on other grounds. In a number of cases,

[1] Gurū Aṅgad: *Vār Mājh*, *ślok* 1 of *pauṛī* 27, *AG*, p. 150.
Gurū Arjan: *Soraṭhi* 13 and 14, *AG*, p. 612; *Mārū* 10, *AG*, p. 1001; *Basant Dutukiā* 1, *AG*, p. 1192. *Mājh*, *Soraṭhi*, *Mārū*, and *Basant* are four of the *rāgs*, or metres, to which the hymns of the *Ādi Granth* are set.

[2] Panegyrics of the bards. The *bhaṭṭs*, or bards, whose *savayyās* have been included in the *Ādi Granth* were contemporaries of Gurū Arjan.

[3] Rāi Balvaṇḍ and Sattā the Ḍūm: *Vār Rāmakalī* (1–2), *AG*, p. 966. Kal the Poet: *Savayye Mahale Pahile ke* (7), *AG*, p. 1390; *Savayye Mahale Tīje ke* (1) *AG*, p. 1392; *Savayye Mahale Chauthe ke* (12), *AG*, p. 1398. Nal the Poet: *Savayye Mahale Chauthe ke* (4), *AG*, p. 1399. There is also a mention of his name in the *Sadu* of Sundar, *AG*, p. 923.

[4] loc. cit., *AG*, pp. 966–7.

[5] Literally 'birth-evidences', or 'evidences of his life'.

[6] See *infra*, p. 153.

however, there is an evident possibility that some historical fact may lie beneath a superstructure of legend. Not all of these possibilities can be satisfactorily tested, but our task must be to examine them all and wherever possible to affirm or reject them.

This must be our method for there is no other way in which a reconstruction of the events of Gurū Nānak's life can be attempted. In spite of their manifest shortcomings we are bound to rely on the janam-sākhīs for almost all of our information concerning these events, for there is nothing to replace them and little to supplement them. There is no piece of external evidence which can be accorded complete trust and, as we have already noted, such indications as his own works contain are at best only hints.

References to Gurū Nānak may be found in other works, but none of these carry us beyond the janam-sākhīs. The *Dabistān*, which of all non-Sikh works containing references to Gurū Nānak lies nearest to his time, is no nearer than the older janam-sākhīs and it is clear that Mohsin Fānī relied largely upon Sikh informants.[1] Much of the chapter in the *Dabistān* entitled 'Nānak-panthīs' deals with the life of Gurū Nānak, but the account which it gives of him amounts to little more than a series of legends. At one point it does offer significant support to a janam-sākhī tradition,[2] but as far as Gurū Nānak is concerned it is more important as a description of the seventeenth-century Sikh understanding of him than as a contribution to authentic biography.

Independent traditions concerning the life of Gurū Nānak did, of course, emerge, but there is no indication that any of them possessed more than the remotest of connexions with historical fact. Beyond the Pañjāb Gurū Nānak's name became a part of the hagiography of the later bhakti movement. Mahīpati's *Bhaktalīlāmrit*, written in A.D. 1774, testifies to both the extent and the nature of his reputation.

> Whoever shows some wonderful event, be he a *bhakta* of God or the chief of the yogīs, his reputation spreads widely and others continue the history of his sect. Hence in that country [the Pañjāb] there are many *bairāgīs* belonging to the sect of Nānak who give the *mantra* to the people and make the dull and ignorant remember God.
>
> If one listens to the lives of the saints, his greatest sins are burnt away; the giver of salvation is pleased with him, and keeps him in the world of Vaikunth.[3]

[1] The Persian *Dabistān-i-Mazāhib* was written in the mid-seventeenth century and is generally attributed to Mohsin Fānī. It appears that the author was personally acquainted with Gurū Hargobind, the sixth Gurū, and he explicitly claims a close acquaintance with Gurū Hari Rāi, the seventh Gurū. (Ganda Singh, English translation of the chapter 'Nānak-panthīs' published under the title *Nanak Panthis or the Sikhs and Sikhism of the 17th Century*, pp. 13, 21.)

[2] The tradition that Gurū Nānak was for a period employed as a steward by Daulat Khān Lodī. Ganda Singh, op. cit., p. 4. See *infra*, p. 108.

[3] Mahīpati, *Bhaktalīlāmrit*, 'The Story of Nānak', 177–9, translated from the Marathi by J. E. Abbot, N. R. Godbole, and J. F. Edwards, p. 195.

For Mahīpati Gurū Nānak was one of the great *bhagats* and his chapter 'The Story of Nānak' is a collection of appropriate legends. Muslim writers also referred to him, but apart from the *Dabistān* their interest appears to have developed later and to have been, for the most part, a polemical one. Colonel Malcolm, who collected the material for his *Sketch of the Sikhs* in 1805, refers to the existence of Muslim accounts of Gurū Nānak, but dismisses them as efforts to misrepresent and denigrate.[1] In other cases the concern of Muslim writers was evidently to claim Gurū Nānak as a believer in the doctrines of Islam.[2]

These independent traditions are almost totally valueless as sources of authentic information and accordingly we are bound to depend on the intensely interesting but largely unreliable janam-sākhīs for practically all of our information concerning the events of the Gurū's life. The best we can hope to do is to discern the historically possible in the midst of accumulated legend, and to test such possibilities against whatever criteria may be available. The outcome must inevitably be that there is little we can categorically affirm concerning the details of his life. There can, however, be no question concerning the basic facts that he was born in the Pañjāb almost five hundred years ago, spent a period in travel, composed the works which are attributed to him in the *Ādi Granth*, and ensured the perpetuation of his teachings by appointing a successor. These are beyond all doubt.

The precise manner in which the janam-sākhīs developed is not known for certain, but it is possible to reconstruct a likely pattern. The beginnings would be the remembered facts about the Gurū which would have circulated orally among the first generation of his followers. With the passage of time these facts would inevitably be embellished by reverent imaginations and practically all of them would undergo gradual change.

It would be remembered, for example, that the Gurū had spent many years travelling outside the Pañjāb. Some of the places he had visited might well be known, but it is unlikely that there would be any reliable knowledge of his complete itinerary. There would doubtless be many gaps in the account and these would soon be filled with the names of places which such a traveller might be expected to visit. These would include the important centres of pilgrimage, both Hindu and Muslim, and names which figured prominently in the current folklore of the Pañjāb. This is not to say that Gurū Nānak did not visit any of these places. On the contrary it is safe to assume that he must surely have visited at least some of them. The point here is that in many cases the name of a certain town or locality will have been added to the collection of *sākhīs*, not because there existed any reliable

[1] J. Malcolm, loc. cit., pp. 4–5.

[2] An example of this interpretation appears in G͟hulām Husain K͟hān's *Siyar-ul-Mutakhirin*, trans. J. Briggs, vol. i, pp. 110–11. The *Siyar-ul-Mutakhirin* was written about the year A.D. 1785.

information in this respect but because the popular imagination believed that he must surely have visited such a place on his travels. In most cases it is impossible to say with anything approaching certainty that he did or did not visit a particular place. Even when the incident which is located in a certain setting is manifestly unhistorical it does not necessarily follow that Gurū Nānak did not pass that way. On the other hand, the fact that an incident bears the marks of probability does not necessarily mean that the location given in the janam-sākhīs is the correct one.

In addition to these remembered facts and their embellishments, stories would have gathered around certain references in his works. It seems clear that this must have happened in the case of *Vār Rāmakalī*, *śloks* 2–7 of *pauṛī* 12.[1] In these six *śloks*, as they appear in the *Ādi Granth*, Gurū Nānak speaks successively as Īśar, Gorakh, Gopīchand, Charapaṭ, Bharatharī, and finally himself. The *śloks* were evidently intended for yogīs of the Nāth sect and this would explain the names used.[2] Subsequently these names must have suggested that Gurū Nānak had actually met these renowned figures and as a result there would have developed the story of his discourse with the Siddhs on Mount Sumeru which we find in stanzas 28–31 of Bhāī Gurdās's *Vār* 1,[3] *sākhī* 50 of the *Purātan Janam-sākhī*,[4] and *goṣṭ* 117 of the *Miharbān Janam-sākhī*.[5] Other similar verses would have assisted the process, notably *Rāmakalī* 4,[6] which refers to Gorakhnāth, and *Rāmakalī* 5,[7] which mentions Machhendranāth. In the *Purātan* janam-sākhīs these two compositions are responsible for a separate *sākhī* involving the two Nāths,[8] but in the *Miharbān Janam-sākhī* they are a part of the lengthy discourse on Mount Sumeru which extends from *goṣṭ* 117 to *goṣṭ* 124.[9]

Obviously there can be no question of historical truth in the story for Gurū Nānak and Gorakhnāth certainly were not contemporaries and Mount Sumeru exists only in legend. The only evident explanation is that a general acceptance of the popular belief in the immortal existence of the nine Nāths and of the eighty-four Siddhs in the fastnesses of the Himālayas[10]

[1] *AG*, pp. 952–3.

[2] Gorakhnāth, Gopīnāth, and Charapaṭnāth appear in the first of the lists of the nine Nāths given by G. W. Briggs, *Gorakhnāth and the Kānphaṭa Yogīs*, p. 136. Īśa is a name of Śiva, the *Ādināth* or 'Primal Master' of the Nāth sect. Bharatharī, or Bhartṛharī, is said to have been a disciple of Gorakhnāth and to have founded the Bairāg sub-sect of the Kānphaṭ order. According to tradition he was a king of Ujjain who abdicated his throne to become a yogī. Ibid., p. 65.

[3] See *infra*, pp. 34–35.

[4] *Pur JS*, pp. 94–97.

[5] *Mih JS*, pp. 384–91. The tradition concerning a discourse on Mount Sumeru is discussed below, pp. 119–22.

[6] *AG*, p. 877. *Rāmakalī* is one of the *Ādi Granth* metres.

[7] *AG*, p. 877.

[8] *Pur JS*, *sākhī* 46, pp. 84–86.

[9] *Mih JS*, pp. 384–413. The discourse as recorded in this janam-sākhī also includes *Āsā* 37 and 38 (*AG*, pp. 359–60), both of which refer to Bharatharī (ibid., pp. 405–9).

[10] The immortal existence of the nine Nāths and the immortal existence of the eighty-four Siddhs constitute two separate traditions, but in the janam-sākhīs the two are confused. See Glossary, p. 243, *Nāth*.

combined with these references in Gurū Nānak's works to produce a story of his having visited them there. The differences in the *Purātan* and *Miharbān* accounts indicate that there must have been an evolution over a period of time, but there seems to be no doubt that the real genesis of the story lay in these compositions which were originally addressed to Nāth yogīs.[1]

The influence of popular belief in this particular case illustrates a fundamental axiom which applies to such works as the janam-sākhīs. All such works will reflect, to some extent, the context in which they evolved, a context which will include not only current beliefs and attitudes but also current needs. In the case of the janam-sākhīs the relevant context is the situation of the Sikh community during the closing years of the sixteenth century and the early decades of the seventeenth century. It can be safely assumed that the janam-sākhīs will express in some measure the beliefs of the community during this period, its more insistent needs, and the answers which it was giving to questions which confronted it. An example of this feature is the recurrent reference to relationships between Hindus and Muslims, and specifically the insistence upon the identity of the Hindu and Muslim ways of salvation. The janam-sākhī attitude towards this issue is most strikingly expressed in the famous pronouncement attributed to Gurū Nānak at the time of his emergence from the waters of the Veīn.

> *nā ko hindū hai nā ko musalamān hai.*
> There is neither Hindu nor Mussulman.[2]

It is quite possible that this aphorism derives from an authentic utterance by Gurū Nānak, but the general unreliability of the janam-sākhīs forbids a positive affirmation on this point. There can, however, be no doubt that it represents a particular doctrinal conviction held by the Sikh community during the early seventeenth century and that this conviction has contributed to the content of the janam-sākhīs. Another example of a theme which evidently reflects both a particular situation and an interpretation of it is the fate of those who place their trust in caste status and the fulfilment of prescribed caste custom.[3]

[1] The story of Kauḍā the Savage (*Pur JS*, *sākhī* 44) appears to be another illustration, the link in this case being the word *kaṛāhā* (cauldron), and likewise the story of Kaliyug (*Pur JS*, *sākhī* 24) where the origin appears to be the exposition of the futility of earthly rewards given in Gurū Nānak's *Sirī Rāgu* 1 (*AG*, p. 14). See also *infra*, p. 83 and Rattan Singh Jaggi, *Vichār-dhārā*, p. 15. The popular story of Sajjaṇ the *Ṭhag* may also owe its origin to this particular process. In a few cases a particular reference or verse has given rise to two different stories. *Basant* 3 (*AG*, p. 1169), which concerns the futility of purified cooking-squares, has produced two entirely different stories in the *Purātan* and *Miharbān* accounts. (*Pur JS*, *sākhī* 38, p. 72; *Mih JS*, *goṣṭ* 41, pp. 120–3.)

[2] *Pur JS*, p. 16. See *infra*, pp. 38, 107. Cf. also *BG* 1. 33; *Mih JS*, p. 489.

[3] Cf. *infra*, pp. 45, 52.

This observation should not suggest that at such points the janam-sākhīs are necessarily in conflict with the teachings of Gurū Nānak. In some instances it seems clear that this is the case, as for example in the measure of deference which the janam-sākhīs pay to sādhūs and faqīrs. Gurū Nānak commended a certain kind of sādhū or faqīr, but not the conventional variety which finds favour in some of the janam-sākhī stories.[1] In other cases, of which the denunciation of caste pretensions serves as an example, there is obvious consonance. The relevant issue at this point is not so much the question of conflict or consonance as the circumstances which prompted certain emphases and the extent to which such emphases have moulded the janam-sākhī traditions.

The contemporary needs of the community can also be regarded as the source of the most prominent of all janam-sākhī characteristics, namely the wonder story. The most cursory reading of any of the janam-sākhīs will soon reveal the dominance of this feature and of the impulse which it represents. Such stories are a compelling need in the popular piety of all religions and the janam-sākhīs provide a natural response. Substantial portions of all the janam-sākhīs can be explained by reference to this necessity.

In this way remembered facts, devout imaginations, suggestive references in Gurū Nānak's works, contemporary beliefs and needs, and the mutations which inevitably result from oral repetition must have combined to create a stock of *sākhīs* or isolated incidents concerning the life of Gurū Nānak. The next step would be to group a number of these *sākhīs* into some sort of chronological pattern and to give the pattern a measure of stability by committing the selected *sākhīs* to writing. Such a selection would still be open to alteration, but to a lesser extent than was inevitably the case while the *sākhīs* were still circulating orally. A selection once recorded would be copied, the copy would be copied, and so a tradition would be established, though still subject to modification by drawing on the oral stock, or perhaps on a different written tradition.

The manuscripts which we now possess are the products of the latter stage in the evolution, being copies of earlier collections rather than original compilations. They fall into four recognizable, though overlapping, traditions:

1. *Purātan.*
2. *Miharbān.*
3. *Bālā*, or *Bhāī Bālā.*
4. The *Gyān-ratanāvalī*, or *Manī Siṅgh Janam-sākhī.*

Of the four the least reliable is the *Bālā* tradition, but its influence has been immense. Ever since the days of Macauliffe, author of the six-volume

[1] Cf. *infra*, pp. 62, 83, 133–4.

work entitled *The Sikh Religion*, it has been the *Purātan* tradition which has been accorded the greatest measure of reliability and which has been used as the basis of all the better biographies. There is now reason to believe that this opinion should be revised and that the *Miharbān Janam-sākhī*, hitherto dismissed as sectarian polemic, should be regarded as at least equal in reliability to the *Purātan* tradition. This description is, however, a relative one. It should not be taken to imply anything resembling consistent reliability.

One important work which does not fit easily into this classification is the first *Vār* of Bhāī Gurdās. It is not a janam-sākhī in the normally accepted sense as apart from four incidents it offers very little information about Gurū Nānak's life. In so far as it does present a pattern it accords with the *Miharbān Janam-sākhī*, but the two could not be said to belong to a common tradition. The primary purpose of this *vār* is to extol the greatness of the first six Gurūs and to serve this purpose in the case of Gurū Nānak, Bhāī Gurdās has made a very limited selection from the available material. In this qualified sense it may be referred to as a janam-sākhī, but it would be unduly optimistic to expect from the relevant stanzas more than the barest sketch of the Gurū's life. Nevertheless, it certainly warrants our closest attention because of its relative nearness to the time of Gurū Nānak, and no treatment of the janam-sākhīs would be complete without it.

Bhāī Gurdās's Vār I

Bhāī Gurdās Bhallā is a figure of considerable importance in early Sikh history. The date of his birth is not known, but he is said to have been a nephew of the third Gurū, Amar Dās. The year S. 1636 (A.D. 1579) is given as the date of his admission by Gurū Rām Dās to the Sikh community and for a number of years he worked as a missionary in Agra. Gurū Arjan subsequently summoned him back to the Pañjāb and retained him as his amanuensis during the compilation of the *Ādi Granth*. None of his own works were included in the scripture which he transcribed, but his *vārs* are traditionally regarded as 'the key to the *Gurū Granth Sāhib*'[1] and his compositions are specifically approved for recitation in Sikh gurdwārās.[2] After Gurū Arjan's death he became a trusted follower of Gurū Hargobind. His death is said to have taken place in S. 1694 (A.D. 1637).[3]

Bhāī Gurdās's thirty-nine *vārs*[4] and, to a lesser extent, his 556

[1] *Vārān Bhāī Gurdās*, ed. Hazara Singh and Vir Singh, Foreword.

[2] *Sikh Rahit Marayādā*, Śromaṇī Gurduārā Prabandhak Committee (6th ed., 1961), p. 21.

[3] *MK*, p. 311. For a brief account of Bhāī Gurdās's life see Khushwant Singh, *A History of the Sikhs*, vol. i, pp. 310–12.

[4] The published editions of the *vārs* include forty, but the last of these is by a later writer of the same name. Khushwant Singh, op. cit., p. 312. The *vārs* of Bhāī Gurdās differ in form from those of the *Ādi Granth*. Bhāī Gurdās's *vārs* accord more with the customary form, an heroic ode of several stanzas (*pauṛīs*), but no *śloks*.

compositions in the *kabitt* poetic form are of considerable interest as an exposition of contemporary Sikh belief, but they contain relatively little biographical material. In the case of Gurū Nānak such material is confined to *Vār* 1, stanzas 23–45, and *Vār* 11, stanzas 13–14.[1] The second of these extracts is of comparatively slight importance and consequently Bhāī Gurdās's contribution to the biography of Gurū Nānak is almost entirely limited to the twenty-three stanzas of *Vār* 1.

It is clear that these stanzas must have been composed during the first half of the seventeenth century, but impossible to give them an exact date. According to the *Gyān-ratanāvalī* Bhāī Gurdās wrote his account of the life of Gurū Nānak in response to a request made by some Sikhs 'at the time when the fifth Master established the canon of *Srī Granth Sāhib*'.[2] This would mean in, or soon after, A.D. 1604. The *Gyān-ratanāvalī* was, however, written more than a century later than the compilation of the *Ādi Granth*, and the prologue which contains this statement appears to have been written even later than the main work. It has been argued that *Vār* 1 must have been written after A.D. 1628 as stanza 48 contains, with reference to Gurū Hargobind, the line:

> This heroic Gurū was a conqueror of armies, a mighty warrior and one supremely generous.

Gurū Hargobind's first battle, a skirmish with some troops of the Emperor Shāhjahān, took place in 1628 and it is accordingly held that the *vār* must have been written after this date.[3] Such an argument can, however, apply only to the stanza in which the line occurs, for there is no indication that the *vārs* were composed as complete units.

The only safe conclusion is that the twenty-three stanzas would have been composed before A.D. 1637. They may well have been written appreciably earlier, but there is no trustworthy evidence which establishes this beyond doubt and the legendary details which they contain suggest a later rather than an earlier date. The most which can be said with assurance is that this brief account of Gurū Nānak's life was written at some time during a period extending from the close of the sixteenth century to the year 1637, a period which began sixty years after the Gurū's death and ended one hundred years after that date.

The Purātan Janam-sākhīs

The term *Purātan Janam-sākhī*, or 'Ancient Janam-sākhī', is open to some misunderstanding as it has been used in two different senses. Strictly

[1] Other direct references to him are to be found in *Vār* 24. 1–4, and *Vār* 26. 16, 30–31, but with the exception of a line from *Vār*. 24. 1 which refers to his residence in Kartārpur, and another from *Vār*. 24. 4 which describes the levelling of caste within the community established by the Gurū, their content is exclusively eulogistic.

[2] *GR*, p. 3. See *infra*, p. 25.

[3] *Mih JS*, Introductory Essays, p. 62.

speaking it designates no single known work, but rather a small group of janam-sākhīs which are clearly from a common source which has never been found. It is, however, generally used with reference to the composite work which was compiled by Bhāī Vir Singh and first published in 1926. The usage in this present study corresponds to the second of these meanings. The first of them is covered by the plural form *Purātan* janam-sākhīs, or by the term 'the *Purātan* tradition'.

Of the extant *Purātan* janam-sākhīs the two most important are the *Colebrooke* and *Hāfizābād* versions. The first of these was discovered in 1872 by Dr. Trumpp while examining the Gurmukhī manuscripts in the possession of the India Office Library, London.[1] The manuscript had been donated to the Library of East India House by H. T. Colebrooke, probably in 1815 or 1816, and is accordingly known either by his name or as the *Valāitvālī Janam-sākhī*, 'the janam-sākhī from overseas'.

Trumpp's work was published in 1877 and his information aroused the interest of Sikh scholars in the Pañjāb. In 1883 some Amritsar Sikhs petitioned the Lieutenant-Governor of the Pañjāb, Sir Charles Aitcheson, to have the manuscript brought to India for inspection. The petition was granted and in the autumn of the same year the manuscript was sent to the Pañjāb and made available for scrutiny in Lahore and Amritsar. Learning of the Sikhs' desire to have it photographed, Sir Charles made arrangements to have this done at government expense. The manuscript was photographed and printed by means of a zincographic process in 1885 and copies were given to selected institutions as gifts.[2] In the meantime the Lahore Singh Sabhā, a distinguished reform society of Sikhs, had made a copy from the manuscript and this had been lithographed in Lahore in 1884.

In the same year that the photozincograph facsimiles of the *Colebrooke Janam-sākhī* were produced, Macauliffe published another version of the same janam-sākhī. This second version had been acquired the previous year in the town of Hāfizābād by Bhāī Gurmukh Singh of Oriental College, Lahore. Gurmukh Singh passed the manuscript on to Macauliffe who divided off the individual words and had it lithographed at his own expense.[3] The version was designated the *Hāfizābād Janam-sākhī* by Gurmukh Siṅgh and this is its usual title, but it is also referred to as the *Macauliffe-vālī Janam-sākhī*. Gurmukh Singh reported in his introduction to the lithographed edition that there were pages missing from the end of the manuscript and that Macauliffe had used the *Colebrooke Janam-sākhī* to complete the edition.[4]

[1] E. Trumpp, *The Ādi Granth*, p. ii. The manuscript is IOL, MS. Panj. B6.

[2] *Photozincograph Facsimile*, prefatory note, p. iii. Gurmukh Singh, Introduction to Macauliffe's edition of the *Hāfizābād Janam-sākhi*, pp. 3–4. *Pur JS*, Introduction, pp. u–a.

[3] Gurmukh Singh, op. cit., pp. 4–5. The town of Hāfizābād is in Gujranwālā District, West Pakistan. The manuscript is no longer traceable.

[4] Ibid., p. 9.

These were the two manuscripts which Vir Singh used for practically the whole of his composite *Purātan Janam-sākhī*. For the most part the two versions are very close, with only occasional words or phrases differing, but there are a few significant differences. Of the two, the *Hāfizābād* manuscript appears to be closer to the common source, although it is clear that it is not itself the original of the *Purātan* group. This original *Purātan* janam-sākhī has never been found. Macauliffe and Kahn Singh have attributed it to a certain Sevā Dās,[1] but there is no reference to such a person in the janam-sākhī which Macauliffe published and it is clear from a comment which he makes that the information was not based upon anything he had himself seen.[2]

Neither the *Colebrooke* nor the *Hāfizābād Janam-sākhī* bears an explicit date, but a reference in the *Colebrooke* manuscript clearly points to A.D. 1635 as the date of the original composition.[3] The fact that the reference is missing from the *Hāfizābād* manuscript seriously weakens its claims to authenticity, but there are other factors which suggest the same period. One such is the inclusion of works by Gurū Arjan which are erroneously attributed to Gurū Nānak, and another is the evident fact that the author had not seen Bhāī Gurdās's *Vār* 1. It is inconceivable that had he done so he would have omitted reference to the Baghdad incident which Bhāī Gurdās records. This does not prove that the janam-sākhī predated the *Vār*, but it does point to a period which preceded the general dissemination of Bhāī Gurdās's works. Thirdly, there is the obvious age of the language and of the script, both of which resemble those of the Kartārpur version of the *Ādi Granth*.[4] None of these factors could be regarded as determinative, but the second and third are of some significance, particularly the third. It seems safe to conclude that the *Purātan* janam-sākhī must have been committed to writing during the first half of the seventeenth century.

Since the discovery of the *Colebrooke* and *Hāfizābād* janam-sākhīs several other *Purātan* manuscripts have been found. Of these one deserves special mention as it diverges significantly from other janam-sākhīs of this group. It is a manuscript which was acquired by the India Office Library in 1907 and is listed in its catalogue as MSS. Pañjābī B40.[5] This B40 manuscript follows the *Hāfizābād Janam-sākhī* in the early *sākhīs*, but after the *sākhī* which describes Gurū Nānak's departure from Sultānpur it diverges and only a limited amount of the remaining material corresponds even remotely

[1] Macauliffe, *The Sikh Religion*, vol. i, p. lxxxvi. Kahn Singh, *MK*, p. 172 Kahn Singh worked in collaboration with Macauliffe. His reference to Sevā Dās is brief and cryptic.

[2] Macauliffe's comment is as follows: 'The late Sir Atar Singh, Chief of Bhadaur, gave the author this information.' Op. cit., vol. i, p. lxxxvi, n. 1.

[3] *Pur JS*, pp. 116–17.

[4] E. Trumpp, *The Ādi Granth*, p. ii. *Pur JS*, pp. a, e.

[5] It should not be confused with MSS. Pañjābī B41 which belongs to the *Bālā* group of janam-sākhīs.

to the two main *Purātan* manuscripts.[1] Some of the *sākhīs* suggest a connexion with the *Bālā* tradition, but only a very indirect one, the versions recorded in this manuscript having been withdrawn from the oral stock appreciably earlier than the corresponding *Bālā* tradition *sākhīs*. Bhāī Bālā, the person who figures so prominently in the *Bālā* tradition as a companion of Gurū Nānak and from whom the tradition takes its name, is nowhere mentioned. At a few points the text represents an earlier version of what is recorded in the extant version of the *Miharbān Janam-sākhī*. Several of the *sākhīs* are simply discourses rather than incidents and bear appropriately vague titles. Unlike the principal *Purātan* manuscripts it includes the famous story of how Gurū Nānak pretended to water his Lahore fields from Hardwār,[2] and it also refers to a Baghdad visit.[3] The collection follows no logical order after the departure from Sultānpur, simply recording *sākhīs* as isolated incidents.

This manuscript is important, for it represents a more primitive collection than either the *Colebrooke* or *Hāfizābād* janam-sākhīs. Although there is little to distinguish the three as far as language is concerned, the *sākhīs* of this version are, for the most part, more rudimentary than those of the *Colebrooke* and *Hāfizābād* manuscripts. Several of them consist of little more than a verse by Gurū Nānak, with a very brief introduction added to give it a setting. Whether it may be regarded as a version of the *Purātan* tradition is perhaps open to some doubt. If it is to be assigned to any of the recognizable traditions then it must certainly be included within the *Purātan* group, but it would be more accurate to speak of an affiliation with the *Purātan* tradition rather than of inclusion within it.

The Miharbān Janam-sākhī

Of the four traditions the most neglected has been that of the *Miharbān Janam-sākhī*. Until relatively recent years this was inevitably the case as no copy of any substantial portion of the janam-sākhī was known to exist. The absence of such a copy was not, however, regarded as a serious misfortune, for the janam-sākhī had long since acquired a disagreeable reputation. Soḍhī Miharbān, to whom the janam-sākhī is attributed, was closely associated with the Mīṇā sect, and from this association the janam-sākhī derived its unfortunate reputation.[4] The Mīṇās were inimical to the

[1] Examples of correspondence are provided by the following *sākhīs*: Kaliyug, folio 44; Saidpur, folio 66; the wealthy man's flags, folio 189; the first half of the *sākhī* concerning Rājā Śivanābh, corresponding to the *Pur JS sākhī* 41, folio 138.

[2] Loc. cit., folio 76. See *infra*, p. 55.

[3] Loc. cit., folio 200. The *sākhī* does not, however, correspond to Bhāī Gurdās's account of the Gurū's visit to Baghdad (see *infra*, p. 35). According to this manuscript the discourse in Baghdad is said to have been with Sheikh Sharaf.

[4] The Mīṇās were the followers of Prithī Chand (A.D. 1558–1619) the eldest son of the fourth Gurū, Rām Dās. Prithī Chand's behaviour was evidently unsatisfactory as he was passed over in favour of his youngest brother, Arjan, when his father chose a successor.

Gurūs from the period of Gurū Arjan onwards and it has been assumed that this hostility must have informed Miharbān's account of the life of Gurū Nānak. According to the prologue of the *Gyān-ratanāvalī* it was the Mīṇā practice of interpolating the traditions concerning Gurū Nānak which prompted Gurū Arjan to commission Bhāī Gurdās's account and which subsequently persuaded Bhāī Manī Siṅgh to write the *Gyān-ratanāvalī* itself.[1] The reference in the prologue of the *Gyān-ratanāvalī* seemed to point directly to the *Miharbān Janam-sākhī* and in the absence of an extant copy of the work there was no evident reason for modifying the hostility which had traditionally been accorded to it.

In 1940, however, a manuscript copy of half of the janam-sākhī was discovered at Damdamā Sāhib.[2] This manuscript comprises the first three *pothīs*, or volumes, of the six which constituted the complete janam-sākhī.[3] The first three are entitled *Pothī Sach-khaṇḍ*, *Pothī Harijī*, and *Pothī Chatarbhuj* respectively, and according to the colophon of *Pothī Sach-khaṇḍ* these three were followed by *Keśo Rāi Pothī*, *Abhai Pad Pothī*, and finally *Prem Pad Pothī*.[4] The script is Gurmukhī, but the language is basically Braj with an admixture of words drawn from Eastern and Western Pañjābī, Persian, and Multānī.[5]

Pothī Sach-khaṇḍ, the first volume of the janam-sākhī, is obviously the most important part of the complete work. It is the only *pothī* which is directly attributed to Miharbān himself[6] and it is the only one which contains any appreciable amount of biographical material. The second and

He disputed the succession and following Gurū Arjan's execution in 1606 made further attempts to secure the title. At some point he and his followers were branded 'Mīṇās' and the name stuck. The Mīṇās were a robber tribe of the Gurgāon area, and in Pañjābī the word had come to mean a dissembling rogue, one who took care to conceal his evil intentions. Following the death of Prithī Chand the leadership of the sect passed to his son Miharbān (1581–1640). The Mīṇās were subsequently execrated by Gurū Gobind Singh and declared by him to be one of the five groups with whom orthodox Sikhs were to have no dealings. The sect is now extinct.

1 *GR*, pp. 3–4. See *infra*, p. 25.

2 Damdamā Sāhib, originally called Sābo kī Talvaṇḍī, is eighteen miles south of Bhaṭiṇḍā. It acquired importance in Sikh history as a result of a visit by Gurū Gobind Singh following the Battle of Muktsar in 1705. The manuscript is now in the possession of Khalsa College, Amritsar (MS. no. SHR: 427 of the College's Sikh History Research Department). In 1961 Khalsa College acquired a second manuscript (no. SHR: 2190) which covers a much smaller portion of the total janam-sākhī, but which supplies some material which is missing in the first manuscript.

3 The first *pothī* was published by the Sikh History Research Department of Khalsa College, Amritsar, in 1962 under the title *Janam Sākhī Sri Gurū Nānak Dev Ji* (edited by Kirpal Singh and Shamsher Singh Ashok). The two remaining *pothīs* are forthcoming. The published edition of the first *pothī* incorporates the material which is missing from the Damdamā Sāhib manuscript but supplied by the second Khalsa College manuscript.

4 *Mih JS*, p. 519.

5 It is an example of *Sādhukkaṛī*, or *Sant Bhāṣā*. See *infra*, p. 153.

6 The compiling of the other two sections of the manuscript is attributed, as the titles of the two *pothīs* indicate, to Harijī and Chatarbhuj. Harijī was Miharbān's second son and his successor as *gurū* of the Mīṇās. Chatarbhuj was his third son.

third volumes contain little other than discourse and interpretation of scripture, and it is evident that the same must apply to almost all that was contained in the remaining three volumes which have never been found. Practically all that is of any biographical importance will almost certainly have been incorporated in the first volume. The two which follow it add only an occasional point of interest and it may be safely assumed that the same would have applied to the remaining three volumes.

Even in the case of *Pothī Sach-khaṇḍ* it is at once evident that Miharbān's primary purpose was the exposition of Gurū Nānak's works, and that biographical incidents were included more as settings for discourses than for their own sake. Most of the *goṣṭs*, or 'discourses', into which the *pothī* is divided offer only a few such details and then proceed to discourse, quotations from Gurū Nānak's works, and lengthy interpretations of such quotations. In a few cases an event is described at some length, but in many more no biographical details are given at all. This means that only a small proportion of the janam-sākhī is directly relevant to our biographical concern. There is, however, nothing surprising in this, for all of the janam-sākhīs use most biographical incidents as settings for utterances by Gurū Nānak. In this respect Miharbān's janam-sākhī differs only in that it offers much more extensive interpretations of the scriptures which it quotes.

Pothī Sach-khaṇḍ is accordingly the important portion of the complete *Miharbān Janam-sākhī*, and it provides a valuable addition to the janam-sākhī literature. With such a manuscript available it is possible to determine whether or not Miharbān's account of the life of Gurū Nānak deserves the condemnation which it has traditionally received. An examination of it indicates that Miharbān has been largely misjudged. It is true that certain features of the janam-sākhī could give offence,[1] but such features are by no means as conspicuous as the janam-sākhī's reputation would suggest. The tone, far from being one of denigration, is manifestly one of enthusiastic homage and places this janam-sākhī firmly within the same hagiographic category as the other janam-sākhīs. This is indeed what might have been anticipated. The Mīṇās were schismatics, not heretics, and although they certainly bore enmity towards Gurū Arjan and his successors there was no evident reason why they should have sought to malign Gurū Nānak.

[1] Examples from *Pothī Sach-khaṇḍ* are the claim that Gurū Nānak was a reincarnation of the first Rājā Janak (*Mih JS*, p. 8) and the statement that Gurū Nānak originally began his travels with the intention of finding a *gurū* (ibid., pp. 111, 361). An example from *Pothī Harijī* is its claim that Gurū Nānak remarried following the conclusion of his travels. (Khalsa College MS. no. SHR: 427, folio 387b.) The belief that Gurū Nānak was a reincarnation of Rājā Janak is not confined to the *Miharbān* tradition. There is a *Purātan* janam-sākhī in Hoshiarpur which makes the same claim. (Shamsher Singh Ashok, *Pañjābī hath-likhatān dī sūchī*, vol. ii, no. 92, p. 230.) It is possible that the *Colebrooke Janam-sākhī* may have originally included this story as folios 2–6 are missing from the manuscript (*Photozincograph Facsimile*, prefatory note, p. iii).

According to the colophons at the end of all three *pothīs* the copying of manuscript obtained from Damdamā Sāhib was completed in S. 1885 (A.D. 1828).[1] The colophon of *Pothī Harijī* implies that it is a copy made from the original, a claim which must be treated with some caution. The text is not pure in that it contains references which would not have been possible in the early or mid-seventeenth century,[2] and there are also indications of subsequent alterations by sādhūs of the Udāsī sect.[3]

The date of the original version of *Pothī Sach-khaṇḍ* cannot be determined with certainty, but it seems likely that it would have been finally compiled between A.D. 1640, the year of Miharbān's death, and 1650, the date ascribed to *Pothī Harijī*.[4] The introduction to *Pothī Sach-khaṇḍ*[5] appears to have been written after his death, and the production of *Pothī Harijī* and *Pothī Chatarbhuj* in successive years[6] suggests that the whole collection may have been compiled in a single operation extending over a number of years.

This, or course, applied only to the compilation. The actual composition must have extended over many years of Miharbān's lifetime and been recorded during that time as individual discourses.[7] This means that the composition of Miharbān's janam-sākhī must have taken place during the same period as Bhāī Gurdās's *Vār* 1 and the original *Purātan* janam-sākhī, and that accordingly there can be little to distinguish the three as far as age is concerned. All of them, it appears, had their beginnings in oral traditions which developed during the second half of the sixteenth century, and all three evidently emerged in their present form, or something resembling it, during the first half of the seventeenth century.

The Bālā *janam-sākhīs*

The janam-sākhīs of the *Bālā*, or *Bhāī Bālā*, tradition deserve notice, not because they possess any intrinsic reliability, but because of the immense influence they have exercised in determining what has generally been accepted as the authoritative account of Gurū Nānak's life. Throughout the nineteenth century, until the discovery of the *Purātan* manuscripts, the authority of the *Bālā* version was unchallenged, and even after the *Purātan* tradition had won general acceptance the *Bālā* janam-sākhīs continued to supply many of the incidents required to fill out the relatively

[1] *Mih JS*, p. ix. [2] Ibid., p. ix.

[3] Ibid., Introductory Essays, p. 83. The Udāsīs are an order of celibate ascetics which originally gathered around Sirī Chand, one of Gurū Nānak's two sons. The order still claims numerous followers. There is an important Udāsī temple adjacent to the Golden Temple in Amritsar and many Udāsī sādhūs are to be found in Hardwār. See J. C. Archer, *The Sikhs in relation to Hindus, Moslems, Christians, and Ahmadiyyas*, pp. 226–8.

[4] *Mih JS*, p. ix. [5] Ibid., p. 1. [6] Ibid., p. ix.

[7] This assumption is supported by a work entitled *Goṣṭān Miharvān jī diān*, evidently written during the seventeenth century and attributed to Harijī (Kirpal Singh, *Mih JS*, Introduction, p. vii).

brief accounts given by the *Purātan* manuscripts. Even Macauliffe used them, in spite of his slighting remarks concerning the claims of the *Bālā* version to be the earliest of all janam-sākhīs.[1]

The *Bālā* version is, however, the least trustworthy of all the janam-sākhī traditions. Errors of fact occur with considerable frequency[2] and the fabulous material which it incorporates far exceeds that of the other janam-sākhīs, both in quantity and in degree. The legendary accretions are particularly prominent in its description of Gurū Nānak's mountain-climbing expeditions and of his visits to various Puranic regions (*khaṇḍs*) and continents (*dīps*).[3] A determined assault was made on the *Bālā* tradition by Karam Singh in 1913,[4] but later authors have generally continued to follow the Macauliffe pattern of using *Bālā* material to augment the *Purātan* account.

If one asks for a janam-sākhī in a Pañjāb bazar bookshop today the book which will be offered will almost invariably be a modern edition of the *Bālā* version. Ever since the janam-sākhīs began to be printed the *Bālā* tradition has monopolized the Pañjābī market, and with the passing years these printed editions have grown progressively bulkier. An edition lithographed in 1871 is, for the most part, a copy of a version which is found in several extant *Bālā* manuscripts,[5] but another edition lithographed in the same year by Dīvān Būṭā Singh of Lahore is substantially longer,[6] and yet another produced in 1890 is longer still.[7] Finally we have the letterpress version which still sells well in Pañjāb bookshops.[8] It is to the earliest of the lithographed editions, the one which was published by Hāfaz Qutub Dīn of Lahore in 1871, that reference will normally be made in the section

[1] Macauliffe, i. lxxvii–ix.

[2] Karam Singh provides a lengthy list in his *Kattak ki Visākh*, pp. 36–138.

[3] *Bālā JS*, pp. 200 ff. See especially pp. 265–8. An illustration of the *Bālā* variety of fantasy is its account of Gurū Nānak's ride on a fish measuring thirty-five *kos* in length and five *kos* in breadth. The fish turns out to be a former Sikh who had been reincarnated in this form as a result of Gurū Nānak having once commented that he writhed like a fish whenever he was instructed to do anything (ibid., pp. 137–40).

[4] Karam Singh, *Kattak ki Visākh*, Amritsar, 1913. The book was primarily intended to prove that Gurū Nānak was born in the month of Vaisākh, and not in Kārtik as popularly believed, but practically the whole of the book consists of a vigorous attack upon the *Bālā* janam-sākhīs, the source of the Kārtik tradition.

[5] Published in Lahore by Hāfaz Qutub Dīn in S. 1928 (A.D. 1871). There is a copy of this edition in the IOL (Panj. 1522). Also in the IOL are two reprints, one dated A.D. 1874 (IOL, Panj. 30. E. 3) and the other A.D. 1886 (IOL, Panj. 1523). Although this edition generally follows the IOL manuscript Panj. B41 it is not, as Trumpp claimed, 'nearly identical' (E. Trumpp, *The Ādi Granth*, p. lii, n. 1). It contains four substantial interpolations from a *Purātan* source, it omits some portions which appear derogatory to Gurū Nānak, and it adds an account of the Gurū's death.

[6] *Bālā Janam-sākhī*, Mālik Dīvān Būṭā Singh, Lahore, S. 1928 (A.D. 1871). There is a copy in the IOL (Panj. 31.1.9) and another in the BM (14162. d. 3). A reprint was published in A.D. 1890 (IOL, Panj. 31.1.7).

[7] *Bālā Janam-sākhī*, Maulvī Maibūb Ahmad, Lahore, A.D. 1890 (IOL, Panj. 31.1.10).

[8] Copies available in London are IOL, Panj. H. 18, and BM, 14162 d. 26.

dealing with the life of Gurū Nānak.[1] Occasional reference will also be made to two other editions. These are the Dīvān Būṭā Singh edition which, to distinguish it from the Hāfaz Qutub Dīn edition, will be referred to as 'the expanded 1871 edition', and, as a representative of the modern group, an edition published by Munshī Gulāb Singh and Sons of Lahore in A.D. 1942.

One reason which does much to explain the popularity of the *Bālā* version is its claim that the original *Bālā Janam-sākhī* was dictated in the presence of Gurū Aṅgad by Bhāī Bālā, a companion of Gurū Nānak, and that accordingly it represents an eye-witness account of the life of the first Gurū. This claim can be dismissed without hesitation, but the question then arises of a satisfactory substitute explanation to account for the origin of the *Bālā* janam-sākhīs. Two theories have been advanced. One is that the original janam-sākhī was composed by the heretical sect of Hindālīs during the first half of the seventeenth century; and the other is that a janam-sākhī of unknown but early origin was interpolated by the Hindālīs.[2]

There can be no doubt that the *Bālā Janam-sākhī* as it has survived in manuscript form is a Hindālī version of the life of Gurū Nānak.[3] This is not evident from the printed editions, for the publishers have purged almost all the references which expressed or seemed to imply Hindālī enmity towards Gurū Nānak, but the manuscript versions have whole *sākhīs* and a number of briefer references which were clearly intended to exalt Bābā Hindāl (and consequently the sect bearing his name) and to denigrate Gurū Nānak at the expense of Kabīr and Hindāl. Were these derogatory references an integral part of a Hindālī janam-sākhī deliberately composed as a contribution to the sect's campaign against the orthodox Sikhs, or should they be regarded as interpolations? Of the alternatives the former appears to be the more likely, but the issue is debatable. It is an issue of interest rather than of real importance and the same judgement can be applied to the question of whether or not a person called Bhāī Bālā actually existed. The actual existence of Bhāī Bālā is certainly a possibility, in spite of the failure of Bhāī Gurdās or of any other janam-sākhī tradition to mention

[1] The abbreviation *Bālā JS* refers to this edition.

[2] The heretical sect of Hindālīs, or Nirañjanīs, developed out of the enmity of a certain Bidhī Chand, the son of Bābā Hindāl of Jaṇḍiālā and a contemporary of Gurū Hargobind (1595–1644). Hindāl himself is said to have been converted by Gurū Amar Dās and to have displayed such loyalty, particularly through his service in the Gurū's kitchen (*laṅgar*), that he was appointed to a position of authority in the community. His son Bidhī Chand, however, married a Muslim woman and evidently responded to the reproaches of the Sikhs by turning apostate. Jaṇḍiālā became a centre of malignant opposition to the Gurūs and the mutual enmity which developed persisted until the Hindālī sect eventually declined into insignificance. During the period of Mughal persecution in the eighteenth century the Hindālīs disclaimed the title of Sikh and when Aḥmad Shāh Abdālī descended upon the Pañjāb they gave him their active support against the Khālsā (*MK*, p. 535. *A Glossary of the Tribes and Castes of the Punjab etc*, vol. ii, pp. 325–6).

[3] Macauliffe implies the existence of two separate janam-sākhīs, a *Bālā Janam-sākhī* (i, p. lxxix) and a *Hindālī Janam-sākhī* (i, p. lxxxi). This is incorrect.

him, and it is remotely possible that there was an association between a person of this name and Gurū Nānak.[1] It is not, however, possible to connect the extant *Bālā* janam-sākhīs with any such association except in the most distant and conjectural sense. The dominance of the manifestly fabulous within the *Bālā* tradition demolishes any such possibility and this verdict must hold until a more primitive *Bālā* version is discovered.[2] In a few cases the *Bālā* tradition evidently carries us further back than the other janam-sākhīs,[3] but for the most part it represents a selection from the common pool after it had become well stocked with fabulous incidents. It is a fascinating collection, but it is of only limited help in the search for the historical Nānak.

An important work based upon the *Bālā* tradition is Santokh Singh's *Gur Nānak Prakāś*, commonly called the *Nānak Prakāś*. This is a much later account of the life of Gurū Nānak, having been completed in 1823, but like its principal source it has acquired considerable importance as a result of its great popularity and consequent influence.[4] Relying as it does upon an untrustworthy source the *Nānak Prakāś* is itself unreliable and warrants mention only because its influence has been so extensive.[5]

The Gyān-ratanāvalī, *or* Manī Singh Janam-sākhī

The fourth and evidently the latest of the more important collections of *sākhīs* is the *Gyān-ratanāvalī*, a janam-sākhī attributed to Bhāī Manī Singh which has suffered from a surprising measure of neglect. It has not been totally ignored in the manner of the *Miharbān Janam-sākhī* and indeed it evidently gathered to itself a considerable measure of respect. It was, however, a reputation based on awe rather than upon usage and the practical attention it has received has been relatively slight. This is difficult to understand, for unlike the *Miharbān Janam-sākhī* it has had no taint of

[1] The possibility receives some support from a brief work entitled *Sūchak prasaṅg gurū kā* attributed to Bhāī Bahilo. Shamsher Singh Ashok, *Pañjābī hath-likhatān dī sūchī*, vol. i, p. 361.

[2] The oldest so far found is a Hindālī manuscript which is said to bear the date S. 1715 (A.D. 1658). Rattan Singh Jaggi, *Dasam Granth dā paurāṇik adhiain*, p. 59.

[3] Its account of 'the country ruled by women' is a clear example (IOL, MS. Panj. B41, folios 70b–71b). The 1871 printed edition departs from the manuscript at this point and reproduces instead the *Purātan* version of the story (*Bālā JS*, *sākhī* 25, pp. 102–8). The *Bālā* version of the story of Rājā Śivanābh appears to be another illustration (*Bālā JS*, pp. 120–3). See *infra*, p. 74, numbers 46 and 54.

[4] Santokh Singh did not accept the absolute authenticity of the *Bālā* account, but he did accept its claim to have been originally written at the behest of Gurū Aṅgad and accordingly followed it very closely in the *Nānak Prakāś*.

[5] Its lengthy sequel, the *Gur Pratāp Sūray*, commonly referred to as the *Sūraj Prākāś*, which carries the account up to the tenth Gurū, contains a somewhat higher proportion of historical fact, but is untrustworthy nonetheless. The *Surāj Prakāś* was completed in 1844. Both works are in metre and have been edited in thirteen volumes by Bhāī Vir Singh. For a note on Santokh Singh's life see Macauliffe, i, pp. lxxvi–lxxvii.

heresy attached to it. On the contrary, it has been accepted as the work of one who ranks high amongst loyal Sikhs and who wrote the janam-sākhī with the express intention of correcting heretical accounts of Gurū Nānak's life.

Perhaps the most likely explanation for the neglect is that the original collection of *sākhīs* was made during a period of political disturbance which would have inhibited its circulation. These circumstances would not necessarily have had the same effect upon the *Bālā* janam-sākhīs, for the first half of the eighteenth century was the period of Hindālī influence. By the time more settled conditions returned the *Bālā* version had evidently established itself as the apparently authentic account and the need for other versions was no longer recognized.

Bhāī Manī Singh was a famous Sikh of Gurū Gobind Singh's time[1] and the circumstances which are said to have led him to write his janam-sākhī are set out in a prologue. In this prologue it is recorded that some Sikhs once approached him with the request that he should prepare an authentic account of Gurū Nānak's life. This, they assured him, was essential as the Mīṇās[2] had maliciously interpolated objectionable things in the current account and that as a result the Sikhs' faith in the Gurū was declining. Manī Singh referred them to Bhāī Gurdās's first *vār*, but this, they maintained, was too brief. What was required was an 'expanded commentary' on the *vār*. Manī Singh protested that such a task was beyond his limited capacities, but finally agreed to make the attempt.

> Just as swimmers fix reeds in the river so that those who do not know the way may also cross, so I shall take Bhāī Gurdās's *vār* as my basis and in accordance with it, and with the accounts which I have heard at the court of the tenth Master, I shall relate to you whatever commentary issues from my humble mind.[3]

At the end of the janam-sākhī there is an epilogue in which it is stated that the completed work was taken to Gurū Gobind Singh for his *imprimatur*. The Gurū, it is said, duly signed it and commended it as a means of acquiring knowledge of Sikh belief.[4]

This is the *Gyān-ratanāvalī's* own account of its origin. The claim is that Manī Singh took *Vār* 1 as his basis, that he supplemented it with *sākhīs* he had heard related at the court of Gurū Gobind Singh, and that he presented the complete work to the Gurū for his approval. Gurū Gobind Singh was Gurū from 1675 until 1708. If the janam-sākhī's own claim is to be accepted its date of composition must lie within the intervening period.

The claim is difficult to test as the version of the *Gyān-ratanāvalī* which we now possess is certainly not the work of Manī Singh. It may perhaps

1 *MK*, p. 712, and Macauliffe, i, pp. lxxiv–lxxvi give brief biographies.

2 See *supra*, p. 18, n. 4. 3 *GR*, pp. 3–4. 4 Ibid., *sākhī* 225, p. 592.

incorporate portions of a collection prepared by him, but the available manuscripts record a composite product which has drawn on more than one source and which has obviously been put together much later than the time of Manī Singh.

Three reasons point to this conclusion. In the first place, there are several references to Manī Singh in the third person which clearly imply that the writer of the *Gyān-ratanāvalī* is another person. In the prologue and at various points in the narrative[1] the author makes references which suggest that he is intended to be understood as one who was present while Manī Singh was relating the account.

Secondly, there is the comparative modernity of the *Gyān-ratanāvalī's* language. This cannot be blamed on the printers who lithographed the work in 1891 and 1907 as the manuscript copies possess the same characteristic.[2]

Thirdly, there is manifest lack of homogeneity in the work. Parts of the janam-sākhī are consistent and follow a relatively logical sequence, but there are groups of *sākhīs* and a number of individual ones which disrupt the basic pattern and which have obviously been drawn from extraneous sources. Some of this later material appears to be the result of simple interpolation, but most of it has been properly integrated into the janam-sākhī.

Most of the extraneous material is easily recognizable and its incidence divides the complete work into two distinct parts. The first part covers the period of the Gurū's early life, and of his travels in eastern and southern India. Most of this first section represents an independent selection of *sākhīs* which may well be a revised version of material dating back to the early eighteenth century, perhaps even to Manī Singh himself. Several of the *sākhīs* are also included in both the *Purātan* and *Bālā* versions[3] and just as these two versions differ in their presentation, so the *Gyān-ratanāvalī* account differs from both. A number are also to be found in the *Miharbān Janam-sākhī* as well and in these instances all four versions offer varying accounts. These differences which distinguish individual *sākhīs* from corresponding accounts in other known collections indicate an independent selection from the common stock of oral *sākhīs*.

In addition to the independent material, however, there are in this first part several *sākhīs* which have been borrowed from the *Bālā* tradition,[4] and in the second part the *Gyān-ratanāvalī* becomes, in substance, a *Bālā*

[1] e.g. *GR*, pp. 340, 516.

[2] Writing in 1885 Gurmukh Singh observed: 'This janam-sākhī is popularly attributed to Bhāī Manī Singh, although someone else wrote it because its language is modern.' He adds the comment: 'If Bhāī Manī Singh himself wrote a janam-sākhī it is no longer extant.' Introduction to Macauliffe's edition of the *Hāfizābād Janam-sākhi*, pp. 2–3.

[3] See *infra*, pp. 73–76.

[4] *GR*, pp. 46–48, 135, 194–200, 213, 214, 220–1, 237–42.

janam-sākhī. The change occurs with the sudden appearance of Bhāī Bālā in the *sākhī* which describes Gurū Nānak's return to his home village of Talvaṇḍī after his travels to the east and south.[1] In the first part the person of Bhāī Bālā has been dropped from the *sākhīs* which have been taken from *Bālā* sources,[2] but following the arrival in Talvaṇḍī he is introduced into the narrative and continues in it for most of the remainder of the janam-sākhī. A logical sequence of events is maintained during the first few *sākhīs* which follow his irruption,[3] but the record soon loses its coherence and assumes the characteristic disarray of the *Bālā* tradition. At one point Bhāī Bālā disappears and for a time the record reverts to the pattern of the first half of the janam-sākhī. It retains, however, a strong *Bālā* flavour.[4]

The second half of the janam-sākhī is accordingly an amalgam. Some of it continues the earlier pattern of an independent selection from the current stock, presented in a logical sequence, and the remainder is evidently material subsequently introduced from *Bālā* sources. This means that we have in the extant version of the *Gyān-ratanāvalī* two contrasting elements. The first half (with the evident exception of the prologue and a number of other individual *sākhīs*) represents an independent selection from the common stock of *sākhīs*, and the second combines this first element with substantial borrowings from the *Bālā* tradition. With the exception of a few minor points both elements have been integrated into a single janam-sākhī by an editor who provided an introduction and a conclusion, and who refers to Manī Singh in the third person. The language of the janam-sākhī and its relationship to the *Bālā* tradition suggest that this was probably done in the late eighteenth or early nineteenth century, although some individual *sākhīs* may have been added later. The first element representing the independent selection would, however, be older and may possibly go back as far as the time of Gurū Gobind Singh.

The value of the *Gyān-ratanāvalī* lies chiefly in this first element and as far as this material is concerned the janam-sākhī is a rather more satisfactory collection than those of the *Bālā* group. It has an order which the *Bālā* janam-sākhīs lack, it avoids many of their errors, and it offers appreciably less that is plainly fantastic. In spite of this, however, its usefulness is not much greater as far as efforts to reconstruct Gurū Nānak's biography are concerned. It does at times have a negative value in that its variant

[1] *GR*, p. 264. In some copies, including the edition lithographed in 1891, Bhāī Bālā appears prior to this point in a group of *sākhīs* which describe Gurū Nānak's meeting with Sālas Rāi, a jeweller in a town called Biṣambarpur (*GR*, *sākhīs* 99–107, pp. 247–59). The same *sākhīs* appear, in almost exactly the same words, in the expanded 1871 version of the *Bālā* tradition (Dīvān Būṭā Singh, Lahore, *sākhīs* 74–75, pp. 183–93). See *infra*, pp. 84–85.

[2] In one case (the Gayā *sākhī*, *GR*, p. 214) the omission of Bhāī Bālā's name has left an obvious hiatus, but for the most part the *sākhīs* have been successfully woven into the narrative.

[3] *GR*, *sākhīs* 110–20, pp. 264–85.

[4] *GR*, pp. 401–516.

account will strengthen a case against the historicity of a particular incident recorded in the older janam-sākhīs, and at a very few points, such as the date of birth question, it makes a positive contribution of some significance. In so far as it adds to what Bhāī Gurdās's *Vār* I contains it represents a relatively late selection from the fund of oral *sākhīs*, interesting for this reason and sober by comparison with the *Bālā* presentation, but still a supplementary source of only occasional usefulness.

The two versions of the Mahimā Prakāś

Two works which deserve a brief mention are the *Mahimā Prakāś Vāratak* and the *Mahimā Prakāś Kavitā*. The earlier of the two, the *Mahimā Prakāś Vāratak*, was written in 1741 by Bāwā Kirpāl Singh Bhallā, and the later longer version, the *Mahimā Prakāś Kavitā*, in 1776 by Sarūp Dās Bhallā, a descendant of Gurū Amar Dās.[1] The two accounts are basically the same, but the prose version, the *Vāratak*, is appreciably shorter, having only twenty *sākhīs* devoted to Gurū Nānak as opposed to sixty-five in the metrical version.

Neither work deals exclusively with Gurū Nānak, the remainder in each case concerning the lives of the Gurūs who followed him. The two versions occupy positions of importance in the history of Sikh tradition, for they were composed during a period which, although generally obscure, was certainly significant in terms of the development of such tradition. Like the *Gyān-ratanāvalī*, however, both are too recent to be regarded as primary sources for the life of Gurū Nānak. The portion of the *Mahimā Prakāś Vāratak* dealing with Gurū Nānak was printed privately in 1959,[2] but neither version has yet been published in full.

The relative value of the different janam-sākhī traditions

An attempt must now be made to assess the relative value of the different janam-sākhī traditions as sources for a biography of Gurū Nānak. As we have already indicated, the janam-sākhīs of the *Bālā* tradition are particularly unreliable, and the relatively late *Gyān-ratanāvalī* offers little which is not available in earlier janam-sākhī sources. Accordingly, these two sources may be summarily excluded and the discussion confined to Bhāī Gurdās's *Vār* I and the janam-sākhīs of the *Miharbān* and *Purātan* traditions. The *Bālā* janam-sākhīs and the *Gyān-ratanāvalī* will not, of course, be totally excluded from the analysis of the events of Gurū Nānak's life,

[1] The date S. 1833 (A.D. 1776) given in the text of the *Mahimā Prakāś Kavitā* refers only to the portion dealing with Gurū Nānak (Khalsa College, Amritsar, MS. SHR: 2300A, folio 145a).

[2] *Jīvan kathā Srī Gurū Nānak Dev Jī Mahimā Prakāś* (*Vāratak*) *vichon*, ed. Kirpal Singh, Dehra Dun, 1959.

for notwithstanding their limitations they do have a contribution to make.

The account of Gurū Nānak's life given in Bhāī Gurdās's *Vār* 1, and supplemented in *Vār* 11, is a very brief one, but within the limited range which it covers this account has generally been accepted as the most reliable available. There are three reasons for this reputation. The first and basic one is the indisputable fact that the author was a Sikh of impeccable orthodoxy who had close associations with the more prominent of his Sikh contemporaries. These would have included not only Gurū Arjan and Gurū Hargobind, but also older disciples whose memories might have extended back to the time of Gurū Nānak himself. Secondly, there is the coherence of the travel itinerary which may be deduced from the first *vār*. Thirdly, there is the belief that there is less of the miraculous in this account, and accordingly less that warrants a measure of scepticism. Khushwant Singh is expressing a generally accepted conclusion when he says of the events of Gurū Nānak's life, 'whatever reference he makes in the *Vārs* must be considered authentic'.[1]

The importance of the first reason should not be minimized, but we are nevertheless unable to accept the conclusion without some qualification. The belief that the account given in *Vār* 1 contains less of the miraculous than the janam-sākhīs is an illusion created by its limited range. If the comparison is narrowed down to the three incidents which are common to the *vār* and to either or both of the two older janam-sākhī traditions[2] it is at once evident that Bhāī Gurdās's account contains almost as many miraculous or otherwise unacceptable details as the *Purātan* version and, in one instance, more than that of the *Miharbān Janam-sākhī*. In the encounter with the eighty-four Siddhs on Mount Sumeru there is the anachronistic reference to Gorakhnāth and also the story of the jewels by the lakeside which the *Miharbān* account lacks. In Mecca we have the moving mosque, and in Achal Baṭālā the yogīs turning into lions, wolves, birds, and snakes.[3]

These details must prompt a measure of caution and constrain us to qualify Khushwant Singh's conclusion. We may attach a greater degree of trust to Bhāī Gurdās's account than to those of the *Purātan* and *Miharbān* janam-sākhīs, but it cannot be an unqualified trust. We must, moreover, conclude that even if the two *vārs* are the most reliable they are also the least satisfactory. The chief reason for this is the brevity of the account which they provide. The author's primary purpose was obviously to extol the Gurū rather than to provide a comprehensive record of his life, and so the *vārs* must disappoint us if we seek in them anything more than a brief

[1] Khushwant Singh, *A History of the Sikhs*, vol. i, p. 301.

[2] The Mount Sumeru, Mecca, and Achal Baṭālā incidents. See *infra*, p. 75, numbers 72, 79, and 90.

[3] See *infra*, p. 35. In Bhāī Gurdās's version it is Mecca itself which moves.

sketch of a small part of his travels and the names of a number of his followers. They retain a value in these respects, but it is to the janam-sākhīs that we must look for most of our material.

This restricts the discussion to the *Miharbān* and *Purātan* traditions. One point which at once becomes clear in any comparison of these two traditions is that as far as their biographical content is concerned they share a common heritage and a common distinction from the janam-sākhīs of the *Bālā* tradition. It is remotely possible that this is a result of one having copied from the other, but much more likely that they share a common source, or sources, of *sākhīs*. The similarities between the two accounts establish the connexion beyond all doubt, and the differences indicate that there is unlikely to have been any direct copying of one by the other. The parallels are marked, but so too are the divergences and it is on the basis of these divergences that an effort must be made to assess their relative values.

The most apparent difference is the greater length of the *Miharbān Janam-sākhī*. We are here concerned with the biographical content of the two janam-sākhīs and this means that the disparity is not nearly as great as might appear at first sight. Most of the *Miharbān Janam-sākhī* covers discourse, scripture, and interpretation, and the strictly biographical content is comparatively small. It is, however, greater than that of the *Purātan* janam-sākhīs. In the account of Gurū Nānak's marriage, for example, we find in the *Miharbān* version a lengthy catalogue of details which almost certainly owes its origin to an understanding of how marriages are usually conducted rather than to an authentic knowledge of the manner in which this particular marriage took place.[1] In the *Purātan* janam-sākhīs, on the other hand, the account of Gurū Nānak's marriage is dealt with in a single, brief sentence: 'When Bābā (Nānak) turned twelve he was married.'[2]

This is an extreme case, but Miharbān's accounts are generally longer. There are two possible reasons for this. The first is that the *Miharbān Janam-sākhī* may have drawn from the common pool of *sākhīs* later than the original *Purātan* version and that the individual *sākhīs* had been expanded in the meantime. This would mean that the *Purātan* version was a more primitive one, nearer to the time when memory still played a significant part, and was consequently more reliable.

The second possibility is that the additions represent the embellishments of a more sophisticated mind. There can be no doubt that the *Miharbān Janam-sākhī* is the work of a person of appreciably more learning than the person or persons responsible for the *Purātan* compilation. The less sophisticated mind would be content with the tradition as he found it, whereas a person such as Miharbān might feel compelled to embroider a simple account with details which do not materially affect the basic

[1] *Mih JS*, *goṣṭ* 11, pp. 29–33. [2] *Pur JS*, *sākhī* 3, p. 6.

elements of the account. The nature of the differences lends support to this latter possibility, but it may well be that both are true and that the *Purātan* version does carry us a little further back in the evolutionary process.

The other differences tend, however, to support the claims of the *Miharbān Janam-sākhī*. In the first place there is the fact that Miharbān is more careful with his material than whoever was responsible for the *Purātan* collection. This applies not just to his quotations from scripture, but also to his use of place-names and the names of people with whom Gurū Nānak is purported to have conversed. We do not find in his account such places as 'the land of Āsā'[1] or 'the land of Dhanāsarī',[2] and Gurū Nānak is said to have conversed not with Pīr Bahāuddīn[3] but with a descendant.[4] In this respect, however, the difference between Miharbān's account and that of the *Purātan* janam-sākhīs is one of degree, not an absolute one. His mistakes with scripture may be understandable,[5] but they are there nevertheless. There may be no lands of Āsā and Dhanāsarī, but there are numerous unidentified towns, deserts, and jungles. A conversation with a descendant of Pīr Bahāuddīn[6] cannot be given the summary treatment required in the case of a conversation with Bahāuddīn himself,[7] but an interview with Islām S͟hāh shows that Miharbān is also liable to record anachronisms.[8]

Secondly, although both accounts contain substantial quantities of the miraculous, the miracle stories recorded in the *Miharbān-Janam-sākhī* are, on the whole, less grotesque than those of the *Purātan* tradition. There is no description of Mardānā being turned into a lamb,[9] no reference to the victory of an army of insects possessing human faculties over an army of men,[10] no conversation with a man who had been reincarnated as a wolf,[11] no mention of Bahāuddīn's magic prayer-mat,[12] and no account of Rājā Śivanābh killing and stewing his son at Gurū Nānak's command.[13] Miharbān's janam-sākhī is by no means devoid of this kind of fantasy, but in general his miracles are of a more subdued nature.

[1] *Pur JS*, p. 40.
[2] Ibid., p. 78.
[3] Ibid., pp. 82, 108.
[4] *Mih JS*, p. 434. The word used is *potā* which generally designates a son's son, but which may be used of a more remote descendant in the direct male line.
[5] All but one of the extracts which he erroneously ascribes to Gurū Nānak appear in the *Ādi Granth* as parts of *vārs*. The *vārs* of the *Ādi Granth* are almost all composite works including the compositions of different Gurūs, and although the components are all identified a mistake made with *vār* material is more excusable than one involving a verse which plainly bears its author's title. The one exception, Gurū Amar Dās's *ślok* 104, is also explicable. It occurs in the collection of Sheikh Farīd's *śloks* and the same collection also includes *śloks* by Gurū Nānak.
[6] *Mih JS*, p. 434.
[7] *Pur JS*, pp. 82–84, 108–10. Bahāuddīn is believed to have died in A.D. 1266 (T. W. Beale, *An Oriental Biographical Dictionary*, p. 97).
[8] *Mih JS*, p. 114. See *infra*, p. 80.
[9] *Pur JS*, p. 34. According to the janam-sākhīs Mardānā the Bard was Gurū Nānak's companion during his travels.
[10] Ibid., p. 39.
[11] Ibid., p. 71.
[12] Ibid., pp. 82–84.
[13] Ibid., p. 88.

Thirdly, Miharbān offers a more satisfactory chronology and a more likely travel itinerary than the *Purātan* janam-sākhīs. According to Miharbān's *Pothī Sach-khaṇḍ* Gurū Nānak made two major journeys, followed by a brief excursion. During the first journey he travelled eastwards as far as Jagannāth Purī, southwards to Rāmeśwaram and perhaps to Ceylon, and then back to the Pañjāb up the west coast, calling at Ujjain and Bīkāner on the way. The second took him northwards into the Himālayas, westwards to Mecca, and then back through Sindh. The brief excursion took him no further than Pāk Paṭṭan.

This is much more likely than the traditional pattern of the *Purātan* account which follows the four cardinal points of the compass. It is not at all likely that Gurū Nānak would have returned home after an eastern journey and then gone to the south, and nor does it seem possible that he would have had sufficient time for such extensive travels.[1] Miharbān's description of a single all-embracing visit to the holy places of India is inherently more probable and offers a more reasonable time schedule. Moreover, Miharbān is supported by the brief outline which Bhāī Gurdās gives.

Fourthly, it is worth noting that Miharbān, for all his schismatic connexions, was a grandson of Gurū Rām Dās and a great-grandson of Gurū Amar Dās. The relationship would probably have meant access to relatively reliable traditions which might well have been denied to whoever gathered the *Purātan* material. This is an assumption, not a proven fact, but it is a reasonable assumption. These points would seem to indicate that of the three oldest sources the *Miharbān Janam-sākhī* is the most important. Before any conclusions are drawn, however, two of the arguments must be qualified. The second is qualified by the fact that the India Office Library manuscript B40, to which we have granted a *Purātan* affiliation, omits all but one of the miracles which are listed above;[2] and the force of the third is greatly reduced by the existence of another possibility which is much more likely than either the itinerary offered by the *Purātan* tradition on the one hand or that of Miharbān on the other. This third possibility is that neither of the collections is based upon a knowledge of the actual routes followed by Gurū Nānak in his travels, but rather that both represent patterns which were evolved by grouping the available *sākhīs* in a reasonable

[1] The likelihood appears to be that the *Purātan* pattern represents a later expression of the ancient *digvijaya* tradition. The term was primarily applied to a monarch's military triumphs in all four directions, but it had also acquired a hagiographic usage. In this latter sense it described the spiritual triumphs of a great saint, again with reference to the four cardinal points of the compass. Śaṅkara's biographies provide the most important illustrations of this usage and it seems that the *Purātan* pattern of Gurū Nānak's travels provides another example. I owe this suggestion to Professor A. L. Basham.

[2] The exception is the changing of Mardānā into a sheep (IOL, MS. Panj. B40, folio 83). This manuscript agrees with the *Bālā* and *Gyān-ratanāvalī* versions in having him turned into a ram, not a lamb.

sequence.[1] Miharbān's more rational grouping probably amounts to no more than another example of his greater sophistication.

Even with these qualifications the arguments in favour of the *Miharbān* version still seem to indicate that of the three oldest sources it is the most satisfactory. The margin dividing the *Purātan* manuscripts and the *Miharbān Janam-sākhī* is, however, slender, and with the India Office Library B40 manuscript added to the *Purātan* group it virtually disappears. The differences are important not so much as a yardstick for measuring relative superiority, as a means of testing the reliability of individual *sākhīs*. Agreement between all versions may strengthen the claims of a *sākhī* and disagreement will have the opposite effect. Occasionally this factor is of appreciable significance, although generally in the negative sense.

Two things may be said with assurance. The first is that the normal practice of relying on the *Purātan* janam-sākhīs cannot produce reliable biography. The second is that any effort to use the *Miharbān Janam-sākhī* in the same way will be equally unsatisfactory. The janam-sākhīs must be regarded as examples of hagiography and any inclination to treat them as biographies will distort both our understanding of Gurū Nānak and our appreciation of the true value of the janam-sākhīs themselves. It is a value which includes the provision of strictly limited source material for the life of Gurū Nānak, but which is by no means limited to this function. It consists rather in the testimony which the janam-sākhīs give to the impact and continuing influence of the Gurū's personality, and even more in the evidence they offer of Sikh belief and understanding at particular points in the community's history. Having made this acknowledgement we must turn back to them. We are compelled to use the janam-sākhīs as best we can, for there is nothing better, but we must do so in the full understanding that they are thoroughly inadequate sources.

[1] See *infra*, p. 145.

3

THE LIFE OF GURŪ NĀNAK ACCORDING TO THE JANAM-SĀKHĪS

THE ideal method of relating the janam-sākhī testimony to the life of Gurū Nānak would be to provide a connected account which harmonized in a single narrative the accounts given in our three principal sources. This, however, is impossible. The selection of incidents offered by Bhāī Gurdās can, by reason of its brevity, be assimilated with either of the two janam-sākhī narratives, but apart from the period covering the Gurū's childhood and early manhood it is not possible to fuse the accounts recorded in the *Miharbān* and *Purātan* traditions. Up to the point where Gurū Nānak sets out from Sultānpur on his travels there is relatively close correspondence and a harmony of the two versions could, if necessary, be provided. Following his departure from Sultānpur, however, the two narratives diverge so radically that reconciliation is out of the question. For the period of the Gurū's eastern and southern travels there is no correspondence at all. In the case of his northern and western journeys there are a number of incidents in common, but there remain crucial differences in sequence. It is accordingly necessary to set out the testimonies of our three principal sources as three separate accounts. Having done this we shall seek to analyse the material which they provide.

The life of Gurū Nānak according to Bhāī Gurdās

Bhāī Gurdās's account of the life of Gurū Nānak is to be found in stanzas 23–45 of his first *vār*, and in stanzas 13–14 of his eleventh *vār* he gives a list of the Gurū's more important followers. Stanzas 23 and 24 of the first *vār* provide little more than eloquent panegyric, but stanza 25 begins with the line:

> Bābā (Nānak) visited the places of pilgrimage; he went round seeing them all on festival days.

None of these centres are named, but it is clear from the description which follows that the line is meant to indicate a journey of considerable length.[1]

The first reference to a particular event comes in stanza 28 where it is related that the Gurū ascended Mount Sumeru and there held discourse

[1] *BG*, I. 25–27.

with Gorakhnāth and the other eighty-three Siddhs.[1] The Siddhs questioned Gurū Nānak concerning the condition of the world below and received in reply a report of darkness, sin, and corruption. They then sought to persuade him to enter their sect and sent him to a nearby lakeside in order that he might be tempted by the masses of jewels which he would find in the lake. Their efforts failed, however, and the Gurū emerged victorious from the debate.[2]

Next he proceeded to Mecca and there went to sleep with his feet pointing towards the *miharāb*.[3] Observing this evident blasphemy a Muslim named Jīvaṇ kicked him and dragged his feet away from the direction of the *miharāb*. When he did this, however, the whole of Mecca miraculously moved in the same direction as his feet. A discourse followed in which Gurū Nānak emphasized that Rām and Rahīm, Hindu and Muslim names for God, designate one and the same God.[4]

Having left his sandals in Mecca as a relic,[5] the Gurū proceeded on to Medina,[6] and from there to Baghdad where, with Mardānā the Bard, he camped outside the city. From there he uttered the call to prayer whereupon the city at once became silent. A *pīr* named Dastgīr went out to investigate the newcomer's credentials and entered into a debate with him. In response to Dastgīr's request for enlightenment the Gurū took the *pīr's* son, ascended with him into the air, and in the twinkling of an eye revealed to him the multitude of heavens and underworlds. The two then descended into the regions below the earth and from there brought a bowl of *kaṛāh prasād*, the sacramental food of the Sikhs.[7]

Having returned to the Pañjāb Gurū Nānak proceeded to Kartārpur and there began to lead a settled life, surrounded by his followers. His sons proved rebellious and the seal of succession was accordingly set upon Aṅgad.[8]

On one occasion Gurū Nānak travelled from Kartārpur to the village of Achal Baṭālā[9] where many yogīs had gathered for the annual Śivrātri fair. In the debate which ensued the yogīs sought to overwhelm him with an impressive display of miracles. Disdaining to use the same methods, the Gurū eventually overcame them with his insistence upon the Name of God as the true source of power.[10]

From Achal Baṭālā he travelled south to Multān, but before he could enter the city some *pīrs* came out to him bearing a cup filled with milk. Gurū Nānak responded by plucking a jasmine flower and laying it on the surface of the milk.[11]

[1] See *supra*, p. 11, n. 10.
[2] *BG*, 1. 28–31.
[3] The niche in a mosque which indicates the direction of the *Ka'bah*.
[4] *BG*, 1. 32–33.
[5] *BG*, 1. 34.
[6] The reference to Medina comes in 1. 37, but the visit should presumably be placed after the Mecca visit.
[7] *BG*, 1. 35–36.
[8] *BG*, 1. 38.
[9] Four miles east of Baṭālā in Gurdāspur District.
[10] *BG*, 1. 39–44.
[11] *BG*, 1. 44. For the meaning of this gesture see *infra*, p. 142.

Following the Multān visit the Gurū returned to Kartārpur and settled down once again. There his glory daily increased and his fame spread throughout the world. Before he died he appointed his disciple Lahiṇā to succeed him as Gurū Aṅgad and then, merging his spirit in the spirit of his successor, he passed away.[1]

The life of Gurū Nānak according to the Purātan *janam-sākhīs*[2]

1 Bābā Nānak was born in the month of Vaisākh, S. 1526 (A.D. 1469). The date is given as the third day of the light half of the month, and the birth is said to have taken place during the last watch before dawn. His father, Kālū, was a khatrī of the Bedī sub-caste who lived in the village of Rāi Bhoi dī Talvaṇḍī and it was there that Nānak was born. His mother's name is not given. During his infancy he played with other children, but unlike them he had a concern for spiritual things and from the age of five began to utter mysterious sayings. The local Hindus declared that a god had been incarnated in human form, and the Muslims that a true follower of God had been born.

2 When he turned seven Nānak was taken to a paṇḍit to learn how to read. After only one day he gave up reading and when the paṇḍit asked him why he had lapsed into silence Nānak instructed him at length in the vanity of worldly learning and the contrasting value of the divine Name of God. The paṇḍit was greatly impressed and permitted him to return home.

3 The child now began to manifest disturbing signs of withdrawal from the world. He was set to learning 'Turkī'[3] at the age of nine, but returned home and continued to sit in silence.[4] The local people suggested to Kālū that he should have Nānak married. Kālū took their advice, a betrothal was arranged at the house of Mūlā, a khatrī of the Choṇā sub-caste, and at the age of twelve Bābā Nānak was duly married. No reference is made to where Mūlā lived or to where the marriage took place, and nor is the bride's name given. Nānak now took up a worldly occupation, but his heart was not in it and he spent his time consorting with faqīrs.

4 Two miracles are related of this period. On one occasion he went to sleep while grazing the family buffaloes and the unattended animals ruined a field of standing wheat. The aggrieved owner of the field haled the negligent Nānak before Rāi Bulār, the landlord of the village. Gurū Nānak insisted, however, that no damage had been done, and a messenger

[1] *BG*, 1. 45.

[2] The figure in the margin indicates the number of each *sākhī* as given in Vir Singh's *Purātan Janam-sākhī*. For a translation of the *Colebrooke Janam-sākhī* see E. Trumpp, *The Ādi Granth*, pp. vii–xlv.

[3] Persian.

[4] The IOL manuscript Panj. B40 inserts before the reference to Kālū's effort to have him taught 'Turkī' a very brief reference to his having been invested with the sacred thread (*janeū*) at the age of nine. Loc. cit., folio 6a.

despatched by Rāi Bulār found that the ruined crop had been miraculously
restored. On another occasion Rāi Bulār happened upon Nānak sleeping in 5
the shadow of a tree and was greatly impressed to observe that the shadow did not move with the declining sun.[1] The same *sākhī* also records the birth of Gurū Nānak's two sons, Lakhmī Dās and Sirī Chand.

Nānak's habitual withdrawal from the world continued to cause grave 6
concern and both his parents remonstrated with him unsuccessfully. Some 7
of the Bedīs suggested consulting a physician, but this merely prompted utterances concerning the nature of what the Gurū regarded as the real
illness afflicting mankind. The family problem was eventually solved by 8
Nānak's brother-in-law, Jai Rām,[2] who was the steward of Nawāb Daulat Khān of Sultānpur. Jai Rām sent a letter inviting Nānak to Sultānpur. The invitation was accepted and Gurū Nānak departed, comforting his forlorn wife with a promise that he would call her as soon as his work in Sultānpur prospered.

As soon as Nānak arrived in Sultānpur Jai Rām petitioned Daulat Khān 9
to grant his brother-in-law an audience. The request was granted and as a result of the interview Daulat Khān formed a very favourable impression of Nānak. He presented him with a robe of honour and issued instructions that he should be given employment. The nature of the employment is not specified beyond the fact that it was evidently understood to be clerical work. The *sākhī* records that each morning the Gurū would first take his orders from the court and then would 'sit down to write'.[3] In the following *sākhī* Daulat Khān refers to him as 'a good vazīr' and uses the same word to describe him in *sākhī* 11.

During this period Gurū Nānak lived a very simple life, keeping only enough of his food allowance to meet his own limited needs and devoting the remainder to God's work.[4] Mardānā the Ḍūm[5] came from Talvaṇḍī to join him and was followed by others. All were commended to Daulat Khān by Nānak and received employment as a result. The group regularly sang the praises of God until late into the night, and during the last watch of the night the Gurū would go to the river and bathe.

One day Nānak went to the river[6] and removing his clothes left them in 10
the care of a servant. While he was bathing messengers of God came and he was transported by them to the divine court. There he was given a cup of nectar (*amrit*) and with it came the command, 'Nānak, this is the cup of My Name (*Nām*). Drink it.' This he did and was charged to go into the world and preach the divine Name.

[1] Rāi Bulār's relationship to Rāi Bhoi is not specified.
[2] Gurū Nānak's sister is not named.
[3] *Pur JS*, p. 14.
[4] That is, giving it to sādhūs and faqīrs.
[5] A depressed sub-caste of Muslim genealogists and musicians, also called Mirāsīs.
[6] The name of the river is not given.

In the meantime the servant had become anxious at his master's failure to emerge from the water. He returned to the town and informed Daulat Khān of the apparent tragedy. Daulat Khān rode out at once and had the river dragged, but Nānak's body was not to be found. Three days later, however, the missing Nānak suddenly reappeared at the point where he had entered the river. Daulat Khān joined the crowd which gathered, but Gurū Nānak evidently remained silent, for the people explained to the Nawāb that he had sustained injury in the river. Hearing this Daulat Khān departed with a heavy heart and Nānak, wearing only a loin-cloth, went with Mardānā to live with some faqīrs.

11 For one day Gurū Nānak maintained his silence and then on the following day he spoke, saying: 'There is neither Hindu nor Mussulman.' This was reported to Daulat Khān, but dismissed as the sort of utterance one might expect to hear from a faqīr. His qāzī, however, took a more serious view of what appeared to be a clear rejection of Islam's claims to superiority. Daulat Khān agreed to question Nānak on the subject, but found nothing offensive in the reply which he received.

It so happened that the appointed time for the second daily prayer came while Gurū Nānak was being examined. Everyone present arose and went to the mosque, and Nānak went with them. There he caused even greater offence to the qāzī by laughing out loud during the reading of *namāz*. The qāzī protested angrily to Daulat Khān, but Nānak explained that he had done so because the qāzī had been thinking, not of the prayer he was uttering, but of a new-born filly he had left in the compound, dangerously near a well. The qāzī was now convinced of Nānak's powers and made his submission. The people all followed his example and Daulat Khān was so impressed that he offered to surrender his entire authority and all his property to the Gurū. When he returned home he found that his treasury had been miraculously filled.[1] Gurū Nānak then left Sultānpur, taking with him Mardānā the Bard.

After leaving the town the Gurū and Mardānā first proceeded to a wilderness and for some time deliberately avoided all inhabited places. On one occasion Mardānā became hungry and was sent ahead to a village of Uppal khatrīs to receive the generous offerings they would make. On another occasion Mardānā entered a town where reverence, clothing, and money were lavished upon him. He returned laden to the Gurū, but was told to throw the offerings away as they were unnecessary encumbrances.

13 Journeying on they came to the house of a certain Sheikh Sajjaṇ. The house was situated out in the country and its owner had built both a temple and a mosque. These were ostensibly for the convenience of Hindu and Muslim travellers, but Sajjaṇ was a *ṭhag*[2] and his real purpose was to lure

[1] The IOL manuscript Panj. B40 omits this point.

[2] In its strict sense the word *ṭhag*, or thug, designates a member of the cult of ritual

travellers into his house in order that he might murder them and so acquire their wealth. His method of despatching his guests was to throw them into a well. Bābā Nānak and Mardānā were welcomed in the usual way and when night came they were invited to take rest. Before doing so the Gurū sang a hymn. The words which he sang convicted Sajjaṇ of his sin and falling at the Gurū's feet he implored forgiveness. This was granted on condition that he made restitution for all he had stolen. The *Hāfizābād* manuscript adds that the first *dharmsālā* was built there.[1]

After leaving Sajjaṇ they travelled to Pāṇīpat where Gurū Nānak held 14
a successful discourse with Sheikh Sharaf, the *Pīr* of Pāṇīpat. The name of
the *Pīr*'s disciple is given as Sheikh Ṭaṭihar. From Pāṇīpat they proceeded 15
on to Delhi where they encountered some mahouts employed by Sultan Ibrāhīm Beg.[2] The mahouts were bewailing the death of the elephant which had provided their employment. At the Gurū's bidding they stroked the dead animal's face and uttered, 'Vāhigurū!'[3] The elephant was instantly restored to life and the sultan, hearing of the miracle, asked for a repetition of it. The elephant duly died again, but Gurū Nānak made no effort to revive it. His cryptic explanation was, however, understood by the sultan and accepted as a thoroughly laudable one.

These early incidents were evidently a part of the Gurū's first journey 16
(*udāsī*), but this is not explicitly declared to have begun until after the Delhi visit. *Sākhī* 16 records that the first journey was to the east and that on this occasion the Gurū's companion was Mardānā. It also details the bizarre dress which he adopted for this journey. It is given as an ochre garment and a white one, a slipper on one foot and a wooden sandal on the other, a faqīr's *kafnī*[4] and a necklace of bones around his neck, a *qalandar's* hat on his head, and a saffron mark (*tilak*) on his forehead. His food is said to have consisted of air. The same *sākhī* also refers to a certain Sheikh Bajīd whom they happened to observe being transported in a litter and then being massaged and fanned by servants. In response to Mardānā's inquiry concerning the inequalities of the human condition Bābā Nānak replied, 'Joy and pain come in accordance with the deeds of one's previous existence.'

Travelling on they reached Banāras where they sat down in a public 17
square. A paṇḍit named Chatur Dās, who happened to pass, observed with surprise that Gurū Nānak had neither *śālgrām*, *tulsī-mālā*, rosary, nor sectarian mark. A discourse ensued, ending with a complete recitation of the lengthy work entitled *Oaṅkāru*[5] and with the conversion of Chatur Dās.

murderers who strangled and robbed in the name of the goddess Kālī. In the janam-sākhīs, however, it means any highwayman or violent robber.

[1] i.e. the first Sikh *dharmsālā*, or first building dedicated to Sikh worship and service.

[2] This is the *Hāfizābād* reading. The *Colebrooke* manuscript gives his name as Braham Beg.

[3] 'Wonderful Lord.' A characteristic Sikh name of God which originated after the time of Gurū Nānak.

[4] A piece of cloth worn round the waist.

[5] *AG*, pp. 929–38.

18 The next incident is set in a place which the *Purātan* janam-sākhīs refer to simply as Nānakmatā.[1] It was evidently a Nāth centre and the Siddhs[2] who were there at the time observed that a banyan tree which had stood withered for many years suddenly became green when the Gurū sat beneath it. They sought to persuade him to join their order, but ended by hailing him as one exalted.

19 The next four *sākhīs* are given no explicit geographical location. The first concerns a community of traders who were busy celebrating the birth of a son to their leading merchant and who ignored Mardānā in spite of his obvious hunger. Gurū Nānak is said to have smiled when Mardānā reported their ungracious behaviour and to have informed him that the new arrival would depart next morning. The prophecy proved to be correct, for the next day the community was lamenting the death of the infant.

20 The second unlocated *sākhī* briefly describes a watchman who, because he sought to give the visitors the best food he had available, received an undefined 'royal authority'.

21 The third is the story of a disciple whom the Gurū won while staying in a village during a rainy season. One day the new disciple's neighbour accompanied him to meet the Gurū, but on the way stopped instead at a prostitute's house. Thereafter the two would go out together, one to the Gurū and the other to his mistress, until one day they decided to test the merits of the radically different habits they were following. That same day the neighbour discovered a pot filled with coal, but containing also a gold coin, whereas the disciple had the misfortune to pierce his foot with a thorn. Gurū Nānak explained to them that the neighbour's gift of a gold coin to a sādhū in his previous existence had earned him a pot of gold coins. The disciple, on the other hand, had performed deeds meriting an impaling stake. The neighbour's subsequent immorality had, however, converted all but the original gold coin to coal, and the disciple's piety had reduced the impaling stake to a thorn.

22 The fourth of the unlocated *sākhīs* describes an encounter with some *ṭhags*. Like Sajjaṇ the *Ṭhag* (in the *Purātan* version) these *ṭhags* decided that the evident brightness of the Gurū's face must surely mean the possession of much concealed wealth on his person. Before killing the travellers, however, the *ṭhags* were persuaded to send two of their number to a funeral pyre which could be seen burning in the distance. There they observed angels of Rām snatch a body from messengers of Yam.[3] One of the angels explained that the man had been a monstrous sinner, and that accordingly

[1] The later janam-sākhīs add that it was formerly called Gorakhmatā (e.g. *GR*, p. 203). It is identified with a location in Nainī Tāl District, fifteen miles north-west of Pīlībhīt. Gurū Hargobind is said to have visited it (*MK*, p. 519). Bhāī Gurdās and Miharbān make no reference to the place or the incident.

[2] In this context the term Siddh designates a Nāth or Kānphaṭ yogī. See *supra*, p. 11, n. 10.

[3] The god of the dead.

he should really have been the rightful property of Yam. 'The smoke of his funeral pyre has, however, been seen by that divine *gurū* whom you came to kill, and as a result he has gained access to Paradise.' The *ṭhags* were appalled to think that they had been about to kill one who imparted salvation simply by seeing smoke. They made their submission and were pardoned on condition that they took up honest agriculture and devoted any surplus they might have to renunciate *bhagats*.

Sākhī 23 is set in a land called Kaurū,[1] or Kāvarū,[2] a land ruled by female 23
magicians. The queen's name is given as Nūr Shāh. Mardānā went ahead to beg for food and was turned into a lamb by one of the enchantresses. Gurū Nānak, following him, caused a pot to adhere to the woman's head, and told Mardānā to restore himself by saying 'Vāhigurū' and bowing down. The female magicians all converged on Gurū Nānak when they heard what he had done, some riding on trees, some on deerskins, some on the moon, several on a wall, and some on a whole grove of trees. When their efforts to enchant him failed Nūr Shāh herself came and tried magic and various sensual temptations. All failed and the women finally submitted.

Next the Gurū and Mardānā came to a wilderness where they rested. 24
At God's command Kaliyug came to try and deceive the Gurū.[3] To Mardānā's inexpressible terror a great darkness fell and trees were swept away. Next there appeared fire, with smoke ascending on all sides from four abysses of fire. Black clouds then gathered and rain began to fall. Finally, Kaliyug appeared in the form of a demon giant so tall that the top of its head reached to the heavens. It advanced towards them, but the nearer it came the smaller it grew, until eventually it assumed the form of a man and Kaliyug stood before Gurū Nānak in a posture of respect. In the discourse which followed he sought to tempt him with offers of a beautiful palace, of jewels, of women, of the power to work miracles, and finally of temporal sovereignty. All were rejected by the Gurū, and Kaliyug finally made his submission and asked for salvation.

Having left Kaliyug, the travellers came next to a city of insects. Where- 25
ever they looked everything was black and Mardānā was once again in the extremities of terror. Gurū Nānak related to him a macabre story of how a rājā had once shown disrespect to the insects, and of how they had first destroyed his army with poison and then revivified it with nectar.

Sākhīs 26 and 27 obviously constitute a single story. The first concerns a 26
village which refused hospitality, and the second a village which gave it 27

[1] *Pur JS*, p. 33.

[2] *Pur JS*, p. 34.

[3] *Kaliyug*, the fourth and last in the cycle of *yugs* or cosmic eras, is the period of ultimate degeneracy. In this janam-sākhī context the meaning appears to be a manifestation in material form of all the characteristic evils and vices of the fourth *yug*. The evident impossibility of such a being subsequently led to the tradition that Kaliyug was the name of an evil person who lived in Jagannāth Purī and was converted by the Gurū. *MK*, p. 232. Teja Singh, *Sikhism: Its Ideals and Institutions*, p. 37.

liberally. After leaving the second village Gurū Nānak uttered the pronouncement: 'May this town be uprooted and its inhabitants scattered.' When Mardānā observed that this was strange justice indeed, he explained that the inhabitants of the first village would, if dispersed, corrupt others, whereas those of the second would spread true beliefs.

28 After this they reached the land of Āsā and there found the famous Sūfī Sheikh Farīd sitting in a jungle. Three incidents are recorded of the period which they spent with Sheikh Farīd. In the first a devout person offered the two holy men a cup of milk, having surreptitiously dropped four gold coins into it. When he returned later he discovered a gold cup filled with gold coins and realized that by offering worldly things instead of an open heart he had received a worldly reward and so had missed a great opportunity. The second describes a problem which was bothering the people of Āsā. The Rājā of Āsā, Śyām Sundar,[1] had recently died, but in spite of persistent efforts his skull would not burn. The astrologers had been consulted and had declared that he was in affliction as a result of once having told a lie, and that his salvation could not be effected until a sādhū set foot in the kingdom. For this reason Farīd and the Gurū were welcomed when they arrived. Farīd declined the honour and insisted that Gurū Nānak should be the one to pass through the gate which had been erected at the point of entry into the kingdom. The Gurū did so, the rājā's skull duly burst, and his soul went free. The third incident describes how Sheikh Farīd threw away a wooden *chapātī* which he had previously kept in order to have an excuse for refusing food. The rājā's unfortunate experience had shown him what would happen if he were to persist with this falsehood. The *sākhī* concludes with the statement that there is a *mañjī*[2] in the land of Āsā.

29 Much of *sākhī* 29 is incoherent, and the *Colebrooke* and *Hāfizābād* versions differ considerably. It concerns a visit to a land called Bisīar where everyone refused hospitality except a carpenter named Jhaṇḍā. Sitting on 'an island in the ocean',[3] Gurū Nānak composed a work called the *Jugāvalī* which he delivered to Jhaṇḍā. There is an obscure reference to a city called Chhuṭhaghāṭakā, and there is said to be a *mañjī* in Bisīar.

30 During these travels hunger was never a problem for the Gurū, who could subsist on air alone, but for Mardānā it was different. After leaving Bisīar they entered a great desert and here Mardānā's hunger became so extreme that he could proceed no further. Gurū Nānak showed him a tree

[1] This is the name given by the *Hāfizābād* manuscript. The *Colebrooke* manuscript gives Samundar.

[2] Literally a small string bed. Gurū Amar Dās, the third Gurū, is said to have divided his Sikhs into twenty-two districts, each under a superintendent (*mahant*). These districts were called *mañjīs* (*MK*, pp. 634, 750). References to *mañjīs* in the janam-sākhīs are anachronisms. The *mañjīs* were later superseded by the *masand* system of the fourth Gurū, Rām Dās (Teja Singh and Ganda Singh, *A Short History of the Sikhs*, vol. i, p. 27, n. 1).

[3] Literally 'a sandbank in the ocean'. *Pur JS*, p. 46.

which would provide him with fruit, but strictly enjoined him to take none with him when they proceeded on. Mardānā disobeyed the command and later ate some of what he had brought with him. He at once collapsed and Gurū Nānak explained that it was poisonous fruit which had turned to nectar because of the word he had spoken. He then cured him by placing his foot on his forehead.[1]

After twelve years of wandering they eventually arrived back at Tal- 31
vaṇḍī and stopped in the jungle at a distance of two *kos* from the village. Mardānā was given permission to enter the village, and was instructed to go to Kālū's house as well as his own. He was, however, to refrain from mentioning Nānak's name. In the village he received a reverent yet warm welcome. When asked where Nānak was he replied, 'Brethren, when the Bābā was in Sultānpur I was with him, but since then I have had no news of him.' The Gurū's mother refused to believe this and when he left the village she followed him at a distance. A touching reunion with her son followed. Kālū galloped after her as soon as he received the news and did his best to persuade Nānak to remain in Talvaṇḍī. The Gurū insisted, however, that they had renounced the world and that the settled life was not their calling.

Leaving Talvaṇḍī, Gurū Nānak and Mardānā visited the Rāvī and 32
Chenāb rivers, and then proceeded south towards Pāk Paṭṭan.[2] In a jungle, three *kos* outside the town, they encountered Sheikh Kamāl, a disciple of Sheikh Braham who was the contemporary successor of the famous Sūfī Sheikh Farīd. Kamāl informed his master and Sheikh Braham went out to converse at length with the Gurū.

From Pāk Paṭṭan the two travellers moved north-east and passing 33
through Dīpālpur,[3] Kaṅganpur,[4] Kasūr,[5] and Paṭṭī,[6] entered Goindvāl.[7]
There no one would give them shelter except a faqīr who was a leper and
who, as a result of the meeting, was healed. They then travelled on through 34
Sultānpur,[8] Vairovāl,[9] and Jalālābād,[10] and entered a village called Kiṛīān
Paṭhāṇān[11] where the Gurū made more disciples.

From there they moved north through Baṭālā to Saidpur, or Sayyidpur, 35
the modern Eminābād in Gujranwālā District. By this time they had been

[1] The IOL manuscript Panj. B40, folios 30–32, places this *sākhī* immediately after *sākhī* 12 of the principal *Purātan* manuscripts, combining the two in a single *sākhī*. This corresponds with Miharbān's arrangement (see *infra*, p. 55). It is not possible to say whether the compiler of the B40 manuscript intended the incident to be placed at the beginning or the end of the first journey as it is the only incident he records between the departure from Sultānpur and the return to Talvaṇḍī, twelve years later.

[2] Montgomery District.

[3] Montgomery District.

[4] A village in Chūṇīā tahsīl, Lahore District.

[5] Lahore District.

[6] A village in Kasūr tahsīl.

[7] Taran Tāran tahsīl, Amritsar District.

[8] Kapūrthalā District. See *sākhī* 8.

[9] Taran Tāran tahsīl.

[10] There is a town of this name in Ferozepore District, but it is a common name and the itinerary which is being followed suggests a village in Amritsar District.

[11] Amritsar District (Macauliffe i, 108).

joined by some faqīrs and all were hungry. Gurū Nānak himself asked the townsfolk for food, but the Paṭhāns who lived there were all busy celebrating marriages and paid no heed to his requests. This lack of response made him exceedingly angry and in his wrath he uttered the verse which begins, *jaisī mai āvai khasam kī bāṇī.*[1]

A brāhmaṇ who had evidently heard the verse, and who had recognized it as a summons to Bābur the Mughal to punish the town, brought an offering of fruit and asked the Gurū to retract his curse. Gurū Nānak replied that what had been uttered could not be recalled, but assured the brāhmaṇ that if he were to remove his family to a pool twelve *kos*[2] away they would all be saved. The following day Bābur arrived and fell upon Saidpur. Everyone in it, Muslim as well as Hindu, was slaughtered, houses were looted and then razed to the ground, and the surrounding countryside was devastated.

At some stage the Gurū and Mardānā were seized and committed to the Saidpur prison under the supervision of a certain Mīr Khān. Both were made to do forced labour, Gurū Nānak as a coolie and Mardānā as a horse attendant. Mīr Khān, when he came to watch the prisoners, was startled to observe that the Gurū's load remained suspended a full cubit above his head and that the horse followed Mardānā without a halter. This information was conveyed to Bābur who declared, 'Had I known there were such faqīrs here I should not have destroyed the town.' He accompanied Mīr Khān to where the prisoners were working and observed that a hand-mill which had been issued to Gurū Nānak turned without any assistance.

Bābur then approached the Gurū who uttered two verses. Hearing these the Mughal fell and kissed his feet, and offered him a favour. Gurū Nānak asked for all the prisoners to be released, and Bābur at once issued orders to free them and restore their property. The prisoners, however, refused to go unless Gurū Nānak accompanied them. Mardānā subsequently asked why so many had suffered for the sins of one[3] and was told that he would be given his reply after he had slept under a nearby tree. While he was sleeping ants were attracted by a drop of grease which had fallen on his chest. One of the ants bit him and, without awaking, Mardānā brushed them away, killing them all as he did so. This, Gurū Nānak subsequently informed him, was his answer.

To this the *Hāfizābād* manuscript adds a lengthy account of the manner in which Bābur, who was really a clandestine *qalandar*, was impressed by the Gurū. When asked to free the prisoners he agreed to do so on condition that his throne should endure for ever. Gurū Nānak would promise only

[1] *Tilaṅg* 5, *AG*, p. 722.

[2] *Colebrooke* manuscript. The *Hāfizābād* manuscript gives two *kos* (*Pur JS*, p. 59).

[3] The identity of the culprit is not indicated.

that the kingdom would endure 'for a time'. This was accepted as sufficient and the prisoners were all released.

Leaving Saidpur, Gurū Nānak and Mardānā passed through Pasrūr[1] and 36
came to the small fortress of a local celebrity named Mīā Miṭhā. They stopped in a grove at a distance of one *kos* and when Mīā Miṭhā was informed of the Guru's arrival he boasted that he would skim him as cream is skimmed off milk. Gurū Nānak replied that he would squeeze Mīā Miṭhā as he squeezed juice from a lemon. A debate followed and Mīā Miṭhā finally made his submission.

Next Gurū Nānak proceeded to Lahore where his coming was brought 37
to the notice of a wealthy Dhuppaṛ khatrī named Dunī Chand who happened to be celebrating his father's *śrāddh*.[2] In response to Dunī Chand's invitation Gurū Nānak came and, upon arrival, asked him what point there was in feeding brāhmaṇs when his father, in whose memory the *śrāddh* was being held, had not eaten for three days. Dunī Chand at once asked where his father was to be found, and was informed that he had been born as a wolf and was lying under a certain bush five *kos* away. Taking some food he went in search of his reincarnated father and was told by the wolf that the unfortunate rebirth was the result of having coveted some boiling fish when at the point of death.

Dunī Chand subsequently took Gurū Nānak to his house. Over the door were seven flags, each representing a *lākh* of rupees. The Gurū made no comment, but gave his host a needle with the request that he return it in the hereafter. 'Good God!' exclaimed his wife when he told her what the Gurū had said. 'Will this needle accompany you to the hereafter?' Appreciating the force of her rhetorical question Dunī Chand took the needle back to Gurū Nānak, who asked him, 'If a needle cannot go there, how can these flags get there?'

Sākhī 38 provides the setting for a denunciation of unnecessary cere- 38
monial purity. An excessively scrupulous brāhmaṇ refused Gurū Nānak's food and tried to dig a cooking-square which would satisfy his own notions of purity. After digging all day and everywhere turning up bones he finally made his submission.

The next incident evidently belongs to a later period, for it describes 39
Gurū Nānak's practice of daily communal *kīrtan*.[3] The Gurū happened to observe that a boy aged seven had become a regular attender at *kīrtan* and one day asked him why he engaged in such serious practices at such an early age. In reply the boy related that the necessity of doing so had been impressed upon him as a result of his having observed how when he

[1] Siālkoṭ District.

[2] A ceremony in which food and other commodities are offered to brāhmaṇs on behalf of deceased forebears.

[3] The singing of songs in praise of God.

kindled a fire the small sticks were consumed first. The boy's name is not given.

The two *sākhīs* which conclude the *Purātan* account of the first journey
40 are recorded in the *Hāfizābād* manuscript, but not the *Colebrooke*. According to the first of them, Gurū Nānak took up residence on the banks of a river near Talvaṇḍī where crowds of people flocked to see him. A local official (*karoṛīā*) who lived in a neighbouring village concluded that Nānak was taking advantage of this popularity to corrupt both Hindus and Muslims, and that accordingly he should be imprisoned. He set out to make the arrest, but on the way was struck blind. This convinced him that Nānak must indeed be a great *pīr* and, greatly chastened, he remounted his horse, only to fall off again. The people who had observed these misfortunes assured him that the only proper way to approach a great *pīr* was on foot. This he did and was so impressed by the Gurū that he decided to build for him a village which was to be called Kartārpur.

41 The second of the *Hāfizābād sākhīs* relates the story of Bhāgīrath and an unnamed shopkeeper. A poor Sikh once came to the Gurū asking for financial assistance in order that he might have his daughter married. Gurū Nānak acceded to the request and dispatched another Sikh, Bhāgīrath, to Lahore with instructions to purchase everything that would be required, and to return at all costs that same day. Failure to do so would mean forfeiting his opportunity of salvation.

The shopkeeper to whom he went for his purchases provided him with everything except a set of bangles, informing him that these could not possibly be ready until the next day. When Bhāgīrath insisted that delay was more than his salvation was worth the shopkeeper became curious and decided to visit this gurū who could evidently give or withold salvation as he pleased. He provided a set of bangles from his own house and set off with Bhāgīrath. While they were still on the way the Gurū's voice came to them. The shopkeeper was instantly convinced and spent three years with Gurū Nānak before returning to Lahore.

When he eventually did return it was to entrust his property to other shopkeepers. He then embarked on a ship, sailed to the city where Rājā Śivanābh lived, and there established a trading business. He lived a life of great piety there, but it was not one which accorded with the superstitious practices of the local people. These people were not Hindus and they made a point of defiling any Hindus who went there. The shopkeeper did not observe local practices, but nor did he follow Hindu customs and so eventually he was reported to the rājā. Śivanābh summoned him, demanded an explanation, and was given a description of Gurū Nānak. This aroused a great longing in him for an opportunity to meet the Gurū. The shopkeeper replied that the proper place to meet him was in his own heart, but before leaving he comforted the rājā with the assurance that the Gurū would one day come to him in person. He warned him, however, that there could be no knowing the guise in which he would come.

After the shopkeeper had sailed away Rājā Śivanābh devised a method of testing all visiting faqīrs. Summoning a number of alluring women he instructed them to exercise their charms on any faqīrs or sādhūs who might arrive, knowing full well that in this degenerate age only the perfect Gurū would be able to resist such advances.

Sākhī 42 opens with the announcement that Gurū Nānak's second journey 42
was to the south. The *Purātan* janam-sākhīs are confused concerning the number and names of his companions on this journey. The *Hāfizābād* manuscript usually gives their number as two and their names as Saido and Gheho, both Jaṭs, but in one place it refers to three companions named Saido, Gheho, and Sīho, again all Jaṭs,[1] in another simply to Saido and Sīho,[2] and in yet another it adds the name of Mardānā.[3] The *Colebrooke* manuscript usually names them Saido a Jaṭ and Sīho a Gheho,[4] but in one place refers to them as Saido and Gheho.[5]

The first visit was to a country called Dhanāsarī where the Gurū's companions encountered Khwājā Khizar.[6] They had previously come to the conclusion that Gurū Nānak's frequent visits to the river were for the purpose of worshipping this deity, and had themselves begun worshipping him. One night, however, they met Khwājā Khizar himself taking an offering to the Gurū whom he worshipped daily. While in Dhanāsarī Gurū 43
Nānak conducted a successful discourse with Anabhī, the superior of a very influential Jain monastery. He then completed *Mājh kī Vār*[7] and proceeded on.

The next recorded incident is set on 'an island in the ocean, in foreign 44
parts, where a savage man exercised tyrannical rule'. The savage seized the Gurū and set about cooking him in a cauldron. Instead of becoming hot, however, the cauldron became cooler. Perceiving this the cannibal fell at the Gurū's feet and asked for salvation. Sīho administered baptism and so he became a Sikh. The savage's name is not given.

The *sākhī* which follows is both confused and fantastic. It concerns a 45
meeting with Makhdūm Bahāuddīn whom Gurū Nānak encountered sporting in the sea on his prayer-mat. After this Gurū Nānak is said to have 46
travelled out into the ocean to converse with Machhendranāth and Gorakhnāth.

[1] *Pur JS*, p. 81, n. **.
[2] Ibid., p. 86.
[3] Ibid., p. 81, n. ‡‡.
[4] In this case Gheho evidently means Ghei, a khatrī sub-caste.
[5] *Pur JS*, p. 79.
[6] A mythical Muslim saint who in many parts of India has been identified with a river god or with a spirit of wells and streams. *Encyclopaedia of Islam*, vol. ii, p. 865. R. C. Temple, *The Legends of the Panjab*, vol. i, p. 221.
[7] *AG*, pp. 137–50.

47 *Sākhī* 47 records another crossing of the ocean, this time to the kingdom of Śivanābh in Siṅghalādīp.[1] When Gurū Nānak arrived there Śivanābh's garden, which had remained withered for years, suddenly blossomed. The gardener reported this to the rājā who at once sent his alluring women to test the new arrival. Later Śivanābh came himself and after questioning the Gurū invited him to his palace. Bābā Nānak replied that he did not travel on foot, but that he required as his mount one who was of royal blood and ruler of a city. Śivanābh at once offered himself and the Gurū proceeded to the palace on the rājā's back.

At the palace Śivanābh and his wife, Chandarakalā, asked him what he wished to eat. In reply the Gurū asked for human flesh and specified that it was to be that of 'a son who is of royal parentage and twelve years old'. Śivanābh consulted his own son's horoscope and discovered that he was, as required, twelve years of age. Both the boy and his wife agreed that the Gurū's wish should be met, and while the mother held his arms and the wife his feet Śivanābh proceeded to cut his son's throat. The boy's body was then stewed and placed before the Gurū who instructed them to shut their eyes, utter 'Vāhigurū', and begin to eat. This they did and when they opened their eyes again the Gurū had disappeared. As a result of this experience the rājā became insane, but twelve months later was vouchsafed a *darśan*[2] and became a Sikh.

The partly incoherent conclusion of this *sākhī* records that while in Siṅghalādīp Gurū Nānak composed a work entitled the *Prāṇ Saṅgalī*. A group of believers met regularly in the *dharmsālā* and there secret teachings were revealed. Rājā Śivanābh received a *mañjī*[3] and Gurū Nānak departed.

48 The final *sākhī* of the second journey describes how Gurū Nānak wrecked the hut of an hospitable carpenter. The reason for this seemingly ungrateful action was revealed when the carpenter discovered under the remains of his broken bed four pots of gold.

49 The third journey was to the north and Gurū Nānak's companions this time were Hassū, a blacksmith, and Sīhān, a calico-printer. On his head and feet he wore leather and round his whole body he bound rope. The small group first travelled to Kashmir where a paṇḍit named Braham Dās came to meet them wearing an idol round his neck and bringing with him two camels loaded with Purāṇas. The discourse which followed converted him and he threw away his idol.

His conversion was, however, incomplete and one day Bābā Nānak told him to take a *gurū*. For this purpose he directed Braham Dās to some faqīrs

[1] Ceylon.

[2] An audience and, in contexts such as this, specifically an audience with a person of spiritual stature. It is not clear whether the writer intends this to be understood as another meeting or as a vision.

[3] See *supra*, p. 42, n. 2.

out in a tract of waste land, and they in turn sent him on to a nearby temple. There a woman in crimson beat him severely with a shoe and the wailing paṇḍit returned to the faqīrs to be informed that he had just met *Māyā*, the *gurū* he had hitherto served. This completed Braham Dās's conversion. He threw away his books and became a humble servant of the pious.

After leaving Kashmir, Gurū Nānak traversed many mountains and 50
eventually ascended Mount Sumeru where he conversed with Śiva, Gorakhnāth, Bharatharī, Gopīchand, and Charapaṭ. The Siddhs sent him to fill a pot with water, but when it kept filling with jewels the Gurū broke it, repaired it, exorcised the spell with a *ślok*, and then filled it with water.

A lengthy discourse followed, at the end of which the Siddhs suggested that Nānak should proceed to the village of Achal where many Siddhs would be gathered for a fair. The journey, they informed him, would take them three days as they travelled on the wind. They then departed, obviously expecting to arrive well before him. The Gurū, however, was transported there in an instant and at their arrival the Siddhs from Mount Sumeru were amazed to hear from others at the fair that Nānak had appeared three days previously. A brief discourse followed.

The fourth journey took Gurū Nānak westwards to Mecca, evidently 51
without a regular companion. For this journey he wore leather shoes, pajama, a blue garment, and a necklace of bones. Having reached his destination he went to sleep with his feet in the direction of Mecca[1] and a qāzī named Rukandīn, who happened to observe him in this position, rebuked him severely. The Gurū suggested that the qāzī should drag his feet round and leave them pointing in a direction away from God and the *Ka'bah*. Rukandīn complied and was amazed to discover that as he moved the Gurū's feet the *miharāb* moved with them. He summoned Pīr Pataliā and the three engaged in discourse. At its conclusion Gurū Nānak uttered 'Vāhigurū' and water appeared in the wells, thus fulfilling a prophecy contained in the Muslim scriptures that Nānak, a *darveś*, would come and cause water to spring in the wells of Mecca.

The fifth journey was a much shorter one than any of the previous four. 52
On this occasion the Gurū travelled to Gorakh-haṭaṛī where he met Siddhs and held the discourse which is recorded in the work entitled *Siddh Goṣṭ*.[2] The Siddhs sought to impress him with displays of their magical power, but without success.

Sākhī 53 describes the conversion of Lahiṇā who was subsequently to 53
become Gurū Aṅgad. Lahiṇā lived in Khaḍūr[3] where he was the priest

[1] This may indicate the *Ka'bah*, or it may mean that the original *sākhī* was not set in Mecca. See *infra*, pp. 123–4. The B40 manuscript records that it was with his feet towards the *miharāb* that Gurū Nānak went to sleep (loc. cit., folio 51).

[2] *AG*, pp. 938–46.

[3] Amritsar District.

of the Tehaṇā (Trehaṇ) khatrīs. In the same town there lived a Bḥallā khatrī who was a Sikh, the only person there who did not worship the goddess Durgā. One day Lahiṇā happened to overhear him reciting the *Japjī*[1] and this so impressed him that, having learnt the identity of the author, he went at once and became a disciple. The service which he rendered to his master was particularly devoted. He regularly scoured the Gurū's pots and waved the fan, and on one occasion willingly ruined a new suit of clothes in order to obey a command to bring in some wet grass. The *sākhī* also refers to Durgā's practice of coming every eighth day to serve the Gurū, and terminates with an incoherent story concerning a maid-servant who once sought to waken the Gurū by licking his feet.

54 Gorakhnāth once visited Gurū Nānak and the Gurū devised a test to show how many true followers he had. The two set out walking, followed by the Sikhs. At the Gurū's command copper coins appeared on the ground, and many of his followers picked them up and departed. Next silver coins appeared and then gold coins. Each time he lost more Sikhs and after the appearance of the gold coins only two remained. Further on they came to a burning funeral pyre. Over the corpse there was a sheet and from it there issued a foul smell. The Gurū asked if there was anyone prepared to eat the corpse and at this one of the two remaining Sikhs fled, leaving only Lahiṇā to obey the command. Lahiṇā asked which end he should begin to eat and was instructed to start at the feet. Raising the sheet he found Gurū Nānak lying there. Gorakhnāth, impressed by this display of loyal obedience, declared, 'He who is born from a part (*aṅg*) of you will be your Gurū', and the name Aṅgad was accordingly bestowed upon Lahiṇā.

55 In *sākhī* 55 Makhdūm Bahāuddīn reappears, this time as the *Pīr* of Multān and as one near death. Realizing that his end was near he sent a *ślok* to Gurū Nānak in Talvaṇḍī, informing him of the fact, and received in reply another *ślok* with the comment, 'You go and I shall follow after forty days'. Loudly lamenting the prospect of forty days of darkness Makhdūm Bahāuddīn passed away.

56 Gurū Nānak was also aware of approaching death. Before it took place
he appointed Aṅgad as his successor by laying five copper coins in front of
him and prostrating himself before him. The news at once spread that he
57 was about to die, and Hindus and Muslims flocked for a last audience. He
then went and sat under a withered acacia, which at once blossomed, and
his family gathered around him weeping. His sons asked what would
become of them and were assured that they would be cared for. A dispute
then arose between the Muslims and the Hindus, the former claiming that
they would bury the Gurū's body and the latter that they would cremate it.
The Gurū himself settled the argument by instructing the Hindus to lay
flowers on his right and the Muslims to place them at his left. Whichever

[1] *AG*, pp. 1–8.

side's flowers were still fresh on the following day should have his body to dispose of as they wished. The assembled followers then sang *Kīrtan Sohilā*[1] and *Āratī*,[2] and the concluding *ślok* of the *Japjī*.[3] Gurū Nānak covered himself with a sheet and went to sleep. When the sheet was raised the body had gone and the flowers on both sides were still fresh. The Hindus took their share away and the Muslims did likewise. The date was the tenth day of the light half of Asū, S. 1595, and it was at Kartārpur that Gurū Nānak passed away.

The life of Gurū Nānak according to the Miharbān Janam-sākhī (Pothī Sach-khaṇḍ)

The *Purātan Janam-sākhī* contains only fifty-seven *sākhīs* and accordingly it has been possible to include them all in the outline given above. In the case of Miharbān's *Pothī Sach-khaṇḍ* this is not possible, but the exclusion of some individual *goṣṭs* need not involve any significant omissions as far as the biography of Gurū Nānak is concerned. Several of the *goṣṭs* offer no biographical details and frequently a single episode is spread over more than one *goṣṭ*.[4]

The first three *goṣṭs* of the *Miharbān Janam-sākhī* recount the greatness 1–3
of the first Rājā Janak and describe an interview with God wherein Janak is informed that he is to return to the world once again. His name is to be Nānak and his task is to be the salvation of the world from the evils and degeneracy into which it has fallen.

The details of Gurū Nānak's birth are given in the fourth *goṣṭ*. His 4
father was Kālū, a Bedī khatrī, and his mother's name is given as Tiparā. The Damdamā Sāhib manuscript gives the village of Chāhalāvāle[5] as the place where the birth took place,[6] but the second Khalsa College manuscript omits this detail and in *goṣṭ* 17 the Damdamā Sāhib manuscript gives 'Talvaṇḍī Rāi Bhoe kī' as the birthplace.[7] The date given in the Damdamā Sāhib manuscript is a moonlit night in the month of Vaisākh, S. 1526, and the second manuscript adds that it was the third day.[8] The hour is said to have been the last watch of the night. There was great celebration both in heaven and in the village, and Hindus and Muslims of all tribes and ranks

[1] *AG*, p. 12. [2] Ibid., pp. 13, 663. [3] Ibid., p. 8.

[4] The *Miharbān Janam-sākhī* is divided, not into *sākhīs*, but into *goṣṭs* (discourses). The figures in the margin indicate the number of each *goṣṭ* as given in the edition of *Pothī Sach-khaṇḍ* edited by Kirpal Singh and Shamsher Singh Ashok and published under the title *Janam Sākhī Srī Gurū Nānak Dev Jī* by the Sikh History Research Department of Khalsa College, Amritsar, in 1962.

[5] The village of Chāhal in the area of Thāṇā Barakī, Lahore District, is traditionally regarded as the home of Gurū Nānak's maternal grandparents. *MK*, p. 345.

[6] *Mih JS*, pp. 9, 10. [7] *Mih JS*, p. 52. Also *goṣṭ* 141, p. 470.

[8] *Mih JS*, p. 9, n. 5.

came to offer their congratulations. On the ninth day after his birth he was given his name. Various faculties are recorded as having developed with consecutive months during the first year, at eighteen months, and with each year up to the age of five when he began to give utterance to spiritual wisdom. Hindus declared that he was the image of God, and Muslims that truly he was a godly child.

5 At the age of seven Nānak was taken to a paṇḍit to learn how to read. The paṇḍit wrote out the alphabet for him, but the child kept silent and refused to repeat it. A discourse followed based, as in the *Purātan* account, on the verse *Sirī Rāgu* 6,[1] and at its conclusion the paṇḍit acknowledged that one so wise should certainly be permitted to decide what was best for himself.

6 When he was eight years old Nānak would play with groups of other children and give them instruction in the things of God. During this period Kālū decided that he should learn 'Turkī'[2] and summoned a mullah for this purpose. This time Nānak applied himself to his studies and startled both the mullah and the village with his incredible progress. Within a matter of days he had mastered not only Persian but also Hindvī, Arabic, and accounting. After this he became silent and refused to communicate with anyone. The mullah was called again and with some difficulty managed to persuade Nānak to speak. When he did eventually speak it was to utter a verse expounding the transient nature of man's worldly abode.[3] Hearing it the mullah saluted him as a blessed child.

7 When he reached the age of nine arrangements were made for him to be invested with the sacred thread (*janeū*). It appears that he did not actually refuse it, as *goṣṭ* 11 makes reference to his wearing it,[4] but the occasion provided him with an opportunity to criticize external ritual, and to affirm inward acceptance of the divine Name and praises offered to God as the only true *janeū*.

8 The next recorded incident is the restoration of the crop ruined by Nānak's buffaloes. This is said to have occurred at the age of about ten or twelve and is substantially the same as in the *Purātan* account.[5] One significant difference is that the landlord's name is given as Rāi Bhoā, not Rāi Bulār. Two minor differences are that the field is said to have contained paddy, not wheat, and that the reason given for Nānak's negligence is
9 meditation, not sleep. *Goṣṭ* 9 relates the story of the tree's stationary
10 shadow[6] and in *goṣṭ* 10 Rāi Bhoā discusses with Kālū the significance of this

[1] *AG*, p. 16. *Sirī Rāgu* is the first of the *rāgs* in the *Ādi Granth*.

[2] Persian. It is also referred to as *Musalamānī*.

[3] *Tilaṅg* 1, *AG*, p. 721. [4] *Mih JS*, p. 29. [5] See *supra*, pp. 36–37.

[6] See *supra*, p. 37. Neither the *Miharbān* nor the *Purātan* account contains the popular story of how a cobra was once observed to be protecting the sleeping child from the sun's rays with its distended hood. This miracle appears in later janam-sākhīs. See *infra*, pp. 73, 77.

incident and that of the restored field. The owner of the field is summoned to ascertain that he had told the truth and Rāi Bhoā assures Kālū that Nānak is obviously no ordinary son. Nānak's age at the time when Rāi Bhoā observed the stationary shadow is given as thirteen or fourteen.

About the time of his sixteenth birthday Gurū Nānak was betrothed to 11
the daughter of Mūlā, a Choṇā (khatrī) of Baṭālā. The betrothal ceremony is said to have been held on the first day of the dark half of Vaisākh, S. 1542. The wedding took place in Baṭālā soon afterwards and when it was over Nānak returned with his family to Talvaṇḍī. In *goṣṭ* 22 his wife's name is given as Ghumī.[1]

At the age of twenty Gurū Nānak lapsed into silence and inactivity, and 13
his mother's efforts to rouse him were unavailing. In the following *goṣṭ* he 14
explains that his silence is the result of having no godly people to converse
with.[2] *Goṣṭ* 15 records that he neither ate, drank, nor spoke for four or five 15–16
days[3] and that eventually the anxious townsfolk persuaded Kālū to summon a physician. The physician duly came and feeling the patient's pulse pronounced it a case of madness. Nānak's reply was essentially the same as that given in the *Purātan* version,[4] and the physician acknowledged him as Gurū.

Next family pressure was tried. Gurū Nānak was summoned before a 17
family conclave and the Bedīs remonstrated with him, seeking to persuade him to take up agriculture. The effort was unsuccessful and so too was
another which the family made when he was twenty-two. 18

When Gurū Nānak was twenty-seven or twenty-eight his two sons, 22
Lakhmī Dās and Sirī Chand were born. At the age of thirty his renunciate tendencies became even more pronounced and he abandoned all other
activity in favour of discussions with yogīs and sannyāsīs. Efforts made by 22–23
both his father and mother to persuade him to take up agriculture, shopkeeping, trade, or civil service employment met with the usual negative response.

Eventually Jai Rām, his brother-in-law, came to the rescue with his 24
suggestion that Nānak should join him in Sultānpur. The invitation was accepted and Gurū Nānak departed, leaving his wife in the meantime but taking Mardānā the Ḍūm with him. Jai Rām is described as an Uppal

[1] *Mih JS*, p. 67.

[2] This *goṣṭ* is evidently out of sequence as it gives his age as twenty-six. The second Khalsa College manuscript gives it as *goṣṭ* 21 and the two versions differ appreciably. *Mih JS*, p. 40, n. 4.

[3] This is the reading of the second Khalsa College manuscript. The Damdamā Sāhib manuscript gives four months. *Mih JS*, p. 45, n. 8.

[4] Both versions give as his reply *Malār* 7 and 8, *AG*, pp. 1256–7; *Vār Malār*, *śloks* 1 and 2 of *pauṛī* 3, *AG*, p. 1280 (the second of which is by Gurū Aṅgad); and a verse which is not in the *Ādi Granth*. The *Purātan* manuscripts add *Gauṛī* 17, *AG*, p. 156, and a *ślok* which is not in the *Ādi Granth*. The greater length of the Miharbān account is, as usual, chiefly the result of the interpretation which is added to the quotations.

khatrī and as Daulat <u>Kh</u>ān Lodī's steward. The Damdamā Sāhib manuscript gives his home as <u>Kh</u>ānpur and the second manuscript as Sultānpur.
The name of his wife, Gurū Nānak's sister, is not recorded. Gurū Nānak's
age at the time is given as thirty-five years, six and a half months.

His meeting with Jai Rām and his interview with Daulat <u>Kh</u>ān are
described in some detail. At the interview he presented to the Nawāb a fine
Iraqi horse and an offering of money, and in return received a robe of
honour. Daulat <u>Kh</u>ān pronounced himself highly pleased with the new
arrival and commanded that all authority over his province and property
be entrusted to Nānak. This was evidently to be understood as compli-
mentary hyperbole as the employment to which he was actually assigned
was in Daulat <u>Kh</u>ān's commissariat. His daily life, combining pious exercises with proper fulfilment of his secular duties, is also described.

25–26   It was not long, however, before doubts began to arise in the Gurū's
mind. He continued to fulfil his responsibilities in the commissariat, but his
mind turned increasingly to spiritual things, even while he was engaged in his
27   quartermaster duties. In a discourse with his cook he expressed his concern
at his involvement in worldly affairs. Eventually the climax of his developing spiritual crisis came with the summons to the court of God, received
while he was taking his regular early-morning bathe in the river.

28–29   As in the *Purātan* account the river is not named, but the author indicates that it was in the direction of Goindvāl. One morning Nānak plunged
in as usual, but did not reappear, having been transported to the divine
court. Miharbān's version is characteristically diffuse, occupying four times
the space of the *Purātan* account without making any significant additions
to it. The river was dragged without success and on the third day Nānak
emerged to the acclamation of the crowd, gave away his belongings, and
joined a group of faqīrs. The people were perplexed and many concluded
that he must be possessed. Some of the common folk, observing that he
appeared to be conforming to neither Hindu or Muslim practice, asked him
what path he was now following. He replied, 'There is neither Hindu nor
Mussulman so whose path shall I follow? I shall follow God's path. God
is neither Hindu nor Mussulman and the path which I follow is God's.'[1]

32   This comment was communicated to the local qāzī and at his request
Nānak was summoned before Daulat <u>Kh</u>ān to answer for it. Once again
Miharbān provides an account which is appreciably longer than that of
the *Purātan* janam-sākhīs, but which adds nothing except extra quotations
from Gurū Nānak's works, protracted expositions, and incidental details of
no importance. The Gurū successfully answered the qāzī's charge, humbled him by reading his thoughts during *namāz*, and expounded to him
and to Daulat <u>Kh</u>ān the meaning of true *namāz*. At the conclusion
of the exposition Daulat <u>Kh</u>ān prostrated himself adoringly and Gurū

[1] *Mih JS*, p. 92.

Nānak assured him that he had attained salvation. Taking the dust of the Gurū's feet Daulat Khān returned home. No reference is made to his treasury having been miraculously filled.

Bābā Nānak and Mardānā then set out on the first journey (*udāsī*), having 34
spent two years in Sultānpur.[1] As in the *Purātan* janam-sākhīs the account
of this journey begins with a description of how Mardānā would enter a 35
village to ask for food whenever necessary, and of how the Gurū commanded him to throw away the money and clothing which a generous village had bestowed upon him as offerings.[2] Following this experience they entered a wilderness devoid of human habitation. Mardānā became apprehensive, but the Gurū calmed his fears by assuring him that no place where the divine Name was repeated could be uninhabited. Some days later there
occurred the incident of the forbidden fruit.[3] 36

After a conversation with some herons Gurū Nānak and Mardānā 37
reached Delhi where they observed food being distributed to mendicants on 38
behalf of the king, whose name is given as Salem Shāh Paṭhān. The Gurū preached to the people on the necessity of the divine Name and the entire population became his Sikhs. There is no mention of a resurrected elephant.

Leaving Delhi they proceeded on to the Ganges where, as it happened 39–40
to be a festival day, they observed thousands of people bathing in the river. The festival which was being celebrated was that of Baisākhī and the pilgrims were throwing water in the direction of the rising sun. Gurū Nānak also entered the river and began splashing water in the opposite direction. This provoked offended demands for an explanation. The Gurū responded by asking his questioners to whom they thought they were conveying water and they replied that they were sending it to their ancestors in heaven. Gurū Nānak then informed them that he was, in the same manner, watering his fields near Lahore. When this brought a scornful rejoinder he answered that if their water could travel as far as heaven his could certainly reach Lahore. This silenced them for they now realized that they were conversing with a person of exalted spiritual insight. Continuing the discourse on the banks of the river he emphasized the futility of *mantras* and cooking-

[1] In other words, according to Miharbān Gurū Nānak began his travels at the age of thirty-seven and a half.

[2] The *Purātan* manuscripts explicitly state that the first *udāsī* began after they had left Delhi (see *supra*, p. 39). It seems clear, however, that the four preceding *sākhīs* must belong to the first *udāsī*.

[3] Both the assurance concerning the Name and Mardānā's disobedient consumption of extra fruit are related in the *Purātan* janam-sākhīs (see *supra*, pp. 42–43), but the *sākhī* which includes them is placed at the end of the *Purātan's* first journey. Miharbān's setting is more logical. In both cases Mardānā promises to follow the Gurū if he will be patient with one who, unlike the Gurū himself, is subject to human limitations, and the terms in which the discourses are conducted fit the early stages of a journey more appropriately than the concluding stages.

squares.[1] Two more discourses follow. The first of these, another discourse
41 on cooking-squares, provides a setting for the verse *Basant* 3,[2] which in
42 the *Purātan* janam-sākhīs is set in an entirely different incident.[3] The
second refers to Hardwār as the location of these discussions.

43 From Hardwār Gurū Nānak and Mardānā moved on to Prayāg (Allahābād) where the Gurū's fame had preceded him and a large crowd had
gathered to pay their respects. After a discourse with some devout people
44–50 they proceeded on to Banāras where the Gurū engaged in several discourses
with paṇḍits and groups of devout believers. The first of these was with a
49 single paṇḍit, but he is not named. On another occasion the entire population of Banāras, and specifically all of the paṇḍits in the city, are said to
have been present at a discourse held on the Bisarāti (Viśrānti) Ghāṭ, and
at the conclusion of the discourse all of the paṇḍits became Sikhs.

51 After leaving Banāras they came to the city of Rājā Harināth in 'the east
country' where, to begin with, Gurū Nānak observed silence and was consequently mistaken for a *monī*.[4] Hearing of his arrival the rājā himself went
on foot to meet him, listened to his instruction, and asked if he might
accompany him as a disciple. He was, however, told to practise piety while
yet remaining a rājā.

52 From Rājā Harināth's unnamed city they proceeded 'to where Gusāī
Kambīr's house was'. Kabīr went out to meet Bābā Nānak and in the discourse which followed acknowledged him as the supreme Gurū. In reply
Gurū Nānak uttered his *Gauṛī Aṣṭapadī* 8,[5] a composition which if it were
to be applied to Kabīr would imply very high praise of him.

54 Travelling eastwards from where Kabīr lived they came next to Hājīpur
Paṭṇā where the Gurū discoursed with and converted a group of Vaiṣṇavas.
55 Continuing to the east they entered an unnamed city where Gurū Nānak
observed his common practice of initial silence and subsequently instructed the members of the town council in the nature of 'the true food',
namely God Himself.

56 From that city they turned south and, entering a wilderness, met and
57 conversed with an unidentified rājā. Next they arrived at another unnamed
city where Gurū Nānak's presence exercised an attraction so compulsive
that eventually the whole city gathered to pay him homage and declared
58 him to be an incarnation of God. In the following *goṣṭ* they are back in 'the
east country'. There they visited Ayodhyā where, after the Gurū had con-
59 ducted two discourses, 'all the *bhagats* gathered at God's command and
came to meet him—Nāmdev, Jaidev, Kabīr, Trilochan, Ravidās, Saiṇ,

[1] The conclusion of *goṣṭ* 40, which describes the pilgrims who accepted his teaching as the first Sikhs, is evidently an interpolation by sādhūs of the Udāsī sect. Its language is more modern, it conflicts with the earlier reference to the conversion of Delhi, and it affirms the adoption of celibacy.

[2] *AG*, p. 1169.

[3] *Sākhī* 38. See *supra*, p. 45.

[4] A faqīr or sādhū who observes complete silence.

[5] *AG*, p. 224.

Sadhnā, Dhannā, Beṇī'. A lengthy discourse followed, based on *Sirī Rāgu*
10–12,[1] at the end of which the *bhagats* hailed him and departed for heaven.
There they reported their experience to God who, well pleased to hear their 60
praises, summoned Nānak to an interview.

Leaving Ayodhyā they travelled down to Jagannāth where they met 61
Rājā Bharatharī, the famous yogī.[2] *Goṣṭ* 62 records that they spent three 62
years in 'the east country' and that having seen it all they turned south.
Jagannāth Purī is accordingly the eastern terminus in Miharbān's account
and after this visit we find Gurū Nānak travelling south, presumably down
the east coast of India.

From Jagannāth Purī the Gurū and Mardānā travelled a considerable
distance and eventually came to a temple surrounded by a desert. There a
piece of brick happened to fall on Gurū Nānak after he had been meditating
and the consequent pain greatly distressed him as he had believed his
meditation would free him from such suffering. While he was lamenting
this the voice of God was heard assuring him that all who live in the world
must experience pain of this kind.

Two strange incidents follow. The first relates how the thirsty travellers 63
were led to water by a jackal, and how Gurū Nānak, entering the water,
travelled thence to the court of God and returned with food. In the second 64
story Gurū Nānak cures a fit of depression in Mardānā by revealing to him
that the stars are worlds in which dwell those *bhagats* who have served
God faithfully.[3]

Their journey southwards finally brought them to Rāmeśwaram where 65
Gurū Nānak recited the hymn in the *Dhanāsarī* metre entitled *Āratī*[4] and 66
held discourse with the worshippers of the idol installed there. Proceeding 67
on from Rāmeśwaram beyond Setu-bandha ('Adam's Bridge') they entered
a foreign country in which an unknown language was spoken. There they
passed through a series of regions in all of which the one God was worshipped. The first two of these were human kingdoms, but the remainder
were areas inhabited only by either spirits or animals. In all of them they
found the one God worshipped and Gurū Nānak gave praise accordingly.

Next they met Kaliyug who appeared to them as a man carrying fire in 68
his hand and raw meat in his mouth. He is an altogether milder being than
the *Purātan* version[5] and explains his coming as simply the result of his
desire to see a great *bhagat*. A more fearsome monster is encountered in the 69
next *goṣṭ* where a high mountain turns out to be a massive creature. Gurū

[1] *AG*, pp. 17–18.

[2] See *supra*, p. 11, n. 2.

[3] Both *goṣṭs* are obviously later additions. The occurrences which they describe are altogether out of harmony with Miharbān's comparative restraint and their style is uncharacteristic in that they contain neither quotation nor interpretation. *Goṣṭs* 69 and 72 are also examples of later additions.

[4] *AG*, pp. 13, 663. In later traditions this hymn is set in Jagannāth Purī.

[5] See *supra*, p. 41.

Nānak distended himself to the equivalent size, seized the creature, and was about to eat it when Mardānā intervened and begged him to free it. His request was granted, but he was greatly upset to learn that he had been instrumental in freeing *Kāl* (Death). Gurū Nānak assured him, however, that it was really God who had spoken through him.[1]

71 Their next experience was the encounter with the cannibals who were
unable to heat their cauldron.[2] In Miharbān's account it is Mardānā whom
72 the savages try to boil. Following this the Gurū turned a deceitful people
to righteousness by causing a harvest to grow without moisture after local
śakti practices had failed to produce the necessary rain. Gurū Nānak renamed the country Sādiq and the people, following their rājā's example, all
became Sikhs. A *dharmsālā* was built and the Sikh devotional discipline
was adopted.[3]

73 Next, still in 'the south country', they met Sajjaṇ the *ṭhag*.[4] After his
exposure and confession his *dharmsālā* of blood was destroyed and a new
one built in its place. This is followed by a series of unimportant discourses,
most of which are held in wildernesses or various unidentified cities of
74 the south and none of which add any significant details. *Goṣṭ* 74, a discourse with God, is said to have taken place 'in a city of *ṭhags* in the south
75 country'. *Goṣṭ* 75 purports to be a discourse held in a desert with a certain
78, 83 Rājā Mitr Sain, and *goṣṭ* 78 concerns a Rājā Jagannāth. In *goṣṭ* 83 a storm
which kills all the birds in a grove where Gurū Nānak happened to be
sitting prompts a soliloquy on death. The birds are revived in the following
goṣṭ.

87–95 This group of south country *goṣṭs* is followed by another group which are
said to have taken place in the city of Ujjain or the area to the south covered
by the modern Indore District. This is still regarded as 'the south country'.
In the second of these Mardānā's name reappears, having been absent since
87 *goṣṭ* 72. The first of the Ujjain *goṣṭs* records a meeting with Bharatharī,[5]
88 but the discourse is with God. Gurū Nānak and Mardānā then left the city
89 and came to 'Vijhṇī where there are elephants'.[6] From there they continued
on to the Narabad river where Gurū Nānak conversed with a converted and
earnest sanyāsī named Chiti Giri.

90 After leaving the Narabad they turned north again and on the way back
to Ujjain fell among *ṭhags* who surmised that the Gurū must be a person
of much wealth who had disguised himself as a faqīr in order to conceal the

[1] These two *goṣṭs* are missing from the Damdamā Sāhib manuscript. The latter is, like *goṣṭs* 63 and 64, a later addition to the janam-sākhī, and for the same reasons.

[2] See *supra*, p. 47.

[3] The pattern of *goṣṭ* 72 resembles that of *goṣṭs* 63, 64, and 69, and like them appears to be a later addition.

[4] See *supra*, pp. 38–39.

[5] Cf. *goṣṭ* 61.

[6] Evidently the Vindhyā Mountains, which means that Miharbān is taking the travellers south again.

fact. The *ṭhags* of the *Purātan's sākhī* 22 based a like conclusion upon their conviction that a bright face must indicate a full pocket.[1] This appears, however, to be an entirely different story. There is no struggle on a funeral pyre as in the *Purātan* incident and the customary quotations differ. In Miharbān's account all that is required to effect the *ṭhags'* conversion is the recitation of an appropriate hymn.[2]

Goṣṭ 91 contains in its alleged meeting with Bharatharī a common kind 91
of anachronism and it also provides some unusually specific details concerning the location of the meeting.[3] The discourse on this occasion is said to have been held with celibate sādhūs, but Bharatharī is referred to in the introductory portion and appears as a participant during the latter part of
the conversation. Two more discourses with Bharatharī follow, then one 92–93
with God, and finally one with a group of Sikhs. 94, 95

Leaving Ujjain, Gurū Nānak and Mardānā continued their travels in 96–99
'the south country' and eventually, after a number of discourses with sundry people in various unnamed places, reached 'the Bīkāner country in
Rājputān'. Here they moved around for some time, holding discourses with 100–6
people both in Bīkāner city and in the surrounding countryside. After 107
leaving Bīkāner they entered 'the land of Soraṭhi'. Mardānā asked the Gurū if this meant they were in the land of the Soraṭhi who was associated with Bīje[4] and received an affirmative reply. This indicates Saurashtra[5] and means that Miharbān has taken them in a southerly direction once again.

Eventually, after spending five years in 'the south country', the travellers 109
moved on to the north and came to Mathurā. There they visited the Keśo Rāi temple, bathed in the Yamunā, and then proceeded to the eastern part of the town where a large convocation of sādhūs had gathered. After the usual discourse the sādhūs all became Sikhs.

From Mathurā they moved on to Kurukshetra where a festival was in 112
progress and many people were bathing. Gurū Nānak's arrival there brought a large crowd, and a discourse on the ineffectiveness of their
bathing. Finally they arrived back in Sultānpur where they received an 113
affectionate welcome from Daulat Khān Lodī. Three discourses followed, 114
in the second of which Daulat Khān declared that although God was 'the Master of hearts' no one had ever seen Him and that here on earth the title
belonged to Gurū Nānak. The Gurū also conversed with some pious people 116
and was acclaimed a *pīr* by both Hindus and Muslims.

After this interlude in Sultānpur Gurū Nānak set out through 'the north 117
country' to Mount Sumeru, evidently travelling alone. The only place

[1] *Pur JS*, p. 32. See *supra*, p. 40.

[2] *Dhanāsarī Chhant* 3, *AG*, pp. 689–90. The genesis of the story is obviously connected with the word *mūṭhārīe* (*mūṭhāṇā*: to cheat, plunder, rob) which occurs in the first line and which would evoke associations of *ṭhagī* (thuggee).

[3] See *infra*, p. 91.

[4] The reference is to one of the famous Rājpūt cycles.

[5] *MK*, p. 175.

named on his journey there is a temple of Durgā. Climbing Mount Sumeru, Gurū Nānak found all nine Siddhs seated there—Gorakhnāth, Machhendranāth, Īśarnāth, Charapaṭnāth, Baraṅgnāth, Ghoṛācholī, Bālgundāī, Bharatharī, and Gopīchand. When Gorakhnāth asked the identity of the visitor his disciples replied, 'This is Nānak Bedī, a *pīr* and a *bhagat* who is a householder. Nānak Bedī is a great *bhagat*.' Gorakhnāth then addressed Gurū Nānak, asking him from where he had come. The Gurū replied that he had come from *Āsā-andesā* ('Hope and Fear') and that he dwelt there as a water-fowl floats on water. Gorakhnāth commented that a water-fowl knows all that is taking place along the river and asked him to tell them what was happening in the present evil age (*Kaliyug*). Gurū Nānak responded with three *śloks*, all of them describing a condition of degeneracy.

> There is a famine of truth, falsehood prevails, and in the darkness of *Kaliyug* men have become ghouls. . . .[1]
>
> The *Kaliyug* is a knife, kings are butchers, *dharma* has taken wings and flown. . . .[2]
>
> Men give as charity the money they have acquired by sinful means. . . .[3]

The discourse then takes up *Vār Rāmakalī*, *śloks* 2–7 of *pauṛī* 12,[4] and in
118–24 the succession of *goṣṭs* which follows there are quoted other *śabads* and
śloks which imply an audience of Nāths.

125 The series concluded with a discourse in God's court, after which Gurū
126 Nānak descended to 'this world' again and journeyed to Gorakh-haṭaṛī.
He arrived there during a fair, conversed with 'the yogīs' *gurū*', and continued on. No reference is made to any attempt by the yogīs to overawe him with magic.

127 Leaving 'the north country', where he had spent one year, Gurū Nānak
entered 'the west country' and proceeded towards Multān. Mardānā reappears in the janam-sākhī at this point and a group of Multān *goṣṭs* follows.
131 One of these was with a descendant of Pīr Bahāuddīn, and in the next *goṣṭ*
132 it is recorded that the Gurū visited the Pīr's tomb where, according to the
people's report, he paid homage.

135 From Multān Gurū Nānak set out on a pilgrimage to Mecca. On the
way he came to a village which belonged to a mullah and entering the village mosque without removing his shoes he lay down with his feet in the direction of the *Ka'bah*. When the mullah and his congregation entered the mosque for the *pesī*, the second prayer, they discovered him lying in this sacrilegious position. The mullah demanded an explanation and the

[1] *Vār Āsā*, *ślok* 1 of *pauṛī* 11, *AG*, p. 468.
[2] *Vār Mājh*, *ślok* 1 of *pauṛī* 16, *AG*, p. 145.
[3] *Vār Rāmakalī*, *ślok* 1 of *pauṛī* 11, *AG*, p. 951.
[4] *AG*, pp. 952–3.

Gurū replied, 'Bābā Sāhib, turn my shoes in that direction where the house of God will not go. Place my shoes in that direction where the *Ka'bah* is not.' The mullah did not accept the challenge. He first performed the office and then gave orders for the Gurū to be thrown into prison. Gurū Nānak asked for permission to make a single comment and when it was granted declared that God alone and not his accuser was the true Mullah. He then recited *Sirī Rāgu* 28:

> He is the true Mullah who has caused the world to blossom and be verdant. . . .[1]

The mullah, evidently acknowledging defeat, retired to the graveyard and there expired.

Proceeding on from the mullah's village he met two faqīrs who were 136
going to Mecca and who suggested that they should all travel together.[2] Further on, when they reached a village, the Gurū asked them their names. They informed him that they were called Rahīm and Karīm, and inquired what his name was. When he told them it was Nānak they commented with evident surprise that it sounded like a Hindu name. The Gurū replied that he was indeed a Hindu, and when he added that he was a khatrī and a Bedī they at last recognized him as the renowned faqīr of Sultānpur fame and became very respectful. When he refused food which the Muslim villagers brought, excusing himself on the grounds that he was fasting, word quickly spread that a great *darveś* had arrived and he was acclaimed by the village.

Next morning they all set out again and on the road the two faqīrs asked him how he, a Hindu, could hope to visit Mecca. He replied that if God so willed then it would come to pass. The faqīrs were carrying paper, pen, and ink, and at this point they wrote down the date. Gurū Nānak was then transported to Mecca in an instant. His two companions arrived on foot some months later and discovered the Gurū already there. When they asked the local people his date of arrival they were given the very date they had written down and as a result word soon spread in Mecca that a great *darveś* had arrived. Gurū Nānak remained there for twelve months.

After having visited Mecca and seen 'the west country' Gurū Nānak 138
travelled eastwards to Hiṅglāj.[3] There the pilgrims were unable to recognize his religion or his caste. They also observed that he seemed to neither sleep, walk, eat, nor drink.

Continuing on to the east he arrived back in the Pañjāb and passing 139
through Gorakh-haṭaṛī came to Saidpur. He had spent three years in 'the west country' and had seen all of it, including Rome, Syria, Kābul, and

[1] *AG*, p. 24.

[2] Mardānā disappears following *goṣṭ* 135 and does not reappear in the record until *goṣṭ* 139.

[3] The *pīṭh-sthān* in the Makrān Coast Range about eighty miles west of the Indus Delta and some twelve miles inland.

Peshāwar.[1] When he reached Saidpur Mardānā suggested that they should enter the town to seek alms. This they did and discovered that weddings were being celebrated everywhere. No one, however, paid any attention to them. No food was offered to them, nor any place to rest, and wherever they asked they were ignored or refused. As punishment for its callousness the Gurū called down Bābur upon the town, invoking his coming by the utterance of the verse *Tilaṅg* 5.[2]

As in the *Purātan* version the pronouncement of the curse came to the knowledge of a certain brāhmaṇ who was a friend of faqīrs. Knowing that God invariably heeds the request of a faqīr he hastened to the Gurū and, presenting him with a basket of fruit, begged him to be merciful. Gurū Nānak reminded him that the town had inflicted harm on faqīrs, thereby implying that the imminent punishment was merited. The brāhmaṇ, however, was told to take his family and go to a pool out in the waste land at a distance of fifteen *kos*. Bābur then fell upon the city and all save the brāhmaṇ and his family were massacred. 'And so Saidpur was devastated in accordance with the utterance given by the Gurū.'

140 Next day Gurū Nānak and Mardānā returned to Saidpur and the Gurū commented, 'Mardānā, see what has befallen Saidpur Saloī. Behold the will of God in what has taken place.' They looked upon Saidpur and there was nothing to be seen. From there they travelled to Ṭillā Bālgundāī. The following day Bābur also arrived there and, in accordance with an implied warning which Gurū Nānak had given the arrogant yogīs, assaulted the village.

141 After witnessing the sack of Saidpur and visiting Ṭillā, Gurū Nānak at last turned towards his home in Talvaṇḍī. They stopped at a distance of two *kos* from the village and Mardānā asked if he might continue on into the village. Permission was granted on condition that he was not to mention the name of Nānak and that if anyone should ask for news of him he was to give the following answer: 'Brother, since the time when Bābā Nānak left Sultānpur we, being separated from him, have continually held his name in remembrance. If anyone knows his whereabouts it is God.'

In the village the people showed great respect to him. He went to Kālū's house and prostrated himself before the Gurū's mother When she and others asked where Nānak was he replied that he did not know but was looking for him. After further conversation he departed and the Gurū's mother said to herself, 'There is meaning in his having come and then departed again. He has gone to Nānak.' Taking sweets, fruit, and clothing, she followed Mardānā out into the jungle called Sāndal Bār and there the
142–5 reunion took place. A series of discourses followed in which both his

[1] Rome and Syria must be later additions to the janam-sākhī. The names are found in the later janam-sākhīs. Kābul and Peshāwar may also be later additions.

[2] *AG*, pp. 722–3.

parents unsuccessfully sought to persuade him to abandon his itinerant way of life and settle in Talvaṇḍī.

After leaving Talvaṇḍī Gurū Nānak moved south through the Mājhā[1] 147
to Pāk Paṭṭan, passing through a number of villages on the way and stopping two *kos* short of the town. The account of his meeting with Sheikh Kamāl, who was out gathering firewood, and of the first discourse with Sheikh Ibrāhīm is essentially the same as the *Purātan*'s *sākhī* 32,[2] except that Mardānā appears to be absent in the Miharbān version. Most of the scripture quotations are the same and both put Gurū Amar Dās's *ślok* 104[3] into Gurū Nānak's mouth on this occasion. Miharbān extends the meeting
with Sheikh Ibrāhīm over two more *goṣṭs*, but adds only scripture and 148–9
interpretation.

From Pāk Paṭṭan Gurū Nānak travelled north to Dīpālpur where a pious 151
merchant presented him with some dried fruit and some mangoes. The Gurū asked him why he was offering fruit from both Khurāsān and Hindustān together. The merchant explained that the mangoes were the first of a consignment which had just arrived from Delhi and in order that his business might prosper he wanted Gurū Nānak to be the first to taste them. The raisins had been left by Bābur's army, which had been in Dīpālpur, and some had been saved for any man of God who might come. Gurū Nānak tried a sample from each and then blessed both the donor and the town, reciting a *ślok* which is really by Gurū Aṅgad.[4] He then proceeded on through the areas of Shergaṛh, Mustafābād, Chuṇīān, Talvaṇḍī, Kaṅganpur, Harī, Kasūr, Rohevāl, Nanīer, Bahikiṛīā, and finally reached Khokhovāl.

The following *goṣṭ*, which is set in Khokhovāl, relates a series of bizarre 152
incidents, essentially disconnected but loosely linked by the presence of a brāhmaṇ boy. The language is later and the collection is evidently a subsequent addition.

Leaving Khokhovāl, Gurū Nānak moved through Kiṛīān Paṭhāṇān to 153
the village of Pokho.[5] The area so attracted him that he settled there on the banks of the Rāvī and soon crowds were coming to pay their respects. The local official,[6] however, was sceptical and, as in the *Purātan* version, set off to imprison the corrupter of Hindus and Muslims. The results were the same, except that the fall came first and blindness second, and that a third effort to proceed on horseback produced a pain in his stomach. When he continued on foot all was well. After his interview he donated some fertile

[1] The Bārī Doāb between the Rāvī and Beās rivers.

[2] See *supra*, p. 43.

[3] *AG*, p. 1383.

[4] *Vār Soraṭhi*, *ślok* 2 of *pauṛī* 28, *AG*, p. 653.

[5] Pokho dī Randhāvī, or Pakho, near the town of Dehrā Bābā Nānak. Gurū Nānak's father-in-law is said to have lived here before moving to Baṭālā.

[6] The *karoṛīā* of the *Purātan sākhī* 40. See *supra*, p. 46. The Miharbān account also describes him as a *karoṛīā*.

land for a village and built a *dharmsālā*. Gurū Nānak settled there, naming the new village Kartārpur.

At this point *Pothī Sach-khaṇḍ* concludes.

Summaries

The three best available accounts of the life of Gurū Nānak have now been set out in some detail. In so far as they include references to specific dates, recognizable places, and people of some significance they may be summarized as follows:

Bhāī Gurdās's Vār 1

Gurū Nānak's visit to 'all the centres of pilgrimage'.
Mount Sumeru.
Mecca.
Medina.
Baghdad.
Kartārpur, on the right bank of the Rāvī, immediately opposite Dehrā Bābā Nānak.
Gurū Aṅgad appointed successor.
Achal Baṭālā, four miles east of Baṭālā.
Multān.
Kartārpur.

The Purātan *Janam-sākhīs*

Gurū Nānak was born in the light half of the month of Vaisākh, S. 1526 (A.D. 1469) in the village of Rāi Bhoi dī Talvaṇḍī where his father, Kālū, a Bedī khatrī, lived. The landlord of the village during his childhood was Rāi Bulār.

At the age of twelve he was married to the daughter of Mūlā, a Choṇā khatrī. Two sons, Lakhmī Dās and Sirī Chand, were subsequently born.

His brother-in-law Jai Rām, the steward of Daulat Khān, invited him to Sultānpur where he was given employment in Daulat Khān's service.

From Sultānpur he left on his first journey accompanied by Mardānā, a Ḍūm from Talvaṇḍī. This journey was to the eastern parts of India and included, in the following sequence:

Pāṇīpat (Sheikh Sharaf)
Delhi (Sultan Ibrāhīm Lodī)
Banāras
Nānakmatā
Kaurū or Kāvarū, evidently Kāmrūp in Assam (Nūr Shāh)
Talvaṇḍī, twelve years after leaving Sultānpur
Pāk Paṭṭan (Sheikh Ibrāhīm)
Goindvāl
Saidpur, or modern Eminābād (Bābur)
Lahore
Kartārpur

His second journey was to the south and his companions are variously given as Saido and Gheho; Saido and Sīho; Saido, Gheho, and Sīho; or Saido, Sīho, and Mardānā.

Ceylon (Rājā Śivanābh)

The third journey was to the north. His companions' names are given as Hassū Lohār and Sīhān Chhīmbā.

Kashmir
Mount Sumeru
Achal

The fourth journey was to the west. No regular companions are named.

Mecca (Qāzī Rukan-dīn)

The fifth journey was a brief one to Gorakh-haṭaṛī, perhaps the Nāth centre in modern Peshāwar. No companion is named.

Lahiṇā of Khaḍūr became a disciple, was subsequently renamed Aṅgad, and was eventually designated successor to the office of Gurū by Gurū Nānak himself.

Gurū Nānak died at Kartārpur on the tenth day of the light half of Asū, S. 1595 (A.D. 1538).

The *Purātan* janam-sākhīs also indicate that the Gurū was acquainted with Pīr Bahāuddīn of Multān.[1] Two prominent omissions from the places named are Baghdad[2] and Jagannāth Purī. The only dates of significance which are mentioned are those of his birth and death, and (by obvious implication) that of his marriage which would have been in A.D. 1481 or 1482. Two which may be added are those of the accession of Sultan Ibrāhīm Lodī in 1517[3] and Bābur's sack of Saidpur in 1520.[4] This at once involves a contradiction, as Gurū Nānak is said to have returned to Talvaṇḍī twelve years after the journey began,[5] and the journey is said to have begun after the occasion of Gurū Nānak's meeting with Ibrāhīm Lodī in Delhi.[6] One of the dates must be rejected forthwith and of the two incidents the one which has the greater claims to probability is obviously the Saidpur visit. The Delhi *sākhī* can have no claims whatsoever and accordingly the 1517 date may be summarily eliminated.

[1] The IOL manuscript Panj. B40, folio 53, includes a discourse with Bahāuddīn's *potā* (grandson, or perhaps a remoter descendant in the male line), not with Bahāuddīn himself. The name of the *potā* is given as Rukandīn. Miharbān, who also has such a discourse, does not name the *potā*, referring to him simply as *Pīr Bahāvadī dā potā* or as *pīrzādā* (*Mih JS*, p. 434. See *supra*, p. 60). In the *Colebrooke* and *Hāfizābād* manuscripts Rukandīn is the name of the Mecca qāzī who sought to drag Gurū Nānak's feet away from the direction of the *Ka'bah*. See *supra*, p. 49.

[2] The IOL manuscript Panj. B40, folio 200, includes a *sākhī* describing a discourse held in Baghdad. The other participant's name is given as Sheikh Sharaf.

[3] *Sākhī* 15. See *supra*, p. 39.

[4] *Sākhī* 35. See *supra*, p. 44.

[5] *Pur JS*, p. 48.

[6] Ibid., p. 25.

The Miharbān Janam-sākhī

Gurū Nānak was born in the light half of the month of Vaisākh, S. 1526 (A.D. 1469), the son of Kālū, a Bedī khatrī, and Tiparā. The place where the birth took place is variously said to have been the village of Chāhalāvāle and Kālū's village, Rāi Bhoe kī Talvaṇḍī. The name of the contemporary landlord of the latter village is given as Rāi Bhoā.

At about the time of his sixteenth birthday Gurū Nānak was married in Baṭālā to Ghumī, the daughter of Mūlā, a Choṇā khatrī of Baṭālā. Two sons, Lakhmī Dās and Sirī Chand, were born when he was twenty-seven or twenty-eight years of age.

At the age of thirty-five years, six and a half months, he went to Sultānpur in response to an invitation from his brother-in-law Jai Rām, an Uppal khatrī and steward of Daulat K͟hān Lodī. There he was given employment in Daulat K͟hān's commissariat.

After two years in Sultānpur he left on his first journey, accompanied by Mardānā. This journey was to the east of India and then from there to the far south. It included the following places:

Delhi (Salīm Shāh Paṭhān)
Hardwār
Allahābād
Banāras
Hājīpur Paṭṇā
Ayodhyā
Jagannāth Purī
Rāmeśwaram
A 'land of darkness' beyond Adam's Bridge (evidently Ceylon)
Ujjain (Rājā Bharatharī)
Vindhyā Mountains
Narabad River
Ujjain
Bīkāner
Saurāshtra
Mathurā
Kurukshetra
Sultānpur (Daulat K͟hān Lodī)

The second journey was to the north and then to the west.

Mount Sumeru
Gorakh-haṭaṛī
Multān (a descendant of Pīr Bahāuddīn)
Mecca
Hiṅglāj
Gorakh-haṭaṛī
Saidpur (Bābur)
Ṭillā Bālgundāī (Bābur)

Talvaṇḍī
Pāk Paṭṭan (Sheikh Ibrāhīm)
Dīpālpur
Khokhovāl
Pokho and Kartārpur

In Miharbān's account the notable omissions are Kāmrūp and Baghdad. Nānakmatā is also missing and Ceylon is not mentioned by name. The significant dates, stated or plainly implied, are the Gurū's birth in S. 1526 (A.D. 1469), his marriage (A.D. 1485), his move from Talvaṇḍī to Sultānpur (A.D. 1504), and his departure from there on his first journey (A.D. 1506). To these may be added the date of the attack on Saidpur (A.D. 1520) which means that according to Miharbān's account all of Gurū Nānak's travels outside the Pañjāb took place within the space of fourteen years and between the ages of thirty-seven and fifty-three. The period spent in 'the east country' was three years, in the south five years, in the north one year, and in the west three years, a total of twelve years. This leaves a balance of two years to be allocated to the initial journey from Sultānpur to 'the east country', and the gap between the departure from 'the south country' and the commencement of the second journey. The pattern would then be as follows:

From Sultānpur to 'the east country'	1506–7
Travels in 'the east country'	1507–10
Travels in 'the south country'	1510–15
The journey from 'the south country' to 'the north country' via Sultānpur	1515–16
Travels in 'the north country'	1516–17
Travels in 'the west country'	1517–20

4

THE LIFE OF GURŪ NĀNAK

THE three accounts set out in the previous section provide practically all of the material available for a reconstruction of the events of the life of Gurū Nānak. None of them can be accepted as it stands and our task must now be to seek and apply means of identifying what may be affirmed, what must be rejected, and what falls between the two. There is obviously much that must be rejected as impossible, and in contrast there is regrettably little which may be accepted without reserve. Some of the remaining material may be regarded as probable, but considerably more of it must be classified as unlikely. Finally there is a certain amount from which we must withhold judgement, material which records what is inherently possible, but for which there is no support other than that offered by the janam-sākhīs themselves.

We have here five categories which we may designate the established, the probable, the possible, the improbable, and the impossible. Into these five we must strive to fit the manifold traditions concerning the life of Gurū Nānak. In order to do so it is first necessary to determine the criteria which should be used.

The first criterion, and one which enables us to discard substantial portions of all the janam-sākhī accounts, is the incidence of the miraculous or plainly fantastic. It is, however, one which must be used with some caution. The inclusion of a miracle does not necessarily mean that the whole *sākhī* must be rejected. In most cases this is required, but in others the possibility of a substratum of truth must be borne in mind. The use of this approach should not, of course, suggest that legend possesses no significance and deserves to be wholly ignored. Legendary accretions frequently reflect the piety engendered by great religious figures and as such serve to communicate, in some measure, an impression of their power to attract and inspire.[1] In a study of this nature, however, legend must wherever possible be identified and set aside. The strict, at times ruthless, approach is as much required in a quest for the historical Nānak as it has been required in the quest of the historical Jesus.

A second criterion is the testimony of external sources. In most cases

[1] Tor Andrae, *Mohammed: The Man and His Faith*, Harper Torchbooks, New York, 1960, p. 31. H. D. Lewis and Robert Lawson Slater, *World Religions: Meeting Points and Major Issues*, p. 53.

where this criterion applies to the janam-sākhī accounts of Gurū Nānak's life it demands a negative judgement. The two important exceptions are the incidents involving Daulat Khān Lodī and the Emperor Bābur. There is also an inscription in Baghdad which requires careful consideration.

A third criterion which may be used is Gurū Nānak's own work as recorded in the *Ādi Granth*. This too offers us disappointingly little help for, as we have already observed, explicit references to the events of his life are entirely absent and implicit hints are few. The most important of these concern the connexion with Bābur and Gurū Nānak's relationships with Nāth yogīs. In other cases the help which his works offer us is generally negative. Occasionally it is possible to reject an incident because it is conspicuously out of accord with clearly stated doctrine or with the personality which emerges from his works as a whole.[1]

A fourth criterion is the measure of agreement or, conversely, disagreement which we find in the different janam-sakhis. This alone can rarely determine a particular issue, but in some cases it should certainly influence our judgement. One such instance is the story of Sajjaṇ the *ṭhag*.

In cases where there is disagreement between the different janam-sākhīs, or where only one janam-sākhī records a particular detail or incident, a fifth criterion is the relative reliability of the different janam-sākhīs. This criterion is of little use in issues which concern only the *Purātan* and *Miharbān* janam-sākhīs or *Vār* 1, but it certainly applies whenever the more recent janam-sākhīs enter the discussion. In general the testimony of the three older sources must be preferred to that of either the *Gyān-ratanāvalī* or the *Bālā* janam-sākhīs.

Sixthly, a measure of trust may be attached to genealogical references. Family relationships in the Pañjāb can normally be traced back accurately for several generations and it is reasonable to assume that at least the immediate family connexions of Gurū Nānak would still be known at the time when the older janam-sākhīs were committed to writing.

Finally there is a geographic criterion in the sense that a greater degree of confidence can be placed in details relating to Gurū Nānak's life within the Pañjāb than to those which concern his travels beyond the province.

[1] The so-called contextual argument is of use only in the case of the verses which refer to Bābur, and even here it must be qualified. According to this argument a *sākhī* is entitled to acceptance if the theme of the verse which it incorporates corresponds with the content of the *sākhī*. The argument is unacceptable for two reasons. In the first place it assumes a highly improbable degree of poetic spontaneity, particularly in the case of *sākhīs* relating to the Gurū's childhood. Secondly, such cases of correspondence are subject to a much more likely explanation. There seems to be little doubt that almost all *sākhīs* which are in significant accord with a particular verse should be regarded as examples of stories which have evolved out of a suggestive reference in a verse. The origin may be the theme of the complete verse, or it may be a single word. In some cases it may be the name or the nature of the person to whom the verse appears to be addressed. See *supra*, pp. 11–12 and *infra*, pp. 86–87, 119. It is possible that in a few instances a verse has been subsequently attached to a developed *sākhī* as a result of an evident affinity between the two.

This applies particularly to the period of his later years. The accounts of his childhood are all heavily charged with legend, but there is much that rings true in the brief accounts given of his Kartārpur period. This is to be expected, for the janam-sākhīs we are using must have emerged at a remove of only one or two generations from Gurū Nānak's death.

The relevance of this particular criterion is pointed up by the marked contrast between the geographical exactitude which characterizes the janam-sākhī accounts of his movements within the Pañjāb and the vagueness of those which describe his travels elsewhere. This certainly does not mean that we can accept a particular event as authentic simply because it is set in a recognizable and accurately described Pañjāb location, but it does enhance the possibility of acceptance. In the case of Gurū Nānak's travels beyond the Pañjāb the place-names are almost all either well-known capitals and centres of pilgrimage, or they are unidentifiable and evidently non-existent places such as 'Dhanāsarī'. Many of the *sākhīs* describing incidents which occurred during his journeys are unlocated or are said to have taken place in 'a certain city' or 'a certain country'. A high proportion are placed in deserts or jungles, and a number are said to have occurred on islands in the ocean. The incidence of the fantastic is particularly high in these latter cases. All *sākhīs* with indefinite oceanic settings must be regarded with marked scepticism.

The vagueness also emerges in such details as the names of Gurū Nānak's associates. In the case of the *Purātan's* southern journey the manuscripts disagree not just between themselves but also within their own individual accounts. There is the same evident uncertainty in the names of the people with whom Gurū Nānak is said to have conversed. Discourses with Sheikh Farīd, Sheikh Sharaf, and Pīr Bahāuddīn are anachronisms, but the names are at least those of real people, each of whom would have left a line of spiritual successors. This is more than can be said for such names as Nūr Shāh, Khwājā Khizar, and the eighty-four Siddhs. Such vagueness need not necessarily demand a definite rejection of a particular *sākhī*, but it must certainly weaken its claims to authenticity.

A synopsis of the janam-sākhī traditions concerning the life of Gurū Nānak

These are the seven principal criteria which will be used in this effort to reconstruct the events of the life of Gurū Nānak. Before proceeding to do so, however, it will be convenient to set out, in the form of a chart, a conspectus of the various *sākhīs* which have been used in Bhāī Gurdās's *Vār* 1 and the *Purātan* and *Miharbān* janam-sākhīs,[1] together with the correspond-

[1] In the case of the *Miharbān Janam-sākhī* numbers up to and including 153 represent *goṣṭs* from *Pothī Sach-khaṇḍ*, and numbers 172, 173 and 180 *goṣṭs* from *Pothī Harijī*.

ing *sākhīs* from the *Gyān-ratanāvalī* and *Bālā* versions. To these have been added a few *sākhīs* which do not appear in any of the three older sources, but which are included in most modern biographies of Gurū Nānak. A column has also been added to indicate which of the *sākhīs* have been used by Macauliffe in the first volume of his *The Sikh Religion*. Macauliffe's account is generally based upon the *Purātan* janam-sākhīs, but the author added several other incidents, mainly from the *Bālā* tradition, and in many cases he expanded the *Purātan* account with material drawn from *Bālā* sources. Occasionally he used the *Gyān-ratanāvalī* in the same way and added anything extra which was to be found in Bhāī Gurdās's *Vār* 1.

For this chart the *Miharbān Janam-sākhī* has been taken as the standard and the individual *sākhīs* are listed in the order in which they occur in that janam-sākhī. *Sākhīs* which do not appear in the *Miharbān* version but which include a specific chronological indication have been inserted in their appropriate places. Other *sākhīs* are listed as 'Miscellaneous *sākhīs*'. Each figure indicates the number of the relevant *sākhī*, *goṣṭ*, or *pauṛī* in the janam-sākhī under which it is listed, and the numbers given under 'Macauliffe' are those of the appropriate page numbers in volume i of *The Sikh Religion*.[1] The numbers which appear consecutively in the first column have been added by the writer for ease of reference in the discussion which follows.

The edition of the *Gyān-ratanāvalī* which has been used is the one which was lithographed in Lahore by Charāguddīn and Sarājuddīn in A.D. 1891. *Sākhīs* included in that edition which have obviously been borrowed from the *Bālā* tradition have been bracketed.

Three editions of the *Bālā* version have been included in the chart. These are: (*a*) the Hāfaz Qutub Dīn edition, lithographed in A.D. 1871, which generally follows the India Office Library manuscript Panj. B41 and the British Museum manuscript Or. 2754. I.; (*b*) the expanded 1871 edition lithographed by Dīvān Būṭā Singh, Lahore; and (*c*) a modern version published by Munshī Gulāb Singh and Sons of Lahore in A.D. 1942. *Sākhīs* have been listed under the third of these only if they do not appear in either of the 1871 editions. Numbers listed under (*a*) which are bracketed indicate *sākhīs* which have been taken direct from the *Purātan* tradition and do not appear in the India Office Library or British Museum manuscripts. An error has been made in the indexing of (*b*), the expanded 1871 edition, as a result of which the numbers 165–74 inclusive have been used twice in allocating consecutive numbers to *sākhīs*. In the chart such *sākhīs* are distinguished by the use of either (1) or (2).

It must be emphasized that although most *sākhīs* appear in the chart under more than one source, the different versions normally give differing

[1] One incident (number 93) is recorded in volume ii of *The Sikh Religion*.

accounts of the same incident. Occasionally the differences are such as to destroy practically all resemblances between two accounts. It should also be noted that the *sākhīs* listed in the chart do not cover the total range of all traditions concerning the life of Gurū Nānak. The selection is, however, an extensive one and includes all the important incidents from the older janam-sākhīs.

Sākhī	Mih JS	Pur JS	Vār 1	GR	Bālā janam-sākhīs a	b	c	Macauliffe
1. The birth of Gurū Nānak	4	1		27	2	2		1
2. Recitation of *Sapat Ślokī Gitā*				(31)		2		
3. Instruction by the paṇḍit	5	2		33–34	3	3		2
4. Instruction by the mullah	6	3		45		4		11
5. Investiture with the sacred thread	7			44		5		16
6. The restored field	8	4		46–47		6		15
7. The tree's stationary shadow	9	5		48	4	7		19
8. The cobra's shadow					4	8		19
9. Marriage of Jai Rām and Nānakī					7	13		18
10. Betrothal and marriage	11–12	3		50	11–12	17–18		18
11. The physician convinced	15–16	7		48		11		26
12. The true field	17							
13. The true merchandise	22	6		49		10		23
14. Birth of Lakhmī Dās and Sirī Chand	22	5		51	13	20, 25		29
15. The true harvest	23	6		49		10		21
16. *Kharā saudā*: the feeding of Sant Ren and the faqīrs					6	12		30
17. The *loṭā* and ring presented to a faqīr					8	14		32
18. Bhāgīrath and Mansukh		41		52		19		145
19. Mansukh and Rājā Śivanābh		41		82		27		146
20. To Sultānpur	24	8		53	9	15		32
21. Work in Daulat Khān's commissariat	25–27	9		54	10	16		33
22. Immersion in the river: his call	28–29	10		56	13	21–23		33
23. Nānak accused of embezzlement					10	25		42
24. The mullah seeks to exorcize his evil spirit					15	27		36
25. Discourse with the qāzī	30–32	11		57–58	15	28–29		37
26. Departure from Sultānpur	34	11		61	16	34		43
27. Mardānā commanded to throw offerings away	35	12				176		44
28. Mardānā eats the forbidden fruit	36	30			24	177		94
29. Nānak cooks meat at Kurukshetra				(62)	71	249		47
30. Discourse with Sheikh Sharaf of Pāṇīpat		14		65	(66)			52
31. Delhi: the real alms	38							
32. Delhi: the sultan's elephant resurrected		15		66–68		236		56
33. Sheikh Bajīd		16						58

Sākhī	Mih JS	Pur JS	Vār 1	GR	Bālā janam-sākhīs a	Bālā janam-sākhīs b	Bālā janam-sākhīs c	Macauliffe
34. Hardwār: the watering of his fields	39–40			71			81	50
35. Mount Govardhan, Mathurā, and Brindāban				(69–70)		251–2		57
36. Nānakmatā		18		72	23	90		59
37. Allahābād	43							
38. Banāras: discourses with paṇḍits	44–50			74		253		
39. Banāras: discourse with Chatur Dās		17				196		61
40. Rājā Harināth	51							
41. Meeting with Kabīr	52							
42. Hājīpur Paṭṇā	54			77				
43. Ayodhyā: discourse with 'all the *bhagats*'	59–60							
44. Ayodhyā: discourse with paṇḍits				(75)		255		
45. Gayā				(76)		254		64
46. The country ruled by women		23		84	(25)	170(1)		73
47. Dacca					24			
48. Jagannāth Purī	61			78–79		254		81
49. The brick falls from the temple	62							
50. The jackal and the food from God's court	63							
51. The *bhagats* revealed in the stars	64							
52. Rāmeśwaram	65–66				60	{ 158 227		
53. The yogī of Jāpāpaṭan (Jaffna)				85–86				
54. Ceylon: Rājā Śivanābh and the *Prāṇ Saṅgalī*		47		87–91	29	169(1)		154
55. A girl turned into a boy				(92–94)		173–4(1)		
56. The meeting with Kaliyug	68	24		81	(26)	165(2)		78
57. The struggle with *Kāl*	69							
58. The cannibals' cauldron	71	44		83	30	72–73		152
59. A deceitful people turned to righteousness	72							
60. Sajjaṇ the *ṭhag*	73	13		73	63	239		45
61. Rājā Mitr Sain	75							
62. Rājā Jagannāth	78							
63. Ujjain	87, 91–95							
64. Vindhyā Mountains	88							
65. Narabad River	89							

66. Bīkāner district and city	100–6			108				
67. The land of Soraṭhi (Saurāshtra)	107							
68. Mathurā	109–11							
69. Kurukshetra: discourse on bathing	112							
70. Return to Sultānpur	113–16							
71. The Kashmīrī paṇḍit		49		(114)	(75)	217		163
72. Mount Sumeru	117–25	50	28–31	(139–42)	43–48	111–37		169
73. Gorakh-haṭaṛī	126	52						172
74. Multān: discourse with a descendant of Pīr Bahāuddīn	127–34							
75. The mullah's village	135							
76. Rahīm and Karīm	136							
77. The Mecca pilgrim and the following cloud		51		156				174
78. Mecca: Gurū Nānak's miraculous arrival	136							
79. Mecca: the moving mosque		51	32–34	157	(39)	104		175
80. Medina				(164)	40	106–8		179
81. Baghdad			35–36	161–3		228–31		179
82. Hiṅglāj	138							
83. The sack of Saidpur	139	35		(112)		470		109
84. Discourse with Bābur		35		(112)	73	470		113
85. Bābur attacks Ṭillā Bālgundāī	140							
86. Return to Talvaṇḍī and reunion with parents	141–5	31		110			101	95
87. Pāk Paṭṭan: discourse with Sheikh Ibrāhīm	147–9	32		36–37 (180)	83	258		101
88. The merchant of Dīpālpur	151							
89. The proud official humbled: the founding of Kartārpur	153	40		148–51		55		131
90. Achal Baṭālā: discourse with the Siddhs	173	50	39–44	170–7	61			157
91. Multān: the jasmine petal			44	178		233		180
92. First meeting with Lahiṇā	172	53		169	86	271		182
93. Lahiṇā's clothes ruined		53			86	271		ii. 4
94. Lahiṇā commanded to eat the corpse	180	54			86	279		183
95. Lahiṇā becomes Aṅgad	172	54			86	271		185
96. Death of Ma<u>kh</u>dūm Bahāuddīn		55						186
97. Death of Mardānā				208				181
98. Death of Kālū and Tipārā				216–17		290		

Sākhī	Mih JS	Pur JS	Vār 1	GR	Bālā janam-sākhīs a	b	c	Macauliffe
99. The installation of Gurū Aṅgad		56	45	218	86	293		187
100. The death of Gurū Nānak		57		219	89–90	295–300		188
Miscellaneous Sākhīs								
101. The death of the trader's infant son		19				68		65
102. A watchman receives royal authority		20				160–1		68
103. The coal and the thorn		21						68
104. The *ṭhags* and the funeral pyre		22		120		198		71
105. *Kīṛ nagar*: the city of insects		25			(27)	376		
106. The inhospitable village unmolested		26						80
107. The hospitable village dispersed		27						81
108. The meeting with Sheikh Farīd in Āsā		28			(28)			84
109. Jhaṇḍā Bāḍhī and the *Jugāvalī*		29			34	170(2)		93
110. The leprous faqīr		33				202		107
111. The devotees of Kiṛīān Paṭhāṇān		34						108
112. Discourse with Mīā Miṭhā		36				171(2)		123
113. Dunī Chand and the wolf		37			(74)	62		129
114. Dunī Chand's flags		37			(74)	62		130
115. The brāhmaṇ's cooking-square		38						132
116. A pious boy		39				168(2)		133
117. The meeting with Khwājar Khizar		42				172(2)		147
118. Anabhī the Jain		43						150
119. The meeting with Makhdūm Bahāuddīn		45						153
120. The destruction of the hospitable carpenter's hut		48				167(2)		
121. Sālas Rāi				(99–107)	31	74–75		
122. *Pañjā Sāhib*: the rock stopped							147	171
123. Discourse with Abdul Rahmān of Iran				(119)		193 259–60		
124. Saidpur: Lālo and Bhāgo					19–20	47		43

Sākhīs which must be rejected

Of the *sākhīs* listed in the chart many may be treated in summary manner. A substantial proportion can be discarded at once, most of them in accordance with the first criterion, and many more must be relegated to the 'possible' category. The following may be rejected on the grounds that they are miracle stories without any features which suggest a substratum of truth.

2. Recitation of *Sapat Ślokī Gītā*
6. The restored field
7. The tree's stationary shadow
8. The cobra's shadow
23. Nānak accused of embezzlement
28. Mardānā eats the forbidden fruit
49. The brick falls from the temple
50. The jackal and the food from God's court
51. The *bhagats* revealed in the stars
53. The yogī of Jāpāpaṭan
55. A girl turned into a boy.
56. The meeting with Kaliyug
57. The struggle with *Kāl*
59. A deceitful people turned to righteousness
77. The Mecca pilgrim and the following cloud
78. Mecca: Gurū Nānak's miraculous arrival
94. Lahiṇā commanded to eat the corpse
104. The *ṭhags* and the funeral pyre
105. *Kīṛ nagar*: the city of insects
110. The leprous faqīr
113. Dunī Chand and the wolf.
115. The brāhmaṇ's cooking-square
117. The meeting with K͟hwājar K͟hizar
119. The meeting with Mak͟hdūm Bahāuddīn
120. The destruction of the hospitable carpenter's hut
122. *Pañjā Sāhib*: the rock stopped

Several of these do not appear in the *Vār* or in either of the older janam-sākhī traditions, but have been included here either on account of their prominence in popular biographies of Gurū Nānak or because they provide illustrations of *Bālā* material incorporated in the extant version of the *Gyān-ratanāvalī*. In a number of cases these legends represent not an indigenous development within Sikh tradition, but a borrowing from another source. Number 8, the story of the cobra's shadow, is an obvious example, and another appears to be number 108, the city of insects.[1] In the latter case a legend from an external source, the Persian story of Hazrat Suleimān and a town of ants, may have come to be linked with a suggestive place-name. In Kāṅgṛā District of the Pañjāb there is a village which is now called Baijnāth, but which was formerly known as Kīṛgrām (literally 'insect-village') and which was, for a period, a centre of pilgrimage. It is at least possible that a tradition concerning a visit to the village by Gurū Nānak came to be associated with the Persian legend, and that the *sākhī* entitled *Kīṛ nagar* is the result.[2] The *ślok* which the *sākhī* incorporates must also have participated in the evolution of the story.[3]

A tradition which is accorded particular popularity in modern accounts is number 122, the story of how Gurū Nānak stopped a falling boulder. The story relates that the Gurū once visited Hasan Abdāl, a village in Attock District between Rawalpindi and Peshawar.[4] At the top of a nearby hill there lived a Muslim *darveś* called Bāwā Valī Qandhārī. Water issued from a spring at the summit, but none was available at its foot and Mardānā was accordingly sent up to draw some. Valī Qandhārī had, however, heard of the Gurū's reputation and, piqued by jealousy, he refused access to Mardānā, suggesting that if his master was such a great faqīr he should provide his own water-supply. A second request elicited a similar reply and so the Gurū proceeded to act in accordance with Valī Qandhārī's sarcastic advice. He caused a spring to open at the foot of the hill, whereupon the spring at the summit immediately ceased to flow. Seeing this, the enraged Valī Qandhārī rolled a huge rock down upon the Gurū. The mighty boulder failed, however, to reach its mark, for Gurū Nānak raised his hand and instantly terminated its headlong flight. An impression of his hand was left on the rock and it is for this reason that the place is known as *Pañjā Sāhib*, or the Holy Palm. Some accounts also claim that the flow of water in the spring greatly increased.[5]

The Sikh story concerning Hasan Abdāl is the latest in a line which has successively produced Buddhist, Hindu, and Muslim legends. General Cunningham identified the tank which is filled by the spring with that of the *Nāga* or Serpent King Elāpatra visited by Hsüan Tsang in A.D. 630.[6] The most interesting feature of the Sikh legend is the unusually late date at which it appears to have entered the janam-sākhī traditions. There is, of

[1] See *supra*, p. 41.

[2] The writer owes this suggestion to Professor Pritam Singh of Government College, Ludhiana. For a brief discussion of Puranic elements in the janam-sākhīs see Rattan Singh Jaggi, *Dasam Granth dā Paurāṇik Adhiain*, pp. 58–63.

[3] *Vār Mājh*, *ślok* 1 of *pauṛī* 14, *AG*, p. 144. It includes the line: 'He confers kingship on an insect and reduces armies to ashes.'

[4] It is within the area of ancient remains which surround the site of Taxila. *Imperial Gazetteer of India*, vol. xiii, p. 70.

[5] Sewaram Singh, *The Divine Master*, p. 159.

[6] *Archaeological Survey of India, Report of 1863–4* vol. ii, pp. 135–6.

course, a hand-shaped depression in a rock at Hasan Abdāl and the gurdwara which has been built at the site is regarded as one of the most important of all Sikh temples.[1]

To the twenty-six *sākhīs* listed above the following three must, for all practical purposes, be added.

3. Instruction by the paṇḍit.
4. Instruction by the mullah.
5. Investiture with the sacred thread.

These three concern Gurū Nānak's childhood and the recitation of verses on these occasions obviously falls within the category of miracle stories. It is quite possible that Gurū Nānak was instructed by a paṇḍit and a mullah during his childhood, and that at the appropriate age he was invested with the sacred thread, but there seems to be little doubt that these incidents, like so many others, were introduced in order to provide settings for the verses. Moreover, the information they offer adds nothing to what we already know about Gurū Nānak. His works are not those of an illiterate or semi-literate person[2] and we may assume that his parents would have followed normal practices as far as the sacred thread was concerned.

58. The cannibals' cauldron

The story of the cannibals' efforts to boil Mardānā or, as in the *Purātan* version, Gurū Nānak himself[3] is one of the miracle stories which shows evident signs of having evolved out of references in particular verses, in this case a composition which is by Gurū Arjan and not by Gurū Nānak.[4] It may be argued that even if the story of the recalcitrant cauldron is to be rejected as legendary there still remains a possibility that Gurū Nānak, at some stage in his travels, encountered some savages. The possibility does indeed exist, but this *sākhī* cannot be accepted as evidence of such an encounter. The connexion between the *kaṛāhā*, or cauldron, used by the

[1] The *Gazetteer of the Rawalpindi District 1893–94*, p. 35, states that the 'hand-mark' is 'a rude representation of a hand in relief', and on the following pages stresses that it is *in relief*. G. B. Scott, who himself visited the site, refers to 'a small human hand carved in relief' (*Religion and Short History of the Sikhs 1469–1930*, p. 19). He records a conversation which, he claims, took place during his visit and which concludes as follows:

> 'That's where the Guru put his hand.'
> 'But,' I said, 'the mark of the hand would have been impressed into the rock, not carved outward.'
> However, that was a detail not worth troubling about. Ibid.

The present 'hand-mark' is unmistakably recessed into the rock, not projecting in relief, and it is relatively large, not small (8-in. span and 7½ in. in length). It has been worn smooth by the touch of innumerable hands.

[2] The accusation has, however, been made. Cf. R. C. Śukl, *Hindī Sāhitya kā Itihās* (11th edition), p. 78.

[3] *Pur JS*, *sākhī* 44, p. 81.

[4] *Mārū Mahalā* 5, 14, *AG*, p. 1002.

cannibals, and the occurrence of the same word in Gurū Arjan's *Mārū* 14 offers a much more likely explanation for the whole *sākhī*. The fact that the incident is set outside the Pañjāb and, in the case of the *Purātan* and *Bālā* versions, on 'an island in the ocean'[1] further weakens any claims the *sākhī* may have had to an element of authenticity.

108. The meeting with Sheikh Farīd in Āsā

There is good reason to accept as at least probable the tradition that Gurū Nānak met the contemporary successor of Sheikh Farīd, but this *sākhī* which describes a meeting with Farīd himself is of an entirely different order. As recorded in the *Purātan* janam-sākhīs it recounts two impossible stories set in the non-existent land of Āsā. To these two legends has been added the story of how Sheikh Farīd used to carry a wooden *chapātī* as an excuse for refusing people who offered him food and so unwittingly threatened to upset his ascetic discipline. The story belongs to the traditions which have gathered around Sheikh Farīd.[2] but its inclusion in this *sākhī* does nothing to suggest that there can be any element of historicity in the janam-sākhī incident. On the contrary, it emphasizes its legendary nature, for it indicates that the person concerned is the original Farīd, who died in 1265, and not one of his successors.

The *sākhīs* considered so far have all been rejected on the basis of their almost exclusively miraculous or manifestly fictitious content. Others may be similarly discarded in accordance with our second criterion, the testimony of external sources. This group comprises the following six *sākhīs*:

31. Delhi: the real alms
32. Delhi: the sultan's elephant resurrected

Both of these are set in Delhi and both must be rejected on historical grounds. The first of them, which is to be found only in the *Miharbān Janam-sākhī*, is wide of the historical mark in that it names Salem Shāh Paṭhān as the contemporary sultan of Delhi. The reference is obviously to Jalāl Khān, the second son and successor of Sher Shāh, who adopted the regnal name of Islām Shāh but who is referred to by several of the contemporary chroniclers as Salīm Shāh.[3] Islām Shāh's reign did not begin until 1545, six years after the death of Gurū Nānak. The *sākhī* contains nothing else except the customary discourse and must accordingly be rejected.

The substance of the second Delhi *sākhī* consists of a miracle story which

[1] *Pur JS*, p. 81. *Bālā JS*, p. 123.
[2] Khaliq Ahmad Nizami, *The Life and Times of Shaikh Farid-u'd-din Ganj-i-Shakar*, p. 24, n. 4. Cf. Farīd *ślok* 28, *AG*, p. 1379.
[3] M. A. Rahim, *History of the Afghans in India*, p. 62, n. 1.

must be repudiated as such, but this still leaves open the possibility of a meeting with the sultan. In this case the sultan's name is given as Braham Beg in the *Colebrooke* manuscript and Ibrāhīm Beg in the *Hāfizābād* manuscript.[1] The name is clearly intended to be that of Sultan Ibrāhīm Lodī (1517–26) which means that in this particular instance the *Purātan* tradition comes nearer to historical possibility than Miharbān's account. It is not, however, near enough for, as we have already observed,[2] it is impossible to accept a visit to Delhi at a date later than Ibrāhīm Lodī's accession in 1517 without upsetting the complete pattern of the first journey. Were there any inherent probability in the substance of the *sākhī* it would constitute a sufficient reason for calling that pattern in question forthwith. The substance is, however, plainly impossible and accordingly the *sākhī* may be rejected.

43. Ayodhyā: discourse with 'all the *bhagats*'

Miharbān's description of a meeting with Nāmdev, Jaidev, Kabīr, Trilochan, Ravidās, Saiṇ, Sadhnā, Dhannā, and Beṇī must be rejected for the obvious reason that there can be no possibility of *bhagats* from different centuries and different parts of India ever having gathered in the same place at the same time. Nāmdev, Jaidev, and Trilochan all died well before the birth of Gurū Nānak and the same almost certainly applies to Saiṇ, Sadhnā, and Beṇī also. The *sākhī* has obviously been developed out of the *bhagat bāṇī*[3] of the *Ādi Granth.*

70. Return to Sultānpur

Miharbān records that after returning from the south Gurū Nānak passed through Sultānpur where he renewed his acquaintance with Daulat Khān Lodī. The incident is set in the context of the Gurū's travels and, regardless of which pattern is accepted for this period, it is clear that by this stage Daulat Khān Lodī would have been residing in Lahore, not in Sultānpur. The *sūbah* of Lahore was assigned to Daulat Khān in or shortly after 1500[4] which would certainly be before Gurū Nānak could have returned to the Pañjāb had he followed the itinerary laid down by either Miharbān or the *Purātan* janam-sākhīs. According to Miharbān's chronology this return visit would have taken place in 1516.[5] It is perhaps conceivable that Daulat Khān may have happened to be back in Sultānpur on a visit, but the possibility is remote. Moreover, the tradition is a weak one. It appears only in Miharbān's account.

[1] The *Gyān-ratanāvalī* relates the incident without mentioning the sultan's name (*GR*, *sākhīs* 66–68, pp. 187–94).

[2] See *supra*, p. 65.

[3] The works of various *bhagats* which were incorporated in the *Ādi Granth* by Gurū Arjan.

[4] See *infra*, p. 109.

[5] See *supra*, p. 67.

30. Discourse with Sheikh Sharaf of Pāṇīpat
96. Death of Makhdūm Bahāuddīn

The first of these describes a discourse with Sheikh Sharaf, the Pīr of Pāṇīpat, and the second an exchange of messages between Gurū Nānak and Sheikh Bahāuddīn of Multān shortly before their deaths. Both of these famous Muslim *pīrs* died well before the time of Gurū Nānak.[1] It may be argued that the contacts must have been with successors of the two *pīrs*,[2] but this is not what the janam-sākhīs say. Had the names of the contemporary successors been known they would certainly have been given, for this has been done in the case of Farīd's successor, Sheikh Ibrāhīm.[3] A much more likely explanation is the natural tendency to introduce an association with the acknowledged great in order that the object of the writer's belief or affection may be shown to be even greater. This factor doubtless applies also in the case of number 84, the discourse with Bābur,[4] and in that of number 108, the discourse with Sheikh Farīd.[5] In the case of Farīd the janam-sākhīs present two irreconcilable traditions. Number 108, which names Farīd himself as the person with whom the Gurū conversed, is clearly spurious, whereas number 87, which specifies Sheikh Ibrāhīm, has good claims to at least a measure of authenticity.

This must lead us to reject these two *sākhīs*, for they evidently correspond to number 108 rather than to number 87. This is not to deny that Gurū Nānak must have had contact with some of his more prominent religious contemporaries, and nor does it necessarily mean that successors of these two *pīrs* could not have been amongst these contemporaries whom the Gurū would have met. The point is that these two *sākhīs* do not provide us with evidence of such contacts.

101. The death of the trader's infant son
103. The coal and the thorn

These two *sākhīs* may be discarded in accordance with our third criterion, for both are in evident conflict with what we know of Gurū Nānak's personality and beliefs from his works. The first of them records how the Gurū greeted the prospect of a baby's imminent death not merely with equanimity, but with apparent mirth, a description which is in sharp conflict with the character which emerges from his recorded works. The purpose in this case is clearly to show the fate of those who, like the infant's father, spurn the Gurū, but the illustration is an unfortunate one. The second of the *sākhīs* is based upon a naïve understanding of the doctrine

[1] Sheikh Sharaf is said to have died in A.D. 1324 and Sheikh Bahāuddīn in A.D. 1170. T. W. Beale, *An Oriental Biographical Dictionary*, pp. 17, 97.

[2] This is Macauliffe's interpretation. *The Sikh Religion*, i. 52, 186. Cf. also i. 153.

[3] See *infra*, p. 140.

[4] See *infra*, pp. 134, 138.

[5] See *supra*, p. 80. Other examples are numbers 41 and 43.

of *karma* which would certainly not have accorded with Gurū Nānak's concept. The incident is clearly spurious.

Improbable sākhīs

From the impossible we move to the improbable and here too there are several *sākhīs* which can be relegated without lengthy analyses.

11. The physician convinced
12. The true field
13. The true merchandise
15. The true harvest

These four *sākhīs* are all set in the context of the Gurū's early life in Talvaṇḍī. None of them can be dismissed as absolutely impossible, but there can be little doubt that all four are examples of episodes which evolved as appropriate settings for certain *śabads* or *śloks*. The janam-sākhīs' own claim that the *śabads* and *śloks* were uttered in response to the situations which provide the settings assumes a quality of spontaneity which is difficult to accept, even in a poet as talented as Gurū Nānak.

16. *Kharā saudā*: the feeding of Sant Ren and the faqīrs
17. The *loṭā* and the ring presented to a faqīr

The two stories which concern gifts made by Gurū Nānak to faqīrs are also set in the period of his early life, but it is obvious that they have not developed out of suggestive verses in the manner of the previous four *sākhīs*. These two are narratives, not mere settings, and they are in no way dependent upon extracts from Gurū Nānak's works. Moreover, the stories which they relate, far from seeming intrinsically unlikely, sound like the kind of incident which might well have occurred in the life of a young man of pronounced religious inclinations. The first *sākhī* records how Gurū Nānak was once given a sum of money by his father and sent to use it in trading. The Gurū, however, spent the entire sum in purchasing food for a group of hungry faqīrs whom he happened to meet, and the incident has traditionally been referred to as *kharā saudā*, or the Good Bargain. In the second *sākhī* it is related that Gurū Nānak caused his parents further distress by donating his brass *loṭā* and gold wedding ring to a faqīr whom he happened to encounter.

Neither story can be regarded as impossible, but there is nevertheless a serious objection which must be made against both of them. Both are to be found only in the *Bālā* janam-sākhīs. Had the stories been current at the time when the *Miharbān* and *Purātan* accounts took shape it is highly unlikely that either, much less both, would have omitted them, particularly such an interesting incident as the *kharā saudā* story. The conclusion indicated by their omission is that the two *sākhīs* represent a relatively late tradition. This cannot be established beyond all doubt, but it is certainly a strong likelihood and the fact that the *Gyān-ratanāvalī* also omits them strengthens it. The two *sākhīs* must accordingly be regarded as improbable.

The same argument applies to the following six *sākhīs*:

29. Nānak cooks meat at Kurukshetra
35. Mount Govardhan, Mathurā, and Brindāban
44. Ayodhyā: discourse with paṇḍits
45. Gayā
121. Sālas Rāi
123. Discourse with Abdul Rahmān of Iran

All of these, unlike numbers 16 and 17, do appear in the 1891 edition of the *Gyān-ratanāvalī*, but all are clearly borrowings from the *Bālā* tradition. The first of them, number 29, appears to be a case of a situation evolving in order to give an answer to a later dispute concerning vegetarianism. To provide this answer an appropriate *sākhī* has been built around *Vār Malār*, *śloks* 1 and 2 of *pauṛī* 25.[1] Numbers 44 and 45 give precisely the kind of place one would expect the popular imagination to add to the story of Gurū Nānak's travels. Both Ayodhyā and Gayā are among the seven sacred cities of India and their inclusion within Gurū Nānak's itinerary is altogether natural.

The story of Sālas Rāi, the jeweller of Biṣambarpur who was converted by Gurū Nānak, is one which might well be classified with the categorically rejected. It includes elements of the miraculous[2] and it is set in a city which cannot be satisfactorily identified. Kahn Singh regarded Biṣambarpur as Bishnupur, the ancient city in Bankura District, Bengal,[3] whereas Vir Singh and Teja Singh, evidently following the *Nānak Prakāś*, both name Patna as the city of Sālas Rāi.[4] The compiler of the lithographed version of the *Gyān-ratanāvalī* was apparently unaware of either of these possibilities, for the *sākhīs* which concern Sālas Rāi have been inserted at a point which obviously implies a location in western India.[5] The combination of

[1] *AG*, pp. 1289–90. There are interesting divergences with regard to the meat which Gurū Nānak is said to have cooked. The three *Bālā* manuscripts in London all give goat. (IOL MS. Panj. B41, folio 206b; BM MS. Or. 2754. I, folio 198a; and SOAS MS. 104975, folio 218a.) The 1871 lithographed edition, which follows the IOL and BM manuscripts, reproduces exactly the same wording, but replaces *bakarī* (goat) with *machhī* (fish) (*Bālā JS*, p. 314). The Dīvān Būṭā Singh expanded 1871 edition, p. 534, gives *mirag* (venison) and this is followed by the corresponding *sākhī* which has been interpolated in the 1891 edition of the *Gyān-ratanāvalī* (p. 135).

[2] An inscribed ruby which enabled Mardānā to find Sālas Rāi.

[3] *MK*, p. 140.

[4] Vir Singh, *Gurū Nānak Chamatakār*, vol. i, pp. 185–93. Teja Singh, *Sikhism: Its Ideals and Institutions*, p. 37. Also Khazan Singh, *History and Philosophy of Sikhism*, vol. i, pp. 82–83.

[5] *GR*, *sākhīs* 99–107, pp. 247–59. Gurū Nānak is at this stage travelling northwards from Ceylon to Bikaner.

legendary content, vague geography, and omission from the older collections renders the whole story most improbable. It is remotely possible that some fragment of truth may underlie the tradition, but if so it is unidentifiable.

36. Nānakmatā

In contrast with the story of Sālas Rāi the *sākhī* concerning Nānakmatā is both present in an early janam-sākhī collection and explicit in terms of location. Nānakmatā, which consists of little more than a temple in the jungle, is located in Satārgañj tahsil of Nainī Tāl District, fifteen miles north-west of Pīlībhīt and ten miles west of Khaṭīmā station on the Rohilkhaṇḍ–Kumāon railway.[1] The possibility that the area was visited by Gurū Nānak cannot be ruled out completely, but it seems much more likely that the tradition recorded by the *Purātan* janam-sākhīs can be traced to the existence of an important Udāsī centre at this spot. Udāsī sādhūs, led by a *mahant* named Almast, evidently evicted Nāth yogīs from this centre during the period of Gurū Hargobind (1606–44) and the name Nānakmatā was almost certainly bestowed by them upon the place.[2] The connexion with Nāth yogīs explains the claim made in later janam-sākhī traditions that the original name was Gorakhmatā.[3] This claim may well be true, but it is most unlikely that the original context was an incident involving Gurū Nānak.

40. Rājā Harināth
61. Rājā Mitr Sain
62. Rājā Jagannāth

These three *sākhīs* all name distinguished people with whom, according to Miharbān, Gurū Nānak held discourses in localities well beyond the Pañjāb. There are no details to support the existence of these three persons, none of the other janam-sākhīs mention them, and their sole function appears to be to provide suitable partners for three Miharbān discourses.

41. Meeting with Kabīr

Encounters with Kabīr are to be found in the *Miharbān Janam-sākhī*[4] and in the B40 manuscript.[5] The *Bālā* tradition also introduces Kabīr, but the *sākhīs* which include such references are evidently of Hindālī origin.[6] As they stand the *Miharbān* and B40 accounts can certainly be rejected. They are completely different, they are vague as far as location is concerned,

[1] *MK*, p. 519. *A Glossary of the Tribes and Castes of the Punjab &c*, vol. 1, p. 679.
[2] G. B. Singh, *Srī Gurū Granth Sāhib diān Prāchīn Bīṛān*, pp. 280–1.
[3] *GR*, p. 207.
[4] *Mih JS*, pp. 154–6.
[5] IOL MS. Panj. B40, folios 136 ff.
[6] See *supra*, p. 23.

they offer no recognizably genuine information concerning Kabīr, and their obvious purpose is to exalt Gurū Nānak by having Kabīr acknowledge his superiority. Traditions which record such a meeting are to be found in Kabīr-panthī literature as well as in the Sikh janam-sākhīs,[1] but these must be similarly rejected. Kabīr-panthī traditions concerning the life of Kabīr are notoriously unreliable and can be accepted only when confirmed by other evidence. In this case there is no such evidence. This means that there is no authentic tradition concerning a meeting between Gurū Nānak and Kabīr.[2]

On the other hand, the chance of a meeting between the two cannot be completely ruled out. We may perhaps doubt whether Kabīr really lived to the year 1518, but we cannot reject the possibility of his having done so.[3] This means that if Gurū Nānak travelled through Banāras he may perhaps have met Kabīr. It is, however, pure conjecture, chronologically possible, but completely devoid of evidence. As such it must be classified as highly improbable.

124. Saidpur: Lālo and Bhāgo

The story of Lālo, the carpenter of Saidpur, is one of the most popular in the entire range of *sākhīs* concerning Gurū Nānak. The tradition relates that while Gurū Nānak was staying with this person of low caste a certain Malik Bhāgo gave a feast to which the Gurū was invited. The invitation was, however, refused and eventually Malik Bhāgo had to resort to constraint. When the Gurū was brought to him he demanded an explanation for the refusal. Gurū Nānak in reply took in one hand a quantity of Malik Bhāgo's rich food, and in the other a piece of Lālo's coarse bread. He then squeezed both. From Lālo's bread trickled milk, but from Malik Bhāgo's food there issued blood. The point of the miracle was obviously to demonstrate that Lālo's food had been earned by honest labour, whereas Bhāgo's was the product of extortion and oppression.

The story itself must be dismissed, in spite of modern efforts to rationalize it,[4] but there remains the question of whether there may in fact have been a carpenter in Saidpur around whom this and other lesser legends have gathered. The answer must be that it is extremely unlikely. In the first place Lālo does not appear in the older janam-sākhīs. Secondly, there is a likely explanation for his entry into the developing stock of traditions

[1] Puruṣottam-lāl Śrīvāstava, *Kabīr Sāhitya kā Adhyayan*, p. 311.

[2] Nor is there adequate evidence to establish that Gurū Nānak knew the works of Kabīr, although this has been commonly assumed. There exists a possibility that he did, but the likelihood is that he did not know them. See W. H. McLeod, 'Gurū Nānak and Kabīr' in *Proceedings of the Punjab History Conference*, 1965, pp. 87–92.

[3] See *infra*, p. 155.

[4] e.g. Kartar Singh, *Life of Guru Nanak Dev*, pp. 83–84. Narain Singh, *Guru Nanak Re-interpreted*, p. 151.

concerning Gurū Nānak. In the *Bālā* janam-sākhīs[1] Lālo is associated with the verse *Tilaṅg* 5 which begins:

jaisī mai āvai khasam kī bāṇī taisaṛā karī giānu ve lālo.[2]

All seven lines of the first stanza end in this same way with the words *ve lālo*. *Tilaṅg* 5 is one of the *śabads* which describe the suffering caused by Bābur.[3] The earliest traditions associate all of these *Bābar-vāṇī* verses with his attack on Saidpur and this would mean that the words *ve lālo* would be taken to refer to an audience addressed by Gurū Nānak in Saidpur. The words in this case would mean 'O beloved', a common form of poetic address. The next step must then have been to identify the word *lālo* as a proper noun and so in this manner there evidently developed a tradition concerning Lālo of Saidpur. This hypothesis does not completely destroy the tradition of a Saidpur carpenter called Lālo, but it does render it most improbable.

Possible sākhīs

The third category consists of *sākhīs* which cannot be rejected as inherently improbable or definitely impossible, but which must nevertheless be treated with a considerable degree of caution. They are *sākhīs* which offer only limited opportunities for the application of our criteria, and which accordingly cannot be either affirmed or denied, even in terms of probability or improbability. Many of them must be rejected in part, but in all there is at least some basic detail which requires us to withhold judgement.

The most we can say in these cases is that they generally tend towards the improbable rather than the probable. Many of them are the kind of story which inevitably gathers around a person of acknowledged spiritual stature, and there can be no doubt that several of these *sākhīs* will have entered the body of tradition in this manner. The difficulty is that when such accretions are both rationally and chronologically possible there is generally no means of separating them from incidents of a similar nature which may have a foundation in fact. We may well assume that a majority of such *sākhīs* are subsequent additions and that very few would have any factual connexion with Gurū Nānak, but we do not possess the means of determining which should belong to the majority group and which to the minority.

Many more of the *sākhīs* concern Gurū Nānak's travels, and here doubts must arise from the fact that most of the places named are the very locations which one would expect the popular imagination to associate with the

[1] *Bālā JS*, *sākhī* 21, pp. 88–89.

[2] *AG*, p. 722.

[3] See *infra*, p. 135.

wanderings of a person such as the Gurū. Places such as Hardwār, Allahābād, Banāras, Jagannāth Purī, Rāmeśwaram, and Ujjain are precisely the kind of pilgrimage centres one might anticipate. We cannot, however, assume that Gurū Nānak did not visit any of these places. On the contrary, it is safe to assume that he would have visited at least some of them and in a general sense we may accept the tradition, recorded by Bhāī Gurdās and implied by Miharbān, that Gurū Nānak's travels included visits to famous pilgrimage centres.[1]

What we have is the same problem of separating the likely from the unlikely without the means of identifying either. The fact that the incident or discourse which is set in a certain place is manifestly an invention does not prove that Gurū Nānak did not visit that particular place. We may with good reason decide that most of the *incidents* which are recorded of his travels beyond his own province are products of the imagination, but we must also conclude that Gurū Nānak obviously did make lengthy journeys outside the Pañjāb and that accordingly he must certainly have visited at least some of these places.

Most of the *sākhīs* which we shall classify as 'possible' fall into one or other of these two subdivisions. Either they are the kind of story which one inevitably finds associated with the person of a famous saint, or they concern visits to particular places during the Gurū's travels. The first subdivision includes the following:

27. Mardānā commanded to throw offerings away.
33. Sheikh Bajīd.
102. A watchman receives royal authority.
106. The inhospitable village unmolested.
107. The hospitable village dispersed.
111. The devotees of Kiṛīān Paṭhāṇān.
112. Discourse with Mīā Miṭhā.
114. Dunī Chand's flags.
116. A pious boy.
118. Anabhī the Jain.

Little can be said about any of these. Numbers 106 and 107, which really constitute a single *sākhī*, relate the kind of story which always finds a ready

[1] Gurū Nānak himself offers some support for this tradition.

taṭ tīrath ham nav khaṇḍ dekhe haṭ paṭaṇ bājārā.

Gauṛī 17, *AG*, p. 156

I have seen places of pilgrimage on river banks, *tīraths*, the nine regions of the earth, shops, cities, markets.

The reference to 'the nine regions of the earth', i.e. the whole world, and the context in which the line occurs indicate that we have here an example of hyperbole, but it seems unlikely that Gurū Nānak would have expressed himself in this manner had he not visited places of pilgrimage. For the context see *infra*, p. 177.

welcome in hagiography and the convenient conjunction of an inhospitable village and a hospitable one strongly suggests legend.[1] The episode is one which indicates the narrowness of the distinction between our 'possible' and 'improbable' categories.

In the case of number 114 a comparison of the account given in the India Office Library manuscript B40[2] with that of the *Colebrooke* and *Hāfizābād* janam-sākhīs[3] shows that the incident has been expanded in the latter, but the kernel of the story remains the same in both versions. In both accounts the point of the story concerns the needle which Gurū Nānak delivered to the rich man, and the expansion of the two *Purātan* janam-sākhīs chiefly concerns the quantity of wealth which the rich man possessed. In the B40 version there are only four flags flying, signifying four treasure chests, whereas the *Purātan* account gives seven flags, each representing a *lākh* of rupees. It is also in this latter account that the name Dunī Chand appears. Once again we are confronted with a story which could possibly have roots in an authentic incident but which must prompt a considerable measure of scepticism.

The second sub-division, that of *sākhīs* which refer to specific places visited by Gurū Nānak, is a large one. The *sākhīs* listed here are those which we are obliged to classify without making detailed analyses. In other cases there are factors which make an examination possible and such *sākhīs* will be considered later.

34. Hardwār: the watering of his fields
37. Allahābād
38. Banāras: discourses with paṇḍits
39. Banāras: discourse with Chatur Dās
42. Hājīpur Paṭṇā
48. Jagannāth Purī
52. Rāmeśwaram
63. Ujjain
64. Vindhyā Mountains
65. Narabad River
66. Bīkāner district and city
67. The land of Soraṭhi (Saurāshtra)
68. Mathurā
69. Kurukshetra
71. The Kashmīrī paṇḍit
82. Hiṅglāj
88. The merchant of Dīpālpur
109. Jhaṇḍā Bāḍhī and the *Jugāvalī*

[1] Rattan Singh Jaggi, *Vichār-dhārā*, p. 16.
[2] IOL MS. Panj. B40, folios 189–90.
[3] *Pur JS*, *sākhi* 37, pp. 70–71.

In several cases it is necessary to reject the incident which a *sākhī* relates, but to retain the possibility that Gurū Nānak may have visited the location in which the incident is set. This necessity applies in the case of number 34, the story of how Gurū Nānak confounded the crowds who were devoutly throwing Ganges water towards their forbears.[1] The same story is to be found in earlier Buddhist traditions[2] and is obviously an example of the kind of legend which gains currency among the followers of different religious reformers.[3] The rejection of the actual incident does not, however, mean that the Gurū was never in Hardwār. On the contrary, it is a centre of pilgrimage which, by reason of its fame and proximity to the Pañjāb, he may well have visited.

Other *sākhīs* require, if not total rejection of an incident, at least the setting aside of substantial portions. This applies in the case of number 71, the Kashmīr *sākhī*.[4] It is obviously impossible to accept the story of how Braham Dās was sent in search of a *gurū*, but this certainly does not mean that Gurū Nānak never visited Kashmīr and nor need we conclude that the account of how Braham Dās initially became a convert is necessarily untrue. A considerable degree of doubt will persist as far as the latter aspect is concerned, but in the absence of acceptable evidence either for or against the tradition we must withhold judgement.

Number 109 may also be an example of legend superimposed upon an authentic tradition. The *Purātan Janam-sākhī* presents the story of Jhaṇḍā, the carpenter of Bisīar, as a single *sākhī* which has two distinct parts. Of these the second, which describes the composition of a work called the *Jugāvalī*, may be rejected without hesitation. The *Colebrooke* and *Hāfizā-bād* accounts differ, both are very corrupt, the poem is said to have been composed on 'an island in the ocean', Gurū Nānak's food at the time is said to have been air, reference is made to an unrecognizable city called Chhuṭhaghāṭakā,[5] and the work recorded in the janam-sākhīs under the title *Jugāvalī* is manifestly spurious.

The first part cannot, however, be dismissed in this manner, for it contains neither the inconsistencies nor the evident fantasy of the second part.

[1] See *supra*, p. 55. Khushwant Singh, *A History of the Sikhs*, vol. i, p. 35, gives a translation of the *sākhī* as it is to be found in the modern version of the *Bālā* tradition. The IOL manuscript Panj. B41 (*Bālā* tradition) and both of the 1871 lithographed editions omit the incident, although the expanded 1871 edition does include a discourse on the banks of the Ganges (Dīvān Būṭā Siṅgh 1871 edition, *sākhī* 250, p. 536).

[2] Thomas Watters, *On Yuan Chwang's Travels in India 629–645 A.D.*, London, Royal Asiatic Society, 1904, vol. i, pp. 320–1. I owe this reference to Dr. J. S. Grewal of Chandigarh.

[3] Another example, to which reference will be made later, is Bhāī Gurdās's account of a visit to Multān. See *infra*, p. 142.

[4] *Pur JS*, *sākhī* 49, pp. 90–94. See *supra*, pp. 48–49.

[5] This is the *Colebrooke* variant. The *Hāfizābād* manuscript has Chhuṭāghāṭakā. *Pur JS*, p. 46.

Bisīar may perhaps be a version of Bashahr in the Simla Hills[1] and it is possible that Gurū Nānak may once have met a person called Jhaṇḍā Bāḍhī. The fact that the *Miharbān Janam-sākhī* and the *Gyān-ratanāvalī* both omit the incident weakens the tradition, but there is at least a possibility that an actual encounter may underlie it. This first portion of the *sākhī* is very brief in the *Purātan* account. It merely records that in the inhospitable land of Bisīar only Jhaṇḍā gave shelter to Gurū Nānak and Mardānā, that Jhaṇḍā washed the Gurū's feet, that enlightenment dawned on him while he was drinking the water he had used for the washing, and that the experience led him to abandon wordly concerns in favour of a life of wandering.[2] It must, however, be emphasized that this remains mere possibility and that our acknowledgement of the possibility will be strongly tinged with scepticism. It is a scepticism which must be applied to all the incidents listed in this section.

In most of these travel *sākhīs* the geographical information given amounts to no more than the name of a city or locality. Occasionally, however, extra details are added and in rare instances they are supplied in abundance. Additional details of this kind do not necessarily indicate a sound tradition, even if they happen to be substantially accurate. One of the rare cases of abundant geographical detail is Miharbān's *goṣṭ* 91 which is set in Ujjain and which appears in the chart as a part of number 63. The details which it incorporates indicate a knowledge of the locality, but do nothing to strengthen the tradition. There can be no doubt that they represent the personal knowledge of a more recent visitor, not a report handed down from the Gurū himself.

Two *sākhīs* which do not fit either of our sub-divisions but which should be included in the category of 'possible' *sākhīs* are the following:

97. Death of Mardānā
98. Death of Kālū and Tiparā

Two dominant traditions exist concerning the death of Gurū Nānak's companion Mardānā. One is that he died in the year S. 1591 (A.D. 1534) on the banks of the river Kurram in Afghanistan, and that the last rites were performed there by Gurū Nānak himself.[3] The second is that he died in Kartārpur, before the death of Gurū Nānak but evidently towards the close of the Gurū's life. The first of these must be regarded as highly improbable. It is not recorded in any of the older janam-sākhīs and the evidence all suggests that Gurū Nānak's travelling days were well over

[1] This was Macauliffe's assumption (*The Sikh Religion*, i. 93). It is, however, unlikely. In the *Bālā* janam-sākhīs the location is given as 'on an island in the ocean' (*Bālā JS*, p. 193; IOL MS. Panj. B41, folio 88), a statement which accords with the second part of the *Purātan sākhī* and which strongly implies a legendary setting. Moreover, the resemblance of Bisīar, or Bisīhar as in the *Bālā* version, to Bashahr is not really close.

[2] The tradition is greatly expanded in the *Bālā* janam-sākhīs. See *Bala JS*, *sākhī* 34, pp. 142–57.

[3] *MK*, p. 714.

by 1534. The second tradition, which is to be found in the *Gyān-ratanāvalī*, cannot be regarded as proven, but it is certainly within the realm of possibility.

The *Gyān-ratanāvalī* tradition concerning the deaths of Kālū and Tiparā seems less likely. Gurū Nānak would have been sixty-nine or seventy at the time of his death and if his parents died only shortly before him they must both have attained advanced ages. The possibility exists, but it is one which tends strongly towards the improbable, particularly in view of the fact that the *Bālā* tradition refers in passing to their deaths at an unspecified but obviously much earlier time.[1]

Eighty-seven *sākhīs* out of the total of 124 listed in the chart have now been summarily classified as either possible, improbable, or impossible. The balance of thirty-seven *sākhīs* consists partly of incidents which can in like manner be assigned to the 'probable' category, and partly of *sākhīs* which can be discussed at some length before being classified. For convenience we may group them as follows:

Dates

1. The birth of Gurū Nānak
100. The death of Gurū Nānak

Family relationships

1. The birth of Gurū Nānak
9. The marriage of Jai Rām and Nānakī
10. Betrothal and marriage
14. Birth of Lakhmī Dās and Sirī Chand

Daulat Khān Lodī and Sultānpur

20. To Sultānpur
21. Work in Daulat Khān's commissariat
22. Immersion in the river: his call
24. The mullah seeks to exorcize his evil spirit
25. Discourse with the qāzī
26. Departure from Sultānpur

Visit to Assam

46. The country ruled by women

Visit to Dacca

47. Dacca

[1] *Bālā JS*, p. 288. The *Gyān-ratanāvalī* also records that Gurū Nānak's wife died fifteen days after her husband (*GR*, *sākhī* 219, p. 587). The older janam-sākhīs make no reference to her death.

Rājā Śivanābh and Ceylon

18. Bhāgīrath and Mansukh
19. Mansukh and Rājā Śivanābh
54. Rājā Śivanābh and the *Prāṇ Saṅgalī*

A ṭhag converted and the first dharmsālā built

60. Sajjaṇ the *ṭhag*

Discourse with the Siddhs on Mount Sumeru

72. Mount Sumeru

Mecca and Medina

75. The mullah's village
76. Rahīm and Karīm
79. Mecca: the moving mosque
80. Medina

Visit to Baghdad

81. Baghdad

The Emperor Bābur and the sack of Saidpur

83. The sack of Saidpur
84. Discourse with Bābur
85. Bābur attacks Ṭillā Bālgundāī

The conclusion of the travels

86. Return to Talvaṇḍī and reunion with parents

Visit to Pāk Paṭṭan

87. Pāk Paṭṭan: discourse with Sheikh Ibrāhīm

The founding of Kartārpur

89. The proud official humbled: the founding of Kartārpur

Discourses with Siddhs

73. Gorakh-haṭaṛī
90. Achal Baṭālā

Visits to Multān

74. Multān: discourse with a descendant of Pīr Bahāuddīn
91. Multān: the jasmine petal

Gurū Aṅgad

92. First meeting with Lahiṇā
93. Lahiṇā's clothes ruined
95. Lahiṇā becomes Aṅgad
99. The installation of Gurū Aṅgad

Gurū Nānak's date of birth

The janam-sākhīs agree with regard to the year of Gurū Nānak's birth, but there is a difference concerning the actual month and it is one which has resulted in a protracted controversy. The *Miharbān* and *Purātan* traditions, supported by the *Gyān-ratanāvalī*, record that Gurū Nānak was born on the third day of the light half of the lunar month of Vaisākh, S. 1526, a date which corresponds to 15 April A.D. 1469.[1] The *Bālā* janam-sākhīs, on the other hand, give the date as Kattak *Pūran-māsī*, S. 1526, the full-moon day of the month of Kattak, or Kārtik, more than six months later.[2]

The controversy concerns which of these two dates should be accepted as the birthday of the Gurū. A third is given in the *Mahimā Prakāś Kavitā*:

> *samat bikram nirap ko pandrah sahas pachīs,*
> *vaisākh sudī thit tījā ko parau sant bāp īs.*[3]

This gives the third day of the light half of Vaisākh, S. 1525, exactly one year earlier than the date given in the older janam-sākhīs. There seems to be little doubt that this third date must be an error. The suggestion that Sarūp Dās Bhallā, the author of the *Mahimā Prakāś Kavitā*, was using expired instead of current dating[4] cannot possibly be correct as he gives S. 1596 as the date of Gurū Nānak's death,[5] not S. 1595 as would be required by expired dating. Moreover, the older *Mahimā Prakāś Vāratak* gives the year as S. 1526.[6]

Bhāī Gurdās is silent on this particular issue, although it has been claimed that references in his works point unmistakably to a particular date. Proponents of both sides of the controversy have made this claim, each side

[1] *Mih JS*, p. 9. *Pur JS*, p. 1. IOL MS. Panj. B40, folio 1a. *GR*, p. 41. The word *sudī* (light half) is not used, but the word *chānaṇī* (moonlight) indicates the period of the waxing moon.

[2] *Bālā JS*, p. 7. Kattak and Kārtik both designate the eighth lunar month, Kattak being the form commonly used in Pañjābī and Kārtik the form generally used in Hindī. Kattak *Pūran-māsī*, S. 1526, corresponds to 20 Oct. A.D. 1469.

[3] Khalsa College, Amritsar, MS. SHR: 2300A, folio 5a.

[4] Karam Singh, *Kattak ki Visākh*, p. 224 n. *Gurapurb Niraṇay*, pp. 52–54.

[5] Op. cit., folio 143b.

[6] *Mahimā Prakāś Vāratak*, ed. Kirpal Singh, p. 1. Khalsa College, Amritsar, MS. SHR: 2308, folio 1a. It agrees with the *Mahimā Prakāś Kavitā* as far as the day and the month are concerned.

advancing a different reference in support of its case. A few supporters of the Vaisākh dating have argued that a line from stanza 27 of *Vār* 1 indicates the *first* day of Vaisākh as the correct date.

ghari ghari andari dharamasāl hovai kīratanu sadā visoā.

The claim is that the word *visoā* is a cryptic reference to the Gurū's birth having occurred on the day of the Baisākhī festival.[1] It is a claim which has received little support and there can be no doubt that it is incorrect. The translation should read:

In every house a *dharmsālā* was established and *kīrtan* was sung (as if it were) an unending Baisākhī festival.

From the other side of the controversy has come the claim that the first couplet of Bhāī Gurdās's *Kabitt Savayyā* 345 points to Kattak *Pūran-māsī*.

kārtik māsi rut sarad pūranamāsī
aṭh jām sāṭh gharī āj terī bārī hai.

It is the month of Kārtik, the season of coolness. Today, on this day of the full moon, this day of eight *jāms*,[2] of sixty *gharīs*,[3] it is thy turn.

This, it is argued, refers to Gurū Nānak's turn to enter the world, and on the basis of this interpretation it has been claimed that Bhāī Gurdās here testifies to Kattak *Pūran-māsī* as the date of the Gurū's birth.[4]

It is true that this couplet may be interpreted as a reference to a particular person's birth, but it is also true that it may be interpreted as a conventional reference to the month of Kārtik in the style of the *bārah-māhā*, the 'Twelve Month' or calendar poem. The balance of probability must be held to favour the latter. In the first place there is no reference to Gurū Nānak. Secondly, the form is a common one in Pañjābī literature and it would have been an entirely natural one for Bhāī Gurdās to have used. Thirdly, as one would expect in this particular poetic form, the reference is to the present, not to a past event. And fourthly, as we have already observed, the janam-sākhīs which belong to the Bhāī Gurdās period or soon after all specify Vaisākh. In the light of this fourth point the couplet could be admissible as contrary evidence only if it were to point unambiguously to the Kattak date, and this it certainly does not do. The fact that the poem stands in isolation and is not set in the context of a complete *bārah-māhā* does not affect this conclusion. Farīd's *Āsā* 2, which also makes a conventional reference to Kārtik, is not a part of a *bārah-māhā*.[5]

[1] The point is argued by Teja Singh Overseer in *Khālsā Rahit Prakāś*, pp. 73–75.

[2] *jām*, *yām*, or *pahar*: a period of three hours.

[3] A period of twenty-four minutes.

[4] For this argument see Trilochan Singh, article in the *Sikh Review*, vol. xii, no. 2, Feb. 1964, pp. 22–37.

[5] *AG*, p. 488.

Neither the third day in the light half of Vaisākh nor Kattak *Pūran-māsī* can be accepted as established beyond all doubt, but it is clear that of the two the former is much the more likely. The latter is evidently confined to the *Bālā* tradition and to subsequent works based upon it, notably Santokh Singh's *Nānak Prakāś*. It should be added, however, that the case against Kattak *Pūran-māsī* is, for all its strength, not quite as overwhelming as Macauliffe evidently believed. Macauliffe draws attention to what appears to be an interesting error in the *Nānak Prakāś*. Santokh Singh follows the *Bālā* tradition as usual and gives Kattak *Pūran-māsī* as the date of Gurū Nānak's birth,[1] but he also records that the Gurū lived seventy years, five months, and seven days. Counted back from the date which he gives for the Gurū's death[2] this gives a date close to Vaisākh *sudī* 3.[3] The printed editions of the *Nānak Prakāś* do indeed record that Gurū Nānak lived for seventy years, five months, and seven days,[4] but it is doubtful whether Santokh Singh actually wrote this. Vir Singh adds in a footnote that some manuscript copies of the *Nānak Prākāś* omit this reference.[5] The likelihood appears to be that it has been subsequently interpolated in the *Nānak Prakāś*. The inconsistency is patently obvious as it stands and it seems unlikely that Santokh Singh could have failed to perceive it.

Macauliffe describes the manner in which Kattak *Pūran-māsī* came to be generally adopted by the Sikh community,[6] but says nothing about how it ever came to be included in the *Bālā* tradition in the first place. This is not surprising as anything we may say in this respect must be pure conjecture. Karam Singh's theory was that the Hindālīs inserted it as a part of their effort to denigrate Gurū Nānak at the expense of Bābā Hindāl. His suggestion is that they must have had in mind 'the well-known Pañjāb superstition' that births which occur in the months of Bhādron and Kattak are inauspicious.[7] This is no more than a guess and it is unlikely to be correct. There is no evidence to support it, and it assumes a degree of subtlety which is by no means characteristic of the Hindālīs.

It is accordingly impossible to give any satisfactory explanation for the introduction of Kattak *Pūran-māsī*. There remains a possibility that it entered the tradition for the very good reason that it was the actual date

[1] *Nānak Prakāś*, canto 3 (70). In Vir Singh's edition vol. ii, p. 150.

[2] Asū *vadī* 10, S. 1596, the tenth day of the dark half of Asū, S. 1596.

[3] Macauliffe, *The Sikh Religion*, vol. i, p. lxxxiv. The formula is the exact difference between Vaisākh *sudī* 3, S. 1526, and Asū *sudī* 10, S. 1596 (Karam Singh, *Gurapurb Niraṇay*, p. 51).

[4] *Nānak Prakāś*, canto 57 (90). Vir Singh, vol. iv, p. 1255.

[5] Ibid., p. 1255, n.*.

[6] Macauliffe, i. lxxxiv–vi. He does not, however, give any adequate authority for his account of how Bhāī Sant Singh decided to declare Kattak *Pūran-māsī* the authentic date in order to draw Sikhs away from a Hindu fair which was held at Rām Tīrath on that date. He merely records that he owed his information to Bhāī Gurmukh Singh.

[7] Karam Siṅgh, *Kattak ki Visākh*, pp. 224–5.

of Gurū Nānak's birth, but it is a remote possibility. There can be no doubt that its claims to authenticity are much inferior to those of Vaisākh *sudī* 3. This latter dating has the support of all the better sources, whereas Kattak *Pūran-māsī* can be traced to nothing more reliable than the *Bālā* tradition. Most Sikh scholars now accept the Vaisākh date.[1] The only exceptions of any importance are Gyan Singh[2] and Khazan Singh,[3] writers who belong to generations now long past but whose works still exercise some influence. In Gyan Singh's case the adherence to Kattak *Pūran-māsī* is understandable as he produced his significant work before 1885, the year in which both the *Colebrooke* and the *Hāfizābād* manuscripts were published. Khazan Singh, whose *History and Philosophy of Sikhism* was published in 1914, uses Karam Singh's method in reverse. Just as Karam Singh sought in his *Kattak ki Visākh* to establish the Vaisākh date by attacking the whole of the *Bālā* janam-sākhī tradition as totally unreliable in all respects, so Khazan Singh denied it by affirming the reliability of the *Bālā* janam-sākhīs[4] and repudiating those of the *Purātan* tradition.[5]

The weight of evidence and scholarly opinion is thus strongly on the side of the light half of Vaisākh. If a choice is to be made between the two traditional dates the verdict should certainly go to the Vaisākh tradition. It cannot, however, be regarded as established beyond all doubt. There remains the possibility that *both* traditions are incorrect and that the actual date has been lost. The Vaisākh tradition may be regarded as probable, but not as definitively established.

As there is no dispute concerning the year of Gurū Nānak's birth this controversy would be of relatively slight importance were it not for the fact that a definite date must be acknowledged by the Sikh community in order that the anniversary may be celebrated. Kattak *Pūran-māsī* has been firmly entrenched for almost a century and there is little likelihood that the custom of holding the annual celebrations in November will be abandoned in favour of April.

[1] *MK*, p. 519. Teja Singh and Ganda Singh, *A Short History of the Sikhs*, vol. i, p. 2. Khushwant Singh, *A History of the Sikhs*, vol. i, p. 29. Kala Singh Bedi, *Gurū Nānak Darśan*, p. 45. Gopal Singh, *Sri Guru-Granth Sahib*, vol. i, p. xxxv. Sahib Singh, *Srī Gurū Granth Sāhib Darapaṇ*, vol. x, p. 756. Karam Singh's *Kattak ki Visākh* is devoted exclusively to repudiating the Kattak date.

[2] Gyan Singh, *Panth Prakāś* (6th edition), p. 28; *Tavarīkh Gurū Khālsā* (3rd edition), vol. i, part i, p. 81. These works have been very influential.

[3] Khazan Singh, *History and Philosophy of Sikhism*, vol. i, pp. 30–35. Other writers who have accepted Kattak *Pūran-māsī* are Lajwanti Rama Krishna, *Les Sikhs*, p. 24, and Sewaram Singh, *The Divine Master*, pp. 18–19.

[4] loc. cit., vol. i, pp. 18–19.

[5] 'The whole work seems to be an incoherent collection of traditions, mostly wrong, and the date of birth recorded is apparently based on hearsay.' Ibid., p. 33. Khazan Singh is a very unreliable writer, but his work has been widely used.

Place of birth

If the testimony of the janam-sākhīs is to be accepted, Gurū Nānak's birth-place was his father's village, Rāi Bhoi dī Talvaṇḍī.[1] The name 'Nānak', however, raises doubts as it implies that the birth must have been in the home of the maternal grandparents.[2] Khushwant Singh accepts the implication as established fact:

> The janamsakhis and the *Mahimā Prakāś* state the place of birth to be "in the house of Mehta Kalu Bedi of Talwandi Rai Bhoe." This statement need not be taken literally. The custom of returning to the maternal home for confinement was well-established in Hindu families. The choice of the name confirms the fact of the birth taking place in the mother's parental home, which was in the village of Kahna Katcha. Cunningham supports this view and bases it on an old manuscript, but without giving its reference. Mehervan's janamsakhi mentions Chahleval near Lahore as Nanak's place of birth.[3]

It is true that the name 'Nānak' strongly implies that the birth took place at the home of the Gurū's maternal grandparents, but it is perhaps going too far to affirm this as proven. As Khushwant Singh indicates, all the janam-sākhīs except that of Miharbān specify Rāi Bhoi dī Talvaṇḍī as the place of birth. Miharbān's record is not clear at this point. The Damdamā Sāhib manuscript does indeed name the village of Chāhalāvāle[4] in the *goṣṭ* which describes the Gurū's birth,[5] but elsewhere it states with equal clarity that Rāi Bhoe kī Talvaṇḍī was the place where he was born.[6] Moreover, the second manuscript in the possession of Khalsa College omits the name Chāhalāvāle[7] and is consistent in specifying Rāi Bhoe kī Talvaṇḍī. It is impossible to say whether Chāhalāvāle is an interpolation in the account recorded by the Damdamā Sāhib manuscript or whether the subsequent references are the interpolations. It may even be that both names were in the original and that what we have here is simply a case of confusion.

We must, however, acknowledge that at some stage there was a tradition abroad that the birth-place was Chāhal and that this tradition may possibly have found expression in the original version of the *Miharbān Janam-sākhī*. This tradition, together with the implication borne by the Gurū's name, points to his mother's village as a strong possibility, but in view of the contrary testimonies of the other janam-sākhīs we cannot affirm it as definitely established. The village indicated in this manner would be

[1] The village is now named Nānakiāṇā Sāhib (sometimes spelt Nankana Sahib). It is situated in the Shekhupurā tahsīl of Lahore District, West Pakistan, approximately forty miles west-south-west of Lahore city.

[2] The word *nānā* means 'maternal grandfather' and *nānak* may be used as a common noun to mean 'a mother's family or lineage'.

[3] *A History of the Sikhs*, vol. i, p. 30, n. 11.

[4] The village of Chāhal, the traditional birthplace of Gurū Nānak's mother, is near Barakī in the district and tahsīl of Lahore. *MK*, p. 345.

[5] *Mih JS*, *goṣṭ* 4, p. 9. [6] Ibid., pp. 52 and 470. [7] Ibid., p. 9, n. 4.

Chāhal, not Kahnā Katchā as given by Khushwant Singh and also by Cunningham.[1]

Gurū Nānak's date of death

Just as there is disagreement between the janam-sākhīs concerning the date of Gurū Nānak's birth, so too there is disagreement regarding the date of his death. The divergence is more serious in this latter case, for it involves not simply a difference in the precise date given, but a disagreement concerning the actual year. Three dates are given. The *Purātan* janam-sākhīs give Asū *sudī* 10, S. 1595, the tenth day of the light half of the month of Asū, S. 1595, which would have fallen during September A.D. 1538.[2] The *Gyān-ratanāvalī* also gives Asū *sudī* 10 as the day of the month, but records that the year was S. 1596 (A.D. 1539).[3] The third date is that given in such of the *Bālā* janam-sākhīs as carry their accounts as far as his death. This tradition agrees with the *Gyān-ratanāvalī* as far as the year is concerned, but gives the actual date as Asū *vadī* 10, the tenth day of the *dark* half of Asū, fifteen days earlier than the *Gyān-ratanāvalī* date.[4]

These are the three dates and opinion has been divided concerning which of them has the stronger claims. Some writers have accepted the *Purātan* dating,[5] others follow the *Gyān-ratanāvalī*,[6] and a few the date which is to

[1] J. D. Cunningham, *A History of the Sikhs* (1st edition, 1849), p. 40, n. Khushwant Singh does not state whether he is here following Cunningham and the latter's unidentified manuscript, or whether he bases his statement on some other source. W. L. M'Gregor's *The History of the Sikhs*, which was published in 1846, gives 'the village of Maree, which is near Kot Kutchwa' as the place where the Gurū was born (loc. cit., vol. i, p. 32).

[2] *Pur JS*, p. 115. MS. no. 2310A of the Sikh History Research Department, Khalsa College, Amritsar, is a *Purātan* manuscript which gives S. 1596 as the year of Gurū Nānak's death (loc. cit., folio 185a). This manuscript was, however, written in S. 1829 (A.D. 1772) by which time the 1596 dating was well established in Sikh tradition. The *Colebrooke* and *Hāfizābād* manuscripts obviously represent the authentic *Purātan* tradition at this point and they are supported by the IOL manuscript Panj. B40 (folio 230). Moreover, the Khalsa College manuscript is evidently prone to error as far as recording dates is concerned, for it gives Gurū Nānak's year of birth as S. 1536 (A.D. 1479) instead of S. 1526 (folio 1a). MS. no. 2913 of the Central Public Library, Paṭiālā, is another *Purātan* manuscript which gives S. 1596 (folio 276a). In this case it is obvious that the figure 6 has been written over an original 5.

[3] *GR*, p. 587. Karam Singh, *Gurapurb Niraṇay*, pp. 47–49 and 57, gives 22 September A.D. 1539, as the exact equivalent of Asū *sudī* 10, S. 1596.

[4] SOAS, MS. no. 104975, folio 303. *Bālā JS*, p. 402. The expanded 1871 edition (Dīvān Būṭā Singh, Lahore), p. 587, gives the year as 1546 which may be either a simple error or an unsuccessful attempt made by the printer to convert the date given in the manuscripts to Christian reckoning.

[5] Macauliffe, op. cit., vol. i, p. 191. Indubhusan Banerjee, *Evolution of the Khalsa*, vol. i, p. 22. Volker Moeller, article 'Die Lebensdaten des Glaubensstifters Nanak' in the *Indo-Iranian Journal*, vol. vii, 1964, no. 4, p. 295. Mohan Singh, *A History of Panjabi Literature*, p. 23.

[6] *MK*, p. 519. Teja Singh and Ganda Singh, op. cit., vol. i, p. 17. Khushwant Singh, op. cit., vol. i, p. 37. Karam Singh, *Gurapurb Niraṇay*, p. 57. Sahib Singh, *Srī Gurū Granth Sāhib Darapaṇ*, vol. x, p. 759.

be found in some of the *Bālā* janam-sākhīs.[1] At this point the *Miharbān Janam-sākhī* offers no help as only the first three of its six sections have been found.[2] The last of the six presumably gave a date for the Gurū's death. The two versions of the *Mahimā Prakāś* are once again in conflict, the *Mahimā Prakāś Vāratak* supporting the *Bālā* tradition[3] and the *Mahimā Prakāś Kavitā* offering the same date as the *Gyān-ratanāvalī*.[4]

In an issue involving conflicting evidence from the *Purātan* tradition, the *Gyān-ratanāvalī*, and some *Bālā* janam-sākhīs, the usual procedure would be to accept the *Purātan* testimony as the most likely to be correct. In this particular case, however, the *Bālā* testimony is strengthened by other evidence. Indeed, this other evidence probably predates the references given in some *Bālā* janam-sākhīs, and should accordingly be regarded as the basis of the Asū *vadī* 10 claim. The absence of any account of Gurū Nānak's death in many *Bālā* manuscripts indicates that the date given in some versions has been introduced subsequently, and that the *Bālā* testimony should be regarded as supporting evidence, not as the actual foundation of the claim.

The primary evidence supporting Asū *vadī* 10, S. 1596, is to be found in manuscript copies of the *Ādi Granth*. Many of the extant manuscript copies of the *Ādi Granth* include lists of the dates on which each of the ten Gurūs died, and the testimony of these lists strongly favours the Asū *vadī* 10 dating.[5] It is true that practically all of these manuscripts are later than the period of the *Purātan* tradition, and that a large number must have been copied after the *Gyān-ratanāvalī* emerged, but this claim cannot be made in the case of the manuscript held by the Soḍhī family of Kartārpur,[6] the manuscript which is traditionally believed to be the original copy of the *Ādi Granth* dictated by Gurū Arjan to Bhāī Gurdās in 1603–4. This Kartārpur manuscript contains a list which gives the date of Gurū Nānak's death as Asū *vadī* 10, S. 1596,[7] and it is this entry which must be regarded as the primary evidence for the third of the conflicting dates.[8]

[1] Khazan Singh, op. cit., vol. i, p. 106. Kartar Singh, *Life of Guru Nanak Dev*, p. 263. J. C. Archer, *The Sikhs*, p. 65, unaccountably gives 1540 as the date of Gurū Nānak's death. There is no support for this date.

[2] See *supra*, p. 19.

[3] *Mahimā Prakāś Vāratak*. ed. Kirpal Singh, p. 38. Khalsa College, Amritsar, MS. SHR: 2308, folio 15b.

[4] Khalsa College, Amritsar, MS. SHR: 2300A, folios 143b–4a.

[5] All of the manuscript copies seen by the writer which include such a list give Asū *vadī* 10, S. 1596, as the date of Gurū Nānak's death. There are six such copies in London, five of them in the IOL (MSS. Panj. C3, C5, D2, D3, and F1) and one in the BM. (Or. 2159). If such a list is included it always follows immediately after the *tatkarā* (table of contents).

[6] This is not the Kartārpur in which Gurū Nānak spent his later years, but a town in Jullundur District founded by Gurū Arjan.

[7] *samatu 1596 aṃsū vadī 10 srī bābā nānak dev jī samāṇe*. Loc. cit., folio 25b.

[8] The Kartārpur manuscript is no longer available for public scrutiny, but access has been possible in the past. The author owes this reference to Dr. Bhāī Jodh Singh who himself made a copy from the manuscript.

It must, of course, be acknowledged that the entry in the Kartārpur manuscript may have been made appreciably later than the actual writing of the manuscript, and that accordingly we cannot accept the date it gives as definitely established. The nature of the entry does not, however, suggest a significantly later addition. Were this the case one would expect a uniformity of style in the complete list, whereas what the list actually contains is uniformity of calligraphy and pen in the case of the first four entries,[1] the same calligraphy but a finer pen in the case of Gurū Arjan's own date, and then an entirely different style for the two remaining names.[2] This suggests that the first four entries were made prior to the death of Gurū Arjan in S. 1663 (A.D. 1606). The point cannot be accepted as conclusively proven, but it does appear to be at least a likelihood.

This indicates Asū *vadī* 10, S. 1596, as the most likely of the three conflicting dates. The measure of uncertainty which must be attached to our interpretation of the entry in the Kartārpur manuscript requires a corresponding uncertainty in the case of the date which it gives and we must also acknowledge the possibility that all three dates are incorrect. The convergence upon the month of Asū suggests, however, that this latter possibility is a remote one. We may conclude that Gurū Nānak probably died on the tenth day of the dark half of Asū, S. 1596, a date which corresponds to 7 September, A.D. 1539. All accounts agree that he died in Kartārpur and this may accordingly be accepted as established. Needless to say, the miraculous disappearance of his body is legend. A similar story is recorded in the case of Kabīr.[3]

Family Relationships

The janam-sākhīs all give the names of at least a few of Gurū Nānak's relatives. As one might expect, the briefest list is that which may be compiled from the *Purātan* janam-sākhīs, and the longest that of the *Bālā* janam-sākhīs. The relatives mentioned in the various janam-sākhīs are as follows:

1. *Purātan janam-sākhīs*

Father: Kālū, a Bedī khatrī of Rāi Bhoi dī Talvaṇḍī.[4]
Mother: Referred to but not named.[5]

[1] Gurū Nānak, S. 1596 (A.D. 1539); Gurū Aṅgad, S. 1609 (A.D. 1552); Gurū Amar Dās, S. 1631 (A.D. 1574); Gurū Rām Dās, S. 1638 (A.D. 1581).

[2] Bābā Gurdittā, the elder son of Gurū Hargobind, S. 1695 (A.D. 1638); and Gurū Hargobind, S. 1701 (A.D. 1644). The differences in style and pen were noted by Dr. Jodh Singh when making his copy.

[3] Ahmad Shah, *The Bījak of Kabīr*, p. 28. G. W. Briggs records similar stories in connexion with Daryā Shāh of Uderolā, the founder of the Dayānāth Panth of Kānphaṭ yogīs, and of Ratannāth of Peshawar, a disciple of Bhartṛharī (*Gorakhnāth and the Kānphaṭa Yogīs*, pp. 65, 66).

[4] *Pur JS*, p. 1.

[5] Ibid., p. 8.

Sister:	Referred to but not named.[1]
Sister's husband:	Jai Rām.[2]
Wife:	Referred to but not named.[3]
Wife's father:	Mūlā, a Choṇā khatrī.[4]
Sons:	Lakhmī Dās and Sirī Chand.[5]

2. *Miharbān Janam-sākhī*

Father:	Kālū, a Bedī khatrī of Rāi Bhoe kī Talvaṇḍī.[6]
Mother:	Tiparā.[6]
Sister:	Not mentioned but plainly indicated in a reference to Jai Rām as Gurū Nānak's *bahaṇoī*.[7]
Sister's husband:	Jai Rām, an Uppal khatrī employed as steward by Daulat K͟hān Lodī of Sultānpur.[8]
Wife:	Ghumī.[9]
Wife's father:	Mūlā, a Choṇā khatrī of Baṭālā[10] and formerly of the village Pokho dī Randhāvī.[11]
Sons:	Lakhmī Dās and Sirī Chand.[12]

3. *Gyān-ratanāvalī*

Father:	Kālū, a Bedī khatrī of Rāi Bhoi kī Talvaṇḍī[13]
Mother:	Tripatā.[13]
Sister:	Nānakī.[14]
Sister's husband:	Jai Rām.[14]
Wife:	Referred to but not named.[14]
Wife's father:	Mūlā, a Choṇā khatrī of Baṭālā.[14]
Sons:	Sirī Chand and Lakhmī Dās.[15]

4. *Bālā janam-sākhīs*

Father:	Kālū,[16] or Mahitā Kālū,[17] a Bedī khatrī and *paṭvārī*[18] of Rāi Bhoi dī Talvaṇḍī.
Mother:	Tripatā.[19]

[1] *Pur JS*, p. 13.
[2] Ibid., p. 12.
[3] Ibid., p. 8.
[4] Ibid., p. 6.
[5] Ibid., p.7.
[6] *Mih JS*, p. 9.
[7] Sister's husband. Ibid., p. 72.
[8] Ibid., p. 72.
[9] Ibid., p. 67.
[10] Ibid., p. 29.
[11] Ibid., p. 516.
[12] Ibid., p. 73.
[13] *GR*, p. 45.
[14] Ibid., p. 112.
[15] Ibid., p. 113.
[16] *Bālā JS*, p. 7.
[17] Ibid., p. 8.
[18] The village land accountant. Ibid., p. 14.
[19] Expanded 1871 edition (Dīvān Būṭā Singh, Lahore), p. 5. The *Bālā JS* and the IOL MS. Panj B41 refer to her simply as *Bibī Kālū dī isatrī* (*Bālā JS*, p. 9) or as *Amā Bibī*, 'the Lady Mother' or 'the revered Mother' (ibid., p. 30).

Maternal grandfather:	Rām, a Jhaṅgaṛ khatrī.[1]
Maternal grandmother:	Bhirāī.[1]
Father's brother:	Lālū.[2]
Father's brother's son:	Nand Lāl.[3]
Mother's brother:	Kriṣṇa.[1]
Sister:	Nānakī.[4]
Sister's husband:	Jai Rām, a Paltā khatrī.[4]
Sister's husband's father:	Paramānand.[5]
Wife:	Sulakhaṇī.[6]
Wife's father:	Mūlā, a Choṇā khatrī and *paṭvārī* of Pokho di Randhāvī.[5]
Wife's mother:	Chando Rāṇī.[7]
Sons:	Sirī Chand and Lakhmī Dās.[8]

Family memories are long in the Pañjāb and it is accordingly safe to assume that at least the two older janam-sākhīs are generally reliable in the information they give concerning the family of Gurū Nānak. All of the janam-sākhīs agree that his father was Kālū, a khatrī by caste and a Bedī by sub-caste, who lived in the village of Rāi Bhoi dī Talvaṇḍī. This may be accepted without reservation, and we may regard as at least possible the *Bālā* information that he was a *paṭvārī*, or village land accountant. The statement is confined to the *Bālā* janam-sākhīs, but it does receive some support from the *Miharbān Janam-sākhī* which records that Kālū was employed in *chākarī*[9] and which implies that the position was one which commanded at least a moderate measure of respect.[10] In the same manner we may also accept Tripatā as the name of his mother. The Tiparā form given by Miharbān is obviously a variant and a rather less likely one than the relatively common Tripatā, or Triptā.

His sister's name, which in the *Gyān-ratanāvalī* and the *Bālā* janam-sākhīs

[1] Ibid., p. 36. [2] Ibid., p. 4.
[3] IOL MS. Panj. B41, folio 30a. [4] *Bālā JS*, p. 22. [5] Ibid., p. 30.
[6] The name is used only once in the IOL manuscript B41 and in the *Bālā JS* (*Bālā JS*, p. 48). Elsewhere in these two relatively early *Bālā* versions she is referred to as *Mātā Choṇī*, her family name.
[7] *Bālā JS*, p. 48. [8] Ibid., p. 52.
[9] Employment in civil administration. [10] *Mih JS*, p. 70.

is given as Nānakī, is perhaps a little more doubtful. It is clear that Gurū Nānak had a sister, but neither of the older janam-sākhīs name her, and in the *Gyān-ratanāvalī* the name appears in the context of a brief incident which is plainly legend and which may well be one of the later additions to the janam-sākhī.[1] On the other hand, no source offers an alternative name and it seems reasonable to accept the name Nānakī as at least probable.[2]

All of the janam-sākhīs agree that the sister's husband was called Jai Rām and that he was employed as a *modī*, or steward, by Daulat Khān Lodī of Sultānpur. There is, however, disagreement concerning his sub-caste. Miharbān refers to him as an Uppal khatrī and the *Bālā* janam-sākhīs as a Paltā khatrī. Of these the former appears to be the more likely. Miharbān is almost always more reliable than the *Bālā* record, and in this particular instance it is probable that as a descendant of the third and fourth Gurūs he would have had access to trustworthy information.

The name of Gurū Nānak's wife also seems, at first sight, to present a disagreement. Miharbān calls her Ghumī, whereas the *Bālā* tradition refers to her as Sulakhaṇī. The *Miharbān* form is, however, merely a corruption of Choṇī, the name of her sub-caste and the name which, in accordance with prevailing custom, would have been her usual designation. There is thus no conflict, and although the name Sulakhaṇī does not appear until relatively late in the janam-sākhī records there is no reason to dispute it. Family traditions can be safely trusted in this respect and there is no alternative name offered in the janam-sākhīs.

The janam-sākhīs are, however, in disagreement concerning the time of the Gurū's marriage to Sulakhaṇī, or Mātā Choṇī. The *Bālā* tradition dates it after he had gone to Sultānpur and secured employment there under Daulat Khān,[3] whereas the other three all record it prior to his departure from Talvaṇḍī. The *Purātan* janam-sākhīs give his age as twelve at the time of his marriage (A.D. 1481–2)[4] and the *Gyān-ratanāvalī* as fourteen (A.D. 1483–4).[5] Miharbān gives it as 'fifteen or sixteen' and states that the betrothal ceremony commenced on the first day of the dark half of Vaisākh, S. 1542.[6] The wedding evidently followed soon after, which would mean

[1] *GR*, *sākhī* 50, p. 113. It is recorded that Gurū Nānak caused Nānaki to conceive a son and a daughter by giving her a clove and a cardamom. He then caused his own wife to conceive two sons by giving her two cloves.

[2] This and other doubtful points relating to the family connexions of Gurū Nānak may one day be settled with the aid of the family records kept by the line of Bedī family *pāṇḍās*, or brāhmaṇ genealogists, in Hardwār. The common custom of regularly reporting genealogical details to a family *pāṇḍā* has been followed by the Bedīs and it is reasonable to assume that the details relating to Gurū Nānak's own generation must have once been recorded in Hardwār. Efforts to trace these records have so far failed. but they may yet be uncovered. The Bedī family *pāṇḍā* also serves the Soḍhīs, the family to which all the Gurūs from Gurū Rām Dās onwards belonged.

[3] *Bālā JS*, *sākhī* 12, pp. 43–46.

[4] *Pur JS*, p. 6.

[5] *GR*, p. 112.

[6] *Mih JS*, p. 29.

that both betrothal and marriage took place, according to this account, in A.D. 1485. The *Miharbān Janam-sākhī* and the *Gyān-ratanāvalī* both give Baṭālā as the place where the wedding was held.

The unanimous testimony of the *Miharbān* and *Purātan* janam-sākhīs and the *Gyān-ratanāvalī* is certainly to be preferred to that of the *Bālā* tradition and we may accordingly conclude that the marriage probably took place before Gurū Nānak moved from Talvaṇḍī to Sultānpur. We may also accept Baṭālā as the place where it was held. The actual date must, however, be regarded with more caution. The period indicated by Miharbān and the *Gyān-ratanāvalī* (A.D. 1483–5) would be entirely possible, but both accounts show much evidence of the writers' imaginations and it may be that these were the sources of the dates which they give. Moreover, in their accounts of Gurū Nānak's early life both tend to attach consecutive ages to each successive *sākhī* and there can be no doubt that most, if not all, of these must be rejected.

All four versions are consistent in their descriptions of Gurū Nānak's father-in-law, and we may accordingly accept that he was Mūlā, a khatrī of the Choṇā sub-caste, originally from the village of Pokho di Randhāvī[1] but resident in Baṭālā at the time of the marriage. The *Bālā* account adds that he was a *paṭvārī* which may be correct but is more likely to be a transference from the tradition concerning Kālū.

The janam-sākhīs are also unanimous in naming two sons, Lakhmī Dās and Sirī Chand, as the Gurū's only children and there can be no doubt that this is also correct. The chief difference in the four accounts is that the two older versions imply that Lakhmī Dās was the elder,[2] whereas the two later versions explicitly state that Sirī Chand was born first.

This is as far as the *Miharbān* and *Purātan* janam-sākhīs and the *Gyān-ratanāvalī* take us. The *Bālā* janam-sākhīs add the names of several other relatives, but in the absence of support from any of the other accounts most of these must be regarded with some doubt. Lālū we may perhaps accept as at least probable. It is strange that Miharbān should have omitted all reference to a brother of Kālū had he in fact existed, but the name is firmly implanted in Bedī family tradition.

The traditions of the Bedī family may also be admitted as strong evidence in the case of Kālū's immediate forbears. These traditions record that the parents of Kālū were named Śiv Rām (or perhaps Śiv Narāyan) and Banārasī. Śiv Rām's father's name is given as Rām Narāyan of Dehrā Sāhib in the tahsīl of Taran Tāran, and he in turn is said to have been the son of Abhoj. Kālū's name is also given as Kaliyāṇ Rāi.[3]

[1] On the left bank of the Rāvī, near the town of Dehrā Bābā Nānak.

[2] They refer to both births in a single sentence, naming Lakhmī Dās first and Sirī Chand second.

[3] Kala Singh Bedi, *Gurū Nānak Daraśan*, pp. 268–71. *MK*, p. 830. See also the *Nānak Prakāś*, canto 3: 48, 50. Kala Singh Bedi, op. cit., pp. 271–2, also provides a family tree

Finally there are the names of two people who were not actually related to Gurū Nānak but who were, according to the janam-sākhī accounts, very closely associated with him. The first is Rāi Bulār, traditionally regarded as a son of the Rāi Bhoi, or Rāi Bhoā, whose name generally appears in references to Gurū Nānak's village. Most of the janam-sākhīs record that Rāi Bulār was the village landlord during Gurū Nānak's early years, and that he perceived in the young man signs of spiritual greatness which had evidently escaped Kālū.

The record of the janam-sākhīs concerning Rāi Bulār has been universally accepted, but there are reasons why it should be treated with some caution. In the first place, Miharbān states that the landlord during Gurū Nānak's early life was Rāi Bhoā, not Rāi Bulār.[1] Secondly, the *Purātan* references to Rāi Bulār are to be found in *sākhīs* which are manifestly unhistorical.[2] Thirdly, Bhāi Gurdās makes no mention of him in his list of Gurū Nānak's more important followers.[3]

These reasons do not mean that Rāi Bulār never existed, and nor do they necessarily mean that the role assigned to him in most of the janam-sākhīs must be rejected. What they do indicate is that we can no longer accept the janam-sākhī descriptions of him as beyond doubt. They may be basically correct, but there also exists the definite possibility that they are false.

This does not, however, apply to the second of the two close associates, Mardānā the Mirāsī.[4] Mardānā figures much more prominently in the janam-sākhīs than Rāi Bulār and Bhāī Gurdās refers to him explicitly as one of the Gurū's prominent followers.[5] His association with Gurū Nānak may be accepted without hesitation.

Daulat Khān Lodī and Sultānpur

The janam-sākhīs all record that while still a relatively young man Gurū Nānak spent a period in the town of Sultānpur,[6] working there for Daulat Khān Lodī.[7] The account is basically the same in all four janam-sākhī

showing the descendants of Lakhmī Dās. Sirī Chand, as the founder of the Udāsī sect of sādhūs, was celibate.

[1] *Mih JS*, p. 25.

[2] The restored field (*Pur JS*, *sākhī* 4, pp. 6–7); the tree's stationary shadow (ibid., *sākhī* 5, p. 7). He appears much more frequently in the *Bālā* janam-sākhīs.

[3] *Vār* 11, stanzas 13–14.

[4] Mirāsī or Ḍūm: a depressed Muslim caste of genealogists and musicians.

[5] *Vār*. 11, stanza 13.

[6] The town is situated in the Jullundur Doab, sixteen miles south of Kapūrthalā and near the confluence of the Satluj and Beās rivers. Its situation on the imperial high road between Delhi and Lahore made it a town of considerable importance during Mughal times. It was sacked by Nādir Shāh in 1739 and never recovered its former prosperity. *Punjab State Gazetteers* (*Kapurthala State*), vol. xivA, p. 45.

[7] The *Purātan* janam-sākhīs do not append Lodī, referring to him simply as Nawāb Daulat Khān. There can, however, be no doubt that their reference is to Daulat Khān

traditions. All relate that Gurū Nānak moved to Sultānpur at the invitation of his brother-in-law Jai Rām, who was employed as a steward by Daulat Khān. Jai Rām commended Nānak to his employer and secured for him a position in Daulat Khān's commissariat. Some time later, while bathing in a nearby river,[1] Nānak was carried away to God's presence and there charged with the task of preaching the divine Name. Emerging from the river three days later he uttered the words, 'There is neither Hindu nor Muslim'. The local qāzī regarded this as an insult to the faith of Islam, and Nānak was brought to account before Daulat Khān. After successfully defending himself he left Sultānpur with Mardānā and began his travels.

All of the accounts include miraculous material which must be discarded,[2] but with the exception of the immersion in the river such material concerns only the details of the story and its rejection leaves the basis unaltered. The interview with God during a period of three days spent submerged in the river must also be rejected as it stands, but the incident is one which permits a rational interpretation. It would be entirely reasonable to regard the janam-sākhī accounts as the descendants of an authentic tradition concerning a personally decisive and perhaps ecstatic experience, a climactic culmination of years of searching issuing in illumination and in the conviction that he had been called to proclaim divine truth to the world. With this modification the story becomes wholly credible and we must now decide whether or not it can be accepted.

The evidence in this case leads us to regard the Sultānpur interlude as highly probable. In the first place it concerns events which took place in the Pañjāb. As we have already observed, traditions which relate to incidents or episodes within the province are generally more reliable than those which concern areas beyond its borders, for in such cases the corporate memory of the community can play a significant part. Although legend accumulates quickly it may be doubted whether such an important episode would be completely without foundation.

Secondly, the janam-sākhīs are unanimous as far as the basic details are concerned. Bhāī Gurdās does not refer to this period, but he does mention Daulat Khān as one of Gurū Nānak's followers.[3]

Lodī, and in the case of the *Miharbān Janam-sākhī* and Bhāī Gurdās it is explicit (*Mih JS*, p. 72, and *Vār* 11. 13).

[1] The janam-sākhīs do not name the river, but it would presumably be the Veīn, a small stream which flows past Sultānpur.

[2] Some elements are more accurately described as hagiographic anecdotes rather than as straight miracle stories. A particularly popular one is a late tradition which relates how Gurū Nānak, when distributing commodities in the commissariat, occasionally failed to get past the number thirteen. The word for thirteen (*terān*, or *terah*) is very similar to the word for 'thine' (*terā*) and having uttered the word *terān* the Gurū would sometimes fall into a trance and continue repeating the word *terā*.

[3] *Vār* 11. 13.

Thirdly there is the testimony of the *Dabistān-i-Mazāhib* to strengthen that of the janam-sākhīs.

Before the victory of the late Emperor (Babar) he (Nanak) was a *Modi* to Daulat Khan Lodhi, who was one of the high officials of Ibrahim Khan Emperor of Delhi. And, Modi is an official in charge of the granary.[1]

Fourthly, there is nothing in what we know of Daulat K͟hān Lodī which conflicts with the tradition. He occupied a position of considerable importance during the later years of Sultan Sikandar Lodī (1489–1517) and during the reign of Sikandar's successor, Ibrāhīm Lodī (1517–26), but nothing explicit appears to have been recorded of his early life up to his appointment as governor of Lahore at the very beginning of the sixteenth century. Bābur describes him in a brief, misleading paragraph.

This Tātār Khān, the father of Daulat Khān, was one of six or seven *sardārs* who, sallying out and becoming dominant in Hindūstān, made Buhlūl Pādshāh. He held the country north of the Satluj [*sic*] and Sarhind, the revenues of which exceeded 3 *krūrs*. On Tātār Khān's death, Sl. Sikandar (*Lūdī*), as overlord, took those countries from Tātār Khān's sons and gave Lāhūr only to Daulat Khān. That happened a year or two before I came into the country of Kābul (910 A.H.).[2]

This is incorrect in that it allows no gap between Tātār K͟hān and Daulat K͟hān in the government of Lahore, other than the indefinite reference to 'Tātār Khān's sons'. The *Tārīk͟h-i-Salātīn-i-Afg͟hānā* and the *Tārīk͟h-i-Dāūdī* record that shortly before Bahlūl Lodī's death in 1489 Tātār K͟hān, who had risen in rebellion, was defeated and killed by Nizām K͟hān, the future Sultan Sikandar.[3] The omission of this incident from other chronicles, notably from the *Tabaqāt-i-Akbarī*, raises an element of doubt concerning its authenticity, but it seems clear that there was a break between the termination of Tātār K͟hān's governorship and the beginning of Daulat K͟hān's period, for Daulat K͟hān's appointment must have been made after the incumbent governor, Sa'īd K͟hān Sarwānī, was exiled in 1500 for his part in a conspiracy against Sultan Sikandar.[4] In other words, there must have been at least one other governor between Tātār K͟hān and Daulat K͟hān.

Bābur does, however, confirm that Daulat K͟hān was the son of Tātār K͟hān, and this would mean a connexion with Pañjāb administration prior to 1500. Apart from the janam-sākhīs there appears to be no hint of what

[1] Ganda Singh, *Nanak Panthis*, p. 4. The corresponding reference for Shea and Troyers' translation of the *Dabistān* is vol. ii, p. 247.

[2] A. S. Beveridge, *The Bābur-nāma in English*, vol. i, p. 383.

[3] *Tārik͟h-i-Salātīn-i-Afg͟hānā*, extract translated in N. Roy's *Niamatullah's History of the Afghāns*, part i, pp. 107–9. *Tārik͟h-i-Dāūdī* in Elliot and Dowson, *The History of India as told by its own Historians*, vol. iv, pp. 440–4.

[4] *Tabaqāt-i-Akbarī*, trans. B. De, p. 369. *Tārik͟h-i-K͟hān Jahānī*, in Elliot and Dowson, *The History of India as told by its own Historians*, vol. v, p. 96.

this connexion meant in terms of actual responsibility or achievement. Mrs. Beveridge twice states that he was the founder of Sultānpur,[1] but she does not name her source and neither the Persian chronicles nor the *Bābur-nāma* appear to offer this information. According to the *Kapurthala State Gazetteer* the town was founded in the eleventh century by Sultān Khān Lodī, a general of Sultan Mahmūd of Ghaznī.[2] It goes on to add that this information is 'according to tradition', but of these two possible origins it appears to be the more likely. The difficulty is that Mrs. Beveridge had access to the *Gazetteers* and she was certainly not inclined to make categorical statements without first ascertaining their basis. In one other case, however, she does err in her identification of a Pañjāb town[3] and it seems likely that her statements concerning the origin of Sultānpur represent another such error. It is possible that the janam-sākhīs are the ultimate source of her statements, although none of them records that Daulat Khān founded the town.

The most we can accept concerning Daulat Khān's life prior to his lengthy term as governor of Lahore is that his relationship to Tātār Khān must have meant a position of some standing in the Pañjāb, and that his appointment to Lahore would have been made within the first four years of the sixteenth century. The earliest possible date would be 1500, the year in which Sa'īd Khān Sarwānī was expelled. Bābur's reference to 'a year or two before I came into the country of Kābul' implies 1502 or 1503, as his arrival in Kābul in 910 A.H. corresponds to A.D. 1504. There is, however, an element of vagueness in his expression. An appointment soon after Sa'īd Khān Sarwānī's expulsion seems more likely.

These two conclusions certainly do not establish a connexion between Daulat Khān Lodī and Sultānpur prior to 1500, and if considered apart from the janam-sākhī tradition they do not even imply one. They do, however, render it at least possible. An appointment to Lahore in 1500 or shortly after would fit the chronology of Gurū Nānak's early life in the sense that the association, if it actually took place, must have been prior to this date.

The evidence available seems to indicate a two-fold conclusion. In the first place, we may accept as established the tradition that Gurū Nānak, as a young man, spent a period in Sultānpur, working in the employment of the nawāb of that town. The location of the incident within the Pañjāb and the basic unanimity of the janam-sākhīs appear to justify this conclusion. Secondly, we may accept as probable the claim that this nawāb was Daulat Khān Lodī. In this respect an element of doubt must remain, for it is possible that the connexion may have arisen through Daulat Khān's

[1] A. S. Beveridge, op. cit., vol. i, p. 442, and vol. ii, p. 461, n. 3.

[2] *Punjab State Gazetteers* (*Kapurthala State*), vol. XIVA, p. 45. Muhammad Nazim makes no reference to a general called Sultān Khān Lodī in his *The Life and Times of Sultān Mahmūd of Ghazna*.

[3] See *infra*, p. 133.

undoubted association with Sultānpur in 1524,[1] or through the common tendency to introduce associations with persons of acknowledged stature. The reference in Bhāī Gurdās and the *Dabistān* indicate, however, an unusually strong tradition and the external evidence raises no objections to its acceptance.

The visit to Assam

With the significant exception of Miharbān, all the janam-sākhīs include a *sākhī* which describes a visit to a country ruled by female magicians. The accounts vary in several respects, but the basis of the story is the same in all of them. All relate that Mardānā, who went ahead of the Gurū to beg for food, was put under a spell by one of these enchantresses and turned into a sheep. When the Gurū went in search of him efforts were made to work magic on him also, but to no effect. The women eventually acknowledged his superior power and made their submission to him.[2]

The substance of the *sākhī* must be rejected as a wonder story, but in this particular case we should examine the location ascribed to the incident in order to determine whether or not there may be an element of fact behind the legend. An examination is necessary in this case as such an element has been almost universally assumed. It is this *sākhī*, or more accurately two of the several versions of this *sākhī*, which provide the basis for the common statement that Gurū Nānak's travels extended as far as Assam, a statement which is to be found in practically every modern account of Gurū Nānak.

The two versions which have prompted this acceptance are those of the *Purātan* and *Bālā* janam-sākhīs, particularly the former. In the *Purātan* janam-sākhīs the story is set in a land which is called either Kaurū or Kāvarū,[3] both of which are evidently variants of Kāmrūp. This, at least, is the assumption which has been made by all who accept a visit to Assam and it is a reasonable one. The nature of the *sākhī* appears to confirm this. Assam is famed as a home of the Tantras, and the magic described in the *sākhī* has been taken as a description of tantric practices. All printed editions of the *Bālā* version give the name as Kārū, but in the manuscripts it appears, as in the *Purātan* janam-sākhīs, as Kaurū.[4] The *Bālā* manuscript version records a *sākhī* which differs radically from that of the *Purātan* janam-sākhīs, but it does concern women magicians who turn Mardānā into a sheep and make unsuccessful efforts to overcome the Gurū.[5] These

[1] A. S. Beveridge, op. cit., vol. i, p. 442, and vol. ii, p. 461.

[2] For the *Purātan* version see *supra*, p. 41.

[3] *Pur JS*, pp. 33–34.

[4] IOL MS. Panj. B41, folio 70b.

[5] The *Bālā sākhī* is, for once, much simpler and briefer than that of the *Purātan* janam-sākhīs and evidently represents a more primitive version. There is no reference to a queen called Nūr Shāh, and the miracles described differ from those of the *Purātan* account. According to the *Bālā* story, two women who seek to seduce the Gurū are changed, one

references to Kaurū have been accepted as satisfactory evidence of a visit to Assam and the point has not been challenged.

It must, however, be both challenged and rejected. In the first place, it is clear that Kāmrūp was not ruled by women during the period of Gurū Nānak's lifetime. The kings of western Kāmrūp[1] during the latter decades of the fifteenth century were Chakradhvaj (*c.* 1460–80) and his son Nilambar (*c.* 1480–98), and in eastern Kāmrūp authority was divided between a number of petty chieftains. In 1498 Nilambar was overthrown by Alāuddīn Husain, Sultan of Gaur, and a Muslim garrison was installed in the capital Kāmatapur under a general called Dānīyal. This garrison did not hold the city for long. Some time before 1505 it was attacked by a confederacy of Bhuyān chiefs and completely destroyed. The subsequent period is not entirely clear, but it seems that another king gained the throne, probably Nāgākṣa whom the *Kāmrūpar Buranjī* refers to as king in connexion with the building of the Bilveśvar temple in 1521. Nāgākṣa was evidently succeeded by his son Durlabhendra who was killed in 1540. There is certainly obscurity at this point, but there can be no doubt that the rulers of eastern Kāmrūp were men, not women.

The same applies also to western Kāmrūp where during the period following Nilambar's fall the various chieftains were brought under the authority of the Koche chieftain Hājo. This authority subsequently passed to Hājo's grandson Bisu (1515–40)[2] who greatly extended it and who in 1527 assumed the regnal name of Bisva Siṅgha.[3]

It is accordingly clear that no kingdom within Kāmrūp could have been ruled by women during the time of Gurū Nānak. Nor could it have been the Āhōm kingdom, for it was ruled during this period by King Suhungmung (1497–1539).[4] Indeed there is no likelihood whatsoever that such a kingdom would have been found amongst Kāmrūp's Assamese or tribal neighbours. Matrilineal descent was certainly a feature of Khāsi and Gāro society,[5] but it was not one which produced queens or chieftainesses. The result of this custom was not that women inherited power or property, but that such inheritances descended through them to their sons.[6]

into a ewe and the other into a bitch (ibid., folio 71a). In the earliest of the *Bālā* printed editions most of the manuscript version has been dropped and the *Purātan* version substituted in its place (*Bālā JS*, *sākhī* 25, pp. 102–8).

[1] It is usually referred to as Kāmata during this period.

[2] Hājo had two daughters, Hīra and Jīra, both of whom were married to a certain Haria Mandal. Bisu was the son of Hīra.

[3] E. A. Gait, *A History of Assam* (2nd edition), pp. 42–49. Rai K. L. Barua Bahadur, *Early History of Kāmrūpa*, pp. 283–4. See also N. N. Acharyya, *The History of Medieval Assam* (*A.D. 1228 to 1603*), a thesis submitted for the degree of Doctor of Philosophy in the University of London, 1957; and Francis Buchanan, 'General View of the History of Kamrupa' (Appendix C of S. K. Bhuyan's edition of the *Kāmrūpar Buranjī*, pp. 139–43).

[4] E. A. Gait, op, cit., p. 86.

[5] *Jayantiā Buranjī*, pp. x–xi.

[6] 'The chief of a Khāsi state is succeeded not by his own, but by his sister's son.' E. A. Gait, op. cit., p. 260.

The second reason for rejecting the *sākhī* is that it clearly reflects an earlier legend. Stories concerning *strī-deś*, 'the land of women', were already common currency long before the time of Gurū Nānak or the janam-sākhīs and in a number of traditions *strī-deś* had been identified with Kāmrūp.[1] The land of Kāmrūp was itself identified with an area in Assam or Bhutan, but its true location was in the realm of puranic and tantric mythology where it figured prominently as a symbol of erotic practice and dark magic.

There can be no doubt that it is this legendary land which is to be found in the janam-sākhīs. The *strī-deś*, or *triā-deś*, of the janam-sākhīs does not correspond to anything we know concerning the Assam of the early sixteenth century, but it does correspond closely to the *strī-deś* of puranic and tantric legend. Even the principal divergence separating the different accounts seems to reflect this correspondence, for it is a difference of location. The India Office Library manuscript B40 gives the land an unspecified location 'beside the ocean',[2] the *Gyān-ratanāvalī* places it in the south country immediately before the crossing to Ceylon,[3] and the *Purātan* and *Bālā* versions set it in Kaurū or Kāvarū. Miharbān and Bhāī Gurdās omit it altogether. The Kaurū or Kāvarū of the *Purātan* and *Bālā* janam-sākhīs must be regarded as the Kāmrūp of mythology, not the medieval kingdom of Kāmata or any part of it. Local traditions associated with particular gurdwārās in Assam will almost certainly have derived from the janam-sākhīs. Such traditions will have been planted in the area, as in other parts of India, by khatrī traders, Udāsī sādhūs, or soldiers, and then sustained by the foundation of a *saṅgat* and the erection of a gurdwārā.[4] It is not possible to state categorically that Gurū Nānak never visited Assam, but we must acknowledge that there is no acceptable evidence to support such a visit.

The visit to Dacca

The tradition concerning a visit to Dacca is weak in the janam-sākhīs, but it is one which nevertheless requires an examination as its authenticity has been defended on the basis of external evidence. In the janam-sākhīs such a visit is recorded only in the *Bālā* tradition, and within this tradition there are two conflicting versions of the circumstances. The older of the two sets the story of Mardānā and the forbidden fruit[5] in 'the region of

[1] Hazārī-prasād Dvivedī, *Nāth-sampradāy*, pp. 59–60. In this context the transcribed form is usually Kāmarūpa. Other traditions variously located it in the further regions of Gaṛhwāl-Kumāon, Kulū, near the source of the Satluj, and eastern Tibet. Ibid., p. 59.

[2] IOL MS. Panj. B40, folio 83.

[3] *GR*, pp. 227–30. This location may perhaps indicate a knowledge of Malabar matrilineal customs. Another possibility is that its source can be found in a reference to a *tiriā rāju* which occurs in the *Hakīkat Rāh Mukām Rāje Śivanābh kī*. See *infra*, p. 115.

[4] G. B. Singh, *Srī Gurū Granth Sāhib diān Prāchīn Bīṛān, passim.*

[5] Number 28 in the chart.

Dacca, Bengal'.[1] There can be no doubt that this is a later addition to the *sākhī* for no such location is found in the versions given by the earlier janam-sākhīs. The second appearance of the name is an even more obvious case of interpolation, in this case a recent one made by a publisher or a printer. The modern versions which are available today set the story of Bhūmīā the Landlord in Dacca.[2] This same story is to be found in the expanded 1871 edition, but without a location.[3] The words 'in Dacca' are clearly a recent addition. The reason for the addition was probably the conviction, based upon the external evidence to be mentioned shortly, that Gurū Nānak must have visited the area. The Bhūmīā *sākhī* follows the 'Country ruled by Women' *sākhī* in the expanded 1871 edition; the latter is believed to have taken place in Kāmrūp; subsequent *sākhīs* indicate that Gurū Nānak moved south after visiting Kāmrūp; and therefore Bhūmīā must have lived in Dacca. This appears to have been the line of reasoning which led to the insertion of Dacca in most modern versions of the *Bālā* tradition.

The janam-sākhī references to such a visit can accordingly be rejected, but there remains the evidence which was put forward fifty years ago by Sardar G. B. Singh. In 1915 and 1916 a series of three articles on 'Sikh Relics in Eastern Bengal' were published in the *Dacca Review*.[4] The greater part of these articles relates to the period following the travels of the ninth Gurū, Tegh Bahādur (1621–75), but in the first of them G. B. Singh claimed to have discovered conclusive evidence of a visit to Dacca by Gurū Nānak. This evidence consisted of a well 'out in the waste near Jafarabad, half hidden in bramble growth'.[5] Local tradition held that the well had been dug by Gurū Nānak. In 1915 G. B. Singh evidently accepted this tradition as proof of a visit to the locality and later writers have concurred.[6]

The tradition must, however, be summarily dismissed. Uncorroborated traditions of this kind cannot possibly be accepted and in a subsequent work G. B. Singh explicitly renounced his earlier acceptance of this Dacca tradition.[7] Its origin is apparently to be found in the Sikh monastery which once stood on the site. During the seventeenth century khatrī traders and

[1] IOL MS. Panj. B41, folio 70a. *Bālā JS*, *sākhī* 24, p. 101.

[2] *Bālā* janam-sākhī, Munshi Gulab Singh and Sons, 1942 edition, *sākhī* 89, p. 311.

[3] *Bālā* janam-sākhī, expanded 1871 edition (Divan Buta Singh), *sākhī* 171, p. 358.

[4] *Dacca Review*, vol. v, nos. 7 and 8, Oct. and Nov. 1915, pp. 224–32; vol. v, no. 10, Jan. 1916, pp. 316–22; vol. v, nos. 11 and 12, Feb. and March 1916, pp. 375–8. An article by the same author also appeared in the now defunct *Sikh Review*, July 1915.

[5] Jafarabad, or Zafarabad, the area now occupied by the Dhanmandi Residential Area.

[6] Teja Singh and Ganda Singh, *A Short History of the Sikhs*, vol. i, p. 8, n. 2. Khushwant Singh, *A History of the Sikhs*, vol. i, p. 33. The latter writer refers to Chittagong as well as to Dacca and claims that tablets discovered there mention the stay of the first and ninth Gurūs (op. cit., p. 302). The authority he names is G. B. Singh's series of articles in the *Dacca Review*. The second and third articles do refer to Chittagong, but there is no reference to either Gurū Nānak or to any tablets mentioning him.

[7] G. B. Singh, *Srī Gurū Granth Sāhib diān Prāchīn Bīṛān*, p. 274.

sādhūs of the Udāsī sect travelled to Bengal from the Pañjāb and several Sikh communities (*saṅgat*) were founded in different parts of the province. The well discovered by G. B. Singh had evidently served one of these communities, for adjacent to it were the ruins of a small monastery. It seems safe to assume that the tradition developed within this community and subsequently lingered amongst the inhabitants of the locality after the monastery had been abandoned. The tradition is now completely extinct. The Hindu families which had preserved it left the area in 1947 and the well, although still in existence in 1951, has now disappeared.[1]

Rājā Śivanābh and Ceylon

The tradition that Gurū Nānak visited Ceylon and there met a ruler named Śivanābh is to be found in the *Purātan* and *Bālā* janam-sākhīs and in the *Gyān-ratanāvalī*. In all versions, except that of the earlier *Bālā* janam-sākhīs, it has two parts. The first is the story of how a Sikh trader, whom the *Gyān-ratanāvalī* and later *Bālā* accounts call Mansukh, sailed to the land of Rājā Śivanābh and there converted him to the religion of Gurū Nānak.[2] The second describes how the Gurū himself subsequently journeyed there in order to meet his royal disciple and while there composed a work entitled the *Prāṇ Saṅgalī*.[3] In the *Purātan* version the land is not named in the first part, but in the account of Gurū Nānak's own visit it is identified as Siṅghalādīp (Ceylon).

This tradition is one of the few which can be tested by reference to external evidence, for it specifies not just Ceylon but also the rājā whom, it claims, Gurū Nānak met there. The name Śivanābh indicates that the rājā, if he in fact existed, must have been a Śaivite and this must point to the kingdom of Jaffna. Elsewhere in Ceylon the contemporary dynasties were Buddhist, but in Jaffna the rulers of this period were Śaivites. None of them, however, was named Śivanābh. The two kings who occupied the throne of Jaffna during the time of Gurū Nānak's travels were Pararājasēkharaṇ VI (1478–1519) and Segarājasēkharaṇ VII (1519–61).[4]

Jaffna must accordingly be eliminated, but before concluding that Rājā Śivanābh did not live in Ceylon we must consider the testimony of the

[1] The writer owes this information to Dr. A. H. Dani.

[2] *Pur JS*, *sākhī* 41, pp. 76–78 (*Hāfizābād* MS. only). *GR*, *sākhī* 82, pp. 224–5. The IOL manuscript B41 and the *Bālā JS* do not contain this *sākhī*. In the expanded 1871 edition it is *sākhī* 27, p. 100. For the *Purātan* version see *supra*, pp. 46–47.

[3] *Pur JS*, *sākhī* 47, pp. 86–90. *GR*, *sākhīs* 87–94, pp. 232–43. *Bālā JS*, *sākhī* 29, pp. 120–3.

[4] The University of Ceylon, *History of Ceylon*, vol. i, p. 701. Segarājasēkharaṇ VII assassinated and succeeded his father. For a list of the Jaffna rulers for the period 1467–1620 see Mundaliyar C. Rajanayagam, *Ancient Jaffna*, pp. 373–4. See also V. Vriddhagirisan, *The Nayaks of Tanjore*, p. 78, C. S. Navaratnam, *Tamils and Ceylon*, p. 179, and S. Gnanaprakasar, *Kings of Jaffna in the Portuguese Period*.

Hakīkat Rāh Mukām Rāje Śivanābh kī,[1] a brief work attached to many old manuscript copies of the *Ādi Granth* which purports to be a description of how to get to Rājā Śivanābh's kingdom.[2] The *Hakīkat Rāh* claims that Rājā Śivanābh was the grandfather of Māyādunne. It errs in locating Māyādunne in Jaffna,[3] but he is at least an historical figure and his period is such that his grandfather could conceivably have been alive during the time of Gurū Nānak's travels. Māyādunne's grandfather was not, however, called Śivanābh. He was Parākramabāhu VIII who reigned in Kōṭṭē from 1484 until 1508.[4] Accordingly the *Hakīkat Rāh* must be rejected as evidence of a visit to Ceylon by Gurū Nānak.

What then are we to conclude concerning Rājā Śivanābh? G. B. Singh suggested that he may have been a khatrī landlord who had emigrated to Ceylon from the Pañjāb.[5] There is, however, no evidence whatsoever to support this theory. G. B. Singh makes his suggestion in the context of a reference to the *Hakīkat Rāh* which, as we have just noted, furnishes no confirmation of the tradition.

Our conclusion must be that if Rājā Śivanābh did exist he had no connexion with Ceylon. This seriously weakens the tradition of a visit to Ceylon, but it need not necessarily mean that it is wholly without foundation. We may still assume the possibility of such a visit and apply to it our fourth criterion, the measure of agreement or disagreement which we find in the different janam-sākhīs.

When this criterion is applied the possibility at once begins to crumble. In the first place, there is the failure of Bhāī Gurdās and Miharbān to offer any support to the tradition. Bhāī Gurdās makes no reference at all to any such visit, and although Miharbān's reference to 'a land of darkness' beyond Setu-bandha may be regarded as a clear pointer to Ceylon the description which he gives of the country plainly indicates that it is a product of the imagination.[6] Secondly, there is the fact that the India Office Library manuscript B40 records both the story of the Sikh trader and the subsequent meeting between Gurū Nānak and Rājā Śivanābh without any mention of Siṅghalādīp.[7]

[1] 'The truth (concerning) the way to Rājā Śivanābh's dwelling.'

[2] Almost all of the manuscript copies of the *Ādi Granth* in the British Museum and the India Office Library contain the apocrypha which includes the *Hakīkat Rāh.* In addition to the *Hakīkat Rāh* this apocrypha comprises several *śloks* and a *śabad*, all attributed to Gurū Nānak. This extra material is included at the end of each volume. It follows the *Mundāvaṇī* and Gurū Arjan's concluding *ślok*, but precedes the *Rāgamālā* with which all copies of the *Ādi Granth* end.

[3] Māyādunne was one of the conspirators in an uprising which took place in Kōṭṭē in 1521 and which led to the division of the kingdom of Kōṭṭē. The portion secured by Māyādunne was the territory of Sītāvaka in the south-west of Ceylon. *Çulāvaṃsa*, ii. 224, n. 1

[4] *Epigraphica Zeylanica*, vol. iii, pp. 41, 43. University of Ceylon, *History of Ceylon*, dynastic chart facing p. 851 of vol. i.

[5] *Dacca Review*, vol. v, nos. 11 and 12, Feb.–Mar. 1916.

[6] *Mih JS*, pp. 217–21. See *supra*, p. 57.

[7] IOL MS. Panj. B40, folios 138 ff.

This second point is a most significant one. Its significance lies in the contrast between the B40 and *Purātan* accounts, and in the fact that it is only the later of the two versions which gives the specific geographical location. The B40 account of the Sikh trader's conversion and of his journey to Śivanābh's kingdom corresponds almost exactly to that of the *Purātan*'s *sākhī* 41,[1] and although its treatment of Gurū Nānak's meeting with Śivanābh lacks the same measure of verbal identity and expands the portion which describes the efforts of the rājā's seductive women to tempt the Gurū, the basic details it gives are almost all the same as those of the *Purātan* account. The only exception is the omission of any reference to Siṅghalādīp in the B40 version.

As in the *Hāfizābād* manuscript, the B40 account records that following his conversion the merchant took ship and sailed 'to where Rājā Śivanābh lived'.[2] This nautical reference may be held to indicate Siṅghalādīp, but it is by no means a necessary assumption. On the contrary, it is a common feature of all the janam-sākhīs, except that of Miharbān, that Gurū Nānak is said to have crossed the sea to unspecified islands or lands. Such references are particularly frequent in the *Bālā* janam-sākhīs, but they are also to be found in the *Purātan* account.[3] Geographical inexactitude is generally associated with the historically dubious and this appears to be invariably the case when the inexactitude concerns a location somewhere over the sea. Indeed, references to the *samundar* (ocean) are almost always associated with incidents containing generous measures of the fantastic. The significance of these references is not that they must all point to Ceylon, but rather that their remote settings should prompt an even greater degree of caution.

The likelihood appears to be that the *sākhī* concerning Śivanābh had an early origin, but that it had no specific location in the early traditions, oral or written. This would mean that the whole of the B40 account and the first part of the *Purātan* version (*sākhī* 41) represent an earlier stage in the evolution of the story than the second part of the *Purātan* version (*sākhī* 47) or the later janam-sākhī accounts of the complete episode. It is impossible to identify with complete certainty the manner in which the name Siṅghalādīp came to be attached to the tradition. It may have been the result of visits to the south by Sikh traders, for it is conceivable that the reference to the converted shopkeeper sailing 'to where Rājā Śivanābh lived' may have come to be associated with these later trade contacts. This is one possible explanation and others could be the prominence of Siṅghalādīp in Pañjāb folklore,[4] or the simple fact that if an unspecified maritime location were to be given a name Siṅghalādīp would have been the obvious choice.

[1] *Pur JS*, pp. 74–78 (*Hāfizābād* manuscript only).

[2] B40 MS., folio 140b.

[3] *Pur JS*, *sākhī* 29, p. 46; *sākhī* 45, p. 82; *sākhī* 46, p. 84.

[4] Cf. Mohan Singh, *An Introduction to Panjabi Literature*, p. 186.

The theory that the name Siṅghalādīp was introduced into an earlier tradition also receives support from *Pothī Harijī*, the second section of the *Miharbān Janam-sākhī*.[1] *Pothī Harijī* opens with a lengthy discourse between Gurū Nānak and the paṇḍit of Rājā Śivanābh, but gives no indication of who Śivanābh was or where he lived.[2] In a later *goṣṭ* Śivanābh reappears in a brief discourse which concerns him more directly, but which still makes no reference to his geographical location.[3] The only hint which it offers is the statement that after his conversation with Śivanābh Gurū Nānak returned to Kartārpur.[4] This does not suggest a location as far distant as Ceylon.

The conclusion which follows is irresistible. There was no contemporary ruler in Ceylon called Śivanābh and all the evidence points to a later introduction of the name Siṅghalādīp into *sākhīs* concerning him. The tradition that Gurū Nānak visited Ceylon must accordingly be rejected.

Sajjaṇ the Robber

According to the janam-sākhīs Sajjaṇ was a thief who posed as a pious philanthropist in order to lure unsuspecting travellers to their death.[5] It is an exceedingly popular story and appears in some form or other in all the janam-sākhīs,[6] but it is one which we must nevertheless regard with some considerable doubt.

In the first place, the janam-sākhīs disagree concerning the location of the incident. The *Purātan* version names no place at all, but implies that it must have been in or near the Pañjāb as the meeting is set between Gurū Nānak's departure from Sultānpur and his arrival in Pāṇīpat. This could conceivably be held to accord with the *Bālā* account which gives 'near Tulambā in the district of Multān' as the site.[7] The *Bālā* version differs radically from that of the *Purātan* janam-sākhīs in other respects, but almost all modern accounts, while rejecting the substance of the *Bālā sākhī* accept it as far as this single detail is concerned.[8]

No such compromise is possible, however, in the case of the *Miharbān* and *Gyān-ratanāvalī* versions. The latter names Hastināpur as the location

1 See *supra*, p. 19.

2 Khalsa College, Amritsar, MS. SHR: 427, folio 302a. In this *goṣṭ* he is called Śivanāth.

3 Ibid., *goṣṭ* 171, folios 341b–2a. In this *goṣṭ* the name is Śivanābh.

4 Ibid., folio 342b.

5 *Mih JS*, *goṣṭ* 73, pp. 235–8. *Pur JS*, *sākhī* 13, pp. 21–22. *GR*, *sākhī* 73, pp. 207–10. *Bālā JS*, *sākhī* 63, pp. 290–4. See *supra*, pp. 38–39, 58.

6 Bhāī Gurdās does not refer to it.

7 *Bālā JS*, conclusion of *sākhī* 62, p. 290. The town is also called Makhdūmpur.

8 The modern *Bālā* janam-sākhīs drop the earlier *Bālā* version and follow the *Purātan* account instead (*Bālā* janam-sākhī, Munshi Gulab Singh and Sons, 1942 edition, *sākhī* 67, pp. 269–70).

of the incident[1] and Miharbān sets it in 'the south country'.[2] The precise location is not named in Miharbān's account, but is evidently intended to be somewhere between Rāmeśwaram and Ujjain. It is clear that no definite geographical location can be assigned to the incident and that it should properly belong to the group of miscellaneous *sākhīs* which do not have a precise setting.

The janam-sākhīs also differ with regard to the actual content of the story, although in the case of Miharbān, the *Purātan* janam-sākhīs, and the *Gyān-ratanāvalī* these other differences are of little significance. The *Purātan* version calls Sajjaṇ a sheikh and records that he maintained a temple and a mosque in order to accommodate both Hindus and Muslims.[3] Miharbān's account, on the other hand, gives him no title and makes no reference to either a temple or a mosque, merely describing a handsome *dharmsālā* which had separate drinking facilities for Hindus and Muslims.[4] The *Gyān-ratanāvalī* adds that Gurū Nānak was aware of Sajjaṇ's intentions, having been surreptitiously informed by a bystander as he entered the city that Sajjaṇ was in reality a thug. The same informant added that Sajjaṇ was also in league with the local rājā who customarily received half of the booty.[5]

These are essentially differences of detail and there can be no doubt that all three accounts are relating a common tradition. The *Bālā* version, however, offers much more pronounced variations and indeed the *sākhī* it records is not really the same incident. Sajjaṇ's disguise is described as that of a Vaiṣṇava, not of a sheikh, and although he is obviously intended to be a scoundrel there is no reference to his being a thug. Nor is there any mention of his maintaining a temple and a mosque, of his throwing his victims into a well, or of subsequently building a *dharmsālā*.[6] His practice was evidently to do no more than steal his guests' clothes, for this is what he did to Mardānā's son.[7] The only real links with the story as recorded in the other three versions are his name and his sudden conversion as a result of hearing Gurū Nānak sing the hymn which appears in the *Ādi Granth* as *Sūhī* 3.[8]

Normally a variant of this kind would do no more than suggest that the *Bālā* version can be safely discarded in favour of the accounts given in the other three janam-sākhī traditions. In this particular case, however, the difference is more important, or rather the small area of agreement is

[1] *GR*, p. 207. This anachronistic appearance of the ancient Kuru capital will doubtless be a result of the influence of the *Mahābhārata*. The remains of the city are in Meerut District.

[2] *Mih JS*, p. 235.

[3] *Pur JS*, p. 21.

[4] *Mih JS*, p. 235.

[5] *GR*, p. 207.

[6] The *Bālā JS*, p. 290, refers to the temple and mosque, but the IOL manuscript B41 does not (loc. cit., folio 183b).

[7] Khazan Singh, *History and Philosophy of Sikhism*, vol. i, p. 95, follows this version.

[8] *AG*, p. 729.

important. The story given by Miharbān, the *Purātan* janam-sākhīs, and the *Gyān-ratanāvalī* on the one hand, and the different story given by the *Bālā* version on the other, both have as their key point Gurū Nānak's singing of *Sūhī* 3. This is significant for *Sūhī* 3 contains references which might well indicate the genesis of both stories. The hymn begins:

> Bronze shines brightly, but if I rub it blackness (like) ink (comes off it).
> Even if I clean it a hundred times (outer) cleaning will never remove its inner impurity.

The message which this and subsequent figures convey is that ultimate exposure must inevitably overtake all dissemblers who seek to conceal inner impurity behind an outward show of piety. The refrain then follows:

> They are my real friends who accompany me (now) and who will accompany me (into the hereafter);
> Who, in that place where accounts are called for, will stand up and give (a good) account (of their deeds).

The word used here for 'friends' is *sajaṇ*[1] and it seems likely that the message of the hymn, together with the word *sajaṇ*, produced two separate stories, both concerning an impostor called Sajaṇ, or Sajjaṇ. This cannot be affirmed categorically, but it is at least a strong possibility. Insofar as the two stories agree their agreement may be traced directly to the hymn, and it is when they move out into details which are independent of the hymn that they diverge.

There are accordingly good grounds for questioning the authenticity of the story and to these we may add the fact that Bhāī Gurdās makes no reference either to the incident or to a person called Sajjaṇ. This is not surprising as far as the account of Gurū Nānak's travels given in *Vār* 1 is concerned, but had the tradition been a firm one a reference to Sajjaṇ might well have appeared in *Vār* 11.[2] The *sākhī* cannot be dismissed as totally impossible and nor can we rule out the possibility of a link with an earlier tradition concerning an encounter with a thief of some kind. As it stands, however, it must be classified with the improbable *sākhīs*.

The discourse on Mount Sumeru

The discourse with the Siddhs on Mount Sumeru is one of only three incidents which are to be found in Bhāī Gurdās and in all of the important

[1] *sajaṇ seī nāli mai chaldiā nāli chalanhi;*
jithai lekhā maṅgīai tithai khaṛe dasanhi.
AG, p. 729

[2] Bhāī Gurdās's list of Gurū Nānak's more prominent followers. (*Vār* 11, stanzas 13–14.)

janam-sākhīs.[1] This indicates a very strong tradition and one which cannot be lightly set aside. When Bhāī Gurdās and all of the janam-sākhīs unite in testifying to a particular claim we shall need compelling arguments in order to dismiss it.

In this case, however, the arguments which must be brought against the tradition do compel us to reject it. First, there is the mythical location which is given as the setting for the discourse. Mount Sumeru exists only in legend, not in fact.[2] It has been maintained that in this context Mount Sumeru represents Mount Kailāś,[3] but this is a claim which cannot possibly be sustained. The arguments which have been advanced in support of this identification are, first, a *Purātan* reference to Mahādeo (Śiva) as one of Gurū Nānak's interlocutors;[4] secondly, Bhāī Gurdās's account of how the Siddhs sent the Gurū to draw water from a lake;[5] and thirdly, the reported discovery of images of Gurū Nānak in the Kailāś area. The *Purātan* insertion of Mahādeo's name before that of Gorakhnāth can be traced to Gurū Nānak's use of the name Īśar in the series of *śloks* from *Vār Rāmakalī* which in large measure explain the origin of the Mount Sumeru tradition.[6] Bhāī Gurdās's description of a lake, which has been held to refer to Mānasa-sarovara,[7] must be rejected on rational grounds. Lake Mānasa is not filled with jewels in the manner related by the poet. The third justification concerns the report of an expedition which visited Lake Mānasa and claimed to have discovered images of Gurū Nānak in the four cave temples around the lake.[8] If in fact such images did exist they would certainly have been introduced by sādhūs at a later date.[9]

[1] The Mecca visit (nos. 78–79) and the Achal Baṭālā debate (no. 90) are the others. The association with Daulat Khān Lodī, though not treated as an incident in Bhāī Gurdās, is also referred to by all sources.

[2] Mount Sumeru or, more commonly, Mount Meru is the legendary mountain said to be situated in the centre of the earth. According to the geographical system of the *Purāṇas* the earth was flat and from its central point there arose this mountain. Seven continents (*dvīpas*) lay in concentric circles around it. The inmost of the seven, which was attached to Mount Meru and which included Bhāratavarṣa (India) was named Jambudvīpa. The summit of Mount Meru was believed to reach to the heavens, and the sun and planets revolved around it. The Himālayas were said to be its foothills. A. L. Basham, *The Wonder that was India*, pp. 320, 488–9. The influence of this Puranic mythology is to be found in all the accounts, but in varying degrees. In the *Miharbān Janam-sākhī* it is relatively weak and in the *Bālā* janam-sākhīs very strong.

[3] Vir Singh in his edition of Santokh Singh's *Nānak Prakāś*, vol. iii, p. 689, n.*. Kartar Singh, *Life of Guru Nanak Dev*, p. 190.

[4] *Pur JS*, p. 94. Vir Singh, op. cit., p. 690 n. Kailāś was believed to be the location of Śiva's paradise. Neither Bhāī Gurdās nor Miharbān include this reference.

[5] *Vār* 1. 31.

[6] See *supra*, p. 11, n. 2.

[7] Vir Singh, op. cit., p. 690 n. Kartar Singh, op. cit., pp. 190, 194. The *Pur JS* includes the same legend, but without specifying a lake as the source of water.

[8] Vir Singh, op. cit., pp. 691–2 n. Sewaram Singh, *The Divine Master*, pp. 139–41.

[9] Sewaram Singh also claims as evidence of Gurū Nānak's visit an oral report that the people who worship these images were aware that 'the Great Master . . . had appeared in Ten Forms and had founded the Great *Tirath* at Amritsar' (op. cit., p. 140). Such information could hardly have been derived from Gurū Nānak himself.

The second argument which must be brought against the tradition is the legendary nature not just of its location, but also of the story itself. Gurū Nānak and Gorakhnāth could not possibly have been contemporaries, and nor can it be claimed that the person referred to as Gorakhnāth must have been a Nāth yogī who bore the same name as the sect's founder. The names given to his companions plainly indicate that their origin is to be found in a confused amalgam of the popular traditions concerning the nine immortal Nāths and the eighty-four immortal Siddhs.[1] Bhāī Gurdās explicitly states that the meeting on Mount Sumeru was with the eighty-four Siddhs.[2]

The manner in which this legendary basis is developed varies in the different versions, but in all cases the development shares the nature of the basis. Miharbān relates discourses which surpass in length anything he offers elsewhere. Bhāī Gurdās sets out a denunciation of the degeneracy of life on the plains below and concludes with the miracle of the lake of jewels. The *Purātan* janam-sākhīs relate the story of the jewels and also a miraculous departure from the mountain. The *Bālā* version produces in this and other associated *sākhīs* its most sustained flight of Puranic fancy.

The third objection is the existence of an obvious explanation for the genesis of the whole tradition. There appears to be no doubt that the basic *sākhī* which has provided the foundation for all subsequent expansion of the tradition must have developed out of the *śloks* from *Vār Rāmakalī* which the janam-sākhīs set in the centre of the discourse.[3] This particular point has already been discussed as an illustration of the manner in which much of the janam-sākhī material must have evolved.[4] In the *śloks* from *Vār Rāmakalī* Gurū Nānak speaks successively as Īśar, Gorakh, Gopī-chand, Charapaṭ, Bharatharī, and finally as himself. A discourse with yogīs was obviously implied, and the names used by Gurū Nānak seemed to indicate that these yogīs were none other than the famous Gorakhnāth and other celebrated Siddhs.[5] Around this nucleus there gathered details drawn from Puranic and Nāth mythology, and the result was the legend of the Mount Sumeru discourse as we find it in Bhāī Gurdās and the janam-sākhīs. All accounts have the same nucleus. They differ only in the nature and quantity of the detail which has been added.

The Mount Sumeru *sākhīs* provide us with a tradition which appears in all versions, but which must nevertheless be wholly rejected. This is not to say that Gurū Nānak never visited the Himālayas, nor indeed can we maintain with assurance that he did not penetrate as far as Mount Kailāś

[1] See Glossary for *Nāth*, p. 243, and *Siddh*, p. 245.

[2] *Vār* 1. 28.

[3] *Vār Rāmakalī*, *śloks* 2–7 of *pauṛī* 12, *AG*, pp. 952–3.

[4] See *supra*, pp. 11–12.

[5] Gorakhnāth was of course a Nāth, not a Siddh. This is an illustration of the common confusion of Nāths and Siddhs.

and Lake Mānasa.[1] The conclusion to which our analysis points is that Bhāī Gurdās and the janam-sākhīs do not provide us with acceptable evidence of such a visit, and that accordingly it cannot be a part of the biography which we are seeking to reconstruct.

Mecca and Medina

Although the tradition that Gurū Nānak visited Mecca was summarily dismissed by Trumpp as legend[2] almost all subsequent writers have accepted it and most have regarded it as the terminus of his western travels. Some popular accounts claim that he continued on to Egypt and adjacent African countries, and a few take him into Europe, but most follow the older janam-sākhīs in ending the westward journey at Mecca or Medina.

Once again it is convenient to draw a distinction between the content of the tradition and its geographical setting, and to reject most of the former as legendary. The portion which cannot be summarily set aside in this manner is the discourse recorded by Bhāī Gurdās.

> The qāzīs and mullāhs gathered and began questioning him on religious matters.
> God has unfolded an immense creation! None can comprehend His power!
> Opening their books they asked, 'Which is the greater—the Hindu or the Muslim?'
> Bābā (Nānak) answered the pilgrims, 'Without good deeds both lead only to suffering.
> Neither Hindu nor Muslim finds refuge in (God's) court.
> The safflower's pigment is not fast; it runs when washed in water.
> People are jealous of each other, but Rām and Rahīm[3] are one.
> The world has taken the devil's path.'[4]

This certainly accords with the convictions which we find expressed in the works of Gurū Nānak and it is possible that the tradition has descended from an authentic origin, though not one that took place in Mecca. It can

[1] The possibility of a visit to Tibet has been a recurrent topic for speculation, and support has occasionally been claimed for a particular theory on the basis of a local Tibetan tradition. For a recent example see the *Sikh Review*, vol. xii, no. 37, Jan. 1965, pp. 21–26. Our knowledge of these traditions is confined to reports of travellers who received them as oral traditions, and bearing in mind the linguistic problems normally involved in such communications we must treat these reports with considerable caution. Even when we can accept a report as a substantially accurate account of an existing tradition there will be a strong likelihood that the tradition communicated in this manner represents a later development resulting from the movement of sādhūs between India and Tibet. There remains, however, a small margin of doubt and even if no reports had been received we should still be unable to reject categorically the possibility that Gurū Nānak visited Tibet.

[2] E. Trumpp, *The Ādi Granth*, p. vi.

[3] Hindu and Muslim names for God.

[4] *BG*, 1. 33.

at least be accepted as an accurate representation of Gurū Nānak's teaching concerning the relationship between Hindu beliefs and Islam.

The portion which must be rejected consists of the miraculous events which the janam-sākhīs all associate, in varying forms, with the Mecca visit. These include an instantaneous journey to Mecca,[1] a cloud which followed the Gurū,[2] an issue of fresh water in the wells of the city,[3] and a moving *miharāb*.[4] Of these the last is the most important, for it constitutes in most versions the climax of the episode. Bhāī Gurdās, the *Purātan* janam-sākhīs, the B40 manuscript, and the *Gyān-ratanāvalī* all record that Gurū Nānak, after arriving in Mecca, went to sleep with his feet pointing towards a *miharāb* or, in the case of the *Purātan* version, towards 'Mecca'. A qāzī who happened to observe him in this posture kicked him and demanded an explanation for such blasphemy.[5] In reply the Gurū suggested that the qāzī should drag his feet round and leave them pointing in a direction where God and the *Ka'bah* were not. The qāzī proceeded to do so, but when he moved the Gurū's legs the *miharāb* moved with them. Confounded by this miracle the qāzī fell at his feet.[6]

This story has been rationalized by terminating it at the point where Gurū Nānak suggests that the qāzī should point his feet in a direction where God is not. Although this rationalized version is particularly common in modern accounts it is to be found as far back as Miharbān and evidently provides us with another illustration of the author's relative sophistication. In the *Miharbān Janam-sākhī* the incident is related without the concluding miracle, and the words attributed to Gurū Nānak indicate that the miracle has been deliberately excised.[7]

The second interesting feature of the story of the moving *miharāb* is that it apparently came to be located in Mecca after it had evolved as an explicit tradition. This is the conclusion indicated by a number of inconsistencies in the various versions. One is that the *Miharbān* and *Bālā* versions locate it elsewhere. In the *Miharbān Janam-sākhī* it is set in a village on the way to Mecca,[8] and in the earlier *Bālā* janam-sākhīs the location is given as Medina.[9] A second inconsistency is that the *Purātan* janam-sākhīs, while locating it in Mecca, state that Gurū Nānak went to sleep with his feet

[1] *Mih JS*, p. 453. See *supra*, p. 61. [2] *Pur JS*, p. 99.

[3] Ibid., pp. 99, 104. *Bālā JS*, p. 187.

[4] The niche in a mosque which indicates the direction of the *Ka'bah*.

[5] Bhāī Gurdās calls him Jīvan (*BG* 1. 32), the *Purātan* janam-sākhīs call him Rukan-dīn (*Pur JS*, p. 100), and the B40 manuscript refers to him as a descendant (*potā*) of Makhdūm Bahāuddīn of Multan (loc. cit., folio 53). The *GR*, p. 412, follows Bhāī Gurdās.

[6] *BG* 1. 32. *Pur JS*, pp. 99–102. IOL MS. Panj B40, folios 51–53. *GR*, pp. 408–20.

[7] *Mih JS*, p. 499. The rationalized version is also related in W. L. M'Gregor's *History of the Sikhs*, published in 1846 (loc. cit., vol. i, pp. 36, 159–60).

[8] *Mih JS*, p. 449.

[9] IOL MS. Panj. B41, folio 122a. According to this version Gurū Nānak and Bhāī Bālā both committed the alleged offence. Their feet are said to have been pointing towards the tomb of Muhammad.

pointing towards 'Mecca',[1] a reference which suggests an original setting away from the city. Thirdly, it can be assumed that had the original location been Mecca the Gurū's feet would have been pointing towards the *Ka'bah* rather than a *miharāb*.

All of this concerns, however, the superstructure of the Mecca and Medina traditions and it offers only limited help as far as the basic question is concerned. Did Gurū Nānak visit Mecca and Medina? Regardless of the actual content of the tradition, can its geographical basis be accepted?

In support of the tradition there is the fact that its more significant portion is referred to by all our sources. There is no reference to Medina in the *Miharbān* and *Purātan* versions, but the janam-sākhīs all record a visit to Mecca and Bhāī Gurdās supports them. This means that once again we have a strong tradition and one which cannot be lightly dismissed. The Mount Sumeru *sākhīs* show, however, that a unanimity of this kind is not in itself sufficient to place an incident beyond question and the Mecca *sākhīs* reinforce this conclusion.

The arguments which can be brought against the Mecca tradition are not compelling to the point of absolute certainty, but they are sufficiently strong to raise very grave doubts. In the first place there is the inherent improbability of a non-Muslim entering the city in the manner indicated by the janam-sākhīs. The janam-sākhīs do indeed inform us that Gurū Nānak dressed for the occasion as a Muslim pilgrim, but they also describe additional articles of apparel which implied Hindu affiliations and confused his fellow pilgrims.[2] If we accept the possibility of such a visit we must also accept a complete disguise. This Gurū Nānak may have worn, but it implies a measure of conscious deception which is altogether uncharacteristic of him.

A second reason for questioning the tradition is the fact that Mecca and Medina are precisely the kind of places which one would expect to find figuring in the popular versions of the Gurū's travels. We have already observed how prominently the chief centres of Hindu pilgrimage figure in the descriptions of his journeys beyond the Pañjāb. In the same manner it is to be expected that the principal Muslim centres would also appear in the itinerary. This in itself does not prove that Gurū Nānak did not visit Mecca, but it does provide an alternative theory to account for the genesis of the Mecca and Medina *sākhīs*.

Thirdly, we must note the dominant element of the miraculous in all versions of the story, including that of Bhāī Gurdās. The conclusion which we must draw from this feature is that, despite their unanimity concerning the actual visit, the janam-sākhī descriptions of what took place during the

[1] *Pur JS*, p. 100. See *supra*, p. 49, n. 1.

[2] *Pur JS*, p. 98. In Miharbān's account it is the Gurū's name which marks him as a non-Muslim (*Mih JS*, p. 451).

visit cannot possibly be trusted. Their accounts of the discourses which Gurū Nānak held in the city indicate the same conclusion. Such discourses would have divulged his identity at once and brought either instant expulsion or death.

The first of these three arguments is the significant one and it is an argument which must lead us very near to outright rejection of the tradition. Adventurers such as Burton and Keane have proved the possibility of non-Muslims entering Mecca, but they have also shown that success in such an attempt could be attained only by means of a thorough disguise, both in outward appearance and in behaviour.[1] Gurū Nānak would doubtless have been sufficiently conversant with Muslim belief and practice to have sustained the disguise, but it would have been a violation both of his manifest honesty and of his customary practice of plain speaking. The ban has, it is true, been applied with particular strictness during more recent times. It nevertheless existed during the period of Gurū Nānak's travels and would certainly have prohibited the kind of open entry which the janam-sākhīs describe. We may acknowledge a visit to Mecca as a possibility, but it must be regarded as an exceedingly remote one. The same reasons apply with only slightly less emphasis to the tradition of a Medina visit, and in this case the absence of such a visit in the *Miharbān* and *Purātan* accounts provides an additional argument for rejection. The Mecca and Medina *sākhīs* must accordingly be classified as highly improbable.

The visit to Baghdad

References to a Baghdad visit occur in two of the older janam-sākhīs. Of these the earlier is evidently the *sākhī* describing such a visit which is to be found in the India Office Library manuscript B40.[2] This *sākhī* records a discourse with Sheikh Sharaf who, according to this account, dressed in women's clothing, and applied black collyrium to his eyes and henna to his hands. The discourse which the *sākhī* records consists almost entirely of a recitation by Gurū Nānak of three hymns in the *Dhanāsarī rāg*, none of which is to be found in the *Ādi Granth.*

The second reference occurs in Bhāī Gurdās's *Vār* 1 where two stanzas are devoted to a description of an incident in Baghdad.[3] Bhāī Gurdās's account bears no resemblance whatsoever to the B40 *sākhī*. Instead it records how Gurū Nānak, having arrived with Mardānā at the outskirts of the city, set up camp and then proceeded to utter the call to prayer.[4] Hearing this the astonished inhabitants of the city fell silent, and Gurū

[1] R. F. Burton, *A Pilgrimage to al-Madinah and Mecca*, vol. ii. J. F. Keane, *Six Months in the Hejaz*.

[2] IOL MS. Panj. B40, folios 200–2.

[3] *BG* 1. 35–36. The *Gyān-ratanāvalī* follows this account.

[4] The *bāṅg* normally uttered from a minaret by a *muezzin*.

Nānak was approached by a *pīr* who asked him to what order of faqīrs he belonged. A discussion ensued in the course of which Gurū Nānak assured the *pīr* that there exist many thousands of worlds both below and above the earth. To prove his claim he took the *pīr*'s son and, ascending with him into the air, revealed to him the multitude of heavens and underworlds. From above they descended into the nether regions and brought from there a bowl of *kaṛāh prasād*.[1] Gurū Nānak and Mardānā then left Baghdad and proceeded on their way to Medina and Mecca.

This is the testimony of the janam-sākhīs and it cannot be regarded as a strong one. In the first place there is the absence of any reference to such a visit in the *Miharbān* and *Purātan* janam-sākhīs. It is most unlikely that either would have omitted the tradition had it been known, and in this respect Miharbān's omission is of particular significance. Secondly, there is the fact that the B40 manuscript and Bhāī Gurdās record completely different traditions, the only point in common being the Baghdad location. Thirdly, neither of the traditions appears to offer an intrinsically convincing incident. Within the total range of janam-sākhī traditions Sheikh Sharaf is a ubiquitous figure who is to be found not only in Baghdad, but also in Pāṇīpat,[2] Bidar,[3] and Mecca.[4] In Bhāī Gurdās's account Dastgīr is the name given to the *pīr* with whom Gurū Nānak is said to have held discourse. Dastgīr is one of the more important of the numerous names given to the celebrated Sūfī 'Abd al-Qādir Jīlānī[5] and it seems clear that the name given by Bhāī Gurdās may be traced to this source. 'Abd al-Qādir Jīlānī spent most of his long life in Baghdad and subsequently came to be highly honoured in India as the *Pīr-i-pīrān*.[6] If this identification is correct the conclusion must be that we have in this Baghdad tradition another example of an association with a saint of acknowledged fame, introduced in order to magnify the fame of the Gurū. This is not to suggest that Bhāī Gurdās has related a deliberate falsehood. The likelihood appears to be that he has recorded a *sākhī* which had already evolved in oral tradition, gathering in the process a number of miraculous details. The silence of the *Miharbān* and *Purātan* janam-sākhīs indicates, however, that it could not have gained wide currency.

[1] The sacramental food of the Sikhs.

[2] *Pur JS*, p. 22. See *supra*, p. 39.

[3] IOL MS. Panj. B41, folio 187a.

[4] The *Nasīhat-nāmā* which follows the *Bālā* janam-sākhī in the IOL manuscript Panj. B41 names Sheikh Sharaf as one of the two Muslims with whom Gurū Nānak conversed in Mecca (MS. B41, folio 254).

[5] 'Abd al-Qādir of Jīlān, born 470 H. (A.D. 1077–78), died 561 H. (A.D. 1166), was the founder of the important Qādirī order of Sūfīs. *Encyclopaedia of Islam* (*New Edition*), vol. i, p. 71. See also J. A. Subhan, *Sufism: Its Saints and Shrines*, p. 178. The Qādirī order is particularly influential in India. A. J. Arberry, *Sufism*, p. 85.

[6] J. A. Subhan, op. cit., p. 264. The order was established in India in the fifteenth century by Sayyid Muḥammad Ghawth, tenth in the line of succession. He settled in Uch in A.D. 1428. Ibid.

By itself the testimony of the janam-sākhīs would permit us to classify the Baghdad visit as no more than possible, and the possibility would not be a strong one. In this particular case, however, the janam-sākhīs do not appear to stand alone. As in the case of the Dacca visit the authenticity of the Baghdad tradition has, it is generally believed, been established by the discovery of external evidence. Two inscriptions are said to have been found in Baghdad, both of them recording a visit to the city by Gurū Nānak.

For one of these two inscriptions we are bound to rely solely upon a poem published in 1919. It that year Swami Anand Acharya, who spent his later years living in Norway, published a book of English verse entitled *Snow-birds*,[1] and in this collection he included the following poem:

ON READING AN ARABIC INSCRIPTION IN A SHRINE OUTSIDE THE TOWN OF BAGHDAD, DATED 912 HEJIRA

Upon this simple slab of granite didst thou sit, discoursing of fraternal love and holy light, O Guru Nanak, Prince among India's holy sons!
What song from the source of the Seven Waters thou didst sing to charm the soul of Iran!
What peace from Himalaya's lonely caves and forests thou didst carry to the vine-groves and rose-gardens of Baghdad!
What light from Badrinath's snowy peak thou didst bear to illumine the heart of Balol, thy saintly Persian disciple!
Eight fortnights Balol hearkened to thy words on Life and the Path and Spring Eternal, while the moon waxed and waned in the pomegranate grove beside the grassy desert of the dead.
And after thou hadst left him to return to thy beloved Bharata's land, the fakir, it is said, would speak to none nor listen to the voice of man or angel;
His fame spread far and wide and the Shah came to pay him homage—but the holy man would take no earthly treasures nor hear the praise of kings and courtiers.
Thus lived he—lonely, devoted, thoughtful—for sixty winters, sitting before the stone whereon thy sacred feet had rested;
And ere he left this House of Ignorance he wrote these words upon the stone: 'Here spake the Hindu Guru Nanak to Fakir Balol, and for these sixty winters, since the Guru left Iran, the soul of Balol has rested on the Master's word—like a bee poised on a dawn-lit honey-rose.'[2]

This is the complete text. The author gives no further information concerning the location of the inscription or the circumstances under which it was discovered, and no one has subsequently found anything which corresponds to it.

In the case of the second inscription, however, the location is known and the inscription is accessible. To the south-west of modern Baghdad, in the

[1] London, Macmillan. [2] loc. cit., no. xc, pp. 182–4.

area occupied by the ruins of Old Baghdad, there is to be found the tomb of Bahlūl Dānā, believed to have been the court jester of Hārūn ar-Ras͟hīd. Niebuhr described it as follows:

> Pas loin de là [the tomb of Zobeida] se trouve le tombeau, d'un nommé Bahlul Dâne qui étoit parent du Calife Harun Erraschid et son boufon. On a de lui un livre rempli de petites historiettes, que de pauvres savans racontent encore le soir dans les Caffés. Dans l'inscription inserée au bas de cette page[1] que l'on n'a mise sur son tombeau, que long temps après sa mort, en 501, on le nommoit le Sultan des pauvres en esprit; mais suivant quelques histoires que l'on rapporte de lui il paroit avoir aussi eu ses intervalles de bon sens.[2]

This tomb is now housed in a small two-roomed building. In 1916 some Sikh soldiers discovered in this building a brief inscription which, it is claimed, makes explicit mention of Gurū Nānak.[3] The inscription is set above a niche in the north-eastern corner of the building and below it there is a platform. The discovery was published in the January 1918 issue of the *Loyal Gazette*, Lahore,[4] and since that time has been accepted as conclusive proof of a visit to Baghdad by Gurū Nānak.

The language of the inscription is Ottoman Turkish and efforts to translate it have produced several different versions. Five of these translations are given below:

1. In memory of the Guru, that is the Divine Master Baba Nanak Fakir Aulia, this building has been raised anew, with the help of Seven Saints; and the chronogram reads: 'The blessed disciple has produced a spring of grace'—year 927 H.[5]
2. Guru Murad died. Baba Nanak Fakir helped in constructing this building which is an act of grace from a virtuous follower. 927 A.H.[6]
3. Murad saw the demolished building of Hazrat Rab-i-Majid, Baba Nanak, Fakir Aulia, and rebuilt it with his own hands, so that historic memorial may continue from generation to generation, and His *murid-i-s'eed* (the blessed disciple) may obtain heavenly bliss.—Year 917 H.[7]
4. When Murad saw the building of Baba Nanak, the Prophet of God, fallen in

[1] *hād͟ha qabr sulṭān al-majdhūbīn wa'l-nafs al-muṭmasa sanat khumsumāyah wa-wāḥid.*

[2] Carsten Niebuhr, *Voyage en Arabie et en d'autres pays circonvoisins* (French translation, 1776), tome ii, pp. 245–6. See also J. Oppert, *Expédition Scientifique en Mésopotamie*, tome i, p. 98; and C. Huart, *Histoire de Bagdad dans les Temps Modernes*, Introduction, p. xii. Niebuhr, op. cit., tab. xliv, provides a map of Baghdad which shows the tomb of Bahlūl Dānā as no. 13. The legend has been omitted in Niebuhr, but is supplied in Huart's reproduction of the same map.

[3] The actual words are read as 'Bābā Nānak'. A description of the building, together with a diagram of it, is given in Sewaram Singh, *The Divine Master*, pp. 155–6. Photographs taken in 1964 and 1965 indicate that the building is in considerable disrepair.

[4] Khushwant Singh, *A History of the Sikhs*, vol. i, p. 34, n. 20.

[5] Teja Singh and Ganda Singh, *A Short History of the Sikhs*, vol. i, p. 12.

[6] Indubhusan Banerjee, *Evolution of the Khalsa*, vol. i, p. 73.

[7] Sewaram Singh, *The Divine Master*, p. 157.

ruins, he built a new one instead, with the help of his own hands so that it may stand as a monument in history for generations to come, and that the meritorious act of his fortunate disciple may last for aye.[1]

5. Whoever saw this sacred place of Baba Nanak faqir was granted fulfilment of his heart's desire by the Great God and Seven Angels helped him. Its date lies in line [*sic*] He caused a spring of Grace to flow for His lucky disciple—year 927 H.[2]

The two different readings of the concluding date are the result of an obscure second figure. Normally it should be possible to determine the value of the indistinct figure by calculating the value of the chronogram, but here too there are evidently differences of opinion. Vir Singh sets out the value of the chronogram as follows:

$$27+59+205+215+13+254+144 = 917.$$[3]

The writers who give 927 do not offer interpretations of the chronogram.

There are accordingly radical differences concerning the translation of the inscription and a fundamental disagreement concerning the reading of the date it gives, but no account of Gurū Nānak's travels written since 1918 has disputed the basic contention that the inscription refers to Gurū Nānak and proves that he visited Baghdad. Most writers have also accepted the authenticity of Anand Acharya's Arabic inscription and have inferred that the two inscriptions must describe a common event. The conclusion which follows is that Gurū Nānak conversed with 'Shah Bahlol, a local fakir'[4] or with 'a successor of Bahlol Dana'.[5] Vir Singh has offered a reconstruction based upon the two inscriptions and the account given by Bhāī Gurdās. His theory is that Gurū Nānak visited Baghdad twice. The first visit took place in A.D. 1506–7,[6] on the way to Mecca, and on this occasion the Gurū met Bahlol. The second visit was in A.D. 1511–12[7] and this time the discourse was with Dastgīr. Kahn Singh suggests a discourse with 'the descendants of Pīr Dastgīr, Bahlol, and other holy men'.[8] Several writers add that the discourse took place on the platform which is to be found beneath the inscription in the building which houses the tomb of Bahlūl Dānā. This assumption is evidently based upon the location of the inscription in relation to the platform, and upon Anand Acharya's 'slab of granite'.

Of these two inscriptions the Arabic one described by Anand Acharya must certainly be rejected as evidence of a visit to Baghdad. An inscription corresponding to the translation which he gives has never been discovered

[1] Kartar Singh, *Life of Guru Nanak Dev*, p. 214, n. 1. [2] Ibid.

[3] Vir Singh, *Gurū Nānak Chamatakār*, vol. ii, p. 664, n. *.

[4] Teja Singh and Ganda Singh, op. cit., p. 12.

[5] Kartar Singh, op. cit., p. 215. See also Sewaram Singh, op. cit., p. 155.

[6] 912 H., the date given by Anand Acharya.

[7] Vir Singh's reading of the date on the Turkish inscription. [8] *MK*, p. 622.

by anyone else, and without access to the original it is impossible to accept the Swami's poetic testimony as adequate evidence.

The most likely explanation of the missing original is that Anand Acharya's poem concerns not a separate inscription but the one which is to be found near the tomb of Bahlūl Dānā. The Swami might well have known of its existence and visited its location, for his book was published three years after its discovery. The experience which he records in the title of his poem could have taken place in or shortly after 1916.[1] Within the poem itself there are indications which point to an identification of his 'Arabic inscription' with the Turkish inscription. One such pointer is the name 'Balol' which he gives to the Gurū's disciple. The fact that this corresponds to the name of the court jester whose tomb lies near the Turkish inscription is much more likely to be a result of confusion than of coincidence. The reference to 'a shrine outside the town of Baghdad' also fits the Turkish inscription, and the 'simple slab of granite' may well be a poetic description of the platform beneath the inscription. Bahlūl Dānā's tomb is said to be adjacent to an old cemetery,[2] a location which would explain the Swami's reference to 'the grassy desert of the dead'; and the 'pomegranate grove' may perhaps correspond to the garden which is shown in diagrams of the tomb and its adjacent enclosure.[3]

In view of the translation difficulties which the Turkish inscription has presented the description of it as 'Arabic' need occasion no surprise, and the wording of the Swami's own translation probably arises from these same difficulties. If he did in fact see the Turkish inscription it would have been soon after its discovery and, consequently, prior to the more concerted efforts to produce a translation. The translation which he gives of the 'words upon the stone' is probably a poetic reconstruction, from memory, of an inscription only very imperfectly understood. The likelihood that he would have written from memory could also explain the date which he gives. It seems probable that Anand Acharya's poem represents an imaginative reconstruction of a Baghdad discourse, based upon the writer's recollection of a visit to the tomb of Bahlūl Dānā.

This leaves us with the Turkish inscription and in this connexion there are three basic questions which require answers. First, does the inscription actually refer to Gurū Nānak? Secondly, what date does it give? Thirdly, if it does refer to Gurū Nānak and if it does give a date which accords with the known events of his life, can it be accepted as authentic evidence of a visit to Baghdad? The writer owes the following comment to Dr. V. L. Ménage, Reader in Turkish at the School of Oriental and African Studies, London.

[1] It is also possible that he may have chanced upon the inscription before its reported discovery in 1916.

[2] Sewaram Singh, op. cit., p. 155.

[3] Ibid., p. 156. Vir Singh, op. cit., vol. ii, p. 663.

While in Baghdad in the summer of 1965 Miss D. Collon of the British Museum very kindly took a series of photographs of the inscription [in the tomb of Bahlūl Dānā], the clearest of which I enclose. She tells me that the inscription has been painted over several times with dark green paint, which has chipped in places and so made it difficult to read.

There is no doubt that the language is Ottoman Turkish and that the text is a quatrain, rhyming *aaba*, in the metre *mufta'ilun fā'ilun mufta'ilun fā'ilun*; this is a rather rare but standard metre of classical Persian and Turkish poetry.

Transliterating according to the system of the *Encyclopaedia of Islam*, I read the text as follows (lines 1 and 3 being certain, and line 4 practically certain):

1. Gör ne murād eyledi Ḥaḍret-i Rabb-i Medjīd
2. [five syllables] ola tā ki 'imāret djedīd
3. Yediler imdād edüb geldi ki tārīkhine
4. Yapdî thewāb edjr ede anî mürīd-i sa'īd

sene 917

1. See what the Glorious Lord proposed
2. [ ] that the building should be new.
3. The seven having given help, there came for the chronogram of it:
4. 'The blessed disciple performed a meritorious work; may He recompense it.'

year 917 [A.H. = A.D. 1511–12]

The five translations which you have shown me are all in varying degrees unsatisfactory.[1] Without going into detail, I mention three points which bear closely upon your problem:

(*a*) The word 'Guru' of versions 1 and 2 is a misreading of Turkish *gör* (line 1), 'see'.
(*b*) *murād* (line 1) is not a personal name, as versions 2, 3, and 4 interpret it, but bears its usual lexical meaning 'desire', 'wish'.
(*c*) The expression 'Glorious Lord' of line 1, correctly read in version 3 (i.e. 'Hazrat *Rab-i-Majid*'), and rendered 'Divine Master' in version 1, could not be applied to a human being, however saintly, but must refer to God.

The part of line 2 which I cannot understand is the passage where earlier translators have read *Bābā Nānak fakīr* or, more grammatically, *Bābā Nānak-i fakīr* (either six or seven syllables); and in the photograph the first letters certainly appear to be *bābānānk* and the next word, though not at all clear, might indeed be *fakīr*. But the metre indicates clearly that this section contains only five syllables and that they scan – ◡ ◡ – –. The word *baba* being Turkish, both its vowels are by nature short, but since it is legitimate in poetry to lengthen a short vowel if necessary, the word could be scanned *bābă*. It would, however, be a grave fault of prosody to shorten the long vowel of *Nānak* in order to satisfy the demands of the metre for the third syllable of the line. Hence *Bābă Nānak fakīr* does not fit the metre—and even if the reading is accepted the complete line does

[1] The same five translations are given above, pp. 128–9.

not make sense. I regret that I am unable to suggest the correct reading, but *Baba Nānak* seems to me to be excluded.

The last words of line 3 are an indication to the reader that line 4 constitutes a chronogram, i.e. that the total of the numerical values of the letters in it will reveal the date (by Muslim reckoning) of the event which the inscription commemorates. Vir Singh's calculation, giving 917, is based on two misreadings, the most serious of which arithmetically is *nwāb* = 59 for *t͟hwāb* = 509. My reading of the line gives 27+509+204+20+61+254+144 = 1219. However, the poet's ingenuity has not stopped here. The phrase 'The seven having given help' in line 3 does not refer merely to the Rid͟jāl al-g͟hayb, the invisible Helpers who, in popular Muslim belief, come to the aid of the distressed. It is also a warning that 7 has to be added to the total given by line 4. (Examples of such enigmatic chronograms are given by Salâhaddin Elker, *Kitâbelerde (ebced) hesabinin rolü*, in *Vakiflar Dergisi* iii (Ankara, 1956), 17–25, esp. p. 22.) Thus the date indicated by the quatrain is 1219+7 = 1226 A.H., i.e. 26 January 1811–15 January 1812.

The date in the cartouche below certainly appears in the photograph as 917 (A.D. 1511–12). It is impossible to reconcile this figure with the chronogram. Bearing in mind the points (1) that it would be very surprising to find an Ottoman Turkish inscription of this date in Baghdad (first occupied by the Ottomans only in 1534), (2) that riddling chronograms of this type do not make their appearance, so far as I know, until the eighteenth century, (3) that the figures in the cartouche have evidently been touched up, and (4) that the width of the cartouche seems appropriate to the accommodation of four figures rather than three, I am forced to conclude that the original reading in the cartouche was '1226', and that this is an Ottoman inscription of the early nineteenth century.

To answer your three questions: (1) Does the inscription refer to Gurū Nānak? Almost certainly not. (2) What date does it give? Apparently 1226 A.H. = A.D. 1811–12. (3) Can it be accepted as evidence of a visit by Gurū Nānak to Baghdad? No.

The janam-sākhī traditions offer insufficient evidence and the support hitherto claimed on the basis of the inscription must be withdrawn. Although there remains a possibility that Gurū Nānak visited Baghdad we are now compelled to regard it as an unsubstantiated possibility. The tradition may be classified with the possible *sākhīs*, for Baghdad was certainly not beyond the range of a traveller from India and access to the city would not have been refused as in the case of Mecca. The weakness of the evidence indicates, however, a remote possibility, not a strong one.

Bābur and the sack of Saidpur

Bābur is the only contemporary figure of any significance who is referred to by name in the works of Gurū Nānak, and with the exception of Bhāī Gurdās's *Vār* 1 the principal janam-sākhīs all record that the Gurū was present as a witness when the Mughal army assaulted the town of Saidpur.[1] The *sākhīs* which offer a description of his experiences on this occasion are of very considerable importance as they provide the only reference in the janam-sākhīs to a recognizable and datable event in contemporary Indian history.

The attack upon Saidpur was made during the third of Bābur's preliminary expeditions into North India. Mrs. Beveridge has described it as follows:

> The march out from Kābul may have been as soon as muster and equipment allowed after the return from Lamghān chronicled in the diary. It was made through Bajaur where refractory tribesmen were brought to order. The Indus will have been forded at the usual place where, until the last one of 932 A.H. (1525 AD.), all expeditions crossed on the outward march. Bhīra was traversed in which were Bābur's own Commanders, and advance was made, beyond lands yet occupied, to Sīālkot, 72 miles north of Lāhor and in the Rechna *dū-āb*. It was occupied without resistance; and a further move was made to what the MSS. call Sayyidpūr; this attempted defence, was taken by assault and put to the sword. No place named Sayyidpūr is given in the Gazetteer of India,[2] but the *Ayīn-i-akbarī* mentions a Sidhpūr which from its neighbourhood to Sīālkot may be what Bābur took.
>
> Nothing indicates an intention in Bābur to join battle with Ibrahīm at this time; Lāhor may have been his objective, after he had made a demonstration in force to strengthen his footing in Bhīra. Whatever he may have planned to do beyond Sidhpūr (?) was frustrated by the news which took him back to Kābul and thence to Qandahār, that an incursion into his territory had been made by Shāh Beg.[3]

According to Mrs. Beveridge this expedition was made in 1520.[4] If the janam-sākhīs' claim that Gurū Nānak was present at the sack of Saidpur can be established it follows that he must have returned, at least temporarily, from his travels by that year. The question then arises of whether or not this date assists us in determining the end of his period of travelling.

The janam-sākhīs relate that Gurū Nānak and Mardānā happened to reach Saidpur at a time when its Paṭhān inhabitants were celebrating numerous marriages. The *Purātan* version adds that on this occasion the Gurū was also accompanied by some faqīrs who were weak with hunger.[5] The travellers asked for food, but were everywhere refused. This so enraged the Gurū that he uttered the verse which is recorded in the *Ādi Granth* as *Tilaṅg* 5.[6] A brāhmaṇ who, it seems, had heard the verse and

[1] It is also spelt Sayyidpur. The early janam-sākhīs refer to it as Saidpur, Saidpur Saṇḍeālī, Saidpur Siriālī, and Saidpur Saloī (*Pur JS*, p. 58, n. †; *Mih JS*, p. 463). It is the modern Eminābād, nine miles south-east of Gujranwālā. The *GR* uses the modern name (p. 112).

[2] Saidpur and Eminābād are identified in the *Imperial Gazetteer of India*, vol. 12, p. 24, and also in the *Gazetteer of the Gujranwala District 1893–4*, p. 173.

[3] A. S. Beveridge, *The Bābur-nāma in English*, vol. i, p. 429.

[4] Ibid., p. 428. See also Leyden and Erskine, *Memoirs of Zehir-ed-Din Muhammed Baber* (1st edition, 1826), p. 286.

[5] *Pur JS*, p. 58.

[6] *AG*, p. 722.

who recognized it as a summons to Bābur to punish the ungenerous town, begged him to retract his curse. This the Gurū was unable to do, but he promised the brāhmaṇ that he and his family would be spared if they took refuge at a certain pool some distance outside the town.[1] Bābur then descended upon Saidpur, sacked it, put all of its inhabitants to the sword, and ravaged the surrounding countryside. All this had happened because the churlish people of the town had failed to show proper consideration towards faqīrs.

> Such was the destruction which Bābā (Nānak's) *śabad* brought upon the Paṭhāns. A Great Soul was filled with wrath and because faqīrs believe in God He hears their prayers. God hears the petitions of faqīrs and whatever is in a faqīr's heart He performs.[2]

Miharbān gives the same explanation for the town's misfortune. He concludes, as usual, with a *ślok* of his own.

> Those who do not heed a faqīr's request are tormented in Hell. Behold their condition! The slave of Nānak says, 'The beliefs of faqīrs are true; all else is false.'[3]

After this the two principal accounts diverge. The *Purātan* janam-sākhīs relate an interview with Bābur,[4] whereas the *Miharbān Janam-sākhī* describes an assault by Bābur on Ṭillā Bālgundāī.[5]

It is at once clear that much of what the janam-sākhīs relate must be rejected. The reason they give for the destruction of the town can be dismissed on rational grounds and also because it is completely out of character as far as Gurū Nānak is concerned. Nothing in his works, including the verse which is interpreted as a curse, offer the remotest sign that he could be capable of such vindictive behaviour. Most of the extra *Purātan* material,

[1] 'The Chaḍḍa (*sic* Chaḍḍhā, a khatri sub-caste) hold the *ak* sacred, because they say their forefathers once fought with Babar near Eminabad and all fell, save one who hid under an *ak* bush. He refounded the section and it still performs the *munnan* at Eminabad and worships the *ak*.' *A Glossary of the Tribes and Castes of the Punjab &c*, vol. ii, p. 518. This tradition and the janam-sākhī story evidently have a common origin.

[2] *Pur JS*, p. 59.

[3] *Mih JS*, p. 465.

[4] *Pur JS*, pp. 62–63. The *Hāfizābād* manuscript, which relates a longer interview with Bābur than the *Colebrooke* version, describes him as a clandestine *qalandar* (see *supra*, p. 44). The *Tārīkh-i-Dāūdī* also recounts a legend which depicts Bābur as a *qalandar*. This legend relates how a *qalandar* once visited Sultan Sikandar Lodī in Delhi. The Sultan accorded him due reverence and hospitality, and later learnt, to his great dismay, that he had missed an opportunity of capturing Bābur. The extract is translated in N. Roy's *Niamatullah's History of the Afghans*, part i, p. 123.

[5] A famous Kānphaṭ yogī centre thirteen miles west of Dīnā in Jhelum District. It is variously referred to as Ṭillā Bālgundāī, Bālnāth kā Ṭillā, Ṭillā Ḍaṅgā, Jogīān dā Ṭillā, and Gorakh Ṭillā. See G. W. Briggs, *Gorakhnāth and the Kānphaṭa Yogīs*, pp. 101 ff. Bābur evidently camped below the village on his way into north India in 1525, but the reference in the *Bābur-nāma* makes no mention of any encounter with the inhabitants. A. S. Beveridge, op. cit., vol. ii, pp. 452–3. For the *Purātan* and *Miharbān* accounts of the complete episode see *supra*, pp. 43–45 and 62 respectively.

which describes the actual encounter with Bābur, must also be repudiated as a legendary wonder story, and so too must the *Miharbān Janam-sākhī*'s account of an attack upon Ṭillā Bālgundāī. This latter addition is a clear example of a story which has evolved out of a reference in one of Gurū Nānak's works, in this case the fourth stanza of *Āsā aṣṭapadī* 12.[1]

All of this may be rejected, but it still leaves open the two basic questions. Was Gurū Nānak present during the sack of Saidpur, and did he meet Bābur?

The principal argument which has been advanced in support of his presence at Saidpur, and one which has hitherto been accepted as conclusive, is the fact that Gurū Nānak himself refers directly to Bābur and describes the devastation wrought by his army. These references occur in the hymns *Āsā* 39,[2] *Āsā aṣṭapadī* 11,[3] *Āsā aṣṭapadī* 12,[4] and *Tilaṅg* 5,[5] four verses which are collectively known as the *Bābar-vāṇī*, or 'utterances concerning Bābur'. All four are set by the janam-sākhīs in the context of either the assault on Saidpur or Gurū Nānak's subsequent interview with Bābur soon afterwards.

There can be no doubt that in these verses Gurū Nānak is describing at least one of the Mughal expeditions for he does so explicitly.

> Now that Bābur's authority has been established the princes starve.[6]
>
> Thousands of *pīrs* tried to stop Mīr (Bābur by means of magic) when they heard of his invasion. Resting-places were burnt, rock-like temples (were destroyed), princes were hacked into pieces and trampled in the dust. (In spite of the *pīrs*' efforts) no Mughal was blinded. None of the spells had any effect.[7]
>
> Thou didst spare Khurāsān and spread fear in Hindustān. O Creator, (Thou didst this), but to avoid the blame Thou didst send the Mughal as (the messenger of) Death.[8]

But to which of Bābur's expeditions does he refer? The indications are that the two *aṣṭapadīs*, at least, concern the later invasions of 1524 and 1525–6. Saidpur is nowhere mentioned and the descriptions hardly accord with the limited nature of the 1520 incursion.

In the first place, there is one reference which indicates that the Lodī rule had come to an end prior to the composition of the *aṣṭapadī* in which it occurs.

> The wealth and sensual beauty which had intoxicated them became their enemies. To the messengers (of Death) the command was given to strip

[1] *AG*, pp. 417–18. See below. An *aṣṭapadī* is a poem or hymn of eight, or occasionally more, stanzas. *Rāg Āsā* is one of the principal metres of the *Ādi Granth*.
[2] *AG*, p. 360. [3] *AG*, p. 417. [4] *AG*, pp. 417–18.
[5] *AG*, pp. 722–3. [6] *Āsā Aṣṭ* 11 (5), *AG*, p. 417.
[7] *Āsā Aṣṭ* 12 (4), *AG* pp. 417–18. [8] *Āsā* 39, *AG*, p. 360.

> them of their honour and carry them off. If it seems good to Thee Thou givest glory, and if it pleases Thee Thou givest punishment. Had they paused to think in time, then would they have received the punishment? But the rulers paid no heed, passing their time instead in revelry, and now that Bābur's authority has been established the princes starve.[1]

It seems clear that the reference here must be to the Lodīs, as there are no other 'rulers' or 'princes' to whom it could conceivably apply. These two stanzas bring out the point which Gurū Nānak makes in all four verses. The historical incident expresses for him a religious truth. It is for him an illustration of the truth that God's justice cannot be ignored, that the divine Order (*Hukam*) cannot be defied, that unrighteousness will be punished.[2] The Lodīs had acted in a manner contrary to the divine intention and they paid the inevitable penalty for having done so. This, however, must surely refer to the ultimate overthrow of the dynasty. The 1520 incursion was by no means a decisive defeat for the Lodīs and could scarcely be interpreted as the final penalty for their irresponsibility and unrighteousness.

Secondly, the description given of a battle fought by the Mughals and of the devastation caused by them does not tally with the evident nature of the 1520 expedition.[3]

> The Mughals and Paṭhāns fought each other, wielding swords on the battlefield. One side took aim and fired guns, the other urged on (its) elephants. They whose letters were torn in (God's) court had to die.[4] Hindu, Muslim, Bhaṭṭ, and Ṭhākur women (suffered), some having their *burqās* torn from head to toe, others being slain.[5] They whose handsome husbands failed to return home, how did they pass the night, (what grief they must have endured)![6]

[1] *Āsā Aṣṭ* 11 (4–5), *AG*, p. 417.

[2] In the case of *Āsā* 39 this is only a subsidiary theme and is limited to the last stanza.

> If anyone assumes an exalted name and indulges always in whatever his mind desires, he becomes as a worm in the sight of the Master, regardless of how much corn he pecks up. Die (to self) and you shall truly live. Remember the Name and you shall receive a portion.

The principal theme is the question of why the weak should suffer unmerited torment at the hands of the strong and in this respect the verse has obvious affinities with the Book of Job. God is called to account, just as Job summons Him, and the conclusion which Gurū Nānak reaches is expressed in the line:

> Thou dost unite and Thou dost divide; thus is Thy glory manifested.

The only solution to the problem lies in the absolute nature of the divine will and authority —absolute and ultimately beyond human comprehension. This differs from the point made in the other *Bābar-vāṇī* verses, but both themes directly concern the nature of the divine *Hukam*.

[3] See *supra*, p. 133, the second paragraph of Mrs. Beveridge's note.

[4] The reference is to the custom of making a small tear in obituary notifications.

[5] Literally: becoming inhabitants of the cremation ground.

[6] *Āsā Aṣṭ* 12 (5–6), *AG*, p. 418.

This reads much more like a description of an important battle and the victors' subsequent devastation than simply the account of a siege. A battlefield is explicitly mentioned and the presence of elephants suggests that it was no mere skirmish. The reference to the bereaved wives whose husbands failed to return home also points to a battle rather than to an incident which involved no more than the fall of a small besieged town, and the same indications are evident both in the preceding stanza and in the extract quoted above from *Āsā aṣṭapadī* 11. The episode which appears to correspond most closely to this combination of fixed battle and subsequent devastation is the incursion of 1524. On this occasion Bābur defeated the army led by Bihār Khān Lodī which Ibrāhīm Lodī had sent to Lahore, and then sacked the city.[1] Neither Talvaṇḍī nor Kartārpur is far distant from Lahore and we may assume that if Gurū Nānak were in the Pañjāb at the time he would certainly have been well acquainted with the incident.[2]

The implied destruction of Lodī authority, together with the nature of the warfare described in the *aṣṭapadīs*, plainly suggests that these two works at least were written after 1526 and that they were prompted not by a single event, but rather by the series of events which culminated in the overthrow of the Lodī dynasty. The other two verses offer no clear indications. The fact that both express the same *Hukam* theme as the two *aṣṭapadīs* may imply a date subsequent to the Lodī downfall, but the point is not brought out with sufficient clarity to enable us to attach much significance to it.[3]

There are, accordingly, two principal conclusions which may be drawn from the four *Bābar-vāṇī* compositions. The first is that Gurū Nānak must have personally witnessed devastation caused by Bābur's troops. There is in his descriptions of agony and destruction a vividness and a depth of feeling which can be explained only as expressions of a direct, personal experience. The actual battle described in *Āsā aṣṭapadī* 12 may possibly

[1] A. S. Beveridge, op. cit., vol. i, p. 441.

[2] According to some traditions the cryptic *ślok* which runs:

lāhor saharu jaharu kaharu savā paharu

refers to the 1524 attack on Lahore. Literally translated the *ślok* reads:

Lahore city, poison, violence, a watch and a quarter.

It is number 27 in the collection 'Surplus *śloks* left over from the *Vārs*', *AG*, p. 1412.

[3] *Tilaṅg* 5, *AG*, p. 723, contains an enigmatic line:

He will come in seventy-eight and go in ninety-nine, and another disciple of a warrior will arise.

The usual explanation is that this refers to Bābur's entry into India in S. 1578 (A.D. 1521–22) and to Humāyūn's departure in S. 1597 (A.D. 1540). The *marad kā chelā*, 'disciple of a warrior', is said to refer to Sher Shāh Sūr. (*Śabadārath*, p. 723, n. 4.) The objections to this interpretation are that the third and fourth expeditions evidently took place in A.D. 1520 and 1523–4 respectively, and that although Humāyūn was certainly defeated by Sher Shāh in 1540 the reference would be to an event which followed Gurū Nānak's death.

be based upon hearsay, but even here one is left with an impression of close proximity to the event. The second conclusion is that the four verses were probably composed after 1526 in response to the complete series of invasions, rather than in response to any single event within the series. *Āsā aṣṭapadī* 12, with its battle scene, evidently refers to a specific event, but the nature of the reference points to the 1524 capture of Lahore, not to the 1520 sack of Saidpur.

This does not necessarily mean, however, that there can be no truth in the janam-sākhī traditions concerning Gurū Nānak's presence as a witness during the sack of Saidpur. The support claimed on the basis of his four *śabads* must go, but there remain others. In the first place, the janam-sākhīs all agree on this point. Secondly, the tradition concerns an incident which happened in the Pañjāb during the latter part of the Gurū's life. Thirdly, there appears to be a measure of accuracy in the janam-sākhī descriptions of the actual assault. And fourthly, it seems reasonable to assume that had there been no factual basis for the connexion with Bābur the narrators would surely have chosen the capture of Lahore or the Battle of Pāṇīpat as a setting rather than an obscure town besieged on one of the minor expeditions. These factors indicate a strong tradition and one which has good claims to acceptance. We may conclude from the janam-sākhīs that Gurū Nānak was probably in the Pañjāb during 1520, and from the *Bābar-vāṇī* verses that he was almost certainly there in 1526.

The same cannot, however, be said for the claim that Gurū Nānak actually met Bābur. The *Miharbān Janam-sākhī* omits it, the *Purātan* janam-sākhīs give divergent accounts,[1] and the familiar tendency to introduce interviews with the acknowledged great offers a much more likely explanation of its origin. It cannot be ruled out as completely impossible, but it certainly appears to be most unlikely.

The founding of Kartārpur

The *sākhīs* which describe the founding of Kartārpur raise two issues. First, there is the question of whether or not the account they give of the origin of the village can be accepted; and secondly, that of the incident's location within the total framework of the Gurū's travels.

In these *sākhīs* we have both a Pañjāb setting and general agreement amongst the janam-sākhīs as far as the content of the incident is concerned, but we also have a number of minor miracles. According to the janam-sākhī accounts a certain rich official[2] set out with the intention of apprehending the Gurū, but was persuaded to forsake enmity for reverence after

[1] *Pur JS*, p. 65.

[2] He is referred to by the janam-sākhīs as a *karoṛī*, a high-ranking revenue collector of the Mughal period. The term came into use in the time of Akbar and is accordingly an anachronism in the janam-sākhīs.

being smitten on the way with blindness and other afflictions.[1] This aspect of the story must be rejected, but its elimination leaves the essence of the *sākhī* unaffected. With the miraculous element excluded we are left with a brief account of a man of substance who in some manner developed a great reverence for the Gurū, and who gave this reverence practical expression either by building the small village of Kartārpur, or, more likely, by donating the land on which it was subsequently built, and by erecting a *dharmsālā*.

There can be no doubt that Kartārpur, if not positively founded by or for Gurū Nānak, was at least transformed from insignificance to importance by his arrival there. The tradition that he actually founded the village, or that it was founded for him, appears to be much the stronger of the alternatives, for the janam-sākhīs are here dealing with an issue which has a local setting and which should evidently be placed in the last two decades of the Gurū's life. The land for such a village would have had to be procured in some manner and there is nothing which leads us to doubt the story that it was donated by a wealthy Sikh. To this simple statement of the village's origin miraculous elements were subsequently added in its oral transmission. Stripped of them the story offers no difficulties and can be accepted.

This disposes of the first question. The second one arises because the janam-sākhīs, while generally agreeing as far as the actual content of the *sākhī* is concerned, disagree regarding the point at which they introduce the incident. For Miharbān the founding of the village marks the completion of the Gurū's major travels,[2] whereas the *Hāfizābād* janam-sākhī places it at the conclusion of the first of the *Purātan* tradition's five journeys.[3] The *Gyān-ratanāvalī* offers yet another alternative by setting it at the end of the Gurū's visit to the north.[4]

This seems to present us with three possibilities, but in all probability there are only two. The acknowledgement of three possibilities assumes that the different travel itineraries can be compared and a decision made in favour of one of them. As we shall see, however, the likelihood is that all three should be rejected and accordingly the question at this point is whether the founding of Kartārpur took place at some unknown point during the Gurū's two decades of travel, or whether it took place after their conclusion. The *Hāfizābād* janam-sakhi and the *Gyān-ratanāvalī* offer the first alternative, and the *Miharbān Janam-sākhī* the second.

There is no evidence which will either establish the one or disprove the other, but the second appears the more likely. Even if Miharbān's chronology is suspect it is at least a more likely pattern than that developed by the *Purātan* tradition. Moreover, this particular incident is, in a sense, outside

[1] See *supra*, pp. 46, 63–64. See also *BG* 24. 1.
[2] *Mih JS*, p. 516.
[3] *Pur JS*, p. 74. The *Colebrooke* manuscript lacks this *sākhī*.
[4] *GR*, p. 401.

the problem of travel chronology as far as the *Miharbān* version is concerned, as it comes at the conclusion of the travel period. The *Miharbān* alternative is also more satisfactory in that a sustained period of travel seems more likely than two such periods broken by an interlude of settled life at Kartārpur. We may accept that the land was donated by a wealthy follower of the Gurū, and we may add that the village was probably built after the conclusion of the Gurū's travels. This recognizes the stronger likelihood of the *Miharbān* alternative without according it an unqualified acceptance.

The return to Talvaṇḍī

The *sākhīs* which describe Gurū Nānak's return to his home village record nothing of importance apart from the fact that he did return and that he was there reunited with his parents. Their significance lies rather in the differing points at which the janam-sākhīs introduce the incident, a question which has already been considered in connexion with the founding of Kartārpur. The descriptions of Gurū Nānak's reunion with his mother are among the most beautiful passages in the janam-sākhīs.

The visit to Pāk Paṭṭan

There seems to be little doubt that Gurū Nānak must at some time have met Sheikh Ibrāhīm, the contemporary incumbent of the Sūfī line descending from Sheikh Farīd.[1] Pāk Paṭṭan was within easy reach and Sheikh Farīd's reputation would certainly have exercised a powerful attraction. Even without the testimony of the janam-sākhīs such a meeting might well be regarded as a likelihood. There are evident inconsistencies in the janam-sākhī descriptions of the encounter, but they are in substantial agreement as far as the principal details are concerned. We may assume that the discourse which they record owes more to imagination than to an actual knowledge of the event, but there is nothing which suggests that the event itself is open to doubt. Accordingly, we may accept as a strong probability the tradition concerning a meeting in Pāk Paṭṭan with Sheikh Ibrāhīm, the contemporary successor of Sheikh Farīd.

Discourses with Siddhs

The janam-sākhīs record two famous encounters with Siddhs within or near the Pañjāb. Of these one must be regarded with some scepticism, but the other may perhaps be authentic if for Siddhs we read Kānphaṭ or Nāth yogīs.

[1] For an account of the life and work of Sheikh Ibrāhīm see Lajwanti Rama Krishna, *Pañjābī Ṣūfī Poets*, pp. 1–11.

The story of Gurū Nānak's disputation with the Siddhs at Gorakh-haṭaṛī[1] must be regarded with considerable doubt as the *sākhīs* which describe it in the *Purātan* and *Miharbān* versions are both unsatisfactory. In the *Purātan* janam-sākhīs it amounts to no more than a wonder story of how the Siddhs sought to overwhelm him by assuming fearsome forms through the exercise of their occult powers.[2] It appears that the *sākhī* must originally have developed without having any specific location assigned to it, for Bhāī Gurdās sets the same story in the context of the Achal Baṭālā disputation.[3] The *Miharbān Janam-sākhī* gives an entirely different description and one which is equally unsatisfactory. All that it tells us is that a religious fair was being held there and that Gurū Nānak held a discourse with 'the *gurū* of the yogīs'. Gurū Nānak may have visited the locality, but neither of these *sākhīs* can be accepted as sufficient evidence for such a visit.

The Achal Baṭālā encounter, however, has a firmer basis. Bhāī Gurdās,[4] the *Purātan* janam-sākhīs,[5] the India Office Library manuscript B40,[6] the *Gyān-ratanāvalī*,[7] the *Bālā* version,[8] and *Pothī Harijī* of the *Miharbān Janam-sākhī*[9] all record such a dispute, and the fact that Achal Baṭālā is so near Kartārpur enhances the likelihood of the tradition. Bhāī Gurdās and the B40 manuscript both name the occasion as a Śivrātri fair. As usual there are details in the various accounts which must be rejected, but the basis of the tradition appears to be well founded. Gurū Nānak's own works also offer it some support. The location is not named in any of his compositions, but it is clear from many of them that his contacts with Nāth yogīs must have been frequent and it seems evident from such a work as the *Siddh Goṣṭ*[10] that he engaged them in formal debate.

Visits to Multān

Multān, like Pāk Paṭṭan, was a place which would almost certainly have drawn a person such as Gurū Nānak, for it too was a renowned centre of Muslim devotion within easy reach of Talvaṇḍī and Kartārpur. There is, however, nothing which may, with any assurance, be added to this assumption. In the *Purātan* janam-sākhīs the only reference to Multān occurs in the *sākhī* which describes the death of Bahāuddīn, 'the Pīr of Multān'.[11] This does not establish a connexion with the city for, as we have already noted, the reference to Sheikh Bahāuddīn must be regarded as an anachronism.[12] It appears that Miharbān's description of a discourse with the *potā*

[1] Generally identified with an elevated area in Peshāwar. *MK*, Addendum, p. 43, and *A Glossary of the Tribes and Castes of the Punjab*, vol. i, p. 679.

[2] *Pur JS*, pp. 104–6. This version concludes with a verse which is by Gurū Arjan.

[3] *BG* 1. 41.

[4] *BG* 1. 39–44.

[5] *Pur JS*, *sākhī* 50, p. 97.

[6] IOL MS. Panj. B40, folio 117. This janam-sākhī records a second visit to Achal on folio 181.

[7] *GR*, *sākhīs* 170–7, pp. 463–508.

[8] *Bālā JS*, *sākhī* 61, p. 287.

[9] Khalsa College, Amritsar, MS. SHR: 427, *sākhī* 173, folio 344a.

[10] *AG*, pp. 938–46.

[11] *Pur JS*, *sākhī* 55, p. 108.

[12] See *supra*, p. 82.

of Bahāuddīn must likewise be rejected as an anachronism.[1] The term *potā* generally designates a son's son and although it is occasionally used of a descendant further down the male line it is highly unlikely that it will be applied beyond the sixth generation. This brings Miharbān's reference within the bounds of remote possibility, but there is nothing in the discourse which strengthens its claims.

The tradition related by Bhāī Gurdās[2] must also be set aside. The incident which he briefly recounts concerns a symbolic gesture which the *pīrs* of Multān are said to have made when they heard of the Gurū's approach. A cup filled to the brim with milk was sent out to him, the intention being to indicate that the city already held all the holy men it could contain. Gurū Nānak laid a jasmine petal on the milk and returned it, thereby proclaiming that there was still room for one more. This is an example of the kind of anecdote which gains common currency in hagiography. An earlier version of this particular legend is related in connexion with 'Abd al-Qādir Jīlānī (A.D. 1077–1166), the founder of the Qādirī order of Sūfīs.[3] The details differ,[4] but the story is essentially the same.

There is accordingly nothing in the janam-sākhīs which may safely be added to the assumption that Gurū Nānak probably visited Multān. It is possible that he may have had contact with descendants of Sheikh Bāhāuddīn and that to this extent there is an element of truth in the *Purātan* and *Miharbān* accounts. As they stand, however, all of the accounts which describe Multān visits must be rejected. We are left with no more than our initial assumption that the fame and proximity of Multān would almost certainly have led Gurū Nānak to visit the city at least once during his lifetime.

Gurū Aṅgad

The *sākhī* describing the manner in which Gurū Aṅgad was tested and found worthy of the succession has already been rejected,[5] but there can be no doubt that the other basic details recorded by the janam-sākhīs are substantially correct. To say that Gurū Aṅgad succeeded Gurū Nānak is to state the obvious and unchallengeable, for the *Ādi Granth* includes works

[1] *Mih JS*, *goṣṭ* 131, p. 434. See *supra*, p. 60. The IOL MS. Panj. B40, folio 53, also describes a meeting with the *potā* of Bahāuddīn, but sets it in Mecca.

[2] *BG* 1. 44. The story is repeated in the *GR*, *sākhī* 178, p. 508.

[3] J. P. Brown, *The Darvishes or Oriental Spiritualism*, ed. H. A. Rose, pp. 100–11.

[4] According to this version the city was Baghdad, the cup was filled with water, and the flower which 'Abd al-Qādir Jīlānī laid on it was a rose. This legend is given as the origin of the Qādirī custom of wearing an embroidered rose in the cap (J. A. Subhan, *Sufism: Its Saints and Shrines*, pp. 181–2). Another version of the same story is to be found in Parsi tradition (H. Jai Singh, *My Neighbours*, p. 56, following A. R. Wadia, art. 'Dadabhai Naoroji' in *Bhavan's Journal* of 7 Aug. 1960).

[5] See *supra*, p. 77.

by him and Sikh tradition could not possibly be mistaken on such a point.[1] Nor need we doubt the family background which the janam-sākhīs give, for here too tradition would have been reliable. We may accordingly affirm that Gurū Nānak's successor was Lahiṇā, a resident of Khaḍūr[2] and a Trehaṇ khatrī by caste; that he met the Gurū and became a follower after the settlement of Kartārpur; that the Gurū bestowed on him the name of Aṅgad; and that he chose him as his successor in preference to either of his sons.

Gurū Nānak's decision to appoint a formal successor was one of critical importance, for there can be no doubt that it was the establishment of an effective succession of Gurūs which, above all other factors, ensured the transmission of the first Gurū's teachings and the cohesion of the religious community which he had gathered around him. The choosing and formal installation of Aṅgad was the first step in the process which issued in the founding of the Khālsā, and ultimately in the emergence of a Sikh nation. Other factors, such as the clarity of the teachings, the compiling and promulgation of a canon of scripture, the ethnic constitution of the community, and the incentive to greater cohesion provided by Mughal persecution, certainly played very important parts, but it is inconceivable that these elements could have had the same enduring effect without the original bond provided by Gurū Nānak.

The chronology of Gurū Nānak's travels

The analysis of individual *sākhīs* is now complete, but there remains the broader question of the total framework which each janam-sākhī compiler has constructed with the *sākhīs* at his disposal. In this respect none of the janam-sākhīs agree. There is general agreement for the period up to Gurū Nānak's departure from Sultānpur, but for the years which follow this event the *Miharbān*, *Purātan*, and *Gyān-ratanāvalī* accounts all give differing chronologies, and that of the *Bālā* version is fragmented to a degree which appears to render it meaningless. Many of the incidents which provide the substance of these differing chronologies have already been discarded and most of the remainder have been classified as no more than possible *sākhīs*, but there still remains the question of whether or not we can accept in a general sense any of the patterns which are given in the different janam-sākhīs.

In this examination it is possible to work from two fixed points. Neither of these points can be regarded as beyond doubt, but both have been accepted in this study as at least probable. The first may be located about

[1] *Vār Rāmakalī* by Rāi Balvaṇḍ and Sattā the Ḍūm refers to Gurū Nānak's appointment of Gurū Aṅgad in stanzas 1–4 (*AG*, pp. 966–7). See *supra*, p. 8.

[2] Tarn Tāran tahsīl, Amritsar District.

the year 1500. An association with Daulat Khān Lodī has been acknowledged as likely and from this it follows that Gurū Nānak probably began his travels in or about that year. The actual date may have been a few years earlier, but is unlikely to have been much later as it must have been in or soon after 1500 that Daulat Khān received his appointment to Lahore. The second point which we are probably entitled to regard as fixed is 1520, the year in which Bābur sacked Saidpur.

The pattern which has been generally accepted is the one set out in the *Purātan* version. This involves four major journeys (*udāsīs*) to the east, south, north, and west respectively, with a brief concluding excursion to Gorakh-haṭaṛī. The Saidpur *sākhī* is included in the first of these, and between each of the journeys Gurū Nānak returns to the Pañjāb.[1]

The *Miharbān Janam-sākhī*, on the other hand, gathers the various *sākhīs* into only two journeys. The first of these is a round trip to the east and then to the south of India. The second is to the north and west, and includes a visit to Gorakh-haṭaṛī. The Saidpur *sākhī* follows Gurū Nānak's return from the west.[2]

The third grouping, that of the *Gyān-ratanāvalī*, follows the *Miharbān* pattern in a general sense as far as the journey to the east and the south is concerned, but divides the Gurū's subsequent travels into separate northern and western tours. The Saidpur *sākhī* is placed at the beginning of the second, or northern, journey.[3]

Of these three, the *Purātan* pattern is the least likely. The Saidpur *sākhī* follows shortly after the *sākhi* which describes Gurū Nānak's return to Talvaṇḍī at the conclusion of his eastern journey, and this return is said to have taken place twelve years after the departure from Sultānpur.[4] The proximity to the Saidpur incident suggests that this *sākhī* should, according to the *Purātan* reckoning, be placed in 1519 or 1520. This does not accord with the Daulat Khān date. Moreover, it means that the remaining four journeys and the period of consolidation at Kartārpur must all be fitted into the last nineteen or twenty years of the Gurū's life. This seems to be most unlikely.[5]

The *Miharbān Janam-sākhī* is also in conflict with the Daulat Khān date as it indicates that the period of travels began in 1506.[6] It is, however, much nearer to reasonable possibility in placing the Saidpur *sākhī* at the end of the major travels, and in this respect it would appear to offer a more likely chronology than the *Gyān-ratanāvalī* pattern which records the northern and western journeys after the Saidpur incident.

[1] See *supra*, pp. 64–65. [2] See *supra*, p. 66. [3] *GR*, pp. 265–75.

[4] *Pur JS*, p. 48. In specifying twelve years as the length of the journey the *Purātan* janam-sākhīs are evidently following convention. Twelve years was the usual time taken by sādhūs for a *tīrath-yātrā*, or visit to the important pilgrimage centres.

[5] See also *supra*, p. 32.

[6] See *supra*, pp. 55, 67.

Comparisons of this nature imply, however, that we are bound to accept one or other of the three recorded patterns. This is certainly not the case. There is a fourth possibility and it is a much more likely one. In all probability the janam-sākhī chronologies represent not known fact, but rather the results of the compilers' reasoning. In other words, it seems likely that what the janam-sākhīs offer us are structures which have been devised in order to provide logical sequences for the stock of oral *sākhīs* at the compilers' disposal. This process need not have been a wholly conscious one. On the contrary, it is more likely to have been a gradual evolution rather than a deliberate ordering of isolated *sākhīs* at a particular point in time.

This is the conclusion indicated by the India Office Library manuscript B40. In this version the individual *sākhīs* are, for the most part, set down in isolation and only rudimentary efforts have been made to organize them into something resembling a sequence. The manuscript makes it plain that many of the incidents are set outside the Pañjāb, but it does not use them to construct an integrated itinerary. This manuscript offers a more primitive janam-sākhī than the *Miharbān* and *Purātan* janam-sākhīs or the *Gyān-ratanāvalī*, and the contrast between its lack of order and the developed continuity of the later versions strongly suggests that integrated itineraries should be regarded as a characteristic of the later stages of the janam-sākhī evolutionary process.

Such a conclusion should not, of course, imply that Gurū Nānak never travelled. All sources agree that he did and traditions which emerged within a century of his death could hardly have been mistaken in a general issue of such importance. This we can certainly accept, and we may also assume that the period of his travels probably covered the first two decades of the sixteenth century. The probable association with Daulat K͟hān Lodī provides a beginning for the period, and the likelihood that Gurū Nānak was present at Saidpur in 1520 indicates a probable terminus. Certainly he must have been back in the Pañjāb by 1526 at the latest. Within this period, however, it is possible to name neither destination nor sequence. The most we can do is accept as inherently probable Bhāī Gurdās's statement that Gurū Nānak travelled round visiting centres of pilgrimage.[1]

Gurū Nānak's life now falls into three clearly defined periods. The first three decades comprise his childhood and early manhood in Talvaṇḍī and Sultānpur. This first period evidently culminated in an experience of enlightenment and divine call. The fourth and fifth decades are the period of his travels in and possibly beyond India. The remaining two decades were then spent chiefly in Kartārpur, and we may assume that it was during this period that the real foundations of the Sikh community were laid.

[1] *BG* I. 25.

The life of Gurū Nānak

We may now proceed to relate the life of Gurū Nānak.

Gurū Nānak was born in A.D. 1469, probably in the month of April. His father was Kālū, a Bedī khatrī living in the village of Rāi Bhoi dī Talvaṇḍī, and his mother was named Tripatā. Kālū and Tripatā had one other child, a daughter whose name was probably Nānakī and whose husband's name was Jai Rām. Gurū Nānak was married to the daughter of Mūlā, a Choṇā khatrī of Baṭālā who had formerly resided in the village of Pokho di Randhāvī. His wife's name was Sulakhaṇī and two sons, Lakhmī Dās and Sirī Chand, were born to them.

As a young man Gurū Nānak worked in the town of Sultānpur, probably in the employment of Daulat Khān Lodī. This must have been during the last decade of the fifteenth century. While in Sultānpur he experienced a sense of divine call and it was evidently in response to this that he began a period of travelling in and perhaps beyond India, accompanied for at least some of the time by a bard named Mardānā. Neither the pattern nor the extent of his travels can be determined, but it may be assumed that he visited a number of the more important centres of both Hindu and Muslim pilgrimage. The period of travelling probably ended in or shortly before 1520 as it seems likely that Gurū Nānak witnessed Bābur's attack upon the town of Saidpur in that year. It appears, however, that the references he makes to Bābur in his works point rather to the invasions of 1524 and 1525–6.

At some stage a wealthy follower evidently donated land on the right bank of the Rāvī and there the village of Kartārpur was built. This probably took place after the Gurū's travels had ended. For the remainder of his life he lived in Kartārpur, but made brief journeys from there to places within easy reach. These destinations probably included Pāk Paṭṭan and Multān. Contacts with Nāth yogis were frequent and on one occasion the Gurū evidently engaged a group of them in debate at the village of Achal Baṭālā.

During his years in Kartārpur Gurū Nānak must have attracted many disciples, one of whom was Lahiṇā, a Trehaṇ khatrī of Khaḍūr. Lahiṇā must have impressed the Gurū by his devotion and ability, for prior to his death Gurū Nānak renamed him Aṅgad and appointed him as his successor in preference to either of his sons. The Gurū died in Kartārpur towards the end of the fourth decade of the sixteenth century, probably in September 1539.

In this brief account we have everything of any importance which can be affirmed concerning the events of Gurū Nānak's life. It provides us with an outline, but it is a meagre one, leaving lengthy periods covered by no more than a general comment or a single detail. And yet in spite of this paucity of authentic biographical material there is much we can know about Gurū Nānak. In the numerous works by him which are recorded in the *Ādi Granth* we do not find biographical details but we do find a developed theology which points back to a person. It is to his teachings that our search for the historical Nānak must lead us for it is there only that we can hope to find him.

In the janam-sākhīs what we find is the Gurū Nānak of legend and of faith, the image of the Gurū seen through the eyes of popular piety seventy-five or a hundred years after his death. It is an important image, but it is not the primary object of this study. Here we seek the person who lived and taught in the Pañjāb almost five hundred years ago. Of this person the janam-sākhīs provide only glimpses and by their inadequacy force us back to the works preserved in the *Ādi Granth*. It is true, as we have several times observed, that the *śabads* and *śloks* attributed to Gurū Nānak are not sources of detail concerning the events of his life. As one might reasonably expect, however, it is also true that behind these works and the thought which they contain there can be discerned a personality. Our study of his teachings must be, in part at least, an exercise in discernment.

5

THE TEACHINGS OF GURŪ NĀNAK

> Nānak, without the indwelling Name of God one endures suffering throughout the four ages.[1]
>
> What terrible separation it is to be separated from God and what blissful union to be united with Him![2]

TERSE expression is common in the writings of Gurū Nānak and we find examples in these two extracts. Both concern the ultimate purpose of all life and all religion, and set it forth as union with God through the indwelling Name, an inward union which imparts eternal bliss. He who recognizes this, who accepts the proffered means and so attains such union, transcends the cycle of birth and death and passes instead into a condition of beatitude, infinite, eternal, and ultimately inexpressible.

Such a summary statement, however, can have meaning only in the light of a developed understanding of Gurū Nānak's beliefs. Who, or what, is this God with whom union is sought? Of what nature is He? Is He to be conceived in terms of personality? In what way is His being expressed to man? And what is man? Of what nature is his condition that he should seek to transcend it? What are the proffered means and how does he appropriate them? Having appropriated them how can he describe his regenerate condition, in so far as words are able to describe it? These and many other related questions must be answered if we are to reach an adequate understanding of Gurū Nānak's beliefs, of what may properly be called his theology.

Theology is the correct word to use in this connexion, for the whole of Gurū Nānak's thought revolves around his understanding of the nature of God. It was entirely appropriate that Gurū Arjan should place a declaration of the nature of God at the very beginning of the *Ādi Granth* and that it should be called the *Mūl Mantra*, the Basic Credal Statement.[3] Of all Sikh scripture none is more important than Gurū Nānak's *Japjī*, and in this work of surpassing beauty (which significantly follows immediately after the *Mūl Mantra* in the *Ādi Granth*)[4] the theme is God, the One whom men must praise and who yet far exceeds the most exalted conception which the mind of man can form. It is theology which we find in the *śabads* and *śloks* of Gurū Nānak and it is theology of a refined quality.

[1] *Tukhārī Chhant* 2 (4), *AG*, p. 1110.
[2] *Mārū* 1, *AG*, p. 989.
[3] *AG*, p. 1.
[4] *AG*, pp. 1–8.

This theology is not, of course, set out in any systematic form. Gurū Nānak's writings bear witness to his experience of God and the characteristic expression of that experience is the hymn of praise which it engenders. Neither Gurū Nānak nor Gurū Arjan, who compiled the *Ādi Granth*, sought to set out his beliefs in an integrated pattern and we should not expect them to have done so. Theirs was essentially a religion of experience, the 'real' rather than the 'notional'. The latter can, however, do much to impart an understanding of the former. 'Theology', as Professor Basil Willey reminds us, 'is the notional formulation of what the experience seems to mean'.[1] For the purpose of our own understanding an integrated pattern can do much to clarify the nature of Gurū Nānak's belief and accordingly the intention of this section is to seek such a pattern.

The fact that Gurū Nānak's thought is not set out systematically does not mean that it is necessarily inconsistent. On the contrary, one of the great merits of his thought is its very consistency. The accusation of inconsistency has been levelled against him,[2] but we believe that the system outlined in the present chapter will constitute a rebuttal of the charge. One can gauge the importance of this aspect of Gurū Nānak's works by comparing them with those of other *bhagats*. Kabīr's thought, for all its striking qualities, is by no means as consistent doctrinally as that of Gurū Nānak. In Nānak's case the consistency is there even if it is not at once apparent. There is certainly that doctrinal tension which is inevitable in a system upholding both the gracious activity of an absolute God and the necessary participation of man endowed with free will, but the person who seeks to extract the components of Gurū Nānak's thought and to fashion with them a systematic theology does not have to decide between statements which are mutually incompatible. Nor indeed does he have to grapple with the degree of obscurity which is found in so much of Kabīr's thought.

The comparison with Kabīr is an instructive one at this point. Gurū Nānak and Kabīr both offer syntheses and in each case the nature of the synthesis reflects the personality of its author. This is a point of critical importance as far as the subsequent effect of their thought is concerned. Kabīr was above all a mystic and the pattern of his thought is determined by this quality. The result is both profundity and obscurity. Kabīr's works have commanded an immense popularity ever since they were first circulated, but the popularity has been accorded to thoughts in isolation, not to an integrated pattern of belief. It has been the pithy saying, the striking aphorism, which has brought Kabīr his popularity. Those who claim direct allegiance to him, the Kabīr-panthīs, possess a system of belief, but it is one

[1] Basil Willey, *Nineteenth Century Studies*, Penguin edition, p. 104.

[2] J. E. Carpenter, *Theism in Medieval India*, pp. 477–8. J. N. Farquhar, *An Outline of the Religious Literature of India*, p. 337. Nicol Macnicol, *Indian Theism from the Vedic to the Muhammadan Period*, pp. 146, 153. E. Trumpp, *The Ādi Granth*, p. cv.

which only remotely resembles the original teaching of the sect's eponymous founder.

Gurū Nānak, on the other hand, produced a coherent pattern and one which, with some additions by later Gurūs, is followed to this day by orthodox Sikhism. In his own way Gurū Nānak was also a mystic and, as with Kabīr, the climax of his thought is to be found in an ineffable union with God, the Formless One. The climax itself was beyond analysis or expression, but not the path to it, and in this respect Gurū Nānak is much clearer than Kabīr. A person of pronounced mystical inclinations would doubtless find in Kabīr's works something of the depth of meaning which Kabīr himself had experienced, but most men would not. Many could, however, appreciate the pattern which Gurū Nānak sought to expound, for it is expressed in terms which are much more readily understandable. The fact that Gurū Nānak appointed a successor to continue his work is of primary importance as far as the perpetuation of his teachings is concerned, but it is not the only reason to account for the existence of modern Sikhism. The clarity and coherence of his thought have also been factors of fundamental significance.

For Gurū Nānak the meaning and purpose of human existence centres in the divine existence of the Eternal One, He who creates, sustains, and destroys, He who having created reveals Himself in His creation, He who by His grace communicates to man the way of salvation and calls forth the response which enables him to appropriate that salvation. Set over against this sovereign Master is man who, in his unregenerate condition, manifests a corrupt nature cutting him off from the divinely proffered way of salvation. Perverse and wayward, deluded by the transitory attractions of this world and the creature of evil impulses, he lives a life which binds him more firmly to the wheel of transmigration and condemns him to an endless cycle of death and rebirth.

To all men, however, is held out the means of escape from the misery of this self-centred life and continued transmigration. By His divine Order (*Hukam*) God has so created and regulated the world that the perceptive man can see in it an expression of the Creator's nature. The prerequisite perception is awakened in man by the *Gurū*, by the voice of God mystically uttered within. He who hears and responds to the *Gurū* will, through his response, begin to comprehend the Word (*Śabad*) of God made manifest in all that lies around him and in all that he experiences within himself. The necessary response is that of adoring love expressed through meditation on the Name (*Nām*) of God, on the nature of God communicated through His creation and through human experience within the creation. He who submits himself to this exacting discipline is cleansed from his impurities and grows progressively nearer to God. Ascending to higher and yet higher levels of spiritual perception he finally reaches the ultimate, a condition of ineffable union with the Eternal One in which all earthly bonds are dissolved and the cycle of death and rebirth finally brought to an end.

Many of these concepts Gurū Nānak shared with other earlier and contemporary religious figures, including Kabīr.[1] It is at once evident that his thought is closely related to that of the Sant tradition of Northern India and there can be no doubt that much of it was derived directly from this source. This is not, however, a sufficient answer to the question of his antecedents. Three issues require consideration in order to elicit this answer. First, there is the problem of how the Sant tradition itself evolved. Secondly, there is the question of other influences which may have operated upon the thought of Gurū Nānak, a question which chiefly concerns the extent of direct Islamic influence. Thirdly, there is the impact of Gurū Nānak's own originality upon the inheritance which he received. Of these three the second is comparatively unimportant. The system developed by Gurū Nānak is essentially a reworking of the Sant pattern, a reinterpretation which compounded experience and profound insight with a quality of coherence and a power of effective expression.

The Sant tradition of Northern India (the Nirguṇa Sampradāya)[2]

For the vast majority of Gurū Nānak's contemporaries, both Hindu and Muslim, the essence of religion was to be found in external authority and conventional ceremony. In the case of the Hindu community this authority was generally accorded to the brahmaṇs and through them to the Vedas and Purāṇas. The required response consisted in the performance of the customary rites appropriate to a man's station within the caste structure of society. For the Muslim also religion meant loyalty to an objective authority. In his case the authority was the Qur'ān and its exercise the acknowledged function of the qāzīs.

These conventional patterns did not, however, command universal acceptance. Customary religion had received numerous challenges and of the dissenting movements three were of particular importance. There was, first, the tradition of Vaiṣṇava bhakti which had spread to Northern India from the south, and which in the north was associated, above all other names, with that of Rāmānand. For bhakti the essential religious response was love, and in Vaiṣṇava bhakti this love was directed to one of the *avatārs* of Viṣṇu. Secondly, there was the ancient tradition of tantric yoga, expressed in Northern India during this period by the numerous adherents

[1] Cf. also F. R. Allchin, 'The Place of Tulsī Dās in North Indian Devotional Tradition', *JRAS*, parts 3 and 4 (1966), p. 140.

[2] For an explanation of the terms *Sant* and *Nirguṇa Sampradāya* see the Glossary, p. 245. The term *Nirguṇa Pantha* is also commonly used. The North India tradition should not be confused with the Vārkarī sect of Paṇḍharpur in Maharashtra, the exponents of which have commonly been referred to as *sants*. It seems highly probable, however, that Namdev provides a direct link between the two *Sant* traditions. See *infra*, p. 154.

of the Kānphaṭ or Nāth sect of yogīs. The sect was divided into various sub-sects, all claiming allegiance to the semi-legendary Gorakhnāth and all following essentially the same *haṭha-yoga* technique.[1] Thirdly, there were the members of the Sūfī orders, numerically far fewer than the adherents of orthodox Islam, but exercising a perceptible influence on the religious thought and practice of Hindus as well as Muslims.

Within each of these religious groupings there was a recognizable continuity, but none of them was completely insulated. All were to some extent influenced by one or more of the others and underwent corresponding modifications. In one significant case this reciprocal exchange issued not simply in the modification of an existing tradition, but in the emergence of a recognizable synthesis, a new pattern which in various respects strongly resembled other existing patterns but which in its wholeness corresponded to none of them. This was the Sant tradition of Northern India. The new movement was by no means the dominant religious tradition during this period, but it was certainly the most fertile and, as we have already observed, it is of fundamental importance as far as Gurū Nānak's religious antecedents are concerned.

The Sant tradition was essentially a synthesis of the three principal dissenting movements, a compound of elements drawn mainly from Vaiṣṇava bhakti and the *haṭha-yoga* of the Nāth yogīs, with a marginal contribution from Sūfism. For the Sants, as for the Vaiṣṇava *bhagats*, the necessary religious response was love, and for this reason the movement has frequently been regarded as an aspect of Vaiṣṇava bhakti.[2] In several respects, however, the Sants disagreed with traditional bhakti and some of these differences were fundamental. Their love was offered not to an *avatār*, but direct to the supreme God Himself, and their expression of this love was through strictly inward meditation and devotion. It was, moreover, a method which involved suffering, or at least some appreciable difficulties. It was not the easy path of traditional bhakti.

In spite of these differences bhakti elements provided the principal contribution to the Sant synthesis, particularly during the earlier stages of its development. Traces of Nāth influence are by no means absent during these earlier stages, but nor are they prominent and in some cases they may represent subsequent additions. It is not until the time of Kabīr that Nāth concepts assume a significant role. In the thought of Kabīr such concepts

[1] Gorakhnāth must be accepted as an historical figure, but practically all that is related concerning him must be regarded as legend. His period is uncertain, but appears to have been between the ninth and twelfth century A.D. See G. W. Briggs, *Gorakhnāth and the Kānphaṭa Yogīs*, pp. 228 ff., 250; M. Eliade, *Yoga: Immortality and Freedom*, p. 303; Rangey Raghava, *Gorakhnāth aur unkā yug*, pp. 29, 43. For a brief account of the Nāth sect see the Glossary, p. 243. The members of the sect are variously referred to as Nāth yogīs, Kānphaṭ ('split-ear') yogīs, and Gorakhnāthīs.

[2] The frequent use of Rām, as a name of God, and of other Vaiṣṇava names and epithets by the Sants has obviously encouraged this misunderstanding.

are both prominent and integral, and it is accordingly at this point that we encounter the developed synthesis. Nāth influence emerges in much of the basic terminology used by Kabīr (and later by Gurū Nānak), in a rejection of all exterior forms, ceremonies, caste distinctions, sacred languages, and scriptures, in a strong emphasis upon unity as opposed to 'duality', and in the concept of a mystical union which destroys this 'duality'. It is not without significance that the commonest of all terms used by both Kabīr and Gurū Nānak to express this experience of union is *sahaj*, a word which at once carries us back into Nāth theory and beyond the Nāth tradition into the earlier world of tantric Buddhism. The bhakti influence retains its primacy, but the Nāth content of Kabīr's thought is also of fundamental importance.

The Sants were monotheists, but the God whom they addressed and with whom they sought union was in no sense to be understood in anthropomorphic terms. His manifestation was through His immanence in His creation and, in particular, through His indwelling within the human soul. It was there that He, by grace, revealed Himself, and man's proper response was a love expressed through meditation on the divine Name. External authorities and ceremonies were useless for this purpose and religious texts, idol worship, formal religious exercises, pilgrimage, and ritual bathing were all accordingly rejected. The inward way to God was open to all who were prepared to accept the difficulties and the discipline which it would involve, and so caste was rejected also. Great importance was attached to the *gurū*, who might be a human teacher or who might be understood not as a person but as the inner voice of God. No value was accorded to celibacy or asceticism. Hindu and Muslim sectarian notions were spurned, not because the two systems were regarded as basically true, but because both were regarded as radically wrong and ultimately futile.[1]

These beliefs the Sants expressed not in the traditional Sanskrit, but in a language which was closely related to that of the common people to whom they addressed their teachings. Within the tradition and amongst other sādhūs there evolved a language which, with minor modifications, was used by Sants all over northern India. This language has been called *Sādhukkaṛī*. Its basis was Khaṛī Bolī, the dialect spoken around Delhi, and to this were added elements drawn from Old Rajasthānī, Apabhraṃśa, Pañjābī, and Persian.[2] Most of the Sants were from low caste groups and in such cases were generally poorly educated or completely illiterate. For this reason their compositions were usually oral utterances which came to be written down only after a period of circulation.

The first of the great Sants was Nāmdev (A.D. 1270–1350)[3] who lived in

[1] A particularly clear summary of the characteristics of the Sant movement is given by Dr. Charlotte Vaudeville in her *Au Cabaret de l'Amour: Paroles de Kabîr*, pp. 7–9.

[2] Ch. Vaudeville, *Kabīr Granthāvalī* (*Dohā*), Introduction, pp. iv–v. Traces of Marāṭhī influence are evident in the works of Nāmdev and Trilochan.

[3] R. G. Bhandarkar, *Vaisnavism, Saivism, and Minor Religious Systems*, p. 92, disputed

Maharashtra and whose name is closely linked with the Vārkarī sect of Paṇḍharpur. The Vārkarī sect was well within the bhakti tradition and its worship centred on the famous idol of Viṭṭhal[1] which was located in Paṇḍharpur. Elements of traditional Vaiṣṇava bhakti are evident in Nāmdev's work, but his primary emphases are clearly in accord with Sant concepts. His influence extended into northern India as a result of his Hindi works and possibly as a result also of an extended visit to the Pañjāb. Doubts have been expressed concerning the assumption that the author of the Hindī works is the same Nāmdev as the famous Marāṭhī *bhagat* of Paṇḍharpur, but recent comparisons of the Hindī and Marāṭhī compositions have established it as at least a strong probability.[2]

The tradition of a Pañjāb visit must still be regarded as open to some doubt. According to this tradition Nāmdev spent twenty years in Ghuman, a village in the Baṭālā tahsīl of Gurdāspur District. In Ghuman itself the tradition is both strong and old, and there is certainly nothing improbable in a Sant wandering so far from home, but the complete absence of any reference in the older Marāṭhī accounts of Nāmdev's life raises an objection which cannot be overlooked. The tradition may still be regarded as possible, but certainly not as established.

The second of the important Sants was Raidās, an outcaste leather-worker (*chamār*) of Banāras.[3] Chronologically Raidās follows Kabīr, but his work corresponds more closely to that of Nāmdev. It belongs to the earlier stage of the Sant movement, to the stage in which the links with Vaiṣṇava bhakti are much more prominent and the evidence of influence from other sources much slighter. The Vaiṣṇava concept of the divine *avatār* is rejected, and likewise all external ceremonies or aids to worship,[4] but the nature of the devotion offered by these earlier Sants resembles the adoration of the *bhagats* rather than the deeply mystical experience of Kabīr.[5] There is also a stronger emphasis upon the immanence of God in external phenomena than in Kabīr's works.[6] In the latter the emphasis moves more to the inner revelation within the human soul.

these traditional dates, claiming that Nāmdev's works indicate a period one hundred years later. Recent work by Marāṭhī scholars favours the traditional dates. The question is fully discussed by Bhagirath Misra and Rajnarayan Maurya, *Sant Nāmdev kī Padāvalī*, pp. 9–31.

[1] A manifestation of Kriṣṇa.

[2] Bhagirath Misra and Rajnarayan Maurya, op. cit. There are sixty-one of Nāmdev's Hindī verses in the *Ādi Granth*. *Ślok* 241 of the Kabīr *śloks* (*AG*, p. 1377) may be by Nāmdev.

[3] In the *Ādi Granth* he is called Ravidās, and in it there are thirty-nine of his *śabads*. The number is generally given as forty, but *Soraṭhi* 4, *AG*, p. 658, and *Mārū* 2, *AG*, p. 1106, are the same composition. *Ślok* 242 of the Kabīr *śloks* (*AG*, p. 1377) may also be by Ravidās.

[4] Cf. Ravidās, *Dhanāsarī* 3, *AG*, p. 694.

[5] Nāmdev: *Gond* 3, *AG*, p. 873; *Bhairau* 7, *AG*, p. 1164; *Sāraṅg* 3, *AG*, pp. 1252–3. Ravidās: *Soraṭhi* 3, *AG*, pp. 658–9; *Gūjarī* 1, *AG*, p. 525.

[6] Nāmdev: *Tilaṅg* 2, *AG*, p. 727; *Goṇḍ* 2, *AG*, p. 873; *Malār* 1, *AG*, p. 1292. Ravidās: *Sirī Rāgu* 1, *AG*, p. 93; *Malār* 2, *AG*, p. 1293.

Little is known about Raidās's life and all that we can accept is contained in the occasional references which he makes in his works. In several verses he refers to his low caste status as a *chamār*,[1] and in one to his work as a cobbler.[2] Elsewhere he describes how the members of his caste carry away the cattle carcases from Banāras.[3] The tradition that he was a disciple of Rāmānand must be rejected. The traditional link between Rāmānand and Kabīr is barely plausible on chronological grounds, and it is evident that Raidās was younger than Kabīr. This is the conclusion which is indicated by the references which he makes to Kabīr[4] and it places him beyond the time of Rāmānand. Moreover, there is no hint of such a relationship in any of his works.

Raidās makes the characteristic Sant emphases, with an evident stress upon the irrelevancy of caste in all that concerns a man's salvation. An even stronger emphasis, and one which is peculiarly his own, is a recurring note of humility and confession. Raidās is a particularly attractive figure and one who has yet to receive the attention he deserves.

With Kabīr the Sant tradition moves into a more complicated phase. As in the case of Raidās little is known concerning his life, although a considerable quantity of legend has gathered around him.[5] The traditional date of his death, A.D. 1518, appears to be at least a definite likelihood, but his traditional date of birth, A.D. 1398, must be regarded as highly improbable. No definite year can be given to replace it, but a date in the vicinity of 1440 would appear to be reasonable.[6] Kabīr's life was spent in Banāras and his death probably took place in the village of Magahar, twenty-seven miles south-east of Bastī. His caste was that of *julāhā* and it seems clear from his works that he followed, in a somewhat erratic manner, his caste's hereditary occupation of weaving. Recent research has established a Nāth background as a strong probability. It now seems clear that

[1] Ravidās: *Gauṛī* 2, *AG*, p. 345; *Gauṛī Bairāgaṇi* 1, *AG*, p. 346; *Gauṛī Pūrabī* 1, *AG*, p. 346; *Āsā* 3, *AG*, p. 486.

[2] Ravidās: *Soraṭhi* 7, *AG*, p. 659.

[3] Ravidās: *Malār* 1, *AG*, p. 1293. A hymn attributed to the *bhagat* Dhannā and evidently revised by Gurū Arjan repeats this information concerning Raidās (Dhannā, *Āsā* 2, *AG*, p. 487).

[4] Ravidās: *Āsā* 5, *AG*, p. 487; *Mārū* 1, *AG*, p. 1106; *Malār* 2, *AG*, p. 1293.

[5] See Ahmad Shah, *The Bījak of Kabīr*, introductory chapter 'The Life of Kabīr in Legend', pp. 1–28.

[6] Ch. Vaudeville, *Au Cabaret de l'Amour: Paroles de Kabîr*, pp. 10–11. The question of Kabīr's dates is discussed at some length by Parasuram Chaturvedi, *Uttarī Bhārat kī Sant-paramaparā*, pp. 709–33. Chaturvedi decides in favour of A.D. 1448 as the date of Kabīr's death. The principal reason leading him to this conclusion appears to be a memorial in Magahar which is said to bear a date equivalent to A.D. 1450 (see *Archaeological Survey of India (New Series): the Monumental Antiquities and Inscriptions in the North Western Provinces and Oudh*, vol. ii, p. 224). Another reason may perhaps be a desire to maintain the traditional connexion with Rāmānand. The fact that 1518 has been consistently maintained in tradition in spite of its manifest conflict with the Rāmānand relationship is one of the principal arguments in favour of the later date. Another is the convergence of the Hindu and Muslim traditions at this point.

Kabīr belonged to a family of non-celibate yogīs converted only recently, and to a considerable degree superficially, to Islam.[1] The traditional association with Rāmānand cannot be rejected outright, but it is a most unlikely one. It involves chronological difficulties and the only references which Kabīr makes to Rāmānand are to be found in works of doubtful authenticity.[2] The numerous references which Kabīr does make to a *gurū* point unmistakably to the *Satgurū* within, the voice of God within the human soul.

The compositions attributed to Kabīr are seemingly numberless, but only two collections have adequate claims to be regarded as genuine. These are the *Kabīr-granthāvalī* and the selection included in the *Ādi Granth*.[3] To these the *Bījak* may be added, but with reservations. The *Bījak* is later than the other two collections and must be regarded as a Kabīr-panthī recasting rather than as the original work of Kabīr. There can be no doubt that the works included in the two older collections have also been altered in oral transmission, but to an appreciably lesser degree than those of the *Bījak*. The famous translation by Tagore from a collection made by Kshitimohan Sen cannot be accepted as authentic.[4]

The basis of Kabīr's belief was not, as has been commonly supposed, Vaiṣṇava bhakti or Sūfism but tantric yoga. Kabīr's name is certainly a Muslim one, but it has always been clear that his knowledge of Islam was relatively slight. In contrast to this there is a wealth of *haṭha-yoga* terminology and a thought-structure with obvious resemblances to that of the Nāths. In the light of this contrast the theory that Kabīr belonged to a caste which had recently been converted from tantric yoga to Islam is at once convincing.

Kabīr was, however, far from being a Nāth yogī. To this background he brought elements from Vaiṣṇava bhakti and perhaps from Sūfism also. His debt to the *bhagats* is evident in the primacy accorded to love, and his concept of such love as a way of suffering may possibly reflect, in some measure, a debt to the Sūfīs. These and other elements from the same sources he compounded with his own mystical nature and produced the synthesis which is the distinctive religion of Kabīr. It is a religion which in true Sant style renounces all that is mechanical or external, affirming as

[1] Ch. Vaudeville, *Kabīr Granthāvalī (Dohā)*, p. viii.

[2] *Bījak, śabad* 77. Tagore, *One Hundred Poems of Kabir*, no. xxix, p. 36.

[3] The *Ādi Granth* includes 226 *śabads* by Kabīr. Of these 225 are to be found in the *bhagat bāṇī* at the end of the various *rāgs*, and the remaining one is included amongst the works of Gurū Arjan (*Bhairo* 3, *AG*, p. 1136). The total number of Kabīr *śloks* included in the *Adi Granth* is either 237 or 239. The collection entitled *Ślok Bhagat Kabīr jīu ke* (*AG*, pp. 1364–77) has 243, but of these five are by Gurū Arjan (nos. 209, 210, 211, 214, 221), one by Gurū Amar Dās (no. 220), and two (nos. 241 and 242) may possibly be by Nāmdev and Ravidās respectively. Two extra *śloks* by Kabīr are included in the *bhagat bāṇī* of *Rāg Mārū*, *AG*, p. 1105. There are also three longer works: the *Bāvan Akharī* (*AG*, pp. 340–3), the *Thintī* (pp. 343–4), and the 'Seven Days' (pp. 344–5). A number of *śloks* are to be found in *vārs* (*AG*, pp. 509, 555, 947, 948), but all of these are duplicated in the collection at the end of the *Ādi Granth*.

[4] Rabindranath Tagore, *One Hundred Poems of Kabir*.

valid only that which may be experienced inwardly. Within a man's soul God may, by grace, reveal Himself. The revelation comes, however, only to him who has prepared himself to receive it. The way of preparation is the path of love, a love addressed directly to the supreme Lord who is both transcendent and immanent, and a love which will inevitably involve long periods in the anguish of separation. Few will have the courage to undertake it and fewer still the persistence to follow it to the point of revelation. The point at which the revelation occurs cannot be foreseen. It comes at the divine initiative and it comes with suddenness. God, the True Gurū (*Satgurū*), discharges the arrow of the Word (*Śabad*) and man is slain that in death he may find true life. This life is to be found in mystical union, an ineffable experience of dissolution in the divine.[1]

There is inevitably much that must remain obscure in Kabīr's attempts to describe his experiences, for they were of a fundamentally mystical quality and, as Kabīr himself repeats, ultimately inexpressible. There is also a measure of inconsistency in his utterances. In his efforts to impart some impression of his mystical experience he has frequent recourse to monistic terminology, but he uses it in senses which are his own. Monistic concepts certainly influenced him, but it seems clear from what he indicates concerning his own understanding of the nature of his relationship with God that his thought must be regarded as monotheistic, not monistic.[2] The works of Kabīr represent the highly personal record of an individual experience, but they nevertheless place him well within the framework of Sant beliefs.

It was this Sant tradition which provided the basis of Gurū Nānak's thought, an inheritance which, like Kabīr, he reinterpreted in the light of his own personality and experience. This is not to imply that he should be regarded as in any sense a disciple of Kabīr. There is no sound evidence to support the popular tradition that Gurū Nānak met Kabīr and little to suggest that he knew any of his works.[3] It is, however, clear that the Sant tradition was by far the most important element in all that he inherited from his past or absorbed from contemporary patterns.

This leads to the second question concerning the antecedents of the thought of Gurū Nānak, the question of direct influences which operated independently of his Sant inheritance. The dominant issue in this respect must be the extent of his debt to Islamic sources. Nāth beliefs certainly exercised an influence and we encounter many examples of Nāth terminology in his works,[4] but in so far as these influences and terms constitute integral expressions of his own beliefs they represent aspects of the Sant

[1] Ch. Vaudeville, *Au Cabaret de l'Amour: Paroles de Kabîr*, pp. 25–37.

[2] Ch. Vaudeville, art. 'Kabīr and Interior Religion' in *History of Religions*, vol. 3, no. 2, pp. 197–8, and *Au Cabaret de l'Amour: Paroles de Kabîr*, pp. 221–2.

[3] See *supra*, pp. 85–86.

[4] Cf. *Vār Malār*, *slok* 1 of *pauṛī* 27, *AG*, pp. 1290–1.

inheritance. Gurū Nānak himself explicitly rejected Nāth beliefs[1] and his works bear clear witness to open controversy with Nāth yogīs. Nāth concepts were communicated to his thought through Sant channels which transformed their meaning, and in his usage such elements are, for the most part, naturalized. They are recognizably of Nāth derivation but they belong to the Sants, not to the Nāths.

Muslim influence

Sikhism has commonly been regarded as a blend of Hindu beliefs and Islam, and if for Islam we substitute Sūfism there appears, at first sight, to be much to support this view. It is at once evident that many elements in the thought of Gurū Nānak have affinities with Sūfī concepts and this would seem to suggest strong Sūfī influence. In his works we find an emphasis upon the unity of God, a revelation in creation, the paradox of God transcendent as well as immanent, an expression of God in terms of light, a perverse human organ[2] which requires purification, a doctrine of grace, an emphasis upon the suffering involved in separation from the Beloved, a concept of *nām simaran*[3] which appears to combine elements of both the *dhikr* and *murāqabat* of the Sūfīs, an ascent to union through a number of stages, a purging of self and an ultimate union which, although they are nowhere explicitly defined, do not appear to be inconsistent with the Sūfī notions of *fanā'* and *baqā'*. He also shares with many Sūfīs a belief in the needlessness of asceticism on the one hand, and upon the snare of worldly wealth on the other. In a few instances we encounter references which appear to be obvious echoes of the Qur'ān.

The appearance is, however, misleading. Affinities certainly exist, but we cannot assume that they are necessarily the result of Sūfī influence. Other factors suggest that Sūfism was at most a marginal influence, encouraging certain developments but in no case providing the actual source of a significant element.

In the first place, there is the fact that the Pañjābī Sūfism of Gurū Nānak's period had evidently departed radically from the classical pattern of Arab and Persian Sūfism. Gurū Nānak himself indicates this condition in references which place Sūfīs under the same condemnation as the conventional qāzīs and mullahs.[4] Classical Sūfism evidently had little opportunity to influence him, for there is no evidence to suggest that he came in contact with it during his formative years, nor even in subsequent years.

The evidence which can be derived from his works points not to a regular

[1] An arresting example is the verse *Sūhī* 8, *AG*, p. 730. See *infra*, p. 211.

[2] Gurū Nānak's *man* and the *dil-rūh-sirr* complex of the Sūfīs.

[3] 'Remembering the Name.' See *infra*, pp. 214–19.

[4] Cf. *Sirī Rāgu Aṣṭ* 17 (3), *AG*, p. 64; *Vār Mājh, ślok* 1 of *pauṛī* 13, *AG*, p. 143; *Gauṛī Aṣṭ* 14 (7), *AG*, p. 227.

direct contact with members of Sūfī orders, but rather to the kind of informal contact with ordinary Muslims which would have been inevitable in his circumstances. Amongst those Muslims there would certainly be some strict Sunnīs and we can assume that there would also be a number who might fitly be described as Sūfīs. The majority would, however, represent in varying degree the blend of modified orthodoxy and debased Sūfism which was dominant in the Muslim community of the Pañjāb during this period. Such contacts would explain the occasional references which seem to echo the language of the Qur'ān. It is, however, most unlikely that they could have had any significant positive influence upon the thought of Gurū Nānak, for they represented contacts with a version of Islam which he explicitly rejected.

Secondly, there is a conspicuous lack of Sūfī terminology in the works of Gurū Nānak. Even when a Sūfī term makes an appearance it is rarely used in a sense implying the precise meaning which it would possess in Sūfī usage, and in some cases such terms are introduced with the patent intention of providing a reinterpretation of their meaning.[1] This contrasts significantly with a wealth of Sant terminology and imagery derived from Hindu sources. Almost all of his basic terminology is of native Indian derivation. In choosing names of God his preference is strongly for Hindu names, and when dealing with a concept which has obvious affinities with Sūfī belief he will almost always use a non-Sūfī term.

Thirdly, we must observe that although there are certainly strong resemblances to Sūfī thought, almost all of the evident affinities can, with equal cogency, be traced back to native Indian sources. This is not to affirm that we must in all cases seek an Indian source; merely that an apparent affinity need not necessarily point to a Sūfī source.

Fourthly, there is the fact that in some fundamental respects Gurū Nānak's thought is in direct conflict with that of the Sūfīs. The obvious example of this is his acceptance of the doctrines of *karma* and transmigration.

Finally, and most significant of all, an examination of the more important points at which Muslim influence has been claimed can do little to support the claims made in this respect. The Islamic insistence upon the Divine Unity would presumably have strengthened the monotheistic basis of Gurū Nānak's thought, but his monotheism must be regarded primarily as an inheritance from the Bhakti Movement mediated through the Sant tradition. The word *hukam*, which possesses a particular significance in the thought of Gurū Nānak, is certainly an Arabic word, but the concept which it expresses is not a borrowing from Islam.[2] His doctrine of *nām simaran* does not correspond to the Sūfī technique of *dhikr*, and the five *khaṇḍs*, or 'realms', of *Japjī*[3] do not correspond, even remotely, to the *maqāmāt* of the Sūfīs.

[1] e.g. *faqīr* and *darveś*.

[2] See *infra*, pp. 199–203.

[3] *Japjī* 34–37, *AG*, pp. 7–8. See *infra*, pp. 221–24.

Muslim influence upon the thought of Gurū Nānak must accordingly be regarded as relatively slight. This conclusion should not, however, be pressed to the point of totally rejecting all such influence. The Sant tradition had already absorbed a limited measure of Islamic influence and this was obviously mediated to Gurū Nānak as a part of the Sant synthesis. Most of the elements in the thought of Gurū Nānak which suggest Muslim influence evidently descended to him in this indirect manner, for they are elements which he shared with his Sant predecessors. Instances of this are the encouragement which, we must assume, Islam provided in strengthening monotheistic tendencies, and the indeterminate pressure which the egalitarian emphasis of Islam exercised upon the Bhakti Movement. We may also assume that Sūfism, as opposed to orthodox Islam, must have subscribed to the characteristic Sant belief in the omnipresence of God, a feature of fundamental importance in the thought of Gurū Nānak.

To this we must add the likelihood that the Islam of Gurū Nānak's own environment must have exercised some direct influence, although here too stress must be laid upon the apparently limited nature of such influence. Very occasionally an evident borrowing can be detected, an example of which appears to be the 'veil' which conceals the Truth from man's perception.[1] Even here, however, we must observe that the debt is limited to the imagery and that Gurū Nānak imparts his own particular meaning to the Sūfī figure.

The conclusion to which we are led is that Islamic influence evidently operated upon the thought of Gurū Nānak, but that in no case can we accord this influence a fundamental significance. Sūfī and Qur'ānic imagery have certainly made their impress, and there must have been encouragement of tendencies which accorded with Sūfī teaching, but no fundamental components can be traced with assurance to an Islamic source. Gurū Nānak's principal inheritance from the religious background of his period was unquestionably that of the Sant tradition and evidence of other independent influences is relatively slight. We must indeed acknowledge that the antecedents of Sant belief are by no means wholly clear and that within the area of obscurity there may be important features which derived primarily from Sūfī sources. The complexity of the subject leaves some room for doubt and we are accordingly bound to own that at least some of our conclusions must be regarded as tentative, not as definitively established. It appears, however, that Sant belief owes none of its basic constituents to the Sūfīs. For Sant belief the major source is to be found in the Bhakti Movement, with Nāth theory entering as a significant secondary source.[2]

[1] *Japjī* 1, *AG*, p. 1.

[2] For a more detailed treatment of the question of Islamic influence see W. H. McLeod, 'The Influence of Islam upon the Thought of Gurū Nānak' in *History of Religions*, vol. 7, no. 4.

From this conclusion it follows that a common interpretation of the religion of Gurū Nānak must be rejected. It is not correct to interpret it as a conscious effort to reconcile Hindu belief and Islam by means of a synthesis of the two. The intention to reconcile was certainly there, but not by the path of syncretism. Conventional Hindu belief and Islam were not regarded as fundamentally right but as fundamentally wrong.

Neither the *Veda* nor the *Kateb* know the mystery.[1]

The two were to be rejected, not harmonized in a synthesis of their finer elements. True religion lay beyond these two systems, accessible to all men of spiritual perception whether Hindu or Muslim. It was the person who spurned all that was external and who followed instead the interior discipline of *nām simaran* who could be called a 'true' Hindu or a 'true' Muslim. Such a person had in fact transcended both.

It is accordingly incorrect to interpret the religion of Gurū Nānak as a synthesis of Hindu belief and Islam. It is indeed a synthesis, but one in which Islamic elements are relatively unimportant. The pattern evolved by Gurū Nānak is a reworking of the Sant synthesis, one which does not depart far from Sant sources as far as its fundamental components are concerned. The categories employed by Gurū Nānak are the categories of the Sants, the terminology he uses is their terminology, and the doctrines he affirms are their doctrines. This is not to suggest, however, that Gurū Nānak's thought was a precise copy of what earlier Sants had developed. He inherited the components of his thought from the Sants, but he did not transmit his inheritance unchanged. He received a synthesis and he passed it on, but he did so in a form which was in some measure amplified, and in considerable measure clarified and integrated. This applies in particular to his understanding of the manner of divine communication with man. Gurū Nānak's concepts of the *Śabad*, the *Nām*, the *Gurū*, and the *Hukam*[2] carry us beyond anything that the works of earlier Sants offer in any explicit form. It is Sant thought which we find in his works, but it is Sant thought expanded and reinterpreted. The result is a new synthesis, a synthesis which is cast within the pattern of Sant belief but which nevertheless possesses a significant originality and, in contrast with its Sant background, a unique clarity. It possesses, moreover, the quality of survival, for it remains today the substance of a living faith.

The verses which have been used in the following analysis are those which are recorded in the *Ādi Granth*. There have, as one would expect,

[1] *Mārū Solahā* 2 (6), *AG*, p. 1021. *Kateb* designates the Qur'ān. Sikh theology has traditionally interpreted *Kateb* as the four 'Semitic texts', namely the *Torah*, the *Zabūr* (*Psalms*), the *Iñjīl* (Gospel), and the Qur'ān. Cf. also *Vār Āsā*, *ślok* 1 of *pauṛī* 6, *AG*, p. 465, and *BG* 1. 33.

[2] The Word, the Name of God, the divine Preceptor, and the divine Order.

been many other compositions attributed to Gurū Nānak,[1] but none of these have been used as there can be no guarantee, or even likelihood, of their authenticity. The restriction involves no appreciable loss, for the *Ādi Granth* contains a substantial number of works by Gurū Nānak.[2] These can all be accepted as authentic. It is clear that Gurū Arjan compiled the *Ādi Granth* with considerable care and the principal source which he used was a collection which had been recorded at the instance of the third Gurū, Amar Dās, who was only ten years younger than Gurū Nānak.

Two things remain to be added before beginning the analysis. The first must be a strong emphasis upon the primacy of religious concerns in the thought of Gurū Nānak. This has already been observed in the case of the celebrated verses which refer to Bābur where the purpose is not to provide a description of a Mughal invasion but to illustrate the fate of the unrighteous.[3] The message is religious, not political. The Lodīs had sinned and their misfortunes were the penalty for their sins. The same applies to a group of three *śloks* which are commonly quoted as evidence that insecurity and decadence were dominant features of the India of Gurū Nānak's time.[4] The three *śloks* refer to a far broader span of space and time than the period of the Gurū's own lifetime. Their primary application is to the whole of the present cosmic age, not to the contemporary conditions of the Lodī Sultanate or the early Mughal administration. The condition of degeneracy which they express is a characteristic of the *Kaliyug*, the era of ultimate degeneracy in the cosmic cycle, and although the specific conditions of the Gurū's own times would certainly be regarded as a reflection of this perversion they would, in this respect, be no different from those of other historical periods and other places. The issue is that of Truth, the quality which is so conspicuously absent in the *Kaliyug*. The absence of Truth means darkness and the unconquered self brings suffering.

This pursuit of Truth and so of salvation was, for Gurū Nānak, mankind's paramount concern, and as a result his comment on contemporary conditions relates almost exclusively to attitudes, customs, and institutions which obstructed this quest. Political, social, and economic issues find expression in his works only in so far as they relate to the pattern of religious salvation which he upheld, or to contemporary patterns which he rejected. This is not to deny that details relating to such issues can be gleaned from his works, and it is obvious that his teachings have had effects which

[1] The janam-sākhīs contain numerous apocryphal works attributed to Gurū Nānak, the most important of them being the *Prāṇ Saṅgalī* (*Pur JS*, pp. 89, 118).

[2] Kahn Singh, *MK*, p. 327, gives the figure 947 as the total of all Gurū Nānak's *śabads*, *śloks*, *chhants*, *pauṛīs*, etc. in the *Ādi Granth*.

[3] See *supra*, p. 136. Cf. also *Vār Malār*, *ślok* 2 of *pauṛī* 22, *AG*, p. 1288.

[4] *Vār Mājh*, *ślok* 1 of *pauṛī* 16, *AG*, p. 145; *Vār Āsā*, *ślok* 1 of *pauṛī* 11, *AG*, p. 468; and *Vār Rāmakalī*, *ślok* 1 of *pauṛī* 11, *AG*, p. 951. The *Mih JS* sets these *śloks* in the context of the Mount Sumeru discourse. See *supra*, p. 60.

extend far beyond a recognizably religious context. Nor should it suggest that he was uninterested in human joy or human suffering. The *Bābar-vāṇī* verses make it abundantly clear that the wretchedness inflicted by Bābur's army had evoked a deep pity. There remained, however, the conviction of a condition transcending the misery and decay of this life. Gurū Nānak's concern was accordingly for salvation, for personal salvation and for the salvation of others.

Finally, it must be emphasized that this analysis concerns the theology of Gurū Nānak and not the theology of Sikhism. The two are largely but not completely coterminous and at one important point there is divergence. A theology of Gurū Nānak as opposed to Sikh theology must omit the contributions of Gurū Amar Dās, Gurū Rām Dās, Gurū Arjan, and Gurū Gobind Singh, and of concepts which evolved during the eighteenth century. In the case of the third, fourth, and fifth Gurūs the omission concerns amplifications which are certainly valuable, particularly in the case of Gurū Arjan, but which involve no significant modification of the pattern set out by the first Gurū. With Gurū Gobind Singh, however, comes the institution of the Khālsā, and finally the emergence of the belief that with his death in 1708, and the consequent termination of the line of personal Gurūs, the function of the Gurū had been vested in the scripture (the *Ādi Granth*) and in the corporate community (the Khālsā). This is of considerable importance. For modern Sikhism the scripture exists as a channel of communication between God and man, but obviously this could be no part of Gurū Nānak's theology. It must be understood, however, that this doctrine, its significance notwithstanding, is no more than a supplement to the teaching imparted by Gurū Nānak. The theology of Gurū Nānak remains the substance of Sikh belief.

I. THE NATURE OF GOD

1 om sati nāmu karatā purukhu nirabhau niravairu akāl
mūrati ajūnī saibhan gur prasādi[1]

At no point is Gurū Nānak's quality of terseness better illustrated than in the *Mūl Mantra*, the basic theological statement with which the *Ādi Granth* opens. Principal Jodh Singh paraphrases it as follows:

This Being is One. He is eternal. He is immanent in all things and the Sustainer of all things. He is the Creator of all things. He is immanent in His creation. He is without fear and without enmity. This Being is not subject to time. He is

[1] The *Mūl Mantra*, *AG*, p. 1. The title *Mūl Mantra*, or 'Basic *Mantra*', was applied to an abbreviated form of this invocation by Bhāī Gurdās (*BG* 6.19). Gurū Nānāk himself declared that *Harinām*, the Name of God, was the *Mūl Mantra* (*Mārū Solihā* 20, *AG*, p. 1040). The two usages are not in conflict.

beyond birth and death. He is Himself responsible for His own manifestation. (He is known) by the *Gurū's* grace.[1]

Almost all accounts of Sikh belief refer to the *Mūl Mantra* and in Sikh commentaries considerable space is devoted to its exegesis.

In itself, however, the statement conveys relatively little. To a devout Sikh it imparts a wealth of meaning, but only because he has behind him an understanding of what the individual words mean. In themselves the words are not self-explanatory and in isolation may be interpreted in ways which would not accord with a comprehensive statement of Gurū Nānak's theology. The symbol *Om* is particularly open to misinterpretation if it be read without reference to Gurū Nānak's other works[2] and it is by no means self-evident why Dr. Jodh Singh should paraphrase *sati nāmu* as 'He is eternal'. It is in the light of the total range of Gurū Nānak's thought that the *Mūl Mantra* is to be interpreted, for it is the expression of his thought throughout his *śabads* and *śloks* which gives particular meaning and substance to each of the words. The *Mūl Mantra* may well serve both as a starting-point and as a final summary, but much remains to be filled in between the two.

1. *The unity of God*

At the very beginning of the *Mūl Mantra* stands the figure 1 and Sikh tradition is unanimous in accepting this as a declaration of the unity of God.[3] The conclusion is entirely reasonable, for the emphasis is strongly made in Gurū Nānak's works.

> The Lord is manifest in the three worlds. He is the eternal Giver and there is no other.[4]

'There is no other.' It is a characteristic expression of Gurū Nānak which recurs many times. God is for him simply *Ek*, the One.

> There are six systems of philosophy, six *gurūs*, and six patterns of instruction, but the *Gurū* of these *gurūs* is one though His manifestations be many.[5]

This affirmation of unity raises, however, an obvious question. Is this the one of monotheism, or is it the one of monism? Does it refer to the uniqueness of God, to His absolute difference in essence from all other beings; or does it denote the unity which denies ultimate reality to all phenomenal existence?

If we are compelled to choose between these two polar conceptions our

[1] Jodh Singh, *Guramati Niraṇay*, p. 1.

[2] The lengthy poem *Oaṅkāru* in the measure *Rāg Rāmakalī Dakhaṇī*, *AG*, pp. 929–38, provides an elucidation.

[3] Vir Singh, *Santhyā*, p. 3.

[4] *Oaṅkāru* 25, *AG*, p. 933.

[5] *Āsā Sohilā* 2 and *Āsā* 30, *AG*, pp. 12, 357.

choice must settle upon the former alternative. Gurū Nānak's thought cannot be made to conform to the categories of *advaita* doctrine without equating his concept of God with the ultimately unreal *Īśvara* of Śaṅkara's philosophy. The total range of Gurū Nānak's thought makes this equation manifestly impossible and accordingly requires us to reject the monistic alternative.

On the other hand, we must recognize that Gurū Nānak himself explicitly declares notions of 'duality' (*dubidhā*) to be the essence of man's problem, and the overcoming of such notions to be a vital aspect of man's quest for salvation. Moreover, we must also acknowledge the stress which he lays upon divine immanence and upon the fundamental importance of this immanent revelation in the quest for salvation. These aspects of his thought must prompt a measure of caution in our choice of terminology. If the thought of Gurū Nānak is to be designated monotheistic we must be clear that this is not to be construed in the Semitic sense.

The basis of Gurū Nānak's thought is best understood if approached as the thought of one who was essentially a mystic. 'Duality' is to be destroyed, but it is to be a swallowing up in mystical union. The creation does indeed provide a vital revelation of God, but the physical phenomena which impart this revelation are to be regarded as expressions of a God of grace who dwells not only in creation but also beyond it. The ultimate essence of God is beyond all human categories, far transcending all powers of human expression. Only in experience can He be truly known. Man must indeed seek to give human expression to this mystical experience, and Gurū Nānak's works are directed to this very end, but the human expression can communicate no more than a glimpse of the ultimate reality.

Gurū Nānak's own expressions of the experience and of the path to it plainly show that the One of whom he speaks is conceived as a personal God, a God of grace to whom man responds in love. His understanding of God as Creator and his repeated emphasis upon divine grace make this abundantly clear. As in the case of Kabīr monistic language does indeed occur, but the structure of monistic thought can provide no place for Gurū Nānak's concept of God. Strict pantheism is also excluded, for immanence is accompanied in the thought of Gurū Nānak by a notion of transcendence. If a label must be applied then monotheism is the label we must use, but it should be remembered that the vital expression of the One is through the many, through the infinite plurality of the creation.

This stress upon the many as the expression of the One must always be related to the concept of revelation through the created universe. It should not suggest any notion of implicit monotheism expressed through a plurality of deities, except in the sense that the deities of Hindu mythology are occasionally used as symbols to represent particular aspects of the divine activity. It has indeed been argued that Gurū Nānak accepted the *trimūrti*, the Hindu triad, and the justification for this claim is held to be the first couplet of the thirtieth stanza of *Japjī*.[1] Out of context these two lines could be translated:

> In the same manner a Mother conceived and bore three approved disciples—one the creator of the world, one the sustainer, and one who exercises the authority of death.[2]

Most Sikh commentators, however, begin their translations or paraphrases of this passage with some such words as, 'It is believed that . . .' and in the light of both the context and of Gurū Nānak's repeated references to the unity of God there can be no doubt that the addition is warranted. The same stanza continues with an emphatic assertion of the absolute authority of God:

> But Thou dost order (the three) as seems good to Thee and (they act) in accordance with Thy command.[3]

In the next stanza he declares that God Himself is both Creator and Sustainer.

> His abode is in every realm of the universe and every realm is His storehouse. That which He created He created once only and having created it He, the Creator, sustains it. This, Nānak, is the authentic work of the True One.[4]

Gurū Nānak does refer to Brahmā, Viṣṇu, and Śiva in ways which suggest that he accepted their existence as real, but they appear as the creatures of God, deprived of all functions and subject to *māyā* and to death. God did not merely create Brahmā. He created the world also and He it is who sustains it.[5] God is Himself Creator, Sustainer, and Destroyer, and His direct exercise of these functions reduces all demiurges and subordinate deities to meaningless shadows. Elsewhere they lose even this qualified acceptance.

> He, the One, is Himself Brahmā, Viṣṇu and Śiva, and He Himself performs all.[6]

They survive only as convenient illustrations, as conventional figures who will occasionally serve to exemplify a particular point.

As in the works of Kabīr this emphasis upon the unity of God emerges in the names which Gurū Nānak uses. Hari is the most common and there are other Vaiṣṇava names in his works, but there are also Muslim names.

[1] P. D. Barthwal, *The Nirguna School of Hindi Poetry*, p. 255. Indubhusan Banerjee, *The Evolution of the Khalsa*, vol. i, pp. 136–7.

[2] *Japjī* 30, *AG*, p. 7.

[3] Ibid.

[4] Ibid. 31, *AG*, p. 7.

[5] *Mārū Solahā* 15 (14), *AG*, p. 1036.

[6] *Rāmakalī Aṣṭ* 9 (12), *AG*, p. 908.

God is Hari, Rām, and Gopāl, and He is also Allāh, Khudā, and Sāhib.[1] His manifestations may be many, but He alone is and there is no other.

My Master is the One. He is the One, brother, and He alone exists.[2]

2. *Nirguṇa and Saguṇa*

niragunu āpi saragunu bhī ohī.[3]

The words are Gurū Arjan's, but the doctrine which they so concisely express is also Gurū Nānak's. God, the One, is both *nirguṇa* and *saguṇa*, both absolute and conditioned, both unmanifest and manifest.

For Gurū Nānak, God in His primal aspect is *nirguṇa*—absolute, unconditioned, devoid of all attributes.

He who unfolded the three (*guṇa*[4]) has made His abode in the fourth.[5]

In other words, He is beyond the three *guṇa*. In this absolute aspect God is unknowable, completely beyond the range of human comprehension. God is not wholly beyond human perception, however, and for Gurū Nānak the explanation lies in His having endowed Himself with attributes which bring Him within the compass of man's understanding. He, the *nirguṇa*, of His own volition became *saguṇa* in order that man might know Him, and knowing Him enter into a unitive relationship with Him.

From His absolute condition He, the Pure One, became manifest; from *nirguṇa* He became *saguṇa*.[6]

There is at this point some danger of misunderstanding. The term *saguṇa* is generally used in connexion with Vaiṣṇava bhakti and in this customary sense it implies a belief in divine *avatārs*. This is certainly not the meaning which is to be attached to the word in Gurū Nānak's usage, nor in that of any of his successors. In Gurū Nānak's usage the term relates not to anything resembling anthropomorphism, but to his concept of divine immanence. One of the contributors to the commentary on the *Ādi Granth* entitled *Śabadārath Srī Gurū Granth Sāhib Jī* comments as follows on a relevant passage from Gurū Arjan's *Bilāvalu* 117:

In scripture God is said to have two aspects. One is that which He possessed when there was no creation and He existed solely in Himself. His qualities of power or of being unborn cannot thereby be diminished, but we can form no

[1] *Rāmakalī Aṣṭ* 1 (7), *AG*, p. 903. The characteristic Sikh term *Vāhigurū* is not found in Gurū Nānak's compositions. It first appears in the *savayye* of the *bhaṭṭs*. The *bhaṭṭs* whose works appear in the *Ādi Granth* were contemporaries of Gurū Arjan.

[2] *Āsā* 5, p. 350.

[3] Gurū Arjan, *Gaurī Sukhamanī, Aṣṭ* 18 (8), *AG*, p. 287.

[4] The three vital 'qualities' or constituents of cosmic substance which by their varying proportions determine the nature of all that exists.

[5] *Mārū Solahā* 18 (4), *AG*, p. 1038.

[6] *Siddh Goṣṭi* 24, *AG*, p. 940.

impression of them in our mind. This is His *nirguṇa* aspect. Then He created and so revealed Himself in His creation. All the qualities or praiseworthy characteristics which can be attributed to Him are of this *saguṇa* aspect. Both are aspects of the one God.[1]

It is in this *saguṇa* aspect that man can know God and accordingly it is this aspect which is the object of Gurū Nānak's meditation and of his expository utterances. The *nirguṇa* nature of God, for all its fundamental quality, receives little attention for beyond the mere affirmation there is nothing man can say of it. In the ultimate condition of union man does indeed participate in this absolute quality and so in experience it can be ultimately known, but the way to God, the *sādhanā*, must be concerned with the *saguṇa* expression.

3. *Creator*

Gurū Nānak has set out his cosmology in the hymn *Mārū Solahā* 15. It begins:

> For countless aeons there was undivided darkness. There was neither earth nor heavens, but only the infinite Order of God (*Hukam*).[2]

He then details at length the things which did not exist, his point being that apart from God and His *Hukam* there was nothing. It is a striking picture with much that evokes the Genesis conception of primeval chaos. Finally:

> When it pleased Thee Thou didst create the world, establishing Thy creation without visible supports. Thou didst create Brahmā, Viṣṇu and Śiva, and Thou didst spread abroad the allurements of *māyā*.[3]

A number of references to the creative activity of God have already been quoted and there are many more available. The frequency with which they occur is significant in that it brings out a clear and explicit concept of the personality of God. Again the comparison with Kabīr is interesting. An affirmation of the personality of God does emerge from Kabīr's works, but it emerges rather by hint and implication than by explicit statement. References to God as Creator are comparatively scarce and lack the clarity of Gurū Nānak's declarations. The same also applies to other attributes which imply a notion of personality. In Kabīr's works we must often grope; in Nānak's we find clarity.

> Beings of various kinds, colours, and names—He wrote them all with a flowing pen. If anyone knew how to record the number what an immense account it

[1] *Śabadārath*, p. 827, n. ¶. The writer is almost certainly Principal Teja Singh. *Śabadārath* was issued as the work of a panel of commentators, but it is well known that practically the entire commentary was written by Principal Teja Singh.

[2] *AG*, p. 1035.

[3] *AG*, p. 1036.

would be! What power, what beauty of form, what gifts! Who can guess them! With a single command He unfurled creation and by that command there sprang forth thousands of rivers.[1]

The Fearless One, the Formless One, the True Name—the whole world is His creation![2]

4. *Sustainer*

God does not merely create. Having brought the world into being He watches over it and cares for it.

He who created the world watches over it, appointing all to their various tasks.[3]

And in another passage which affirms both His creative and sustaining activity:

True Creator, True Sustainer, and known as the True One! Self-existent, true, ineffable, immeasurable! Uniting both mill stones,[4] He separated them. Without the *Gurū* there is utter darkness. Having created the sun and moon He directs their paths day and night.[5]

Again the attribution of personality is evident. For Gurū Nānak God is a participant in the life of the universe which He has established, watching, directing, and upholding.

The latter passage also indicates the meaning of the term *saibhan* which is used in the *Mūl Mantra* and which is usually translated as 'self-existent'. God created Himself. In human terms this can have no meaning, but human understanding is bounded by strict limitations. The 'self-existence' of God is an affirmation of His absolute nature and beyond this human understanding cannot proceed. God in His fullness is, for Gurū Nānak, far beyond the human intellect and man can no more apprehend that fullness than he can encompass the infinite.

5. *Destroyer*

God, the One, is Brahmā and Viṣṇu, and so too is He Śiva. He who is the Creator and Sustainer is also declared to be God the Destroyer and Recreator.

He who created also destroys; apart from Him there is no other. . . .

Having destroyed He builds and having built He destroys. Casting down He raises up and raising up He casts down. Having filled the sea He causes it to dry up and then fills it again, for He, the One beyond care and anxiety, has the power (to do it).[6]

[1] *Japji* 16, *AG*, p. 3.
[2] *Vār Āsā, ślok* 2 of *pauṛī* 5, *AG*, p. 465.
[3] *Sūhī Chhant* 4 (1), *AG*, p. 765.
[4] i.e. creating heaven and earth.
[5] *Vaḍahaṃsu Dakhaṇī* 3 (1), p. 580.
[6] *Oaṅkāru* 31, 41, *AG*, pp. 934, 935.

Thou art absolute and whatever is in Thy will comes to pass. This world is a pretext.[1] The true Creator pervades the waters, the earth, and all between earth and sky. He, the true Creator, is ineffable, measureless, eternal. The coming (into the world) of a man is fruitful if he meditates single-mindedly (upon the Creator). Breaking down He reconstructs and by His Order He sustains all. Thou art absolute and whatever is in Thy will comes to pass. This world is a pretext.[2]

6. *Sovereign*

Thou art absolute and whatever is in Thy will comes to pass.

The refrain of the stanza from *Vaḍahaṃsu Alāhaṇī* 1 quoted above gathers the creative, sustaining, and destroying activities of God into that basic attribute from which all three flow. God is for Nānak the sovereign Lord, the wielder of absolute authority, the possessor of unqualified power.

Whatever pleases Thee, that Thou doest, and none can gainsay it.[3]

'Whatever pleases Thee.' We have here another of Gurū Nānak's characteristic expressions. Again and again one encounters a variety of forms which may be translated with these words, and repeatedly the same emphasis is made in other ways.

If it pleases Thee Thou dost exalt one to the throne and if it pleases Thee one renounces the world and goes begging. If it pleases Thee floods flow over the desert and the lotus blooms in the sky. If it pleases Thee one crosses the Ocean of Fear and if it pleases Thee (one's boat) fills (with water and sinks) in mid-ocean. If it pleases Thee Thou art a Lord of joy and I am rapt in Thy praises, Thou storehouse of excellences. If it pleases Thee Thou art a fearsome Lord and I go on dying in the cycle of transmigration.[4]

God is accordingly *anāth*, omnipotent, and as He is omnipotent so too is He omniscient.

The sovereign Lord created this visible world. He sees all, comprehends all, and knows all, permeating (all creation) both within and without.[5]

7. *Eternal*

The world, which is the work of God the Creator, is unstable and impermanent, but God Himself is not.

[1] The meaning of this phrase is not clear. Vir Singh's interpretation is probably correct: 'This world is a pretext (i.e. created to be an opportunity) for the liberation of souls.' *Santhyā*, vol. vii, pp. 3533–4.

[2] *Vaḍahaṃsu Alāhaṇī* 1, *AG*, p. 579.

[3] *Gūjarī Aṣṭ* 3 (5), *AG*, p. 504.

[4] *Sūhī Suchajjī*, p. 762. The Ocean of Fear, or the Ocean of Existence, is a conventional image representing the span of human existence with its multitude of attendant impediments which the soul must overcome in order to attain release from the cycle of transmigration.

[5] *Āsā Paṭṭī Likhī* 24, p. 433.

He, the true Lord, is eternally true. He is and will be, for unlike His creation He will not pass away.[1]

God is *abināsī*, eternal. He is *anādi*, without beginning, *akāl*, beyond time, the One who is ever firm and wholly constant. This is a logical corollary of the absolute nature of God, but it requires emphasis because of its importance to Gurū Nānak. To men his repeated appeal was that they should renounce their love of the world and all wordly attachments. These are *māyā*[2] and they are to be renounced, for in the experience of every individual they must inevitably betray the trust which is put in them. Nothing of the world can accompany man after his physical death[3] and so for every individual the world is a vain thing which must pass away. As opposed to this fickle destructible world, however, there stands the eternally constant *achal* God. He is *nirañjan*,[4] the One wholly detached (*atīt*, *alipt*, *niramal*, *niralep*), wholly apart from the *māyā* which He Himself created, wholly perfect.

The Alpha, the Holy One, without beginning and deathless, eternally immutable.[5]

This same concept lies behind the emphasis which Gurū Nānak lays upon God being *ajūnī*, unborn, non-incarnated.

Pervading all (as the heavens extend over all), infinite, absolute, not incarnated.[6]

To be incarnated means to be involved in death, which is the supreme enemy, the characteristic quality of the unstable world and the ultimate antithesis of God's own eternal being. God, however, is beyond death and transmigration.[7] This, by implication, means that there can be no place for a doctrine of *avatārs*,[8] but its primary purpose is to emphasize the total detachment of God from all that is unstable, mutable, or corruptible. The world, caught up in the cycle of birth and death, of endless coming and going, is real but it is *bināsī*, a corruptible reality subject to flux and decay and dissolution, whereas God, in contrast with it, is *abināsī*, *amar*, *achut*, the incorruptible, eternal Reality.

If an individual's affections are transferred from the world to God the result is a relationship which endures to eternity, and the person who is united with God in such a relationship himself participates in the divine immortality. This is Gurū Nānak's constant appeal, that men should

[1] *Japji* 27, p. 6. [2] See *infra*, pp. 185–7. [3] *Bilāvalu Aṣṭ* 2 (1R), *AG*, p. 832.
[4] See *infra*, p. 186. [5] *Japji* 28, *AG*, p. 6. Also stanzas 29–31.
[6] *Oaṅkāru* 20, *AG*, p. 932. [7] *Mārū Solahā* 18 (1–4), *AG*, p. 1038.
[8] Elsewhere the elimination is explicit.

Nānak, in comparison with the Fearless, Formless One, innumerable Rāms are as dust.

Vār Āsā, *ślok* 2 of *pauṛī* 4, *AG*, p. 464.

abandon worldly affections and attach themselves to the eternally tranquil and immutable God.

8. *Formless*

The absolute nature and the eternal being of God are metaphysical qualities and there now arises the question of whether for Gurū Nānak the human understanding of God can proceed from the strictly metaphysical to something more concrete. The answer is a firm negative and a negative which in its firmness rejects not merely idols and *avatārs*, but also anthropomorphic language. He is *arūp*, without form, *niraṅkār*, the Formless One. For Gurū Nānak and for all subsequent Sikh thought this word *Niraṅkār* has been one of the most important names of God. Stanzas 16–19 of *Japjī* all end with the salutation:

> Thou the eternally unchanging Formless One (*niraṅkār*).[1]

In *Soraṭhi* 3 God is addressed in what is, for Gurū Nānak, a thoroughly typical manner.

> Thou the Formless One, beyond fear and enmity, I blend in Thy pure light.[2]

Such significance has been attached to the name *Niraṅkār* that its derivative form *niraṅkārī* has since been used in conjunction with Gurū Nānak's own name to indicate the nature of the salvation which he himself achieved. Nānak Niraṅkārī he is called, Nānak who is one with the Formless One. Gurū Nānak himself used the word in just this sense.

> Perceiving the nature of spiritual reality (lit. the self) he has become *niraṅkārī* (one with the Formless One).[3]

Niraṅkār is the characteristic epithet which Gurū Nānak uses to communicate this particular concept, but elsewhere the formless quality of God is expressed in other language.

> He has neither form (*rūp*) nor material sign (*rekhiā*).[4]

> Thou hast thousands of eyes and yet Thou hast no eye. Thou hast thousands of forms and yet no form, thousands of holy feet and yet no foot, and without a fragrance Thou hast thousands of fragrances.[5] I am dazed by such a wonder.[6]

9. *Ineffable*

God is the Formless One, uncreated, unborn, never incarnated. He cannot be present in an idol, He cannot be revealed by an *avatār*, and He

[1] *Japjī*, *AG*, pp. 3–4.
[2] *Soraṭhi* 3, *AG*, p. 596.
[3] *Āsā Aṣṭ* 8 (7), *AG*, p. 415.
[4] *Sūhī Aṣṭ* 1 (3), *AG*, p. 750.
[5] Lit. nose, noses.
[6] *Dhanāsarī Ārati*, *AG*, pp. 13, 663.

cannot be described in terms appropriate to the human condition. How then can He be apprehended? Is it in fact possible for human understanding to grasp the nature of God, or must man be content with defining Him in negatives, of describing Him in terms of what He is not?

The first answer to this question must be that God is ultimately incomprehensible, ultimately beyond human apprehension. For Gurū Nānak God in His fullness is far beyond the bounds of man's understanding. The intellect of man is strictly limited and any effort it may make to define the wholeness of God must be an effort to circumscribe the infinite, to bring within narrow bounds the One who is boundless. God is ineffable and man's proper and inevitable response to any authentic glimpse of the being of God can only be that of awe (*visamād*), of fear and wonder before Him who is beyond comprehending. He is *agam*, *agochar*, inscrutable, beyond the reach of the intellect; *agah*, unfathomable; *acharaj*, of surpassing wonder; *adriṣṭ*, beyond seeing or perception; *akāl*, beyond time; *alabh*, unsearchable; *anant*, infinite; *apār*, boundless; *abol*, *akah*, *akath*, *alekh*, beyond utterance or describing; *alakh*, ineffable.

> Beyond human grasp or understanding, boundless, infinite, the all-powerful supreme God! He who existed before time began, who has existed throughout all ages, and who shall eternally exist, (He alone is true). Spurn all else as false.[1]

> Beyond understanding, infinite, unreachable, beyond perception, free from death and *karma*, without caste, never incarnate, self-existent, subject to neither love (of worldly things) nor doubt. Thou, the ultimate Truth, to Thee I sacrifice myself. Thou hast neither form, colour, nor material sign, but Thou dost reveal Thyself in the true Word (*Śabad*).[2]

And as God and His dwelling place are beyond all telling so too is that expression of His will which is called the *Hukam*, the divine Order of creation.[3]

> No one has comprehended Thy *Hukam* and none can describe it. Were a hundred poets to gather together their singing could not even approach a description of it. No one has grasped its worth; all but repeat what they have heard.[4]

10. *Immanent*

All this, however, concerns God *in His fullness*. God is infinite and so ultimately beyond apprehension, but this does not necessarily mean that He is wholly unknowable, that He is *totally* beyond the range of human perception. For Gurū Nānak, as for Nāmdev, Kabīr, Raidās, and other

[1] *Āsā Chhant* 3 (1), *AG*, p. 437.
[2] *Soraṭhi* 6, *AG*, p. 597.
[3] See *infra*, pp. 199–203.
[4] *Sirī Rāgu Aṣṭ* 1 (2), *AG*, p. 53.

Sants, there is certainly a revelation of God, partial no doubt but commensurate with the understanding and experience of man and accordingly sufficient for his salvation. The extract from *Soraṭhi* 6 quoted above continues as follows:

> Thou hast neither mother nor father, son, relation, wife, nor sensual desire. Thou art without lineage, free from *māyā*, boundless. Thy light (shines) in all.[1]

And the passage from *Dhanāsarī Āratī* continues:

> Within all there is light and it is Thy light which is in all. Through the *Gurū's* leading the light is revealed. True worship is what pleases Thee.[2]

The figure is that of all-pervading light and its meaning is the all-pervading immanence of God.

> Wondrous, my Master, are Thy ways! Thou dost pervade the waters, the land, and all that is between the heavens and the earth, indwelling in all. Wherever I look there I see Thy light. Of what nature is Thy form? In a single form Thou dost move concealed (in all creation) and yet (in spite of Thy presence) no one person is the same as another.[3]

'Wherever I look. . . .' They are familiar words, both in the works of Gurū Nānak and in those of the Sants who preceded him. Wherever one looks there He is to be seen, for He manifests Himself in His own creation.

> Do not regard the Lord as far off for He is near, He, the One, pervading creation. He is the only One; there is no other. He, the One, pervades all.[4]

God the omnipotent and omniscient is also God the omnipresent.

> Thou art the ocean, the All-knower, the All-seer. How can I, a fish, perceive Thy limit? Wherever I look there Thou art. If I leave Thee I burst and die.[5]

This is accepted as a general truth and one of fundamental importance, but Gurū Nānak, in common with other Sants, goes further. The *Niraṅkār* who is immanent in all creation is specifically immanent in one particular part of creation.

> The Lord pervades every heart. He dwells concealed in the waters, the land, all that is between the heavens and the earth, but through the Word of the *Gurū* He is revealed. By His Grace the *Gurū*, the True *Gurū*, revealed Him to me in this world where all dies, in the nether world, and in the heavens. The non-incarnated Brahmā is and eternally will be. Behold the Lord within yourself![6]

[1] *Soraṭhi* 6, *AG*, p. 597.
[2] *Dhanāsarī Āratī*, *AG*, pp. 13, 663.
[3] *Soraṭhi* 4, *AG*, p. 596.
[4] *Oaṅkāru* 5, *AG*, p. 930.
[5] *Sirī Rāgu* 31, *AG*, p. 25.
[6] *Soraṭhi* 8, *AG*, pp. 597–8.

God who dwells in all creation has His particular abode within the human heart.

> The one *Omkār*, wholly apart, immortal, unborn, without caste, wholly free, ineffable, without form or visible sign, but searching I perceived Him in every heart.[1]

This is no mere aesthetic mystery, no mere source of numinous awe which, however impressive it may be, leaves man essentially where he was. Here we are at the crucial point, the point at which there can exist communication between God and man, and through which there can develop that relationship which means release and salvation. Failure to grasp this is regarded as fatal.

> Wearing ochre garments they wander around, but without the True *Gurū* none have found Thee. Roaming in all countries and in all directions they have grown weary (but their efforts are in vain for) Thou art concealed within.[2]

For Gurū Nānak the saving activity of God is expressed at this point. Here, in the divine Order (*Hukam*), is the inscription of His will for all who are able to read it. Here it is that the Word (*Śabad*) and the Name (*Nām*) acquire the substance which render them meaningful to the human understanding. And here it is that the *Gurū's* voice is to be heard.[3]

> Know Him who creates and destroys the world, know Him by His creation. Do not look far off for the True One, but recognize Him in the guise of the Word in every heart. He who established this creation, recognize Him as the true Word and do not imagine Him to be far distant. He who meditates on the Name finds peace. Without the Name the game (of life) is lost.[4]

> (Thou who art) inscrutable, beyond apprehending, ineffable, infinite, have mercy upon me! Thou who dost pervade the universe, Thy light shines in every heart.[5]

11. *The divine initiative*

In the pattern of salvation which is to be found throughout the works of Gurū Nānak effort on the part of the individual is essential, but it is not the only factor and nor would it appear to be the primary one.

> Nānak, the True King Himself unites (the believer) with Himself.[6]

It is God, says Gurū Nānak, who is responsible for that union which is the climax of the salvation process. Man must participate and unless he does

[1] *Bilāvalu Thitī*, *AG*, p. 838.
[2] *Vār Malār*, *pauṛī* 25, *AG*, p. 1290.
[3] This summary statement will be developed below under *Śabad*, *Nām*, *Gurū*, and *Hukam*, pp. 191 ff.
[4] *Vaḍahaṃsu Alāhaṇī* 4, *AG*, p. 581.
[5] *Bilāvalu* 2, *AG*, p. 795.
[6] *Sirī Rāgu* 10, *AG*, p. 18.

so there can be no release, no union.[1] His participation is, however, dependent upon the prior activity of God, and without this divine initiative the question of human participation does not arise as its need is not recognized.

> Nānak, all we receive is by the grace of the Beneficient One.[2]

This aspect need not be developed here, for it will be dealt with in the section relating to the divine self-expression.[3] At this point it will be sufficient to draw attention to the stress which Gurū Nānak lays upon what is normally referred to as divine grace. It is an aspect which is integral to his total thought and it is one to which constant reference is made in his works. This divine grace is expressed in terms of divine activity made manifest in the created world and within man's inner being. It is not activity at a secondary level, but purposeful activity upon which the attainment of release depends. Nor is it an inflexible activity which could be interpreted as a mythologized version of natural laws. Natural laws are indeed acknowledged and, as we shall see, are regarded as a significant part of God's communication with mankind.[4] They are not, however, the ultimate basis, for behind them lies a will which is expressed in terms of decision, of giving and witholding. Without this divine grace a man is helpless.[5] If, however, God chooses to impart it the way of salvation lies open.

12. *The greatness of God*

The purpose of systematic theology is to construct a consistent framework, to develop a coherently integrated pattern out of what is dispersed throughout the record of an individual or corporate religious experience. In order to do this it is necessary to extract, analyse, and rearrange in a pattern which serves this particular purpose. By itself, however, such a pattern must be inadequate, for it will inevitably lose much of the spirit which prompted the original record. At the beginning of this section on the nature of God it was noted that the characteristic expression of Gurū Nānak's religious experience is the hymn of praise and it is appropriate that the section should close with extracts which convey something of this spirit. It is an impulse which Gurū Nānak shares with all *bhagats*. *Niraṅkār*, the Formless One, is the supreme Lord of the universe, eternal, absolute, ineffable, and yet purposing that man should know Him and find ultimate peace in union with Him. Before such majesty, infinite and yet condescending in mercy to stoop to man, the inevitable response for Gurū Nānak must be that of adoring praise.

> Having heard of Thy greatness everyone speaks of it, but only by seeing Thee can one know the immensity of Thy greatness. No one can know or express

[1] *Vār Sāraṅg*, *ślok* 2 of *pauṛī* 2, *AG*, p. 1238. *Sirī Rāgu* 30 (3), *AG*, p. 25.
[2] *Japjī* 24, *AG*, p. 5.
[3] See *infra*, pp. 204–7.
[4] See *infra*, p. 201.
[5] *Japjī* 7, *AG*, p. 2.

Thy worth. Those who tell of Thee are gathered up into Thee. Great art Thou, my Lord, ineffable and of excellences beyond comprehending. None can encompass the measure of Thy greatness. The exegetes gathered together and expounded the scriptures; all extollers of Thy worth together determined that worth; men of understanding, men of contemplation, *gurūs* and *gurūs' gurūs*, (all proclaimed Thy greatness and yet) not a fragment of Thy greatness could they express. All truth, all (the merits of) austerities, all goodness, all the impressive works of *siddhs*, (all are from Thee). Without Thee none has reached the mystical consummation, but when Thy grace is received no obstacle remains. Thine is a storehouse filled with excellences beyond telling. He to whom Thou givest (support) what need has he of any other help? Nānak declares: Thou art the True One and all is in Thy hands.[1]

In describing only a tiny portion of the glory of the divine Name (men) have wearied themselves and yet failed to discover its worth. If all were to gather together and strive to describe it the glory would be neither heightened nor dimmed. He does not die and there is no occasion to mourn Him. He gives continually and His gifts do not cease. His particular quality is that He alone is, that there neither was nor will be another. His bounty is infinite as He is infinite, He who caused night to follow day. Low is he who forgets the Lord; wretched is he who is without the Name.[2]

II. THE NATURE OF UNREGENERATE MAN

O my Lord, who can comprehend Thy excellences! None can recount my sinfulness.

Many times was I born as a tree, many times as an animal, many times I came in the form of a snake, and many times I flew as a bird.

Many times did I break into city shops, strong buildings, and having burgled them return home. I looked ahead and behind, but how could it be concealed from Thee?

(I have visited) places of pilgrimage on river-banks, *tīraths*, shops, cities, markets; I have seen all regions of the world. Taking scales I have weighed (my merits against my demerits) in my heart.

As the oceans are filled with water, so immense is my sinfulness. Be merciful, show a measure of Thy grace that this sinking stone may cross over. An undying fire burns in my soul, within (my heart) a knife twists. Nānak prays: (Show me Thy grace for he who by it) understands Thy divine Order attains eternal peace.[3]

Man's nature is, for Gurū Nānak, dependent upon his affiliation, and that nature is transformed when his affiliation is transferred from the world to the divine Name. It is the nature of unregenerate man which concerns us at this point, the nature of man in the condition of attachment to the world. This is the condition of pride, of self-centredness, of sin, and so of

[1] *Āsā* 2, *AG*, p. 9. [2] *Āsā* 3, *AG*, p. 9. [3] *Gauṛī* 17, *AG*, p. 156.

death and transmigration. This is the condition which must be transcended if man is to attain release from transmigration.

For Gurū Nānak the key to an understanding of man's nature is an understanding of the human faculty which is called the *man*.[1] Cleanse the *man* and it becomes a fitting abode for the Name. Control it and you will no more wander from the One with whom you seek union. But let it retain its impurity, let it remain unbridled, and the penalty will be Death. Yam, the God of Death, will seize you, bind you, and march you off to his prison. There you will continue to suffer in the round of birth and death.

1. *The* man

> *mani jītai jagu jītu*
> To conquer the *man* is to conquer the world.[2]

The word *man* as used by Gurū Nānak has no satisfactory English translation. It is usually rendered 'mind', but the translation is unsatisfactory as the English word lacks the breadth of meaning and association which *man* possesses in Sant literature and Sikh scripture. It is true that the concept of mind is included within the range of *man* and that it is the dominant concept covered by the word. To translate it in this way alone is, however, inadequate in the context of Gurū Nānak's usage.

Man is a version of *manas*, a word with a lengthy history. In the *Ṛg Veda* it denotes 'soul' and is very close in meaning to *ātman*.[3] In the *Upaniṣads* the two terms tend to diverge, with *manas* moving towards *chitta* and assuming a quality best translated as 'mind',[4] whereas *ātman* becomes identified with the inmost essence in man.[5] In Vedānta *manas* emerges explicitly as an aspect or function of *antaḥkaraṇa*, the seat of collective thought and feeling.

> Vedanta does not regard manas (mind) as a sense (indriya). The same antahkarana, according to its diverse functions, is called manas, buddhi, ahamkara, and citta. In its function as doubt it is called manas, as originating definite cognitions it is called buddhi. As presenting the notion of an ego in consciousness ahamkara, and as producing memory citta.[6]

In these terms Gurū Nānak's understanding of the *man* could be described as synonymous with *antaḥkaraṇa* in that it embraces all of these functions,

[1] Attention is drawn to the italics. This is not the English word 'man', but a transliteration of the word used by Gurū Nānak and pronounced 'mun' as in 'mundane'. It is not translated as no accurate English translation exists.

[2] *Japjī* 28, *AG*, p. 6.

[3] S. Dasgupta, *A History of Indian Philosophy*, vol. i, pp. 25–26. A Berriedale Keith, *The Religion and Philosophy of the Vedas and Upanishads*, vol. ii, pp. 403–4.

[4] Cf. *Chhāndogya Upaniṣad*, vii. 3. i.

[5] S. Dasgupta, op. cit., vol. i, pp. 45–46. Dr. Radhakrishnan identifies the *manas* of the *Upaniṣads* with the *antaḥkaraṇa* and uses 'mind' to translate it, but maintains a close relationship between the two terms (*The Principal Upanisads*, p. 471).

[6] S. Dasgupta, op. cit., vol. i, p. 472, n. 1.

in so far as they are distinguished in his thought, and is used interchangeably with *buddhi*, *chitta*, and *antaḥkaraṇa* itself. The comparison would, however, be misleading for Gurū Nānak was not a Vedāntist. His concept lacks the sophistication of developed Vedānta doctrine and extends to areas which are excluded from the *antaḥkaraṇa* of Vedānta. It comes much closer to the Yoga notion of the *manas* as 'the inner sense'.[1] Even here, however, the marked divergence from Yoga as a developed and integrated philosophy makes comparison risky, although there seems to be no doubt that in this, as in so much else, the Sant concept has roots in Nāth doctrine.

An impression of the range of meaning which the word covers in Gurū Nānak's works can be gathered from the actual contexts in which it is used, and from other terms which are used in similar contexts and which are obviously synonymous with aspects of *man*. It is with the *man* that one makes decisions and particular emphasis is laid upon its function as moral arbiter.

> The *man* acts as the *man* itself dictates. Sometimes it expresses virtue, sometimes sin.[2]

The *man* is the faculty by means of which Truth is apprehended.

> In his *man* is Truth and so Truth is in (the words of) his mouth also.
> With Truth as his banner he finds no obstacle remaining.[3]

And it is with the *man* that one meditates.

> Meditate in your *man*, cleave in union to the One, and the round of birth and death is at an end.[4]

In all of these the translation 'mind' would be appropriate and it is not surprising that such words as *surati*, *chitta*, *budhi*, and *mati* occur in similar contexts.

Other contexts, however, extend the meaning to express what in English is usually covered by 'heart'.

> If the strong smites the strong the *man* is not grieved.[5]

It is difficult to draw precise bounds between 'mind' and 'heart', but emotions of this kind are generally associated with the latter word. We also find the *man* specified as the seat both of such evil qualities as lust and anger, and of the *bhagat's* love for God.

> Within my *man* lurk the five (evil impulses) and so like a wanderer it has no resting place. My *man* has not found its resting place in the merciful Lord, for it is bound to *māyā*, (caught up in) greed, deceit, sin, and hypocrisy.[6]

[1] M. Eliade, *Yoga: Immortality and Freedom*, p. 20.
[2] *Bilāvalu Aṣṭ* 2 (1), *AG*, p. 832.
[3] *Bilāvalu Thitī* 9, *AG*, p. 839.
[4] *Gūjarī Aṣṭ* 1 (4), *AG*, p. 503.
[5] *Āsā* 39, *AG*, p. 360.
[6] *Āsā* 34, *AG*, p. 359.

Elsewhere *ghaṭ*, *hiradā*, *ridā*, *dil*, or *ur* are used interchangeably with *man*, for all are used to designate the specific abode of God within each individual.

Nor is this the limit, for *man* is also used to cover what in English is normally expressed with the word 'soul'. This applies to the usage which refers to the indestructible quality of the *man*. In such cases neither 'mind' nor 'heart' is adequate. The *man* is mind and it is heart, and it is also that human attribute which does not perish with physical death and which man must seek to unite with God, which he must strive to have carried across the Ocean of Existence.

> Be still, my *man*, and you shall not suffer hurt. Sing (His) praises, my *man*, and you shall enter into supreme tranquillity. Sing God's praises and you shall taste His sweetness. Apply the antimony of the *Gurū's* enlightenment (to your inward eyes) and by the light of that lamp which, fed by the Word, illuminates the whole universe you shall slay the five devils.[1] So shall you destroy your fears and in fearlessness you shall cross the dread Ocean of Existence. You shall meet the *Gurū* and find fulfilment. He upon whom God bestows grace finds a fullness of spiritual stature, spiritual joy, and love for God.[2]

Here we find *man* assuming the qualities of *jīv* and *ātmā*.

One solution to this translation problem is to translate *man* as 'mind' in some contexts, 'heart' in others, and 'soul' in yet others. In circumstances where an English word must be found if possible this is perhaps necessary, but such translations will normally fail to bring out the fullness of meaning which the term possesses. It is strictly untranslatable, for there is nothing in English which combines the functions of the mind, the emotions of the heart, and the qualities of the soul. Perhaps the closest we can get is the word 'psyche', but this too is inadequate and liable to mislead. *Man* is mind, heart, and soul. It is the faculty with which one thinks, decides, and feels, the source of all human good and evil, and that one indestructible attribute which must be released from the body and merged in the being of God.

In laying this stress upon the role of the *man* Gurū Nānak stands within a well-developed tradition. Dr. Vaudeville has described the importance which the *man* held for the Siddhs and the Nāths,[3] and to illustrate Kabīr's understanding of it she gives in her *Au Cabaret de l'Amour: Paroles de Kabîr* a translation of his *Gauṛī* 28, in which she renders *man* as 'âme'.

> Le caractère est inhérent à l'âme:
> Qui donc a jamais obtenu le salut en triomphant de son âme?
> Où donc est l'ascète qui a vaincu son âme?
> Dis-moi, qui donc a jamais obtenu la Délivrance par la défaite de l'âme?

[1] The five evil impulses. See *infra*, p. 184.

[2] *Tukhārī Chhant* 6 (3), *AG*, p. 1113.

[3] Ch. Vaudeville, *Kabīr Granthāvalī* (*Dohā*), p. xvi, and *Au Cabaret de l'Amour: Paroles de Kabîr*, p. 211, n. xxxv.

Pourtant, chacun éprouve cette certitude au fond de l'âme;
Le prix de l'amour divin, c'est la victoire sur son âme. . . .

Ceux qui ont pénétré ce mystère, dit Kabîr,
Contemplent en leur âme le Seigneur, le Maître de l'Univers.[1]

Gurū Nānak's understanding of the *man* is essentially that of Kabīr. The *man* of unregenerate man is erratic and leads him into worldly attachments which are the very antithesis of salvation.

The *man* is unsteady, it does not know the way. The man who puts his trust in his own *man* is as one befouled; he does not recognize the Word (*Śabad*).[2]

It is not, however, an inveterate enemy. It is to be restrained but not crushed, for this same *man* is something priceless, the treasury which contains all treasures, the abode of God Himself if man will but recognize it.

The *man* is a priceless pearl. (Dwelling on) the Name of God it has been accorded honour.[3]

In the *man* are the jewels of the Name, its pearls, its rubies, its diamonds. The Name is the true merchandise, the true wealth, deep down in every heart. If the grace of God, the precious One, is upon a man, then with the *Gurū*'s aid he obtains the divine Name.[4]

In unregenerate man, however, the *man* is impure, unrestrained. Its evil propensities are permitted to assert themselves, and in consequence man remains a slave to his passions and so to Death.

The heedless *man* is a wanderer, a vagrant.
Greedy beyond measure, it has indulged its desire by drinking the poison of *māyā*. Never does it find its peace in love of the One. It is like a fish, caught in the gullet by a hook. . . .
The heedless *man* flits hither and thither like a bumble-bee, seeking through its senses to indulge in many foolish evils. Like an elephant it is trapped because of its lust. It is bound and its head jabbed with a goad. . . .
The *man* is ever straying, never held in check. If it be not filled with love for God, He can give it neither honour nor trust. Thou art the omniscient One, the Protector of all. Thou dost uphold Thy creation, watching over all.[5]

2. Haumai

As iron is thrown into a furnace, melted, and recast, so is he who fastens his affections on *māyā* incarnated again and again. Without understanding (of the divine Word) all he gathers is suffering upon suffering. (Through the influence of) *haumai* he transmigrates and wanders in doubt.[6]

[1] loc. cit., p. 89.
[2] *Āsā Aṣṭ* 7 (8), *AG*, p. 415.
[3] *Sirī Rāgu* 22, *AG*, p. 22.
[4] *Sirī Rāgu* 21, *AG*, p. 22.
[5] *Basant Aṣṭ* 2 (1), (2), and (4), *AG*, pp. 1187–8.
[6] *Sūhī Aṣṭ* 4 (1–1R), *AG*, p. 752.

In unregenerate man the dominant impulse is that of *haumai*, a concept which is to be found in the works of Kabīr and those of other Sants, but which receives appreciably more emphasis in those of Gurū Nānak. For Gurū Nānak it is *haumai* which controls the *man* of unregenerate man and so determines the pattern of his life. The results are disastrous, for instead of leading a man to release and salvation his *haumai* will invariably stimulate affections which can only bind him more firmly to the wheel of transmigration.

The usual translation of *haumai*[1] is 'ego', another example of a rendering which is neither incorrect nor entirely satisfactory. The English word is certainly a literal translation,[2] but it is misleading for two reasons. The first is that it has already been appropriated in Indian philosophy to express a notion which has an equally literal original, but which offers a meaning different from that which *haumai* covers in Gurū Nānak's works. In Vedānta *ahaṃkāra* is an expression of *ajñāna*, a 'blending of the unreal associations held up in the mind (*antaḥkaraṇa*) with the real, the false with the true that is the root of illusion'.[3] This definition, in spite of the etymological connexion and the fact that the word has moved away from a neutral meaning, is not what Gurū Nānak meant, for it does not possess the moral content which is so strongly implied in *haumai*. Nor is 'ego' anywhere near *haumai* when used in a Yoga context, for in this case it is clearly neutral and precedes the emergence of *manas* in the evolutionary process.[4]

A second reason why there is a risk of misunderstanding is that the word 'ego' has at least three different usages in the West and that none of them can be said to accord with Gurū Nānak's usage. In its strictly philosophical application the term has a neutral meaning which is certainly not the case with *haumai*; in a psychological context it is too closely identified with Freudian theory; and in its loose popular usage it has become a mixture of 'pride', 'self-confidence', and 'morale'.

Macauliffe's translation was 'pride'.[5] It is true that *garab* and *haṅkār* are closely related to *haumai* and that in certain contexts they may be used in a sense which corresponds to it.

> Casting out pride (*garab*) we ascend to celestial heights. . . . Through His grace (the *Gurū*) reveals (God's) palace (within our own frame). Nānak, casting out our *haumai* (the *Gurū*) unites us with God.[6]

In general, however, *garab* and *haṅkār* must be regarded not as synonyms for *haumai*, but as a result of it.

[1] Or, in relevant contexts, of *hau* or *āp*.

[2] *hau-main*, 'I–I'.

[3] S. Dasgupta, *A History of Indian Philosophy*, vol. i, pp. 458–9.

[4] M. Eliade, *Yoga: Immortality and Freedom*, p. 20. There is, however, an obvious affinity between *haumai* and the *icchā* ('desire') of the *Yoga-vasiṣṭha* (S. Dasgupta, op. cit., vol. ii, p. 264).

[5] e.g. *The Sikh Religion*, vol. i, p. 227. Cf. also Jayaram Misra, *Srī Gurū Granth Daraśan*, p. 120.

[6] *Gauṛī* 9, *AG*, p. 153.

Another possible translation for *haumai* is 'sin'. It is not a literal translation in the way that 'ego' is, but its meaning corresponds closely. In its strict Christian theological usage 'sin' is always singular. It means self-willed disobedience to God, a condition naturally inherent in man and expressing itself in a multitude of ways. It would be difficult to distinguish this condition from *haumai*, for as applied to the individual the two correspond almost exactly. Just as such impulses as pride and greed are properly regarded as the results of sin, so too do we find that the five traditional evil impulses are the offspring of *haumai*. In both cases the evil impulses are regarded as the expressions in an individual's thoughts, feelings, and actions of a condition which determines the direction of those thoughts, feelings, and actions.

There are, however, two serious objections to the use of 'sin' as a translation. The first is that the word 'sin' extends in Christian usage beyond its application to the individual. In Christian theology it also possesses corporate and cosmic connotations. *Haumai*, however, is limited to the individual. The second objection is that 'sin', like 'ego', has its popular usage. It is a usage which is correct in its own right, but which differs from the strict theological definition. In general usage 'sin' refers to what is properly conceived as the result of sin and it is frequently used in the plural. This clearly does not correspond to *haumai*.[1] A discussion of the theological term 'sin' can certainly clarify the meaning of *haumai*, but the word itself does not provide us with a satisfactory translation.

'Self' and 'self-centredness' are also possible translations. In English 'self' can be used in a bad sense which comes close to *haumai* and its meaning in this sense has not been seriously distorted by popular usage. In this particular context, however, it is liable to be misunderstood because in Indian philosophy it has so commonly been used in its neutral sense as a translation of *ātman*. This leaves us with 'self-centredness' which is perhaps the best available, but which is nevertheless unsatisfactory in that it will frequently impart a weaker and more limited meaning than that which *haumai* was intended to give.

It is unfortunate that there is no really satisfactory English equivalent, for in the thought of Gurū Nānak this word *haumai* epitomizes the condition of unregenerate man.

In *haumai* he comes and in *haumai* he goes;
In *haumai* he is born and in *haumai* he dies;
In *haumai* he gives and in *haumai* he takes;
In *haumai* he acquires and in *haumai* he casts away;
In *haumai* he is truthful and in *haumai* he lies;
In *haumai* he pays regard sometimes to virtue and sometimes to evil. . . .[2]

[1] It is covered by such words as *pāp*, *gunāh*, and *aprādh*.
[2] *Vār Āsā*, *ślok* 1 of *pauṛī* 7, *AG*, p. 466.

Everything that a man does is done in the context of this condition which pervades the whole of his activity. Even that which men call right or good is done only if it accords with the individual's *haumai*, and if it is not in accord it is rejected in favour of that which is evil. The result is that the path of salvation is hidden. Attention is absorbed in *māyā* and so the round of birth and death continues. Only when one perceives the true nature of this condition does there come a recognition of the way of salvation.

> (In *haumai*) he fails to perceive the true nature of salvation. In *haumai* there is *māyā* and its shadow (which is doubt). By acting in accordance with *haumai* he causes himself to be born again and again. If he understands his *haumai* he perceives the door (of salvation), but without understanding he argues and disputes. In accordance with the divine Order (*Hukam*) our *karma* is inscribed. He who discerns the nature of the divine Order discerns his *haumai* also.[1]

The person who fails to discern the nature of the divine Order is a *manmukh*. His loyalty is to himself, to the wayward impulses of his own *man* instead of to the voice of the *Gurū*. In contrast to this pattern is that of the *gurmukh*. The *gurmukh* hears and obeys the *Gurū*'s Word; the *manmukh* ignores it. Offered truth, freedom and life, he chooses instead falsehood, bondage, and death, for such is the fate of the man who has not purged *haumai* from his *man*.

> The *manmukh's* mind is clogged with falsehood. He does not meditate on (the Name of) God and so suffers the penalties of sin.[2]

3. *Evil impulses*

The outward expressions of a *man* dominated by *haumai* are the evil passions and by this fruit the *manmukh* is to be known.

> Day and night are the two seasons when he crops his land; lust and anger are his two fields. He waters them with greed, sows in them the seed of untruth, and worldly impulse, his plough-man, cultivates them. His (evil) thoughts are his plough and evil is the crop he reaps, for in accordance with the divine Order he cuts and eats.[3]

Traditionally these evil passions are five in number—*kām* (lust), *krodh* (anger, wrath), *lobh* (covetousness), *moh* (attachment to worldly things), and *haṅkār* (pride). From these five basic impulses spring all the deeds of violence and falsehood which earn an adverse *karma* and so endlessly protract the cycle of transmigration.

[1] *Vār Āsā, ślok* 1 of *pauṛī* 7, *AG*, p. 466.
[2] *Āsā* 24, *AG*, p. 356.
[3] *Vār Rāmakalī, ślok* 1 of *pauṛī* 17, *AG*, p. 955.

My adversaries are five and I am but one. How shall I defend my house, O *man*?
Daily they attack me and plunder me. To whom shall I cry?[1]

Violence, attachment to worldly things, covetousness, and wrath are four streams of fire, and they who fall therein are consumed. Nānak, clinging, through grace, (to the *Gurū*'s feet) one is saved.[2]

Such impulses and the actions which proceed from them are the marks of the *manmukh*, of the self-willed, unregenerate man. They are the outward evidence of an impure *man*, filled not with love for the divine Name, but with love of self. And these are the snares of Yam, of Death.[3] He who falls into them must assuredly suffer the endless misery of death and rebirth.

4. Māyā

My merchant friend, (you who deal in worldly things), in the third watch of the night[4] you fix your attention on wealth and the bloom of youthful beauty, and do not remember the Name of God which brings release. Forgetting the Name of God, the soul is led astray through keeping the company of *māyā*. Absorbed in wealth, intoxicated by bodily beauty, it fritters its opportunity away. You neither adhered to your duty nor performed good deeds. Nānak says: The third watch is the period of the soul's attachment to money and carnal beauty.[5]

A wayward *man* dominated by *haumai* inevitably means involvement in *māyā*.

She who is caught up in greed, covetousness and pride is sunk in *māyā*. Foolish woman! The Lord is not found by such means.[6]

Māyā in the thought of Gurū Nānak is not the cosmic illusion of classical Vedānta. The world is indeed *māyā*, but it is not unreal. It is an illusion only in the sense that it is accepted for what it is not. Delusion is a more appropriate word. The essence of the world is its impermanence. It is real, but it is impermanent, both in the sense that it is itself perishable and in the sense that its attributes cannot follow a man after his physical death. It offers qualities which are accepted as both good and desirable, but which constitute a fraud, a deception. He who accepts the world in this way and who accordingly seeks fulfilment in attachment to worldly things is a victim of *māyā*, of the pretence that these attachments, if not actually Truth itself, are at least not inimical to Truth.

[1] *Gauṛī* 14, *AG*, p. 155.
[2] *Vār Mājh*, *ślok* 2 of *pauṛī* 20, *AG*, p. 147.
[3] See *infra*, p. 188.
[4] i.e. the third stage of human life. The four stages, corresponding in this *śabad* to the four watches of the night, are birth, childhood, adulthood, and death.
[5] *Sirī Rāgu Pahare* 1 (3), *AG*, p. 75.
[6] *Tilaṅg* 4, *AG*, p. 722.

Māyā is basically untruth as opposed to Truth and the expression of this untruth is the world. It is in worldly affections, in the desire to appropriate the things of this world, that man's great temptation lies and succumbing to this temptation means involvement in untruth. The result can only be separation from God and continued transmigration. *Māyā* is *añjan*, literally the black collyrium applied to eyes but traditionally the symbol of darkness and untruth. God, on the other hand, is *nir-añjan*, the One who is wholly apart from all that is false, the One who is Himself Truth. Man must choose one or the other, for Truth and its antithesis cannot coexist.

> The love of gold and silver, women and fragrant scents, horses, couches, and dwellings, sweets and meats—these are all lusts of the flesh. Where in the heart can there be room for the Name?[1]

The question is obviously a rhetorical one. If man accepts the world's attractions, if he accepts the pretences of *māyā*, he must inevitably choose to be separated from God. This is what unregenerate man does. Blinded by ignorance (*agiān*, *avidiā*), led astray by doubt (*bhram*) and forgetfulness (*bhulekhā*), he accepts the world at its own valuation. But it is *māyā*, it is a fraud (*kapaṭ*), a deceit (*chhal*), untruth (*kūṛ*, *jhūṭh*), a snare (*jāl*), and the penalty for accepting it is inexorable. By accepting it man involves himself in *dubidhā*, in 'duality', in all that stands in opposition to union, in that separation which must divide the self-willed *manmukh* from God. Rejecting Life he chooses instead Death.

> *Māyā's* disciple is false; he abhors the Truth. Bound up in duality he transmigrates.[2]

Some of the practical manifestations of *māyā* are set out in the extract quoted above from *Sirī Rāgu* 4. Wealth, women, sons, power, status, worldly honour, comfort, food—these are the attractions which the world extends and which call forth man's lust, greed, and pride.[3] These are the allurements which stimulate his evil impulses and so lead him into the trap.

> For the love of silver and women the fool is entangled in duality and forgets the divine Name.[4]

None of this, however, endures.

> Accumulating *māyā* (wealth, power, status) kings vaunt themselves, but the *māyā* to which they are so attached does not accompany them (after death).[5]

[1] *Sirī Rāgu* 4, *AG*, p. 15.

[2] *Mājh Aṣṭ* 1 (5), *AG*, p. 109.

[3] Macauliffe uses 'Mammon' as a translation of *māyā* (e.g. *The Sikh Religion*, vol. i, p. 22). The word is useful in that it brings out the basic antagonism between *māyā* and God, but it is inadequate for it limits the application of *māyā* to worldly wealth. *Sampad* (riches) is certainly one of the primary manifestations of *māyā* in Gurū Nānak's works, but so too is *kāmaṇ* (woman). Other temptations receive less emphasis, but obviously they are not to be regarded as negligible.

[4] *Āsā Aṣṭ* 9 (2), *AG*, p. 416.

[5] *Prabhātī Aṣṭ* 1 (2), *AG*, p. 1342.

Māyā is, of course, the work of God, for it consists in the creation and is inseparable from it.

> He who created the various colours, kinds and aspects of *māyā*, having brought His creation into being watches over it, the manifestation of His greatness.[1]

Māyā is an interpretation of the creation, or rather a misinterpretation of it, a misunderstanding of its nature and purpose. The creation is both a revelation of God and a snare. What matters is a man's response to it. If he perceives the revelation he is on the way to salvation. If, on the other hand, he regards it as a means of indulging his *haumai* he is on the road to ruin. It can be either his ally or his enemy, an opportunity or a trap, a firm path or a quicksand. Even evil is from God and is to be regarded as an aspect of man's opportunity.

> Many are endlessly afflicted by pain and hunger, but even these, O Beneficent One, are Thy gifts.[2]

Everything depends upon the response which a man makes, and unregenerate man makes the wrong response.

> *Bābā*, having come (into the world) one must depart again, and this world is but a fleeting show. The abode of Truth is found through serving the True One; attainment of Truth comes only by living in accordance with Truth, by following the path of Truth. Falsehood and covetousness disqualify a man and in the hereafter there is no place for him. No one invites him to enter and take his rest; he is like a crow in a deserted house. The cycle of birth and death is the great separation and in it all are destroyed. Involved through greed in the concerns of *māyā* people are led astray, and Death, standing over them, makes them to weep.[3]

5. *The fate of unregenerate man*

> They who have forgotten the Lord and indulged in sensual pleasures—they are the ones whose bodies are diseased.[4]

He who ignores God and follows instead the dictates of *haumai* is as one diseased. A remedy exists, but for the *manmukh* who refuses it the result can only be Death.

> Ineluctable Death smites the head of the false![5]

By Death in this sense Gurū Nānak does not, of course, mean the physical death which inevitably overtakes every person. Physical death, far from

[1] *Japjī* 27, *AG*, p. 6.

[2] *Japjī* 25, *AG*, p. 5. Dr. Vir Singh adds to this couplet the comment: 'Because as a result of this gift many people develop fear, abandon sin, and attain to the higher life.' *Santhyā*, vol. i, p. 120, n. § .

[3] *Vaḍahaṃsu Alāhaṇī* 5, *AG*, pp. 581–2.

[4] *Malār* 7, *AG*, p. 1256.

[5] *Gauṛī Aṣṭ* 14 (5), *AG*, p. 227.

being something to be feared, is for the *gurmukh* a joy to be welcomed when it comes, for it means a perfecting of his union with God. Gurū Nānak's *Gauṛī Dīpakī*[1] which is recited every night by devout Sikhs as a part of *Kīrtan Sohilā*, the Evening Prayer, is a sublime expression of the contentment with which a believer awaits his physical death and final release. The *manmukh*'s Death, however, is not the perfecting of union but the culmination of separation. To illustrate his meaning Gurū Nānak uses a variety of figures. The most common is the Vedic Yam who also figures prominently in the imagery of the Sants.

> Through Thy Name the *man* finds total bliss. Without the Name one goes bound to the city of Yam.[2]

Another is *narak*, the nether region, but demythologized as in Christian theological usage.

> He who forgets the Name must endure suffering. When the divine Order bids him depart how can he remain? He is submerged in the well of Hell (and yet dies as surely) as a fish without water.[3]

The various figures all point to the same thing. Submission to one's *haumai* and entanglement in *māyā* earn a *karma* which perpetuates the transmigratory process. In the constant coming and going there is separation from God and this is Death.

> No one can comprehend the Creator, He who is beyond human grasp, immeasurable. The soul is deluded by *māyā*, drugged by untruth. Ruined by the demands of greed (such a person) repents eternally, but he who serves the One knows Him, and his cycle of birth and death comes to an end. . . .

> Transmigration desolates us, the disease of duality has spread everywhere. A man who is without the Name collapses like a wall of sand. How can one be saved without the Name? (Such a person) must ultimately fall into Hell. . . .

> (The separated soul is like) the broken strings of a rebeck—severed and so giving no music. . . .

> (Man) is caught like a fish in Yam's net. Without the *Gurū*, the Giver, there is no salvation; one endlessly transmigrates. . . .

> (Innumerable people) have died begging *māyā* (to sustain them) but *māyā* accompanies no one (after death). The swan (-soul) mounts up and sadly flies away, leaving *māyā* here. The *man* which pursues untruth is tormented by Yam and with it go its evil qualities. . . .

[1] *AG*, pp. 12 and 157.

[2] *Prabhātī* 1, *AG*, p. 1327. The epithets used by Gurū Nānak are the common ones found in the works of the Sants. In addition to Yam we find Dharamrāj (with his assistants Chitr and Gupt) and Kāl.

[3] *Mārū Solahā* 8 (8), *AG*, p. 1028.

Those who focused their attention on themselves died. Devoid of the Name they received suffering. . . .

One may accumulate gold and silver, but such wealth is as poison, ashes. Gathering riches (a man) regards himself as an exalted person, (but his belief is vain). Caught up in duality he is destroyed.[1]

The fate of unregenerate man is the death of separation. How then can he escape this fate? In what manner is the way of salvation revealed to him and what must he do to appropriate it?

III. THE DIVINE SELF-EXPRESSION

I know that Thou art not afar. I believe that Thou art within. I have recognized the palace of God (within my heart).[2]

In the first section attention was drawn to Gurū Nānak's belief concerning the immanence of God in the human heart, and it was noted that this belief was for him of primary significance, for it is at this point that there may exist communication between God and man.[3] That the indwelling God should speak to man through his mind or what we call his heart is not in itself a remarkable doctrine and in a general sense it was universally accepted by the Sants. It is when we proceed from this point to inquire precisely *how* God communicates with man that we encounter the specific contribution of Gurū Nānak, a contribution which offers the most significant example of his positive originality. This is not to imply that his work is wholly original, for this can never be the case and much of what we find in Gurū Nānak, both in the total range of his thought and at this specific point, undoubtedly represents an inheritance from his contemporary religious environment. Nor does it necessarily mean that any single strand is without parallel elsewhere, for originality can lie as much in the pattern that is woven as in the threads which are used. There may have been earlier Sants who had arrived at similar conclusions concerning the medium of divine communication. In many there is silence at this point and it is possible that the notions which we find developed in the works of Gurū Nānak may have existed in an inchoate form in the minds of Sants who preceded him. It is true that even in Gurū Nānak's works there is not that manifest clarity which conveys an immediate understanding, but developed concepts of the divine self-expression are there nevertheless and exegesis will reveal them.

The obvious comparison is once again Kabīr and, as we have already noted, Kabīr and Gurū Nānak clearly share a common tradition. An outline of

[1] *Oaṅkāru* 6, 32, 39, 42, and 48. *AG*, pp. 930, 934, 935–6, 937.
[2] *Tukhārī Chhant Bārah-māhā* 6, *AG*, p. 1108.
[3] See *supra*, p. 175.

their respective patterns of belief (*sādhanā*) emphasizes the broad similarity of their thought and offers one reason to explain why the two figures have been so closely connected. The correspondence amounts, however, to no more than similarity. It is certainly not identity. Of Kabīr Dr. Vaudeville writes:

> La seule « révélation » valable, pour lui, est celle de la « Parole » (*çabda*) silencieuse que le Parfait Gourou (*Satguru*) prononce au « fond de l'âme » (*antari*) — et ce Gourou est Dieu.[1]

For Gurū Nānak, as for Kabīr, the Word of the *Satgurū* is the true revelation, and for him also this *Gurū* is God. Beyond this basic agreement, however, there is appreciable divergence. To speak of a 'Parole silencieuse' would not actually be incorrect in Gurū Nānak's case, but it would certainly be misleading. Moreover, we find in Gurū Nānak's doctrine of the divine Order (*Hukam*) and in his emphasis upon divine grace elements which carry him beyond Kabīr. The two are certainly within the same tradition, but their respective interpretations of it are by no means identical.

Our analysis at this point must concern six key words: Word (*Śabad*), Name (*Nām*), Divine Preceptor (*Gurū*), Divine Order (*Hukam*), Truth *Sach*), and Grace (*Nadar*).[2] Of these the first five bear a basic identity. In them we have five different words, but we do not have five radically different concepts. Instead we have five different aspects of a single all-embracing concept. This single concept is perhaps best expressed by the last of them, *Sach* or Truth, but in itself the word obviously has little substance and can only acquire it in the context of Gurū Nānak's usage. Frequently these words are used in ways which render them synonymous. All five are expressions of God; all are used to expound the nature, content, and method of the divine communication to men, of the divine truth which when appropriated brings salvation; all share a fundamental identity.

This does not appear to have received the emphasis which it deserves and the result has been an inability to give a satisfactory, coherent answer to the question of *how* in the thought of Gurū Nānak God communicates with man. The question has been allowed to remain a mystery. It is not sufficient to state that the *Gurū* is God, that the *Hukam* is His will, that the *Śabad* is the divine Word, and that the *Nām* represents the sum total of all God's qualities. Not all of these definitions can be accepted without qualification, and even if they could be so accepted the basic question would still remain unanswered. In what way is this divine Word so presented to the human understanding that it can be recognized, accepted, and

[1] Ch. Vaudeville, *Au Cabaret de l'Amour: Paroles de Kabîr*, p. 25.

[2] *Nadar*, or *nazar*, here represents a group of words which have the same or a closely related meaning: *kirpā, prasād, karam* (the Persian word), *bakhśiś, bhāṇā, daiā, mihar, taras*.

followed? This is the fundamental question and in order to answer it we must turn to the analysis of the six words.

Of the six the one which must receive the closest attention is *Hukam*. This it requires, partly because it has generally received much less attention than the other five, partly because it is in Gurū Nānak's use of this word that his development beyond the thought of Kabīr and other *bhagats* is most obvious, but above all because together with *Nadar* it carries us furthest in our efforts to set out Gurū Nānak's answer to the basic question. *Nadar* likewise demands careful scrutiny. It has not been overlooked in the way that *Hukam* is so often passed over, but neither has it normally received the degree of emphasis which it warrants. The translation of this and of the other words which bear the same meaning[1] is invariably the word 'grace', a translation which would appear to be the best available but which can be misleading in certain circumstances. The problem will be dealt with in the appropriate section.

1. Śabad: *the Word*

> None has encompassed Thy bounds so how can I describe Thee with a single tongue? He who meditates on Thy true *Śabad* is joined in union with Thee. . . . The *Gurū*'s *Śabad* is like a (sparkling) gem which reveals Thee by its light. One understands one's own self and through the *Gurū*'s instruction merges in the Truth.[2]

Śabad is one of the terms which evidently descended to Gurū Nānak through Sant channels from Nāth sources. The term has a significant history apart from its Nāth usage, but it appears to have been from this Nāth usage that it passed into Sant currency. In the context of Nāth theory the word is characteristically used in conjunction with *anahad*, or *anahat*, and refers to the mystical 'sound' which is 'heard' at the climax of the *haṭha-yoga* technique. The *anahad śabad* is, according to such theories, a 'soundless sound',[3] a mystical vibration audible only to the adept who has succeeded in awakening the *kuṇḍalinī* and caused it to ascend to the *suṣumṇā*.[4]

[1] *Kirpā, prasād, karam*, and *bakhśiś*. In some contexts *bhāṇā, daiā* and *mihar* may be translated as 'grace' and will always bear meanings closely related to it. *Taras* will normally be translated as 'pity'.

[2] *Vār Malār, pauṛī* 25, *AG*, p. 1290.

[3] 'Unstruck music'—Rabindranath Tagore, *One Hundred Poems of Kabir*, p. 20.

[4] According to the physiological theories of *haṭha-yoga* there are three principal channels (*nāḍī*) which ascend through the human body. These are the *iḍā* and *piṅgalā*, which terminate in the left and right nostrils respectively, and the *suṣumṇā*, or *sukhmanā*, which is held to run through the spinal column. Along the *suṣumṇā* are located six, or eight, *chakra* (discs, wheels, 'lotuses') and at its base, behind the genitals, is the *kuṇḍalinī*, a latent power symbolized by the figure of a sleeping serpent. By means of the *haṭha-yoga* discipline the *kuṇḍalinī* is awakened, and ascending the *suṣumṇā* it pierces each *chakra* in turn, thereby releasing progressively effectual stores of psychic energy. At the

Kabīr's usage distinguishes *Śabad* and *anahad śabad*. The *Śabad* is the *Gurū*'s 'Word', the revelation of God which is given in the depths of the human soul. *Anahad śabad*, however, he uses in a sense very close to that of the Nāths, although the experience which it expresses is, for him, in no way dependent upon the practice of *haṭha-yoga*.[1]

In the case of Gurū Nānak we find that, as with all such words which have Nāth antecedents, the term has travelled even further from its source. The expression *anahad śabad* has moved away to the periphery. It has become a useful figure of speech, a convenient means of conveying some impression of an experience which is strictly inexpressible.

> When one meets the *Gurū* then, casting aside doubt, one understands one's inner being. While yet alive prepare for the place where you must go when you die. (Prepare for it) by subduing the evil which is within you, and then die. Through meditation on the *Gurū* one hears the enchanting unstruck music (*anahad śabad*). When it is heard *haumai* is destroyed. I humble myself before him who serves the *Gurū*. He who repeats the Name of God receives a robe of honour in the (divine) court.[2]

The link with Nāth usage is very slender. Here there is no *kuṇḍalinī*, no *iḍā*, *piṅgalā*, and *suṣumṇā*, no *chakra*, no *prāṇāyām*. The expression, like other Nāth terms which are to be found in Gurū Nānak's works, has been naturalized. Its antecedents no longer cling to it as they do in the case of Kabīr's usage.[3] Moreover, such hints of the old Nāth association usually occur in verses which are obviously addressed to yogīs and which have a manifest dialectic or apologetic purpose. In such cases Gurū Nānak, like any effective apologist, has deliberately expressed himself in terms which would be related to a yogī's understanding.

Gurū Nānak's emphasis is wholly upon the concept of the Word (*Śabad*) as the vehicle of revelation. Inevitably, the Word is described by him more in terms of what it does than in terms of what it actually is. This is entirely natural as it is the function which concerns him and it is in experience that it is to be known rather than in any purely intellectual sense. The function of the Word is that it provides the means whereby man can know both God and the path which leads to Him, the means whereby the individual may secure release from his bonds and so attain union with God. Again and again the Word is declared to be the essential means of salvation.[4] It is for Gurū Nānak the revelation of God and so the only proper

climax of the ascent it pierces the *sahasradala*, 'the lotus of a thousand petals' said to be located at the top of the cranium. The *dasam duār* ('tenth door') then opens and the *jīv* passes into the ineffable condition of *sahaj*, the state of ultimate union with Brahman.

[1] Ch. Vaudeville, *Kabīr Granthāvalī* (*Dohā*), Introduction, pp. xxii–xxiii.

[2] *Sirī Rāgu* 18, *AG*, p. 21.

[3] Cf. Jodh Singh, *Guramati Niraṇay*, pp. 211 ff.

[4] Cf. *Sirī Rāgu* 19, *AG*, p. 21; *Gauṛī* 17, *AG*, p. 228; *Sūhī Aṣṭ* 2 (2), *AG*, p. 751; *Siddh Goṣṭi* 55 and 61, *AG*, pp. 944, 945.

object of man's contemplation. By contemplation of the Word and by the total conforming of one's life to its dictates the *man* is brought under control, self-centredness is cast out, the individual grows ever nearer to God until, ultimately perfected in His likeness, he passes into a condition of union which transcends death and the cycle of transmigration.

> He has neither form, colour, nor material sign, but He is revealed through the true Word (*Śabad*).[1]

> By the *Gurū*'s leading he obtains salvation and is no longer bound (to the wheel of transmigration).
> Meditating on the Word (*Śabad*), (repeating) the Name of God, he is released.[2]

> Without the Word (*Śabad*) one is condemned to wander. Worldly affections cause many to sink (in the Ocean of Existence). O *man*, apply your understanding to the Word (*Śabad*) and cross over. He who has not followed the *Gurū* and so has not understood the divine Name, (such a person) continues to transmigrate.[3]

> Nānak, the Lord, the true Creator, is known by means of the Word (*Śabad*)![4]

Often the word *Śabad* stands by itself and often it is linked with the word *Gurū*. The latter may be regarded as the characteristic form, for the use of *Śabad* by itself normally assumes its connexion with the *Gurū*. The form may be *gurū kā śabad*, 'the *Gurū*'s Word', or it may be *gurū-śabad*, 'the *Gurū*-Word'.[5] The latter carries us nearer the true meaning for it brings out the basic identity of the two terms. The development of this point must, however, await the section devoted to the *Gurū* and in the meantime we must continue to use the expression 'the *Gurū*'s Word', or 'the *Gurū*'s *Śabad*'.

For Gurū Nānak the Word is accordingly the *gurupadeś*, that expression of God's truth which is imparted to man by the *Gurū*. All that concerns God, all that relates to the path which leads to Him is the Word. It is this comprehensive quality which distinguishes his concept of the Word from that of Kabīr. Man's proper response to the divine revelation is, for Gurū Nānak, an inward one, but the revelation itself is by no means confined to a mystical inward experience. There is in his works a much stronger emphasis upon the significance of external circumstances and phenomena as aids to the necessary inward perception. The Word embraces all that is Truth, all that expresses the nature of God and the means of attaining Him, and this may be perceived in the divine laws governing the universe as well as in the ineffable mystical experience.

The difference between the thought of Gurū Nānak and that of Kabīr emerges not so much in their understanding of the ultimate experience of

[1] *Soraṭhi* 6, *AG*, p. 597. [2] *Gauṛī* 6, *AG*, p. 152.
[3] *Sirī Rāgu* 15, *AG*, p. 19. [4] *Dhanāsarī Chhant* 2 (3), *AG*, p. 688.
[5] Cf. *Dhanāsarī Aṣṭ* 1 (8), *AG*, p. 686, and *Rāmakalī* 10, *AG*, p. 879.

union, not so much in their conceptions of the condition of *sahaj*,[1] as in their differing notions of how that condition is to be attained. For neither is the path to God regarded as accessible to all, and both affirm that humanity suffers from a congenital blindness which is overcome in only a minority of cases. In Gurū Nānak's works, however, one can distinguish with much greater clarity the means whereby this spiritual sight is acquired and the path to God followed. There is in his thought relative clarity at a point where in the thought of Kabīr we are obliged to grapple with mystery.

In Kabīr's case, moreover, the experience of enlightenment comes with a suddenness which we do not find in Gurū Nānak's descriptions. Evidently there had come to Kabīr, at some particular point in time, a compelling and shattering illumination. The figure which he uses to describe it is that of the arrow which is discharged by the True Gurū (*Satgurū*) and which pierces the *man*.[2] The arrow represents the Word and the figure clearly illustrates the abruptness with which, according to Kabīr, it is apprehended. Gurū Nānak, by contrast, implies an ascent over a period of time as the normal pattern of an individual's salvation experience, of his apprehension of the Truth and the conforming of his life to it. This is clearly brought out in his doctrine of the five *khaṇḍs* ('realms' or stages in spiritual progress).[3] The *sākhī* which purports to describe the Gurū's divine call during his immersion in the Veīn stream near Sultānpur does not imply any denial of this.[4] The *sākhī* obviously owes much to a reverent imagination, but there is no need to doubt that Gurū Nānak as a young man did experience a definite sense of call. There is nothing, however, to suggest abruptness. On the contrary, the traditions all emphasize the piety of his youth and the call would accordingly come as the climax of a spiritual development.

The difference is not confined to their respective interpretations of the Word, but these interpretations are an illustration of it. Given the initial act of God's favour, the initiative which first arouses within a man the longing for union, the Word is for Gurū Nānak within the range of ordinary human understanding. It is by no means wholly within it, for the Word partakes of the infinity of God, but sufficiently within it to be readily accessible to all who desire it. God Himself is, in His fullness, a mystery far exceeding the comprehension of man, but in His Word He expresses Himself in terms which may be understood and followed. Here we are anticipating much that properly belongs to the section dealing with the divine Order (*Hukam*), but with terms which share a common basis a certain amount of anticipation is unavoidable.[5]

[1] See *infra*, p. 225.

[2] Cf. Kabīr *ślok* 183, *AG*, p. 1374 (= *KG sākhī* 14. 5); *KG sākhī* 1. 9.

[3] *Japjī* 34–37, *AG*, pp. 7–8. See *infra*, pp. 221–4.

[4] See *supra*, pp. 37, 54, 107.

[5] In Sikh usage the term *śabad* is used as a synonym for an *Ādi Granth pad* (hymn or

2. Nām: *the Name of God*

For a diseased world the remedy is the Name. Without Truth the taint remains.[1]

This second category can be discussed with greater brevity than the first, not because it is any less important, but because for all practical purposes Name (*Nām*) is synonymous with Word (*Śabad*). The functions which are affirmed in the case of the Word may without exception be affirmed in the case of the Name also. It too is the revelation of God's being, the only proper object of contemplation, the standard to which the individual's life must conform, the essential means of purification and salvation.

Sacrifices, burnt offerings, charity given to acquire merit, austerities, and *pūjā*, (all are ineffective) and one's body continues to endure continual suffering. Without the Name of God there is no salvation. He who, by the *Gurū*'s aid, (meditates on) the Name (finds) salvation. Without the Name of God birth into this world is fruitless. Without the Name one eats poison, speaks evil, dies without merit, and so transmigrates.[2]

In this and in many other extracts 'Name' could be replaced by 'Word' without altering the sense at all. In other cases the close conjunction of the two terms renders their identity even more obvious.

Eating and drinking we die without knowing (the Truth). Recognizing the Word (*sabadu pachhāniā*) we die (to self) in an instant. The *man* has ceased to wander and it rejoices in this death. By the *Guru*'s grace we have recognized the Name (*nāmu pachhāniā*).[3]

It is obvious that in this context Word and Name are completely synonymous. The same applies to the following extract from *Bhairau* 2.

Without the Word how can one cross the Ocean of Fear? Without the Name the disease of duality has spread throughout the world. Men have sunk (in the Ocean) and so perished.[4]

In some cases, however, there is an implied distinction.

He who meditates on the true Name by means of the *Gurū*'s Word is accepted in the true court (of God) as a true follower of the *Gurū*.[5]

By means of the Word one enshrines the Name in one's heart.[6]

In such cases the Word appears as the medium of communication and the Name as the object of communication. Both remain, however, expressions

verse), the import being that all such *pads* are expressions of the divine *Śabad*. The word occasionally appears in this sense in *Ādi Granth* headings (e.g. *Rāg Mārū*, *AG*, p. 989).

[1] *Dhanāsarī Chhant* 1 (1), *AG*, p. 687.

[2] *Bhairau* 8, *AG*, p. 1127.

[3] *Oaṅkāru* 19, *AG*, p. 932.

[4] *Bhairau* 2, *AG*, p. 1125.

[5] *Āsā* 21, *AG*, p. 355.

[6] *Prabhātī Aṣṭ* 1 (7), *AG*, p. 1242.

of God's Truth and the distinction is a very fine one, normally determined by the context. Almost invariably Truth as mediated by the *Gurū* is referred to as the Word, whereas Truth as received and meditated on by the believer tends to be expressed in terms of the Name. *Gurū ka śabad* and *nām japnā* are both thoroughly characteristic expressions. There is, however, no basic difference involved and occasionally one of the two is used where the other would be expected.

> Following the True *Gurū* one utters the Word which imparts immortality.[1]

Not only is it the Name which is normally used in the context of the believer's utterances but also it is *Nām* which is usually found in association with *amrit*, the nectar of immortality. The substitution is, however, entirely permissible, even if not common.

> Wherever the meaning of *Nām* is to be found in the *Gurū Granth Sāhib* there too is the meaning of *Śabad*.[2]

To all this we must add a couplet from *Japjī* which carries our understanding a stage further.

> Whatever he has made is an expression of His Name. There is no part of creation which is not such an expression.[3]

The creation is an expression of the Creator and so a manifestation of His Truth. We have here a preliminary answer to the question of how the individual is to perceive this Truth which is referred to as the Word or the Name. Look around you and within you, for in all that He has created you will see Him. Understand the nature of what you see and you will understand the nature of God and of the way to Him.

Once again we are verging on what can with greater clarity be treated under *Hukam*, the divine Order. In concluding this section we may note the radical difference between the Name of God and the names of God. Hari, Rām, Parameśvar, Jagadīś, Prabhu, Gopāl, Allāh, Khudā, Sāhib—these are all but names and none are essential. Some do indeed bear a special significance, as in the case of *Niraṅkār* and *Nirañjan*, but even these do not constitute the Name although they express aspects of it. The Name is the total expression of all that God is, and this is Truth. *Sati Nām*—His Name is Truth. Meditate on this and you shall be saved.

3. Gurū: *the Divine Preceptor*

Within Sikhism primary significance is accorded to the doctrine of the *Gurū* and considerable emphasis is laid upon his role as the communicator

[1] *Āsā* 13, *AG*, p. 352.
[2] *Srī Gurū Granth Koś*, pp. 210–11.
[3] *Japjī* 19, *AG*, p. 4.

of divine Truth. But who is the *Gurū*? A contemporary answer is that the *Gurū* is a particular personality, a creative and perfect personality who stands as guide and exemplar.[1] This personality inhabited the ten personal Gurūs and with the death of Gurū Gobind Singh merged in the scripture and in the community.[2] Such an answer is certainly adequate as applied to a follower of Gurū Nānak, but it leaves unanswered the old question of who was the *Gurū* of Gurū Nānak. How was Truth imparted to Gurū Nānak himself?

The significance of the *gurū* in the bhakti tradition is well known and need not detain us here. Within this tradition the ancient respect for one's spiritual teacher had been magnified to the point where the *gurū* had become an object of devotion and his voice accepted as the veritable voice of God. In the case of the Sant tradition this inheritance from southern bhakti was reinforced by that tradition's link with the Nāth movement. In the Buddhist tantric tradition the master occupied a position of exalted authority as the mediator of esoteric knowledge and from this source the same emphasis descended to the Nāths.[3]

It is within the Sant tradition, however, that we encounter a major modification of the traditional doctrine. As we have already seen, there appears to be little doubt that Kabīr had no human *gurū*, but that for him the *Gurū* or *Satgurū* represented the inner voice, the mystical movement of God in the depths of the individual being, the light of God shed abroad in the inmost recesses of the human soul. The *Gurū* remains the vital link, the essential mediator of divine Truth, but no longer a human link.

In Gurū Nānak's case we must first note the characteristic emphasis upon the absolute necessity of the *Gurū*.

> The *Gurū* is the ladder, the dinghy, the raft by means of which one reaches God;
> The *Gurū* is the lake, the ocean, the boat, the sacred place of pilgrimage, the river.
> If it please Thee I am cleansed by bathing in the Lake of Truth.[4]

> Without the *Gurū* there can be no bhakti, no love;
> Without the *Gurū* there is no access to the company of the *sants*;
> Without the *Gurū* one blindly engages in futile endeavour;
> But with the *Gurū* one's *man* is purified, for its filth is purged by the Word.[5]

> When the True *Gurū* is merciful faith is perfected;
> When the True *Gurū* is merciful there is no grief;
> When the True *Gurū* is merciful no sorrow is known;

[1] Teja Singh, *Sikhism: Its Ideals and Institutions*, pp. 17–18.

[2] Ibid., pp. 23–25.

[3] M. Eliade, *Yoga: Immortality and Freedom*, pp. 206–7. P. D. Barthwal, *The Nirguna School of Hindi Poetry*, pp. 114–22.

[4] *Sirī Rāgu* 9, *AG*, p. 17.

[5] *Basant* 6, *AG*, p. 1170.

When the True *Gurū* is merciful the love of God is enjoyed;
When the True *Gurū* is merciful there is no fear of death;
When the True *Gurū* is merciful there is eternal peace;
When the True *Gurū* is merciful the nine treasures are obtained;
When the True *Gurū* is merciful one blends in union with the True One.[1]

He knows fear who fears not (God). Without the *Gurū* there is darkness.[2]

Such passages recur constantly, but there is nothing remarkable in them apart from the quality of Gurū Nānak's expression. Others, however, carry us much further.

Renounce self-centredness and pride, O *man*! Serve Hari the *Gurū*, the Lake (of Immortality), for so you shall obtain honour in His court.[3]

The *Gurū* is God, ineffable, unsearchable. He who follows the *Gurū* comprehends the nature of the universe.[4]

Gurū Arjan makes the point explicitly.

The True *Gurū* is *Nirañjan* (God). Do not believe that He is in the form of a man.[5]

In the words of Dr. Jodh Singh:

All of the human *gurūs* who roam around nowadays have taken instruction from some person or other. Gurū Nānak's *Gurū*, however, was not a person. In the *sākhī* dealing with the Veīn River incident it is clearly stated that Gurū Nānak received the cup of the Name from the true court (of God). He himself has declared:

'*Nirañjan* is the essence of all and His light shines in all places. All is God and nothing is separate from Him. He who is the infinite, supreme God is the *Gurū* whom Nānak has met.'

Soraṭhi

The Tenth Gurū has also declared:

'Know that the eternal and incarnate One is my *Gurū*.'

Chaupaī[6]

This is the first stage in our effort to define Gurū Nānak's doctrine of the *Gurū*. We must, however, examine the nature of this identification of *Gurū* and God, for it requires some clarification. Many passages clearly imply a distinction between God and the *Gurū* and the question of their interpretation must now be considered.

[1] *Vār Mājh, pauṛī* 25, *AG*, p. 149.
[2] *Sirī Rāgu Aṣṭ* 3 (3), *AG*, p. 54.
[3] *Sirī Rāgu* 19, *AG*, p. 21.
[4] *Bhairau* 2, *AG*, p. 1125.
[5] *Rāmakalī* 39, *AG*, p. 895. Cf. also Gurū Arjan's *Goṇḍ* 9, *AG*, p. 864.
[6] Jodh Singh, *Guramati Niraṇay* (7th edition), p. 114. The passage quoted from Gurū Nānak is from his *Soraṭhi* 11, *AG*, p. 599.

He for whom we searched throughout the universe, Him we found by means of the *Gurū*. It is the True *Gurū* who brings us into union with the Lord.[1]

The Master is near at hand and yet, O my wretched soul, you do not perceive Him. It is the True *Gurū* who reveals Him.[2]

Here there is an evident contrast between the agent and the object of revelation. The conclusion which such extracts suggest is that our initial identification of the *Gurū* with God needs some qualification. A strict definition requires us to identify the *Gurū* not with God Himself, but with the voice of God, with the means whereby God imparts truth to man.

This brings us to what is essentially Kabīr's doctrine, but Gurū Nānak takes us one step further. In the case of Kabīr this step may be deduced; with Gurū Nānak it is categorically affirmed. The *Gurū* is in fact the *Śabad*, the Word. In the work entitled *Siddh Goṣṭ* the Siddhs put the following question to Gurū Nānak.

Who is your *gurū*, he of whom you are a disciple?[3]

Gurū Nānak replies:

The Word is the *Gurū* and the mind (which is focused on it) continually is the disciple. By dwelling on the Ineffable One, on Him the eternal *Gurū-Gopāl*, I remain detached. It is only through the Word that I dwell on Him and so through the *Gurū* the fire of *haumai* is extinguished.[4]

The *Gurū* accordingly is God; the *Gurū* is the voice of God; and the *Gurū* is the Word, the Truth of God.[5] Gurū Nānak uses the term in all three senses. One might perhaps raise logical objections to what may, at first sight, appear to be confused usage, but only if one forgets the basic identity which these three senses share in Gurū Nānak's thought. The passage quoted above from *Siddh Goṣṭ* brings out this identity not just with the pronouncement that the Word is the *Gurū*, but also with the reference to the *Gurū-Gopāl*. God Himself is Truth. In order to accommodate this fundamental belief to the limitations both of language and of the human understanding distinctions, if not absolutely essential, are at least very convenient.

4. Hukam: *the Divine Order*

Śabad, *Nām*, and *Gurū*—all three are to be defined as the Truth of God made manifest for the salvation of men, and all three share a fundamental identity. And yet the basic question remains unanswered. How is this Truth

[1] *Sirī Rāgu* 17, *AG*, p. 20.
[2] *Malār Aṣṭ* 3 (8), *AG*, p. 1274.
[3] *Siddh Goṣṭi* 43, *AG*, p. 942.
[4] *Siddh Goṣṭi* 44, *AG*, p. 943.
[5] And in *Bilāvalu* 3, *AG*, p. 795, God is identified with the Word.
Thou art the Word and Thou art its expression.

to be apprehended by man? The fourth key word brings us another stage nearer the answer.

The fundamental importance of the *Hukam* in the thought of Gurū Nānak is emphasized by its exposition at the very beginning of *Japjī*. The first stanza puts the basic question:

> How is Truth to be attained, how the veil of falsehood torn aside?[1]

And the concept of the *Hukam*, the divine Order, provides Gurū Nānak's answer. Truth is to be found through submission to the *Hukam*.

> Nānak, thus it is written: Submit to the *Hukam*, walk in its way.[2]

For Gurū Nānak this is an affirmation of the utmost consequence and one to which we must return. In the next stanza he proceeds to explain the nature of the *Hukam*.

> The *Hukam* is beyond describing, (but this much we can understand that) all forms were created by the *Hukam*, that life was created through the *Hukam*, and that greatness is imparted in accordance with the *Hukam*. Distinctions between what is exalted and what is lowly are the result of the *Hukam* and in accordance with it suffering comes to some and joy to others. Through the *Hukam* one receives blessing and another is condemned to everlasting transmigration. All are within the *Hukam*; none are beyond its authority. Nānak, if anyone comprehends the *Hukam* his *haumai* is purged.[3]

Several conclusions emerge from this description. The first is that just as God Himself is, in His fullness, beyond human comprehending, so too the *Hukam* is, in its total range, more than the understanding of man can grasp. Secondly, however, it can be understood to a sufficient degree and this much at least man can comprehend that it is the source of those differences and distinctions in man's condition which are seemingly beyond human control. It is the principle which determines the giving of differing forms, of greatness, of differences between high and low, misery and happiness, salvation and transmigration.[4] Thirdly, all are subject to the *Hukam*. And fourthly, understanding of this divine principle leads to destruction of self. Stanza 3 again sets it forth as the principle which regulates the universe in accordance with the intention of God.

> God's *Hukam*[5] directs the path—(God) the ever-joyous and carefree.[6]

[1] *Japjī* 1, *AG*, p. 1. [2] Ibid.

[3] *Japjī* 2, *AG*, p. 1. Vir Singh adds to this the note: 'This *haun* (*haumai*) is the veil of falsehood which prevents us from attaining to the Truth. When *haun* is destroyed Truth is attained.' *Santhyā*, vol. i, p. 48. For *haun*, or *haumai*, see *supra*, pp. 181 ff.

[4] Or more specifically the laws which determine who shall attain salvation and who shall continue to transmigrate.

[5] *hukami hukamu*. 'The *Hukam* of Him who exercises the *Hukam*.'

[6] *Japjī* 3, *AG*, p. 2.

Hukam has usually been translated as 'Will'. This is a literal translation, but it is unsuitable in the context of Gurū Nānak's usage for it fails to convey his precise meaning and is liable to be equated with the Islamic doctrine of the Will of God. In the thought of Gurū Nānak the *Hukam* signifies the divinely instituted and maintained principle governing the existence and movement of the universe. It is a constant principle, and to the extent to which it can be comprehended it functions according to a predictable pattern. This regularity and this consistency distinguish it from the Islamic concept. In Islam the divine Will, if not actually capricious is at least 'unpledged',[1] whereas the *Hukam* of Gurū Nānak's usage is definitely pledged and dependable. A better translation is 'divine Order'. This too is inadequate, but it comes nearer to Gurū Nānak's concept than 'Will' and it is not liable to be confused with the Will of Islam.

This divine Order is manifested in a variety of ways. It is represented as the agent of creation:

> By Thy *Hukam* Thou didst create all forms.[2]

It determines the regular cycle of human existence:

> My friend, (you who) trade (in the things of the world), in the first watch of the night, (the first stage of the human life), you are placed in the womb in accordance with the *Hukam*.[3]

All are under it:

> Speaking, seeing, moving, living, and dying—all are transitory. Thou, the True (Lord), having established the *Hukam* placed all under it (literally, in it).[4]

And it gathers into a single principle the sum total of all God's activity:

> (Of itself, i.e. apart from the *Hukam*) the soul does not die and it neither sinks nor crosses over. He who has been active (in creation) is still active. In accordance with the *Hukam* we are born and we die. Ahead and behind the *Hukam* pervades all.[5]

This principle is most immediately perceptible in the laws governing the structure and functioning of the physical universe, but it is by no means limited to this sphere. It is also expressed in moral terms in the law of *karma*.

> One receives in accordance with what one does. What you sow, that you must eat.[6]

> One reaps what one sows and one eats what one earns.[7]

[1] I owe this definition to Canon Kenneth Cragg.
[2] *Vār Mājh*, *ślok* 2 of *pauṛī* 27, *AG*, p. 150.
[3] *Sirī Rāgu Pahare* 1, *AG*, p. 74.
[4] *Vār Mājh*, *ślok* 2 of *pauṛī* 15, *AG*, p. 145.
[5] *Gauṛī* 2, *AG*, p. 151.
[6] *Dhanāsarī* 6, *AG*, p. 662.
[7] *Sūhī* 7, *AG*, p. 730.

This conviction is as much an aspect of the *Hukam* principle as the regular movement of the physical universe. Indeed it is a vital aspect.

> Hear me, O Lord. Each receives joy or sorrow in accordance with what his past deeds have earned him, and what Thou dost give is fair and just. Thine is the creation, but what is my condition! Without Thee I cannot live for a moment. Without my Beloved I suffer torment and there is none to give me aid. Grant that by the *Gurū*'s aid I may drink the nectar (of the Name). We remain entangled in the world which God has created; the supreme deed is to enshrine the Lord in the *man*. Nānak, the bride watches the way (for the Bridegroom's coming). Hear my cry, O God.[1]

The law of *karma* is here explicitly affirmed.[2] The conclusion which must be drawn from it is that each individual should perform those deeds which will, in accordance with the law of *karma*, bring the supreme reward. And 'the supreme deed is to enshrine the Lord in the *man*'.

> (In God's) presence Dharamrāj scrutinises our record of good and evil, and in accordance with our deeds we dwell near Him or far off. The labours of those who meditated on the Name are over. Their countenances are radiant and many others (through association) with them also find release.[3]

> Meditate on the One and harvest the fruit thereof.[4]

An exhortation of this nature assumes, of course, that man has the necessary measure of freedom to make such a decision. Such references clearly imply an area wherein man has the capacity to exercise free will, a capacity which permits him to live in discord with the divine Order instead of in harmony with it. This faculty is obviously of critical importance, for the manner in which it is exercised brings either salvation or continued transmigration. Disharmony is the normal condition, but it does not lead to Truth and its inevitable consequence is continued movement within the cycle of transmigration, with all the attendant sufferings of this condition. Submission, on the other hand, leads to union, the consequence whereof is freedom. He who recognizes the divine Order perceives the Truth; and he who, having recognized it, brings his life into conformity with it ascends to that eternal union with God which is the ultimate beatitude.

> Beloved, he who comprehends the divine Order of the Lord attains Truth and receives honour.[5]

[1] *Tukhārī Chhant Bārah-māhā* 1, *AG*, p. 1107.

[2] Cf. also *Vār Āsā, pauṛī* 10, *AG*, p. 468; *Vār Sūhī, ślok* 2 of *pauṛī* 17, *AG*, p. 791.

[3] *Japjī, ślok, AG*, p. 8. In *Vār Mājh* (*ślok* 2 of *pauṛī* 18, *AG*, p. 146) this *ślok* is attributed to Gurū Aṅgad. The differences between the two versions are insignificant apart from the addition of the word *hor* in the last line of the *Vār Mājh* version.

[4] *Vaḍahaṃsu Alāhaṇī* 2, *AG*, p. 580.

[5] *Soraṭhi Aṣṭ* 3 (6), *AG*, p. 636.

He who meets the True *Gurū* knows Him. He recognises the divine Order and remains ever obedient to the will (of God). He who perceives the divine Order abides in the dwelling-place of Truth. Birth and death (the cycle of transmigration) are destroyed by the Word.[1]

He who recognises the divine Order of the Master needs no other wisdom.[2]

The divine Order, the *Hukam*, is accordingly an all-embracing principle, the sum total of all divinely instituted laws; and it is a revelation of the nature of God. In this latter sense it is identical in meaning with the Word (*Śabad*).

Thou didst create and Thou didst recognise (the true nature of Thy creation). Thou didst separate the heavens from the earth and Thou didst stretch out light in the heavens. Thou didst establish the sky without pillars and so revealed Thy Word.[3]

Again it is a case of basic identity with differing functions postulated only in order to bring out the fundamental truth with greater clarity. The creation is constituted and ordered by the *Hukam* and in this creation, physical and otherwise, the Word is made manifest. Understand this Principle, this divine Order, and you understand God. Look around you and within you and you shall perceive the Word, the Name, Truth. Herein is God revealed as single, as active, and as absolute; as *Niraṅkār*, as *Nirañjan*, as the eternal One beyond all that is transient and corruptible. Meditate on this, conform your life to it, acquire a nature which in accordance with the law of *karma* will carry you beyond the cycle of birth and death. Thus you shall find salvation.

When one meets the True *Gurū* and understands the *Hukam* one attains to Truth. Salvation is not wrought through one's own efforts. Nānak, such a claim would bring destruction, (not salvation).[4]

It is, as we have already noted, an extended process, an ascent, but in the end there is absolute harmony. With the ultimate attainment of Truth, with the *gurmukh* in the final stage of union (*sach khaṇḍ*) there is absolute fulfilment of the divine Order.

As the *Hukam*, so too the deed![5]

5. Sach: *Truth*

Sach, the fifth of Gurū Nānak's characteristic terms, does not require a detailed analysis for it too, as its normal meaning plainly indicates, is used

[1] *Bilāvalu Aṣṭ* 2 (7), *AG*, p. 832.
[2] *Mārū* 7, *AG*, p. 991.
[3] *Vār Malār, pauṛī* 1, *AG*, p. 1279.
[4] *Vār Malār, ślok* 1 of *pauṛī* 25, *AG*, p. 1289.
[5] *Japjī* 37, *AG*, p. 8.

to express the Truth and an analysis would simply mean covering ground which has already been covered.

> One does not reach heaven through mere talk. It is through acting in accordance with Truth (*sachu*) that one finds release.[1]

6. Nadar: *the Divine Grace*

How does God communicate with man? How does man perceive the nature of God and the means of attaining union with Him? An analysis of *Śabad*, *Nām*, *Gurū*, and *Hukam* can bring us well towards an answer, but there remains one significant gap. According to Gurū Nānak God has revealed His Truth in creation, and specifically in the *Hukam* which orders creation. He who perceives this Truth and submits to it will find salvation. But how are we to explain the manifest fact that only a minority of men perceive it? The Truth may be there for all to grasp, but few there be who do in fact lay hold of it.

> Many there be who long for a vision of Thee, but few who meet the *Gurū*, the Word, and so perceive (Thee).[2]

Why are there so few? One explanation is that *karma* determines the issue. Those who in their previous existences have lived lives of relative merit acquire thereby a faculty of perception which enables them to recognize the *Gurū*. This theory has a logical consistency and in one place it would appear to be explicitly affirmed.

> If it is inscribed in the record of one's former deeds then one meets the True *Gurū*.[3]

Karma is one theory and the other is divine grace. According to the latter, the necessary faculty of perception is a gift from God and one which is not ultimately dependent upon the merit of the individual in this or any prior existence.

The latter theory is the one which we must accept, but not at the cost either of maintaining that Gurū Nānak denied the relevance of *karma* as far as this initial perception was concerned, or of admitting that at this point he was inconsistent. Extracts which affirm a belief in divine grace have already been quoted[4] and such affirmations recur with considerable frequency in his writings. The quotation from *Āsā Aṣṭapadī* 19 given above implies an inconsistency, but when the paucity of such references, direct or implied, is compared with the very considerable weight of

[1] *Vār Mājh*, *ślok* 2 of *pauṛī* 7, *AG*, p. 141.
[2] *Basant Aṣṭ* 3 (1R), *AG*, p. 1188.
[3] *Āsā Aṣṭ* 19 (5), *AG*, p. 421. Cf. also *Basant Hiṇḍol* 12 (2), *AG*, p. 1172.
[4] See *supra*, pp. 174, 176, 177.

emphasis which he lays upon his concept of divine grace there can be no doubt that in the last analysis it is this grace which must decide the issue. The solution which he himself provides to the seeming inconsistency is a compromise which does accord a necessary place to *karma* as far as the initial apprehension of the Word is concerned, but which specifies grace as the ultimate determinant. In a significant line from *Japjī* he contrast the two, *karma* and grace. *Karma* is certainly important in that it will produce a favourable or unfavourable birth, but it is through grace that the initial *opportunity* to lay hold of salvation is attained.

> *Karma* determines the nature of our birth (lit. the cloth), but it is through grace that the door of salvation is found.[1]

Even within its own domain the operation of *karma* is not irresistible. The divine Order, of which *karma* is a part, also provides the means of cancelling its effects, and he who brings his life into accord with the divine Order will find the effects of an adverse *karma* obliterated.

Man's understanding of the divine Order will not, however, provide him with an explanation for the fact that the prerequisite perception is awakened in some, whereas others remain blind. There is a point beyond which the human understanding cannot proceed and the giving or evident withholding of perception is an issue which lies beyond that point. It is for Gurū Nānak an ultimate mystery. The characteristic term used to express this mystery is *nadar*, or *nazar*,[2] but as we have already noted[3] the same doctrine is expressed in the words *kirpā* (or *kripā*), *prasād*, *karam* (the Persian word), *bakhśīś*, *bhāṇā*, *daiā* (*dayā*), *mihar*, and *taras*.

> If Thou dost impart Thy grace then by that grace the True *Gurū* is revealed.[4]

> He, the One, dwells within all, but He is revealed to him who receives grace.[5]

> Within us are ignorance, suffering, and doubt, but through the *Gurū*'s wisdom all are cast out. He to whom Thou dost show Thy grace and whom Thou dost bring to Thyself, he it is who meditates on the Name. Thou the Creator art ineffable, immanent in all. He whom Thou dost bring to the Truth, he it is who attains it. Let Nānak sing Thy praises.[6]

In order that the *Gurū*'s voice may be heard there must be a prior gift of perception and this gift comes by God's grace. If He gives it then the Word may be perceived, and if He does not there is nothing a man can do. This in itself is not sufficient for salvation, for even if a man accepts the proffered gift he must engage in a sustained discipline before he can attain ultimate release. The gift is, however, a prerequisite. Why it is given to some and withheld from others no man can say. There is much that must

[1] *Japjī* 4, *AG*, p. 2.
[2] Literally: 'sight', the gracious glance.
[3] See *supra*, p. 190.
[4] *Vār Āsā, pauṛī* 4, *AG*, p. 465.
[5] *Oaṅkāru* 14, *AG*, p. 931.
[6] *Vār Malār, pauṛī* 28, *AG*, p. 1291.

remain hidden from the limited understanding of man and the exercise of God's grace is of this nature. Man is not given a complete understanding. What he is given is a sufficient understanding.

The translation we have used is 'grace', but a note of caution is required for the English word is liable to be misinterpreted in this context. The possibility arises from the fact that its usage in Christian theology assumes the specific Pauline doctrine of grace with its stress upon the universal nature of grace and of its absolute sufficiency for salvation. For a person nurtured in Sikh thought there is no problem, for he will take from the word 'grace' the meaning which is imparted by such words as *nadar* and *kirpā* in the context of Sikh scripture. The possibility of misinterpretation may exist, however, for the person whose background is Christian or western, and who may unconsciously read into the word specifically Christian connotations. 'Election' actually comes closer to Gurū Nānak's concept, but it is hardly a satisfactory alternative for it is too closely associated with neo-Calvinist theology and would almost inevitably be accorded an interpretation which implied an eternal double predestination, leaving no scope for the determinative exercise of the individual's free will. 'Favour' and 'choice' are both appropriate, but yet fail to convey a sufficient depth of meaning, although the word *bhāṇā* which corresponds exactly to the first of these is one of the words which is used to express this particular doctrine.

'Grace' remains the best word to express this aspect of the divine nature whereby there is imparted an initial and prerequisite illumination.

> He whom Thou hast enlightened understands. He to whom Thou hast given insight perceives all.[1]

Without this gift of perception, without a divine initiative, the *Gurū* will not be recognized. The gift alone does not mean automatic or irresistible salvation, for as we have already noted the gift must be actually accepted and the individual's life must be lived in accordance with what it imparts. Many, indeed most, to whom it is given refuse to accept it. Instead of listening to the *Gurū*'s Word they fasten their affections on *māyā*, on the attractions of the world.

The various terms may also be used in a sense which refers to the individual's own effort to conform to the Truth rather than to the prior gift of perception.

> The grace of the Master is on those who have meditated on Him with single mind, and they have found favour in His heart.[2]

Normally, however, the various terms are used with reference to the divine initiative, the prior act of grace whereby God implants the perception which enables the individual to hear and to understand the Word. It is not

[1] *Vār Mājh*, *ślok* 2 of *pauṛī* 27, *AG*, p. 150. [2] *Sirī Rāgu* 27, *AG*, p. 24.

salvation which is given, for this must be attained through the individual's own efforts. It is the prerequisite appreciation of the need for salvation and of the means to be followed in order to attain it—not salvation itself but 'the door of salvation'.

> Just as He, the Lord, is glorious, so too are His gifts glorious, gifts which He gives in accordance with His will. He upon whom the (Lord's) gracious glance rests, he it is who acquires the glory of the True Name.[1]

God has expressed Himself in the Word which He Himself as *Gurū* communicates to man. If by His grace any man be blessed with the perception which enables him to understand the Word he will discern around and within himself the nature of God and the means of attaining union with Him. In this manner the way of salvation is revealed. What must man do to grasp this proffered salvation? What effort must one make, what discipline must one follow in order to appropriate the Truth?

IV. THE DISCIPLINE

It has already been observed how the first stanza of *Japjī* expresses within a single couplet both the problem of salvation and its answer.[2] Stanza 44 of *Oaṅkāru* offers another summary statement. First it poses the problem:

> No one remains, neither kings nor faqīrs, neither poor nor rich. No one can stay when his turn comes round. The way is difficult, frightening, over seas and impassable mountains. I waste away because of the evil within me. Without the necessary merit how can one enter the house (of God)? Those who possess this merit meet the Lord. How can I meet them in love.[3]

Then follows the answer:

> By meditating on God in my heart I shall become like Him. (My heart) is filled with evil, but in it there also dwell redeeming qualities. Without the True *Gurū* these are not perceived and until they are perceived one does not meditate on the Word.[4]

The answer is two-fold. Salvation depends both upon God's grace, which is expressed by the *Gurū* in the Word, and upon the individual's own effort to cleanse himself of all evil and so appropriate the salvation which is offered to him. It is to the second of these which we must now turn, to the *sādhanā* or discipline which Gurū Nānak propounded as the individual's necessary response to the imparted Word. In this section we shall consider first the paths which he rejected and then the one which he affirmed. The goal is union with God. The prerequisite is a recognition of Him in all

[1] *Vār Mājh*, *ślok* 1 of *pauṛī* 19, *AG*, p. 147.
[2] See *supra*, p. 200.
[3] *Oaṅkāru* 44, *AG*, p. 936.
[4] Ibid.

creation and in particular within the human *man*. The way itself is meditation with adoring love upon the divine qualities revealed through such an understanding. The concomitant result is the cleansing and disciplining of the *man*, and a life brought progressively into total accord with the divine Order. And the end result is release from transmigration through the blending of the *man* in a union with God, a union which transcends all human expression. It is a pattern which denies the efficacy of all that is external or mechanical. For Gurū Nānak inward devotion of a specific kind is the way of salvation.

1. *Interior religion*

There is much obscurity in Kabīr, but at one point he is immediately and strikingly clear. No reader can possibly misunderstand his emphasis upon religion as a wholly inward experience, and the imprecations which he bestows upon all who trust in pride of birth or in outward ceremony have lost nothing of their mordant effect. Gurū Nānak does not manifest the same pugnacity, but his attitude in this repect is no less firm and clear. He too lived in an environment which set great store by birth, scriptures, ceremonies, and ascetic practices, and like Kabīr and other Sants he inevitably denounced them as entirely alien to true religion.

> They who read (scriptures) continually and forget (their spiritual duty) suffer the punishment (of spiritual death). For all their wisdom they continue to transmigrate.
> They who remember the Name and make fear (of God) their (spiritual) food —such servants, with the *Gurū*'s aid, dwell in union (with their Master).
> If the *man* is unclean how can it be purified by worshipping stones, visiting places of pilgrimage, living in jungles, wandering around as an ascetic? He who is united with the True One, he it is who acquires (eternal) honour.[1]

The brāhmaṇs do not receive a measure of scorn comparable with that shown by Kabīr, but we are left in no doubt concerning Gurū Nānak's attitude towards brahmanical pretensions.

> Hear me, paṇḍit, you who put your trust in all your religious works. The work which brings peace is meditation upon spiritual reality. You stand up and recite the Śāstras and Vedas, but your actions are those of the world. Inner filth and evil are not cleansed by hypocrisy. You are like a spider caught upside down (in the web you have spun)![2]

> One may have a cooking-square of gold with utensils of gold, (marked off) with lines of silver immensely protracted, water from the Ganges, a fire kindled with flint, and light food soaked in milk. But all these things are of no account, O *man*, unless one be imbued with the true Name. One may

[1] *Dhanāsarī Aṣṭ* 2 (5–6), *AG*, p. 686.

[2] *Soraṭhi Aṣṭ* 2 (1R–2), *AG*, p. 635.

have a hand-written copy of the eighteen Purāṇas and be able to recite the four Vedas by heart, one may bathe on auspicious days, give to each according to the rules prescribed for each caste, fast and observe regulations day and night; one may be a qāzī, a mullah, or a sheikh, a yogī, a *jaṅgam*, or one wearing ochre robes; one may be a householder and live accordingly, but without the understanding (which comes from meditation upon the Name) all are bound and driven off (to the abode of Yam).[1]

According to the *Purātan* janam-sākhīs this latter verse was the one delivered to the extraordinarily scrupulous brāhmaṇ who had refused even the uncooked food offered to him by Gurū Nānak, preferring instead to dig a cooking-square of unimpeachable purity. Wherever he dug, however, he found bones and after digging all day he finally accepted the Gurū's food.[2] The incident has no evident historical basis, but the spirit of the story certainly accords with Gurū Nānak's attitude towards caste status and purity regulations. In him we find the characteristic Sant rejection of caste as a necessary qualification for religious understanding. Gurū Nānak emphatically condemned pride based upon caste status, notions of purity and contamination arising out of caste distinctions, and above all any suggestion that caste standing was either necessary or advantageous in the individual's approach to God.

Perceive (in all men) the light (of God). Do not ask (a man's) caste for in the hereafter there is no caste.[3]

Caste and status are futile, for the One (Lord) watches over all. If anyone exalts himself the true measure of his dignity will be revealed when his record is produced (in the Lord's court).[4]

We who have taken shelter in God are neither high, low, nor in between. We are God's servants.[5]

Impurity, he declared, lay not in differences of birth but in the condition of the individual's *man*.

Your evil mind is a *ḍomaṇī*, your cruelty a *kasaiṇī*, your malicious tongue a *chūhaṛī*, your anger a *chaṇḍālaṛī*,[6] and all have led you astray. Why mark off a cooking-square when the four (outcastes) already keep you company? Let Truth be your manner (of drawing a cooking-square) and righteous

[1] *Basant* 3, *AG*, p. 1169.
[2] *Pur JS*, *sākhī* 38, p. 72. See *supra*, p. 45.
[3] *Āsā* 3, *AG*, p. 349.
[4] *Vār Sirī Rāgu*, *ślok* 1 of *pauṛī* 33, *AG*, p. 83.
[5] *Gūjarī Aṣṭ* 4 (1), *AG*, p. 504.
[6] The female members of four outcaste groups: *Ḍom*, *Kasāī*, *Chūhaṛā*, and *Chaṇḍāl*. The *ḍomanī* evidently refers to the caste of sweepers and corpse-burners which has been regarded as the type of all uncleanness (D. Ibbetson, *Panjab Castes*, no. 654, pp. 333–4). The *Mirāsī* caste of Muslim genealogists and musicians, to which Mardānā belonged, are also called *Ḍoms*, but the reference will not be to this group for it possesses an appreciably higher status than that of the sweeper *Ḍoms* (Ibbetson, op. cit., pp. 234–5).

deeds your lines. Let repeating of the Name be your ritual ablution. Nānak, hereafter it is he who does not teach sinful ways who will be exalted.[1]

This rejection of such notions was common among the Sants and was particularly strong in the case of Kabīr.[2] In Gurū Nānak's case it may have received a practical expression. One of the most attractive aspects of Sikhism is the *laṅgar*, the intercommunal refectory which is always attached to a gurdwārā. There can be little doubt that the institution was developed as a deliberate attack on caste distinction, but it is not entirely clear whether it was first introduced into Sikhism by Gurū Nānak or by the third Gurū, Amar Dās. Although the balance of probability strongly favours the latter there can be no doubt that the *laṅgar* expresses an ideal which we find clearly articulated in Gurū Nānak's works. It was an ideal which his successors faithfully upheld and in 1699 it received sacramental expression in the baptismal ceremony instituted by Gurū Gobind Singh at the founding of the Khālsā.[3]

Other expressions of external religion suffered a similar fate at Gurū Nānak's hands. Trust in the sufficiency of traditional acts of merit is rejected:

The man who possesses knowledge but knows not the *Gurū*, of what use are his good works and ceremonies?[4]

Idolatry is ridiculed:

The Hindus, straying in abysmal forgetfulness, have followed the wrong path. As Nārada (the Sage) taught, so they worship (idols). Blind and dumb (they walk) in pitch darkness, worshipping this ridiculous stone which they have set up. It sinks so how can it carry you across (the Ocean of Existence)?[5]

Gods and goddesses are worshipped, but what can one ask of them and what can they give? The stones (the idols) are washed with water, but they sink in water (and so are useless as vessels to carry you across the Ocean of Existence).[6]

Bathing at places of pilgrimage (*tīrath*) is rejected as completely ineffective:

If anyone goes to bathe at a *tīrath* with an evil heart and the body of a thief, one part (the exterior) is cleansed by the bathing, but the other (the heart) becomes even filthier. Outwardly he is washed like a faqīr's gourd, but

[1] *Vār Sirī Rāgu, ślok* 1 of *pauṛī* 20, *AG*, p. 91.

[2] Kabīr, *Mārū* 9, *AG*, p. 1105; *Bhairau Aṣṭ* 1, *AG* p. 1162; *śloks* 56, 57, and 82, *AG*, pp. 1367, 1368. *KG sākhī* 33. 7.

[3] See also *BG* 1. 23. I owe to Dr. S. Maqbul Ahmad of the Indian Institute of Advanced Study, Simla, the suggestion that the *laṅgar* may be a borrowing from the Sufi *khānaqāh*.

[4] *Sirī Rāgu* 13, *AG*, p. 19. For a condemnation of faith in astrology see *Rāmakalī Aṣṭ* 4, *AG*, p. 904.

[5] *Vār Bihāgaṛā, ślok* 2 of *pauṛī* 20, *AG*, p. 556.

[6] *Soraṭhi Dutukī* 4 (6), *AG*, p. 637.

inside he is poison and impurity. A sādhū[1] possesses goodness even if he does not bathe and a thief, even if he bathes, remains a thief.[2]

Shall I go and bathe at a *tīrath*? The true *tīrath* is the divine Name; it is inner contemplation of the Word and it is true knowledge (*jñān*). The *Gurū*'s *jñān* is the true *tīrath* where every day is an auspicious day. O Lord, Sustainer of the earth, I crave Thy Name eternally. Grant it (I pray Thee).[3]

Nor is salvation to be found in ascetic practices, in abandoning the world to pursue a solitary or an itinerant life, particularly if the renunciation is a hypocritical one designed to provide a life of irresponsible ease.

He who sings songs about God without understanding them; who converts his house into a mosque in order to satisfy his hunger; who, being unemployed, has his ears pierced (so that he can beg as a yogī); who becomes a faqīr and abandons his caste; who is called a *gurū* or *pīr* but who goes around begging—never fall at the feet of such a person.

He who eats what he has earned by his own labour and gives some (to others)—Nānak, he it is who knows the true way.[4]

The last couplet indicates the positive aspect of this particular rejection. Asceticism is rejected; a disciplined worldliness is affirmed. The way of Truth consists, in this respect, of living in the world yet unaffected by the attractions of the world. It is a common emphasis among the Sants and Gurū Nānak uses the conventional figure of the lotus to illustrate it.[5] The refrain of *Sūhī* 8, a verse which was evidently addressed to Kānphaṭ yogīs, is a striking expression of this belief.

The path of true Yoga is found by dwelling in God while yet living in the midst of the world's temptations.[6]

In this context it is to be noted that family attachments are not upheld as good or permissible. On the contrary, they too are of the nature of worldly attachments and are accordingly to be avoided.

Domestic involvement is a whirlpool; the sin (which lies upon us) is a stone which cannot cross over (the Ocean of Existence).[7]

[1] The word is used in its original sense meaning one who has attained self-control. In this context *bhagat* or 'true believer' would serve as synonyms.

[2] *Vār Sūhī, ślok* 2 of *pauṛī* 12, *AG*, p. 789.

[3] *Dhanāsarī Chhant* 1 (1), *AG*, p. 687. This extract is also of interest in that it illustrates Gurū Nānak's usage of *giān* (*jñān*). The word does not normally possess any particular significance in his thought and neither does it appear with any great frequency. When it does appear it usually corresponds to *śabad* as in the extract quoted here. The only instance where it is given a particular significance is in *Japjī* 35 where it is used to designate the second of the five *khaṇḍs*. See *infra*, p. 221.

[4] *Vār Sāraṅg, ślok* 1 of *pauṛī* 22, *AG*, p. 1245.

[5] Cf. *Gauṛī* 5, *AG*, p. 152; *Rāmakalī* 4, *AG*, p. 877. The beauty of the lotus is in no way diminished by the filthy water which may surround it, nor by the mud in which it takes root.

[6] *Sūhī* 8, *AG*, p. 730.

[7] *Mārū* 2, *AG*, pp. 989–90.

It is, however, the attachment, not the family itself, which is to be spurned. Those who love the Name do not need to isolate themselves in order to avoid such attachments.

> Meditation on the True One brings illumination and so one lives detached in the midst of evil. Such is the greatness of the True *Gurū* that even surrounded by wife and sons one can attain salvation.[1]

This freedom from attachment while yet living in the midst of temptations to attachment is the proper pattern for the true believer.[2] Ascetics and yogis wander in vain.

> If I live in a cave in a mountain of gold or remain immersed in water; if I remain buried in the earth, or ascend into the sky, or remain suspended head down; if I clothe myself completely and wash (my clothes) endlessly; if I read the white, red, yellow, and black Vedas at the top of my voice, or remain unwashed[3] (it is all in vain for) all (such practices) are error and evil misconception. Only if one meditates on the Word does *haumai* go.[4]

Qāzīs, paṇḍits, and yogīs in their traditional pursuits are all astray.

> The qāzī utters lies and eats what is unclean;
> The brāhmaṇ takes life and then goes off to bathe ceremoniously;
> The blind yogī does not know the way;
> All three are desolated.[5]

True religion is to be found not in external practices, but in the inward disciplines of love, faith, mercy, and humility, expressed in righteous and compassionate deeds and in the upholding of all that is true.

> The true yogī is he who recognizes the Way, who by the *Gurū*'s grace knows the One.
> The true qāzī is he who turns away (from the world) and by the *Gurū*'s grace dies while yet remaining alive.
> The true brāhmaṇ is he who meditates on Brahman; he saves himself and all his kin.[6]

> Make mercy your mosque, faith your prayer-mat, and righteousness your Qur'ān.
> Make humility your circumcision, uprightness your fasting, and so you will be a (true) Muslim.

[1] *Dhanāsarī* 4, *AG*, p. 661.

[2] Nāmdev's *Rāmakalī* 1, *AG*, p. 972, is an answer to the charge that such a life must be inconsistent with true devotion. Cf. also Kabīr's *śloks* 212 and 213, *AG*, pp. 1375–6, and Raidās's *Bilāvalu* 2, *AG*, p. 858.

[3] This reference is evidently intended to apply to Jain monks. *Vār Mājh*, *ślok* 1 of *pauṛī* 26, *AG*, pp. 149–50, directs a vigorous attack against their beliefs and practices.

[4] *Vār Mājh*, *ślok* 1 of *pauṛī* 4, *AG*, p. 139.

[5] *Dhanāsarī* 7, *AG*, p. 662. Cf. also *Vār Rāmakalī*, *ślok* 1 of *pauṛī* 11, *AG*, p. 951.

[6] Ibid.

Make good works your *Ka'bah*, Truth your *pīr*, and compassion your creed and your prayer.
Make the performance of what pleases (God) your rosary and, Nānak, He will uphold your honour.[1]

(Make the Merciful Lord) your *śālgrām*, your object of worship, O paṇḍit, and good deeds your garland of *tulsī*.
Construct a boat by repeating the Name of God and pray that the Merciful One may show mercy towards you.
Why waste your life in irrigating sterile land? Why plaster a mud wall when it will surely fall?[2]

2. *Loving devotion*

If one gains anything from visiting places of pilgrimage (*tīrath*), from austerities, acts of mercy,[3] and charity, it is of negligible value. He who has heard, believed, and nurtured love in his heart has cleansed himself by bathing at the *tīrath* which is within.[4]

The *tīrath* is within.[5] Religion is inward and its basic expression is love or, more accurately, loving devotion. This loving devotion, a devotion directed to the formless Lord, is the vital response required of all who have perceived the presence of God suffused throughout creation, and in whom has been awakened a longing for union with Him. It is at this point that Gurū Nānak shares with the Sants a particular debt to Vaiṣṇava bhakti. There is in his works the characteristic Vaiṣṇava emphasis upon the abso lute necessity of love in the bhakti sense, commonly expressed in the figure of the bride yearning for her Beloved, the divine Bridegroom.

He who worships the True One with adoring love, who thirsts for the supreme love, who beseeching cries out, he it is who finds peace for in his heart is love.[6]

In addition to the basic bhakti emphasis we find in Gurū Nānak's works the more important of its corollaries. There must be fear of God, a recognition of His infinite immensity and of His absolute authority.

Fear (of God) is of great weight and hard to bear; the wayward mind, with all its effusions, is slight. (And yet) he who carries on his head (fear of God) can bear (its) weight. By grace he meditates on the *Gurū*'s (teaching). Without such fear no one crosses (the Ocean of Existence), but if one dwell in fear to it is added love.[7]

[1] *Vār Mājh*, *ślok* 1 of *pauṛī* 7, *AG*, pp. 140–1.
[2] *Basant Hiṇḍol* 9, *AG*, p. 1171.
[3] The reference is clearly to acts performed with the intention of acquiring merit.
[4] *Japjī* 21, *AG*, p. 4.
[5] Cf. also *Āsā* 32, *AG*, p. 358; *Vār Āsā*, *ślok* 2 of *pauṛī* 10, *AG*, p. 468.
[6] *Gūjarī Aṣṭ* 5 (1), *AG*, p. 505.
[7] *Gauṛī* 1, *AG*, p. 151.

There must be complete surrender to Him, an unconditional submission in faith.

> The Lord is near at hand (within you), foolish bride. Why seek Him without? Let fear be the *salāī*[1] (with which you apply antimony to your) eyes and let your adornment be that of love. She who loves her Master is known to be the bride united with Him. . . .
>
> Go and ask (those who are already the Master's) brides by what means they found Him. (A bride replies:) 'Accept whatever He does as good, put no trust in your own cleverness and abandon the exercise of your own will. Fix your mind on His feet.[2] (Cleave to Him) through whose love the priceless treasure is obtained. Do whatever He says. Anoint yourself with the perfume of total surrender to Him.' Thus replies the bride, 'O sister, by this means the Lord is found.'[3]

And there must be singing of God's praises.

> He who serves Him wins honour (in His court), so sing His praises Nānak, (sing of Him) the Treasury of excellences. Sing His praises, hear them, love Him. . . .[4]
>
> This is the belief which Nānak proclaims: It is through the singing of (His) praises that we find a place in the Lord's court.[5]

All of these are aspects of traditional bhakti and they represent a significant area of agreement between the Vaiṣṇava *bhagats* on the one hand and Gurū Nānak on the other. There are, however, basic differences separating them. In the first place, as we have already observed,[6] there is in Gurū Nānak's works an explicit rejection of *avatārs*. Like the Sants he addressed his devotion direct to God Himself, supreme and non-incarnated, not to any manifestation or intermediary. Secondly, there is Gurū Nānak's understanding of the practical expression of love, enunciated in his interpretation of *nām simaran* or *nām japan*. This interpretation is of fundamental importance. It provides the heart of his discipline and in it we find his distinctive understanding of the believer's proper response.

3. Nām simaran

> This world is entangled in earthly affections and so in the immense suffering of death and rebirth. Flee to the True *Gurū*'s shelter. There repeat the Name of God in your heart and so obtain salvation.[7]
>
> Nānak, he who is steeped in the divine Name is freed from his *haumai*, is gathered up in the True One, meditates on the way of (true) Yoga, finds the

[1] A small metal instrument for applying antimony to eyes.

[2] A conventional figure signifying humble, submissive devotion.

[3] *Tilaṅg* 4, *AG*, p. 722.

[4] *Japjī* 5, *AG*, p. 2.

[5] *Vār Mājh*, *ślok* 2 of *pauṛī* 12, *AG*, p. 143.

[6] See *supra*, p. 171.

[7] *Gūjarī Aṣṭ* 5 (5), *AG*, p. 505.

door of salvation, acquires an understanding of the three worlds, and attains to eternal peace.[1]

If the mind be defiled by sin it is cleansed with love of the Name. Virtue and sin are not mere words; we carry with us the influence of what we have done. As you have sown so will you reap, and in accordance with the divine Order you will transmigrate.[2]

The divine Order (*Hukam*) expressed, as we have already observed, in the law of *karma* ensures that one must reap in accordance with what one sows. In order to banish the influence of committed sin the individual must sow that seed which bears not the baneful fruit of transmigration but the blessed fruit of union. This seed (or, as here, this cleansing agent) is love of the divine Name. Sahib Singh comments as follows on the *Japjī* stanza:

As a result of the influence of *māyā* man falls into evil and his mind is sullied. This impurity separates man from the wholly pure God and the soul undergoes suffering. *Nām simaran* alone is the means whereby the *man* can be instantly cleansed. And so the practice of *simaran* is the means of cleansing the *man* from evil and of uniting it with God.[3]

Vir Singh has a similar comment:

The True *Gurū* has here informed us that the means of restoring purity to the mind or intellect clogged with sin is love of the Name. . . . God is supremely holy. Remembrance of His Name brings the *man* into a condition of meditation on Him. In this way the *antaḥkaraṇa*, coming into contact by means of the Name with the Possessor of the Name, is purified through His holiness. Through *nām simaran* it is separated from other impure inclinations. Thus it is drawn progressively nearer to both the *Hukam* and its Giver, and thus *haumai* is gradually purged.[4]

But how does one 'love the Name'? What is meant in Gurū Nānak's usage by the expressions *nām simaran* or *nām japan*?

Nām has already been dealt with. The divine Name is the revelation of God's being, the sum total of all His attributes, the aggregate of all that may be affirmed concerning Him. The two verbs which are normally attached to *nām* are *japanā* and *simaranā*, neither of which can be satisfactorily translated into English in the context of Gurū Nānak's usage. *Japanā* means 'to repeat' and is used in connexion with the recital of a divine name or *mantra*. In many contexts this literal translation is entirely appropriate, for mechanical repetition of this kind, often with the help of a rosary, was a very common practice. Mere mechanical repetition was not,

[1] *Siddh Goṣṭi* 32, *AG*, p. 941. See also stanza 33.
[2] *Japji* 20, *AG*, p. 4.
[3] Sahib Singh, *Srī Gurū Granth Sāhib Darapaṇ*, vol. i, p. 87.
[4] Vir Singh, *Santhyā*, vol. i, p. 101.

however, Gurū Nānak's practice. Some references might indeed suggest this, as, for example, the following passage from *Japjī*.

> Let every tongue become a *lākh* of tongues, and let every *lākh* become twenty *lākhs*. And then let every tongue utter the Name of God a *lākh* of times. This path is a stairway which leads to the Lord, and having ascended it one passes into union with Him.[1]

Such examples must, however, be read in the context of his general usage. Here it is a case of hyperbole, an effort to convey the immensity of the divine majesty and not a claim that the infinite repetition of a single name or syllable is an assured path to salvation. Gurū Nānak would without doubt have been in complete agreement with the pronouncement of Gurū Amar Dās:

> Everyone goes around saying 'Rām Rām', but Rām is not found in this way.[2]

Simple repetition of this kind is not enough, regardless of how devout the repetition may be or how sophisticated a system may be built around the practice. It is a pattern which can include the repetition of a chosen word or brief formula, but only if the emphasis is upon the interiorising of the utterance, upon the paramount need of understanding the word so uttered and of exposing one's total being to its deepest meanings.

Simaranā, 'to remember' or 'to hold in remembrance', is more helpful, for 'remembering the Name' is nearer to a description of Gurū Nānak's practice than 'repeating the Name'. It too, however, falls short of an adequate description. How then is the practice to be described? Gurū Nānak himself provides a definition.

> Repeating (the Name) of the True God means engrafting (Him) in the *man*.[3]

And the method whereby this engrafting is carried out is meditation—meditation on the nature of God, on His qualities and His attributes as revealed in the Word (*Śabad*).

> God is found through meditation on the *Gurū*'s Word, the sublime utterance.[4]

> By meditating on the Word one crosses the Ocean.[5]

> You who are drowning (in the Ocean of Existence), you have laid waste your own dwelling. Walk in the *Gurū*'s love. Meditating on the true Name you shall find bliss in the palace (of God). Meditate on the true Name and you shall find bliss. Your stay in your father's house[6] is brief. When you go to your real home you shall know the Truth and you shall dwell eternally with your Beloved.[7]

[1] *Japjī* 32, *AG*, p. 7.
[2] *Vār Bihāgaṛā*, *ślok* 1 of *pauṛī* 18, *AG*, p. 555.
[3] *Vaḍahaṃsu Chhant* 2 (5), *AG*, p. 567.
[4] *Oaṅkāru* 47, *AG*, pp. 936–7.
[5] *Prabhātī Aṣṭ* 1 (1R), *AG*, p. 1342.
[6] i.e. in this world. The person addressed is the conventional figure of the bride.
[7] *Dhanāsarī Chhant* 3 (2), *AG*, p. 689.

The worship (*pūjā*) which we offer is meditation on the Name, for without the Name there can be no (true) worship.[1]

This meditation on the nature and qualities of God is the core of Gurū Nānak's religious discipline. The Word reveals the absoluteness of God. Meditate on this and make your submission before Him. The Word reveals the eternally stable permanence of God, the eternity of God. Reflect on this and abandon the fickle, fleeting world. The Word reveals the absolute freedom of God from all that is *māyā*. Meditate on this and so separate yourself from its deceits. The Word reveals the ineffable greatness of God. Reflect on this and humble yourself before Him. It is a meditation which must overflow in words and deeds which accord with the nature of the Name. It is remembrance of God *mani, bach, karami karakai*[2]—in thought, word, and deed.

This is the practical response which a believer is required to make. Meditate in love and you shall grow towards and into Him who is the object of your devotion and your meditation. It is a discipline which has been developed, interpreted, and expounded again and again, both by Gurū Nānak's successors and by devout Sikhs ever since. This should be remembered, for much of the detailed analysis which may be found in Sikh writings is taken from the works of the later Gurūs or represents assumptions based upon what is found in the scriptures. This is not to say that the assumptions are inconsistent with the basis, but merely that the basis as set out in Gurū Nānak's works is a relatively simple version of what the doctrine was later to become. Moreover, in the case of the Gurūs' followers the source of the Word and so the primary means of meditation has of course been the collection of works recorded in the *Ādi Granth.*

This meditation must be individual and it must also have a corporate application. Gurū Nānak emphasized both.

At the ambrosial hour (of dawn) meditate on the greatness of the true Name.[3]

In the company of true believers the joy of God's (presence) is obtained and when one finds the *Gurū* fear of death departs. This is your destiny, that repeating the Name of God in accordance with the *Gurū*'s instructions you find God.[4]

[1] *Gūjari* 1, *AG*, p. 489. In these four quotations the expression used is either *śabad vichāranā* or *nām dhiāunā*. Cf. also *Vaḍahaṃsu Dakhaṇī* 4 (1), *AG*, p. 581; *Tukhārī* 2 (3), *AG*, p. 1110. In contemporary Sikh usage one also encounters the term *nām abhiās*, 'the regular practice of the Name'.

[2] *Pur JS*, p. 4.

[3] *Japjī* 4, *AG*, p. 2. This injunction has been accepted as an explicit commandment by the Sikh community. See the Sikh Book of Discipline, *Sikh Rahit Marayādā* (Śromaṇī Gurduārā Prabandhak Committee, Amritsar, 1961), p. 10. The same regulation lists the sections from the scriptures which should be recited by the individual in the morning and in the evening (pp. 10–11). Another section deals with attendance at the gurdwārā (pp. 14–17). The *Sikh Rahit Marayādā* has been translated in part by C. H. Loehlin, *The Sikhs and their Scriptures* (1st edition), pp. 39–42.

[4] *Soraṭhi* 10, *AG*, p. 598.

The importance of the company of true believers (the *satsaṅg*) as a vehicle of enlightenment which is so strongly stressed by Kabīr receives a corresponding emphasis in Gurū Nānak's works.

> Even if one were to possess infinite wisdom and were to dwell in love and concord with an immense number of people, without the society of the holy there would be no satisfaction, and without the Name there would be misery.[1]

> He who having created (the universe) watches over it dwells in every heart, (yet not beyond perceiving for) by the *Gurū*'s guidance He is made manifest in (the company of) the people of God.[2]

The traditional figure of the sandal tree is also used.

> Such is the nature of the true believer that like the sandal he imparts his fragrance to all (around him).[3]

The activity of the true believer in the *satsaṅg* is the singing of praises rather than the function implied by the word meditation, but *nām simaran* covers both, for both are concerned with God and with the individual's approach to Him. Music has always been used. Mardānā the Bard was Gurū Nānak's companion in at least some of his travels and there can be no reason for rejecting the janam-sākhī references to Gurū Nānak's practice of *kīrtan*, the corporate singing of God's praises.[4] The discipline must also be practised daily.

> Pain is poison but God's Name is the antidote. Let patient contentment be the stone on which you pound it and let your hand be that of charity. Take it daily and your body shall not waste away, and at the end Death itself will be struck down. Take this medicine, for the consuming of it will purge the evil that is in you.[5]

Meditation on the divine Name and the singing of praises must have seemed easy to many, but Gurū Nānak declares them to be otherwise. They are difficult and few are prepared to make the sacrifices which they demand. Those who do accept the discipline, however, find that the reward far outweighs the sacrifice.

> If I repeat the Name I live; if I forget it I die. Repeating the Name of the True One is hard, but if one hungers for it and partakes of it all sadness goes.[6]

This then is the discipline. The human body is a field in which the seed of the divine Name is to be sown. Cultivate it with love, humility, fear of God, true living, purity, and patience, and thus you shall reap your reward.

> Regard your body as a field, your *man* the plough, your actions the ploughing, and effort the irrigation. (In the field) sow the Name as seed, level it with contentment, and fence it with humility.

[1] *Sirī Rāgu* 17, *AG*, p. 20.
[2] *Basant Hiṇḍol* 12, *AG*, p. 1172.
[3] *Tilaṅg* 2, *AG*, p. 721.
[4] See also *BG* I. 38.
[5] *Malār* 8, *AG*, pp. 1256–7.
[6] *Āsā* 3, and *Āsā* 2, *AG*, pp. 9, 349.

Let your actions be those of love. (The seed) will then sprout and you will see your home prosper.[1]

Love is the soil, holiness the water, and truth and contentment the two buffaloes.

Humility is the plough, the mind the ploughman, remembrance (of the Name) the watering, and union (with God) the seed-time.

The Name is the seed and grace the crop. (These constitute Truth whereas) the world is wholly false.

Nānak, if the Merciful One is gracious all separation (from Him) comes to an end.[2]

4. *The concomitant results*

The practice of *nām simaran* results in experiences which develop progressively as meditation draws the individual nearer and nearer to God, and which find their ultimate perfection in the final absorption of the *man* into Him. They are at the same time results of the discipline and necessary aids to it, for they reveal more and more of the true nature of the Name and render the individual capable of rising to progressively greater heights.

The experience of *visamād* is, in this way, both a result of *nām simaran* and a stimulus to more exalted meditation. *Visamād* (Skt. *vismaya*) may mean either an immense awe, a prodigious wonder engendered by the overwhelming, indescribable greatness of God; or it may connote the actual condition of ecstasy resulting from the awe-inspiring vision of the greatness of God. The most sustained expression of *visamād* in Gurū Nānak's works is the lengthy *ślok* from *Āsā dī Vār* which begins with the line *visamādu nād visamādu ved* and in which almost every second word is *visamād*.[3] Stanza 24 of *Japjī* is also an expression of this same awe.

Infinite are the praises (of the Creator), infinite the ways of uttering them. Infinite are His works and infinite His gifts. Infinite is His sight, infinite His hearing, infinite the workings of the divine mind. His creation is boundless, its limits infinite. Many have striven to encompass its infinity; none have succeeded. None there be who know its extent; whatsoever one may say much more yet remains to be said. Great is God and high His station; higher than high His Name. Only he who is of equal height can comprehend its loftiness; therefore God alone comprehends His own greatness. Nānak, all that we receive is the gift of the Gracious One.[4]

This is *visamād*, for Gurū Nānak both the inevitable result of true meditation and the food for even more refined and intense meditation.

The purging of *haumai* and its related impulses is likewise both a result and an essential aid. The further a believer proceeds in meditation on

[1] *Soraṭhi* 2, *AG*, p. 595.

[2] *Vār Rāmakalī*, *ślok* 2 of *pauṛī* 17, *AG*, p. 955. The word 'contentment' refers in these contexts to a condition transcending both pain and pleasure.

[3] *Vār Āsā*, *ślok* 1 of *pauṛī* 3, *AG*, pp. 463–4.

[4] *Japjī* 24, *AG*, p. 5.

the Name the less inclined he is to submit to his own *haumai*; and the less he submits to his own *haumai* the further he progresses towards the goal of ultimate union. The process is described, as in Kabīr,[1] in terms of dying to Self. Two kinds of death have already been noted in the thought of Gurū Nānak[2] and this is a third.

> Because my eyes are turned towards evil I have neither fear of God nor love for Him. Only if the Self is slain can one possess the divine Name. If one dies by means of the Word one dies not again. Without such a death how can one be perfected?[3]

It is a death which is accomplished by the overthrow of the *man*, a death to Self which the true believer dies while yet remaining physically alive. The *man* must remain, but not the self-willed *man* which finds its expression in evil. It must be a redirected *man* and this overthrow, this redirection, is effected through the believer's love for the Name and his meditation on it.

> He who smites his *man* knows the death which takes place while life yet remains. Nānak, through grace he recognises the Gracious One.[4]

> By the *Gurū*'s grace one perceives (the true nature of) the Self and so dies even while remaining alive.[5]

> The *Gurū* is an ocean, a mine of jewels in which lie a multitude of precious stones. I bathe in the seven oceans (of the *Gurū*'s teaching) and my *man* is purified. I bathe in the pure waters when it is the Lord's will and thus by meditation I acquire the five blessings.[6] I abandon lust, anger, deceit, and evil, and enshrine the true Name in my heart. The wave of *haumai* and covetousness has spent itself; the Merciful One has been found. Nānak, there is no *tīrath* like the *Gurū*, (nothing to compare to) the true *Gurū-Gopāl*.[7]

The *man* is cleansed of *haumai* and purged of all evil passions. Purified and disciplined it ceases to be man's enemy and is transformed instead into his ally. No longer does it lead him into the entanglements of *māyā*; no longer does it earn him a disastrous *karma*. Instead it leads him further and further into conformity with the divine Order, further into that same Truth by which it was itself cleansed.

> He who is steeped in fear of the True One casts out pride. Meditating on the Word he comes to a knowledge of God, for if the Word dwells (within) the True One is also within. Body and soul are immersed in (His) love and

[1] Kabīr, *Sorațhi* 6, *AG*, p. 655; *KG*, *sākhī*, *aṅg* 19.

[2] Physical death which comes to all, and Death (personified in Yam) which is the fate of the *manmukh*. See *supra*, pp. 187–8.

[3] *Gauṛī* 7, *AG*, p. 153.

[4] *Prabhātī Aṣṭ* 3 (8), *AG*, p. 1343.

[5] *Oaṅkāru* 41, *AG*, p. 935.

[6] Truth, contentment, compassion, *dharma*, and patience.

[7] *Āsā Chhant* 2 (3), *AG*, p. 437.

(their passions) are cooled. Nānak, the consuming fires of lust and anger are extinguished by the grace of the beloved Giver of grace.[1]

Increasingly the believer becomes *like* God until ultimately he attains to a perfect identity.

He who is immersed in His love day and night knows (Him who is immanent) in the three worlds and throughout all time. He becomes like Him whom he knows. He becomes wholly pure, his body is sanctified, and God dwells in his heart as his only love. Within him is the Word; he is blended in the True One.[2]

5. *The ascent*

With the ever-widening *visamād* and the progressive subjugation of the *man* go a developing sense of joy and peace. It is a path leading onward and upward. The accent is strongly upon ascent to higher and yet higher levels of understanding and experience, an accent which is particularly evident in Gurū Nānak's famous figure of the five *khaṇḍs*.[3]

The pattern which is set out in this figure is sometimes said to represent a Sūfī contribution to the thought of Gurū Nānak, the theory being that its origin is to be found in the *maqāmāt* of the Sūfīs. There is, however, no evidence to establish this conjecture, and the parallel is not really a close one. A much closer one is to be found in the pattern of salvation enunciated in the *Yoga-vasiṣṭha*.[4] Sikh commentators understandably attach considerable importance to the figure of the five *khaṇḍs*, for it is clearly intended to represent the ascent of the *man* to its ultimate goal. There is, however, much that is obscure in Gurū Nānak's exposition and considerable differences of opinion are to be found in the commentaries. In the case of the third and fourth the very names of the *khaṇḍs* are translated in different ways.

Dharam Khaṇḍ, the first, is the clearest of the five.[5] *Dharam* represents here the law of cause and effect. This obviously applies in the physical universe and the person who has reached this initial stage perceives that it applies in a religious and moral sense also. God is just and in His court the true and the false stand revealed.

Giān Khaṇḍ (or *Jñān Khaṇḍ*) is the second stage.[6] It evidently represents a marked widening of the individual's understanding, chiefly due to a developing appreciation of the manifold qualities of the creation and of the significance of great figures who have preceded him. The precise

[1] *Siddh Goṣṭi* 47, *AG*, p. 943.
[2] *Oaṅkāru* 10, *AG*, p. 931.
[3] 'Realms', or stages in spiritual progress. *Japjī* 34–37, *AG*, pp. 7–8.
[4] S. Dasgupta, *A History of Indian Philosophy*, vol. ii, p. 264, provides a summary of the seven stages set out in the *Yoga-vasiṣṭha*, vi, 120.
[5] *Japjī* 34, *AG*, p. 7. *Dharam* is the Pañjābī form of the Sanskrit *dharma*.
[6] *Japjī* 35–36, *AG* p. 7.

significance is not stated, but to some commentators the point is that such an understanding promotes a weakening of the individual's self-centredness.[1] One characteristic which is explicitly stated is the resultant joy of such a state.

> Knowledge shines in the Realm of Knowledge. In it there is joy of sound, sight, and deed.[2]

Saram Khaṇḍ, the third stage,[3] is the least clear and provides the most marked differences in interpretation. There are three views concerning the meaning of the word *saram*. First there are those who claim that it derives from the Sanskrit *śarma* and who accordingly interpret it as the Realm of Effort.[4] Secondly, there are the commentators who would derive it from the Sanskrit *śarman* and who interpret it as the Realm of Bliss.[5] Thirdly, there are those who favour the Persian *śaram* ('shame') and who interpret it as either the Realm of Humility or the Realm of Surrender.[6] The actual description given in *Japjī* does not provide an answer, but indicates rather that by this stage the nature of the religious experience involved is passing beyond the describable.

> There (in that Realm) are fashioned creations of surpassing wonder. None can describe them. Were one to try he would rue the effort.[7]

The only hint comes in the couplet:

> There inner perception and reason are fashioned; there the understanding of a divine hero or a spiritual adept is developed.[8]

The third of the suggested derivations is an attractive one, but the first seems the most likely. It harmonizes better with the above couplet and where Gurū Nānak uses *saram* in another context the meaning clearly seems to be 'effort'.

> Regard your body as a field, your *man* the plough, your actions the ploughing, and effort (*saramu*) the irrigation.[9]

The figure of the ploughman makes much better sense if *saram* is translated

[1] Harnam Singh, *The Japji*, p. 141. [2] *Japjī* 36, *AG* p. 7. [3] Ibid.

[4] *Śabadārath*, p. 7, n. 29. Teja Singh, *The Japji* (English trans.), pp. 13 and 39 ('self-exertion'). Jodh Singh, *The Japji* (English trans.), p. 54. Sahib Singh, *Srī Gurū Granth Sāhib Darapaṇ*, vol. i, p. 124. S. S. Kohli, *A Critical Study of the Adi Granth*, p. 367. Mohan Singh, *Pañjābī Bhākhā te Chhandābandī*, p. 218. *The Sacred Writings of the Sikhs* (UNESCO), p. 49. *Srī Gurū Granth Koś́*, p. 243.

[5] Vir Singh, *Santhyā*, vol. i, p. 167. Khushwant Singh, *Jupji: the Sikh Prayer*, p. 22. Macauliffe, *The Sikh Religion*, vol. i, p. 216 ('happiness'). E. Trumpp, *The Ādi Granth*, p. 12 ('happiness').

[6] Harnam Singh, *The Japji*, p. 143 ('humility'). Gopal Singh, *Sri Guru-Granth Sahib*, p. 11 ('surrender'), although not in his earlier *The Song of Nanak*, p. 11, where his translation is 'the domain of Practice'. This Persian interpretation is general in the older, less important commentaries such as those by Baba Mangal Singh, Gurmukh Singh, and Sant Gulab Singh.

[7] *Japjī* 36, *AG*, pp. 7–8.

[8] Ibid., *AG*, p. 8.

[9] *Soraṭhi* 2, *AG*, p. 595.

as 'effort' and the idea of modesty or humility is covered by the word *garībī* which comes in the following line.

Karam Khaṇḍ is the fourth stage[1] and here there are two principal interpretations. First there is the majority opinion which takes *karam* to be the Persian word meaning 'grace' and which accordingly interprets the fourth stage as the Realm of Grace.[2] Secondly, there is a strong minority opinion represented by Macauliffe,[3] Teja Singh,[4] and Khushwant Singh.[5] All three have regarded *karam* as the Sanskrit *karma* and have translated *Karam Khaṇḍ* as the realm or domain of Action. The Persian school certainly has the weight of numbers to support it, but there is one serious objection to this theory. Grace does indeed occupy a position of primary importance in the thought of Gurū Nānak, but there is no indication in his works that the receipt of grace comes so late in the believer's ascent to union. On the contrary, it extends over the whole process and if any stage is of particular significance with regard to grace it is the very beginning. The Sanskrit interpretation, however, faces an equally strong objection. If *Saram Khaṇḍ* is to be regarded as the Realm of Effort and *Karam Khaṇḍ* as the Realm of Action there is little difference between the two stages.

A third possibility is that *karam* is the Sanskrit word and that it retains the normal meaning of *karma*. In this context the sense could well be that it is in the fourth stage that the *bhagat* begins to reap the reward of a *karma* earned through the faithful practice of *nām simaran*. This would accord with what we are told of the fourth stage, for the emphasis is upon fulfilment and one aspect of this fulfilment is that the *bhagat* is said to pass beyond error and transmigration.[6] Accordingly, an appropriate translation would appear to be the Realm of Fulfilment.

Sach Khaṇḍ is the fifth and final stage. This is the Realm of Truth, the true dwelling-place of the Formless One. Here the believer passes into a unity which can be described only in terms of infinity.

> Realms, worlds, universes exist there.
> Were anyone to number them, of his numbering there could be no end![6]

This is the ultimate climax of the search for Truth, for it is here that there is perfect and absolute accord with the divine Order (*Hukam*).

> As the *Hukam*, so too the deed![6]

[1] *Japjī* 37, *AG*, p. 8.

[2] Vir Singh, op. cit., vol. i, p. 167. Kahn Singh, *MK*, p. 227. Jodh Singh, op. cit., p. 55. Sahib Singh, op. cit., vol. i, p. 125. Sher Singh Gyani, *Guramati Daraśan*, p. 329. Harnam Singh, op. cit., p. 144. Gopal Singh, op. cit., p. 11. S. S. Kohli, op. cit., p. 367. *The Sacred Writings of the Sikhs*, p. 50. *Srī Gurū Granth Koś*, p. 352.

[3] Macauliffe, op. cit., vol. i, p. 216. His translation is 'the realm of action'. Trumpp's translation was 'the region of works' (op. cit., p. 13).

[4] Teja Singh, *The Japji*, pp. 14, 40, and *Śabadārath*, p. 7, n. *.

[5] Khushwant Singh, op. cit., p. 22. Also Jogendra Singh, *Sikh Ceremonies*, p. 40.

[6] *Japjī* 37, *AG*, p. 8.

But it is a condition which can be known only in experience.

To describe it, Nānak, is as hard as steel![1]

6. *The ultimate*

Sach Khaṇḍ is the goal, the ultimate end and purpose of human existence, the final consummation of man's ascent to God. Gurū Nānak's references to this ultimate condition bring out three things. First, it is to be conceived in terms of a union of the individual *man* with the being of God, the supra-soul.[2] Secondly, this union means an end for ever to the transmigratory process, with all its attendant suffering, and instead an eternal, changeless tranquillity.[3] And thirdly, the true nature of this condition must ever elude description. It can be represented by nothing better than inadequate symbols and the broadest of generalizations. Its essential quality can be known only in the actual experience of union.

The characteristic word which Gurū Nānak uses to convey the nature of the ultimate experience is the verb *samāṇā* or *samāuṇā*. It is also used in the sense of 'to fill' or 'to pervade' in the context of the divine immanence, but here its meaning is rather 'to merge' or 'to blend'. *Sachi samāuṇā, śabadi samāuṇā, sahaji samāuṇā*, and *avigati samāuṇā*[4] are examples of the manner in which Gurū Nānak seeks to express the experience of union. It is a blending of the individual light in the Light of God (*jotī joti samāuṇā*),[5] a mingling of the individual drop in the ocean,[6] a dissolution of the individual *ātmā* in the *Paramātmā*.

> If God shows favour one meditates on Him. The *ātmā* is dissolved and is absorbed (in God). (The individual's) *ātmā* becomes one with the *Paramātmā* and inner duality dies within.[7]

It is the *chauthā pad*, the 'fourth state' or absolute condition transcending the three *guṇa*;[8] the *turīā pad* or *turīā avasthā*;[9] the *param pad*;[10] the *amarāpad*;[11] the condition of supreme bliss beyond all that is corruptible and beyond all powers of human expression.

At no point in the whole range of Gurū Nānak's works is the link with the Nāth tradition, and beyond the Nāth tradition with tantric Buddhism, so clearly evident. Of all the terms used by Gurū Nānak in his effort to communicate something of the meaning of the experience the most

[1] *Japjī* 37, *AG*. p. 8.

[2] See *supra*, p. 180.

[3] Cf. *Gauṛī* 10, *AG*, p. 154; *Āsā Aṣṭ* 7 (4), p. 414; *Āsā Paṭṭī Likhī* (29), p. 434; *Sūhī Aṣṭ* 2 (1), p. 751; *Sūhī Chhant* 5 (3), p. 766; *Bilāvalu Aṣṭ* 2 (8), p. 832; *Mārū Solahā* 20 (4), p. 1040; *Sāraṅg* 2, p. 1197.

[4] The suffix '*i*' designates the word 'in'.

[5] *Tukhārī Chhant* 5 (3), *AG*, p. 1112.

[6] *Sirī Rāgu* 22, *AG*, p. 22.

[7] *Dhanāsarī* 4, *AG*, p. 661.

[8] *Dhanāsarī Aṣṭ* 1 (7), *AG*, p. 686; *Bilāvalu Thitī* (18), p. 840.

[9] *Gauṛī* 12, *AG*, p. 154; *Āsā* 22, p. 356.

[10] *Siddh Goṣṭi* (24), *AG*, p. 940; *Prabhātī* 14, p. 1331.

[11] *Tilaṅg* 1, *AG*, p. 725.

common is *sahaj*, the ineffable radiance beyond the *dasam duār*.[1] It is difficult to distinguish his *sahaj* from that of the Nāth yogīs, for in both cases we have a word which must be beyond the understanding of all who have not experienced the condition which it represents.[2] Gurū Nānak was in emphatic disagreement with Nāth method,[3] but in both cases similar claims are made on behalf of the ultimate state called *sahaj*. For both it has a climactic content which unfolds in absolute equipoise and absolute tranquillity, and for both it is a condition existing beyond the cycle of transmigration. The Nāths did indeed seek, in their own terms, to express their experience with some precision, but the descriptions are negatives or logically insoluble paradoxes which can have no real meaning outside the mystical experience which generated them. Moreover, the most characteristic of all such expressions, the *anahad śabad*, is used by Gurū Nānak as one of the symbols expressing the condition as he experienced it.[4]

Comparisons with Nāth descriptions can provide little help without the actual experience, and the same must also apply to any assistance which we may seek from Sūfī sources. The question which arises from the latter comparison is whether Gurū Nānak offers any symbol which seems to correspond in any way to the Sūfī concept of *baqā'*, of a continuing existence within the condition of union with God. The question cannot be finally answered, although there is certainly no evidence of direct Sūfī influence at this point. The image of the soul as a fish swimming in the ocean which is God seems to suggest such a continuing existence,[5] but the commoner figures of water merging in water and light blending in light point to a notion of total absorption. Gurū Nānak's own response would doubtless be that the answer can be found only in personal experience.

We are faced with the ineffable and must be content with descriptions which impart only a fragment of understanding. The condition of union is, as we have already observed many times, one which transcends the cycle of birth and death.

> He who meditates on the divine Name finds peace, for protected by the *Gurū*'s instruction he cannot be consumed by Death.
> Without the Name the cycle of birth and death remains with us and suffering is our lot.[6]
>
> If one meets Him and does not part from Him transmigration ceases, for He is the True One.[7]

[1] *Gaurī Aṣṭ* 15 (2), *AG*, p. 227; *Rāmakalī Aṣṭ* 3, pp. 903–4. For Gurū Nānak's usage of *dasam duār*, 'the tenth door', see *Mārū Solahe* 13 (1), 16 (2), 19 (4), and 20 (2), *AG*, pp. 1033–40 *passim*.

[2] M. Eliade, *Yoga: Immortality and Freedom*, p. 268. Ch. Vaudeville, *Kabīr Granthāvalī* (*Dohā*), pp. xviii–xix.

[3] *Siddh Goṣṭi*, *AG*, pp. 938–46.

[4] *Sirī Rāgu* 18, *AG*, p. 21; *Āsā Chhant* 2 (1), p. 436.

[5] *Sirī Rāgu* 31, *AG*, p. 25.

[6] *Tukhārī Chhant* 2 (3), *AG*, p. 1110.

[7] *Sūhī* 4, *AG*, p. 729.

It is a condition of supreme wonder (*visamād*).

> None can know Thy limits, but understanding comes through the perfect *Gurū*.
> Nānak, immersed in the True One we are intoxicated with wonder, and struck with this wonder we sing His praises.[1]

And it is a condition of peace, of consummate joy and perfect tranquillity, a condition transcending all human telling.

> The body is the palace of God, His temple, His dwelling-place wherein He has shone light infinitely radiant. By the *Gurū*'s word one is summoned within the palace; there one meets with God.[2]

Beyond this is the unutterable.

[1] *Mārū Solahā* 15 (16), *AG*, p. 1036.

[2] *Malār* 5, *AG*, p. 1256.

6

THE PERSON

An analysis of the janam-sākhīs will reveal a few details concerning the life of Gurū Nānak, and exegesis will produce from his works an integrated theology. Our final task must be to seek a synthesis which will unite the glimpses provided by the janam-sākhīs with the personality emerging from the works recorded in the *Ādi Granth*. The result must be to some extent a disappointment, for we do not have the material to provide an adequate impression extending over the complete range of the Gurū's lifetime. The Nānak of faith and legend can be described at great length, but the historical Nānak must remain in large measure hidden. We can, however, form a distinct impression of the Gurū Nānak of a particular period in his lifetime, and it is the period which in terms of his posthumous influence is by far the most important.

One respect in which the janam-sākhīs provide significant help concerns the threefold division of the Gurū's lifetime which may be safely deduced from them. There seems to be little doubt that his seven decades should be divided into, first, a period of approximately three decades covering his childhood and early manhood in Talvaṇḍī and Sultānpur; secondly, a period of two decades spent in travelling; and, finally, two concluding decades of relatively settled existence in the village of Kartārpur.[1] The division into decades is unlikely to correspond exactly with the actual pattern of his life, but can be accepted as a sufficiently accurate method of defining the limits of the three recognizable periods.

It is the third of these periods which evidently emerges through the pages of the *Ādi Granth*. Many of Gurū Nānak's recorded works will have originated during the time of his travels, and some may go back even further, but the Kartārpur years must have been the period of definitive utterance. These were the years when Gurū Nānak was surrounded by disciples who received instruction from him and who presumably recorded what they had received. His compositions, if not actually committed to writing during his lifetime, must certainly have been recorded within a few years of his death. It is, indeed, entirely possible that they may have been first recorded in writing by Gurū Nānak himself, for unlike many of the religious figures of this period he was obviously not illiterate. This,

[1] See *supra*, p. 145.

moreover, was the period in which he gave practical expression to his own ideals, the period in which he combined a life of disciplined devotion with worldly activities, set in the context of normal family life and a regular *satsaṅg*.

Of the first period we know relatively little, for the janam-sākhīs are almost totally unreliable in their accounts of these early decades. This applies particularly, and inevitably, to his childhood years. We may, however, assume a certain amount on the basis of the limited help provided by the janam-sākhīs and our knowledge of contemporary conditions, and in the light of the mature expression recorded in the *Ādi Granth*. We know, for example, that he was a khatrī of the Bedī sub-caste and that accordingly he belonged to a respected family. To this we may add the indisputable fact that he was brought up in a Pañjāb village and that his growth to manhood took place during a relatively settled period. This would mean a life dictated by the agricultural nature of the village economy and consequently by the seasonal round still so characteristic of rural Pañjāb. It would have been a round of contrasting cold and heat, of labour in the fields and enforced rest during the months of summer barrenness, of the striking resurrection of the land and of men's spirits with the breaking of the monsoon rains, and of the regular festivals marking the high points in this annual cycle. All of this would inevitably have constituted the stuff of his childhood experiences and the beauty of his *Bārah-māhā*[1] bears testimony to the manner in which it influenced him. It was presumably a healthy childhood, for there is no evidence of any serious physical illness having ever afflicted him, and the natural diet of the Pañjāb, with its wheat, its milk, and its green vegetables, is one of the best the world can offer. During this period he must also have received a regular schooling, perhaps from a private tutor but more likely in one of the small charitable schools which were attached to some of the mosques and temples at this time. The compositions recorded in the *Ādi Granth* are certainly not the work of an illiterate or semi-literate author.

The later part of this first period is more obscure, for during adolescence and adulthood individual experience diversifies and we can no longer make assumptions on the basis of a regular pattern. At some stage, presumably during adolescence, he was married and two sons were subsequently born to him, but there seems to be every likelihood that the janam-sākhīs are basically correct in depicting this as a time of increasing restlessness and of resort to sādhūs, faqīrs, and other such holy men. This would explain the subsequent years of travel and also seems natural in view of his deep understanding of contemporary religious belief and practice.

We can, however, affirm nothing categorically concerning the stages of

[1] *Tukhārī Chhant Bārah-māhā*, *AG*, pp. 1107–13. The *bārah-māhā* (literally 'twelve-month') is a conventional poetic form based upon the seasonal cycle.

development through which he passed during his growth to maturity, and any assumptions we make must be strictly tentative. It is perhaps reasonable to postulate a growing dissatisfaction with traditional religious beliefs and practices, and a growing attraction towards Sant ideas acquired from sādhūs with whom he happened to come in contact. In doing so, however, we offer little more than conjecture. That dissatisfaction and attraction of this kind did occur is an obvious assumption, but we do not really know when or in what manner this development took place, neither can we trace the procedures whereby he evolved his own interpretation of the Sant tradition. These years are not altogether hidden years, for we can accept the janam-sākhī claim that part of this period was spent in Sultānpur. They are, however, years of general obscurity.

This conclusion applies with even greater force to the second period, the years of travel. Having rejected the janam-sākhī accounts we are once again reduced to assumption and conjecture, neither of which can take us far. It is, of course, evident that during these years he must have lived the life of a wanderer, subsisting as so many have done in India on the charitable offerings of the devout. We may also assume that he would have sought the company of others of similar outlook and that with them he would have engaged in discussion, in the sharing of experiences, and in the singing of God's praises. Much of his time would be devoted to imparting teaching to those who were prepared to hear it, and at other times he would engage in debate people with whose religious beliefs or practices he disagreed. Such debates would have been held with yogīs, with other exponents of pronounced ascetic ideals, and with the upholders of traditional Hindu and Muslim observances. The years of restlessness were presumably succeeded by assurance and tranquillity, and we may assume that it would be during this period that his beliefs took definitive shape.

It must be emphasized that our procedure for this period is based upon assumption and conjecture. Such assumptions do, however, receive a measure of support from Gurū Nānak's own works. In them we encounter a recurrent didactic note, a repeated emphasis upon the value of singing praises in the company of true believers, and expressions which unmistakably evoke the atmosphere of debate. These features must be related primarily to the Kartārpur period, but by no means exclusively. It seems entirely reasonable to suppose that the pattern which they suggest must also have applied to the years of wandering.

It is when we reach the third period of Gurū Nānak's life that we at last pass beyond this dependence upon assumption and conjecture. We move now into a period which was spent in or near the Pañjāb, and which brings us as near as we can approach to the time when the janam-sākhīs were actually compiled. The janam-sākhī records accordingly assume a somewhat greater degree of reliability. They do not in fact tell us much about the events of the period, but this is understandable and significant, for it suggests that authentic knowledge and memory may have acted in some measure as checks upon the proliferation of legend. We also reach in this concluding phase the period in which Gurū Nānak must have communicated to his followers the works which have been recorded in the *Ādi Granth.*

During this third and final period we find Gurū Nānak settled on the banks of the Rāvī in the village of Kartārpur. The Gurū is now more than fifty years old. Behind him lie many years of religious endeavour and the time has come for the application of the ideals which have matured during those preceding years. His fame has spread and in accordance with immemorial tradition prospective disciples have gathered to learn from one whom they can acknowledge as a preceptor and master.

Within the Kartārpur community of those years there was evidently applied a pattern of threefold activity. In the first place there must have been an insistence upon regular disciplined devotion, both individual and corporate. The disciple was required, in imitation of his master, to arise early and devote the 'ambrosial hour'[1] to meditation upon the divine Name. This Gurū Nānak clearly enjoined and accordingly this must have been the discipline which he himself observed. Other hours are not specified, but the emphasis laid upon such meditation and also upon the corporate singing of praises (*kīrtan*) makes it clear that devotional activity must have occupied much of Gurū Nānak's own time and that his disciples would have been expected to follow his example. *Kīrtan* was presumably held both in the early morning, following individual meditation, and also in the evening following the conclusion of the day's work.

A second feature of the Kartārpur pattern would have been the regular instruction imparted by the Gurū. Such instruction would frequently have been given to individual followers, but the form in which we find it recorded in the *Ādi Granth* will correspond more closely to the instruction delivered in the regular gatherings of his disciples. The content would, however, be the same. In both cases there would be the same emphasis upon the greatness of God, upon His gracious self-revelation, upon the perils of the human condition, and upon the paramount necessity of meditation on the divine Name. Trust in conventional external forms would be exposed as essentially futile, sometimes by means of gentle irony and at other times by direct denial of their efficacy. Those who placed their confidence in status conferred by caste or by wealth would be sternly admonished, and any who descended to religious hypocrisy would be roundly condemned.

All of this is plainly evident from his works and so too is the recurrent dialectic strain which suggests frequent debates. Many disputations must

[1] *amrit velā sachu nāu vaḍiāī vīchāru. Japjī* 4, *AG*, p. 2. See *supra*, p. 217.

have been held with Nāth yogīs for, as we have already observed, members of this sect are addressed directly in several polemical compositions. Nāth yogīs would have been natural opponents, both because of the manner in which their theories and practices conflicted with those of Gurū Nānak, and because of the considerable influence which they still exercised over the popular mind of the Pañjāb. On one occasion the Gurū evidently travelled to a neighbouring Nāth centre in order to meet and dispute with yogīs of the sect.[1] It seems clear that they must have absorbed much of his attention and the subsequent decline of their influence in the Pañjāb must be regarded as one of his most striking victories.

The third feature of the Kartārpur pattern would presumably have been regular daily labour. In the works of Gurū Nānak asceticism is explicitly rejected and in its place a disciplined worldliness is set forth as the proper path for the believer. A necessary part of this disciplined worldliness was the insistence that the believer should live on what he had himself laboured to receive.[2] At this point we return once again to assumption, but in the light of Gurū Nānak's pronouncements on this particular subject it seems entirely reasonable to suppose that regular labour must have been a part of the Kartārpur community discipline. Whether Gurū Nānak himself participated is impossible to say. His position as leader of the community would certainly have freed him from any obligation to do so, but a concern to practise in his own life what he exhorted others to do may well have led him to join his followers in their daily labours. His concept of a disciplined worldliness also enjoined a continuation of normal family relationships and we may accordingly accept the janam-sākhī indications that his wife and sons lived with him in Kartārpur during this period.

The impression which emerges is that of a deeply devout believer absorbed in meditation and rejoicing in the manifestations of the divine presence, but refusing to renounce his family or his worldly occupation. Discipline there certainly was, but not renunciation and total withdrawal. The impression is also that of a revered teacher giving expression to his experience in simple direct hymns of superb poetic quality. Around him would be gathered a group of regular disciples, and many more would come for occasional *darśan*, or audience, with the master. And the impression is that of a man, gentle and yet capable of sternness, a man of humour and mild irony who could nevertheless reprimand and if necessary denounce, a man who experienced the inexpressible and who yet maintained an essentially practical participation in the everyday affairs of his community and of the world beyond it.

The combination of piety and practical activity which Gurū Nānak manifested in his own life he bequeathed to his followers and it remains

[1] His visit to Achal.

[2] See *supra*, p. 211.

characteristic of many who own him as Gurū today. At its best it is a piety devoid of superstition and a practical activity compounded with determination and an immense generosity. It explains much that has happened in the Pañjāb during the last four centuries and it explains much that can be witnessed there today.

BIBLIOGRAPHY

English, French, and German (including translations from Persian, Panjabi, etc.)

'ABDUL HALIM, *History of the Lodi Sultans*, Dacca, 1961.

ABU'L FAZL, *Āīn-i-Akbarī*, vol. ii, Eng. trans. H. S. Jarrett, Calcutta, 1891.

—— *Akbarnāma*, vol. i, Eng. trans. H. Beveridge, Calcutta, 1897–1903.

AHMAD SHAH, *The Bījak of Kabīr*, Hamirpur, U.P., 1917.

—— and ORMEROD, E. W., *Hindi Religious Poetry*, Cawnpore, 1925.

ANANDA ACHARYA, *Snow-birds*, London, 1919.

ARBERRY, A. J., *Sufism*, London, 1950.

ARCHER, JOHN CLARK, 'The Bible of the Sikhs', *The Review of Religion*, January 1949.

—— *The Sikhs in relation to Hindus, Moslems, Christians, and Ahmadiyyas*, Princeton, 1946.

ASHRAF, K. M., 'Life and Conditions of the People of Hindustan (1200–1550 A.D.)', *JRASB*, 1935, vol. 1, part i, pp. 103–359; and Jiwan Prakashan, Delhi.

AZIZ AHMAD, *Studies in Islamic Culture in the Indian Environment*, Oxford, 1964.

BADĀUNĪ, *Muntakhab al-Tawārīkh*, vol. i, Eng. trans. G. A. S. Ranking, Calcutta, 1898.

BANERJEE, I. B., *Evolution of the Khalsa*, vol. i, Calcutta, 1936.

BARTH, A. *The Religions of India*, London, 1882.

BARTHWAL, P. D., *The Nirguna School of Hindi Poetry*, Benares, 1936. Also in Hindi translation: *Hindī kāvya men nirguṇa sampradāya*, trans. Paraśu-rām Chaturvedī, Lucknow, S. 2007 (A.D. 1950).

BASHAM, A. L., *The Wonder that was India*, London, 1954.

BEALE, T. W., *An Oriental Biographical Dictionary*, London, 1894.

BEVERIDGE, A. S., *The Bābur-nāma in English*, London, 1921.

BHANDARKAR, R. G., *Vaisnavism, Saivism and Minor Religious Systems*, Strasbourg, 1913.

BINGLEY, A. H., *Sikhs*, Simla, 1899.

BRIGGS, G. W., *The Chamārs*, Calcutta, 1920.

—— *Gorakhnāth and the Kānphaṭa Yogīs*, Calcutta, 1938.

BRIGGS, JOHN (trans.), *History of the Rise of the Mahomedan Power in India till the year A.D. 1612* (Firishta), London, 1829.

—— *The Siyar-ul-Mutakherin* (Ghulām Husain Khān), London, 1832.

BROWN, JOHN P., *The Darvishes, or Oriental Spiritualism* (ed. H. A. Rose), London, 1927.

BROWNE, JAMES, *Indian Tracts, containing a description of the Jungle Terry Districts. . . . Also an History of the Origin and Progress of the Sicks*, London, 1788.

CANDLER, EDMUND, *The Mantle of the East*, Edinburgh and London, 1910.

CARPENTER, J. E., *Theism in Medieval India*, London, 1921.

CHHABRA, G. S., *The Advanced Study in the History of the Punjab*, vol. i, Jullundur, 1960.

CHHAJJU SINGH, *The Ten Gurus and their Teachings*, Lahore, 1903.

COURT, HENRY, *History of the Sikhs*, Lahore, 1888 (Eng. trans. of Sardhā Rām's *Sikhān de rāj dī vitthiā*).

CUNNINGHAM, J. D., *A History of the Sikhs*, London, 1849.
CUST, R. N., 'The Life of Bâbâ Nânak, the Founder of the Sikh Sect', in the *Indian Antiquary*, iii (1874), pp. 295–300.
DALJIT SINGH, *Guru Nanak*, Lahore, 1943.
DASGUPTA, SHASHIBHUSAN, *An Introduction to Tantric Buddhism*, Calcutta, 1958.
—— *Obscure Religious Cults as Background of Bengali Literature*, Calcutta, 1946.
DASGUPTA, SURENDRANATHA, *A History of Indian Philosophy*, Cambridge, 1922–55.
—— *Yoga as Philosophy and Religion*, London, 1924.
DE BARY, WM. T., *et al.* (compilers), *Sources of Indian Tradition*, New York, 1958.
DOWSON, JOHN, *A Classical Dictionary of Hindu Mythology &c*, London, 1961.
ELIADE, MIRCEA, *Yoga: Immortality and Freedom*, London, 1958.
ELLIOT, H. M., and DOWSON, J., *The History of India as told by its own Historians*, vols. iii, iv, and v, London, 1871–3.
FARQUHAR, J. N., *Modern Religious Movements in India*, New York, 1919.
—— *An Outline of the Religious Literature of India*, London, 1920.
FIELD, DOROTHY, *The Religion of the Sikhs*, London, 1914.
FORSTER, GEORGE, *A Journey from Bengal to England &c*, London, 1808.
GANDA SINGH, *Contemporary Sources of Sikh History (1469–1708)*, Amritsar, 1938.
—— (ed.) *Early European Accounts of the Sikhs*, Calcutta, 1962.
—— (trans.) *Nānak Panthīs, or the Sikhs and Sikhism of the 17th Century*, Eng. trans. with original Persian text of a chapter from Muhsin Fānī, *Dabistān-i-Mazāhib*, Madras, 1939.
—— *A Select Bibliography of the Sikhs and Sikhism*, Amritsar, 1965.
GOPAL SINGH, *The Song of Nanak*, Eng. trans. of the *Japjī*, London, 1955.
—— *Sri Guru-Granth Sahib*, Eng. trans. of the *Ādi Granth*, Delhi, 1962.
GORDON, J. J. H., *The Sikhs*, London, 1904.
GREENLEES, DUNCAN, *The Gospel of the Guru-Granth Sahib*, Adyar, Madras, 1952.
GRENARD, FERNAND, *Baber, Fondateur de l'Empire des Indes*, Paris, 1930.
GRIERSON, G. A., *The Modern Vernacular Literature of Hindustan*, Special Number of the *Journal of the Asiatic Society of Bengal*, vol. lvii for 1888, Calcutta, 1889.
GRIFFIN, LEPEL, 'Sikhism and the Sikhs' in *The Great Religions of the World*, New York, 1901.
GURSHARN SINGH BEDI, *The Psalm of Life*, Eng. trans. of the *Japjī*, Amritsar, 1952.
HARBANS SINGH, *The Heritage of the Sikhs*, Bombay, 1964.
HARNAM SINGH, *The Japji*, Delhi, 1957.
HODIVALA, S. H., *Studies in Indo-Muslim History*, Bombay, 1939 and 1957.
HOPKINS, E. W., *The Religions of India*, London, 1896.
IBBETSON, DENZIL, *Panjab Castes*, Lahore, 1916.
IKRAM, S. M. (ed. Ainslie T. Embree), *Muslim Civilization in India*, New York, 1964.
IRFAN HABIB, 'Evidence for Sixteenth-century Agrarian Conditions in the Guru Granth Sahib', *The Indian Economic and Social History Review*, vol. i, no. 3, Jan.–Mar. 1964, pp. 64–72.
JIWAN SINGH, *Japjee Sahib*, Calcutta, 1935.
JODH SINGH, *The Japji*, Amritsar, 1956.
—— 'Religion and religious life as conceived by Guru Nanak' (tract), Anandpur Sahib, 1925.
—— *Some Studies in Sikhism*, Ludhiana, 1953.
JOGENDRA SINGH, *Thus Spake Guru Nanak*, Madras, 1934.
KAPUR SINGH, *Parasharprasna, or the Baisakhi of Guru Gobind Singh*, Jullundur, 1959.

KARTAR SINGH, *Life of Guru Nanak Dev*, Ludhiana, 1958. Also in Panjabi translation: *Jīvan kathā Srī Gurū Nānak Dev Jī*, Lahore, 1947.
KEITH, A. BERRIEDALE, *The Religion and Philosophy of the Vedas and Upanishads*, Cambridge, Mass., 1925.
KHALIQ AHMAD NIZAMI, *The Life and Times of Shaikh Farid-u'd-din Ganj-i-Shakar*, Aligarh, 1955.
KHAZAN SINGH, *History and Philosophy of Sikhism*, Lahore, 1914.
KHUSHWANT SINGH, *A History of the Sikhs*, vol. i, Princeton and London, 1963.
—— *Jupji: the Sikh Prayer*, London, n.d.
—— *The Sikhs*, London, 1953.
KIRPAL SINGH, *A Catalogue of Punjabi and Urdu Manuscripts in the Sikh History Research Department*, Amritsar, 1963.
LAL, K. S., *Twilight of the Sultanate*, London, 1963.
LANE-POOLE, S., *Babar*, Oxford, 1899.
LATIF, MUHAMMAD, *History of the Punjab*, Calcutta, 1891.
LEYDEN, J., and ERSKINE, WM., (trans.), *Memoirs of Zehīr-ed-Dīn Muhammed Baber Emperor of Hindustān*, London, 1826.
LOEHLIN, C. H., *The Sikhs and their Book*, Lucknow, 1946.
—— *The Sikhs and their Scriptures*, Lucknow, 1958.
MACAULIFFE, M. A., *The Sikh Religion*, Oxford, 1909. Vol. i also in Panjabi translation: *Jīvan Srī Gurū Nānak Dev Jī*, trans. Sujān Singh, Amritsar, n.d.
MACDONELL, A. A., *Vedic Mythology*, Strasbourg, 1897.
M'GREGOR, W. L., *The History of the Sikhs*, London, 1846.
MACNICOL, NICOL, *Indian Theism from the Vedic to the Muhammadan Period*, London, 1915.
MAHĪPATI, *Nectar from Indian Saints*, Eng. trans. of Mahīpati's Marāṭhī *Bhaktalīlāmrit* by Justin E. Abbott, N. R. Godbole, and J. F. Edwards, Poona, 1935.
—— *Stories of Indian Saints*, Eng. trans. of Mahīpati's Marāṭhī *Bhaktavījaya* by Justin E. Abbott, and N. R. Godbole, Poona, 1933.
MALCOLM, JOHN, *Sketch of the Sikhs*, London, 1812.
MOELLER, VOLKER, 'Die Lebensdaten des Glaubensstifters Nanak', in *Indo-Iranian Journal*, vol. vii, 1964, no. 4, pp. 284–97.
MOHAMMAD NOOR NABI, *Development of Muslim Religious Thought in India from 1200 A.D. to 1450 A.D.*, Aligarh, 1962.
MOHAN SINGH UBEROI, *A History of Panjabi Literature*, Amritsar, 1956.
—— *An Introduction to Panjabi Literature*, Amritsar, 1951.
—— *Kabīr—His Biography*, Lahore, 1934.
MONIER-WILLIAMS, M., *Brahmanism and Hinduism*, London, 1891.
MUHAMMAD IQBAL, 'Sikhs', art. in *The Encyclopaedia of Islam*, Leyden and London, 1934.
MUHSIN FĀNĪ, *Dabistān-i-Mazāhib*, Eng. trans. *The Dabistan or School of Manners* by David Shea and Anthony Troyer, Paris, 1843.
—— *Nānak Pānthis or the Sikhs and Sikhism of the 17th Century*, Eng. trans. of a portion of the *Dabistān-i-Mazāhib* by Ganda Singh, Madras, 1939.
NARAIN SINGH, *Guru Nanak Re-interpreted*, Amritsar, 1965.
—— *Our Heritage*, Amritsar, n.d.
NARANG, GOKUL CHAND, *The Transformation of Sikhism*, Lahore, 1912.
NICHOLSON, R. A., *The Mystics of Islam*, London, 1963.
NI'MATULLAH, *Niamatullah's History of the Afghans*, Eng. trans. of Ni'matullah's *Makhāzan-i-Afghānī*, part i, by Nirodbhusan Roy, Śantiniketan, 1958.
NIZĀMUDDĪN AHMAD, *Tabaqāt-i-Akbarī*, Eng. trans. by B. De, Calcutta, 1927–40.
OMAN, J. C., *The Mystics, Ascetics, and Saints of India*, London, 1903.

PANDEY, A. B., *The First Afghan Empire in India*, Calcutta, 1956.
—— *Early Medieval India*, Allahabad, 1965.
PANIKKAR, K. M., 'The Ideals of Sikhism' (tract), Amritsar, 1924.
PARKASH SINGH, *The Sikh Gurus and the Temple of Bread*, Amritsar, 1964.
PARRY, R. E., *The Sikhs of the Punjab*, London, 1921.
PAYNE, C. H., *A Short History of the Sikhs*, London, 1915.
PINCOTT, F., 'Sikhism', art. in T. P. Hughes's *A Dictionary of Islam*, London, 1885.
POLLET, GILBERT, *Studies in the Bhakta Māla of Nābhā Dāsa*, thesis presented to the University of London for the degree of Ph.D., 1963.
PRASAD, ISHWARI, *The Life and Times of Humayun*, Calcutta, 1955.
PRINSEP, H. T., *Origin of the Sikh Power in the Punjab and the political life of Muharaja Runjeet Singh*, Calcutta, 1834.
PRITAM SINGH, *Saints and Sages of India*, New Delhi, 1948.
PURAN SINGH, *The Book of the Ten Masters*, London, 1926.
QURESHI, I. H., *The Administration of the Delhi Sultanate*, Lahore, 1944.
RADHAKRISHNAN, S., *Indian Philosophy*, London, 1929.
—— *The Principal Upanisads*, London, 1953.
RAHIM, M. A., *History of the Afghans in India*, Karachi, 1961.
RAMA KRISHNA, LAJWANTI, *Les Sikhs*, Paris, 1933.
—— *Pañjābī Ṣūfī Poets*, Calcutta, 1938.
RANBIR SINGH, *Glimpses of the Divine Masters*, New Delhi, 1965.
RICE, CYPRIAN, *The Persian Sufis*, London, 1964.
RIZVI, SAIYID ATHAR ABBAS, *Muslim Revivalist Movements in Northern India in the Sixteenth and Seventeenth Centuries*, Agra, 1965.
ROSE, H. A. (ed.), *A Glossary of Tribes and Castes of the Punjab and North-West Frontier Province*, Lahore, 1911–19.
ROSS, DAVID, *The Land of the Five Rivers and Sindh*, London, 1883.
SARDUL SINGH CAVEESHAR, *The Sikh Studies*, Lahore, 1937.
SCOTT, G. B., *Religion and Short History of the Sikhs 1469–1930*, London, 1930.
SEN, KSHITIMOHAN, *Medieval Mysticism of India*, London, 1935.
SEWARAM SINGH THAPAR, *Sri Guru Nanak Dev*, Rawalpindi, 1904.
—— *The Divine Master*, Lahore, 1930.
SHARMA, KRISHNA, *Early Indian Bhakti with special reference to Kabir, a Historical Analysis and Re-interpretation*, thesis presented to the University of London for the degree of Ph.D., 1964.
SHER SINGH GYANI, *Philosophy of Sikhism*, Lahore, 1944.
SINGH, G. B., 'Sikh Relics in Eastern Bengal', in the *Dacca Review*, vol. v, nos. 7 and 8, Oct. and Nov. 1915, pp. 224–32; no. 10, Jan. 1916, pp. 316–22; and nos. 11 and 12, Feb. and Mar. 1916, pp. 375–8.
SOHAN SINGH, *The Seeker's Path*, Bombay, 1959.
STEINBACH, H., *The Punjaub*, London, 1845.
STULPNAGEL, C. REBSCH, *The Sikhs*, Lahore, 1870.
SUBHAN, J. A., *Sufism: Its Saints and Shrines*, Lucknow, 1960.
SURINDAR SINGH KOHLI, *A Critical Study of the Adi Granth*, New Delhi, 1961.
—— *Outlines of Sikh Thought*, New Delhi, 1966.
TARA CHAND, *Influence of Islam on Indian Culture*, Allahabad, 1963.
TARAN SINGH, *Guru Nanak as a Poet*, thesis presented to the University of Panjab for the degree of Ph.D., 1959.
DE TASSY, GARCIN, *Histoire de la Littérature Hindoui et Hindoustani*, vol. i, Paris, 1839.
TEJA SINGH, *Essays in Sikhism*, Lahore, 1944.

TEJA SINGH, *Growth of Responsibility in Sikhism*, Bombay, 1948.
—— 'Guru Nanak and his Mission' (tract), Lahore, 1918.
—— *The Japji*, Lahore, 1930.
—— *The Sikh Religion*, Kuala Lumpur, 1937.
—— *Sikhism: Its Ideals and Institutions*, Bombay, 1951.
—— and GANDA SINGH, *A Short History of the Sikhs*, vol. i, Bombay, 1950.
TEMPLE, R. C., *The Legends of the Panjâb*, Bombay and London, 1884–6.
THORNTON, D. M., *Parsi, Jaina and Sikh*, London, 1898.
THORNTON, T. H., *History of the Punjab*, London, 1846.
TITUS, MURRAY T., *Islam in India and Pakistan*, Madras, 1959.
TRIPATHI, R. P., *Some Aspects of Muslim Administration*, Allahabad, 1936.
TRUMPP, ERNEST, *The Ādi Granth*, London, 1877.
VAUDEVILLE, CHARLOTTE, *Au Cabaret de l'Amour: Paroles de Kabîr*, Paris, 1959.
—— *Kabīr Granthāvalī (Dohā)*, Hindi text with French translation, Pondichéry, 1957.
—— 'Kabīr and Interior Religion', in *History of Religions*, vol. iii, no. 2, Winter 1964, pp. 191–201.
WARD, WM., *Account of the Writings, Religion, and Manners of the Hindoos*, vol. iv, 'Account of the Sikhs', pp. 383–406, Serampore, 1811.
—— *A View of the History, Literature, and Mythology of the Hindoos*, vol. iii, chap. ix, London, 1822.
WESTCOTT, G. H., *Kabir and the Kabir Panth*, Cawnpore, 1907.
WILKINS, CHARLES, 'Observations and Inquiries concerning the Seeks and their College at Patna, in the East-Indies', an article reprinted in *Dissertations and Miscellaneous Pieces relating to the History and Antiquities, the Arts, Sciences, and Literature of Asia* by sundry authors, Dublin, 1793.
WILLIAMS, L. RUSHBROOK, *An Empire Builder of the Sixteenth Century*, London, 1918.
WILSON, H. H., *Sketch of the Religious Sects of the Hindus*, Calcutta, 1846.
—— 'A Summary Account of the Civil and Religious Institutions of the Sikhs', *JRAS*, vol. ix (1848), pp. 43–59.
YAHYĀ IBN AHMAD SIRHINDĪ, *Tarīkh-i-Mubārak Shāhī*, Eng. trans. K. K. Basu, Baroda, 1932.
YUSUF HUSAIN, *Glimpses of Medieval Indian Culture*, London, 1959.

ANON., *The History of the Sikhs*, Calcutta, 1846.
Cambridge History of India, vols. 3 and 4.
The Cultural Heritage of India, vol. iv, *The Religions*, Calcutta, 1956.
Encyclopaedia of Islam, Leyden and London, 1913–38. New edition: 1960—in progress.
The History and Culture of the Indian People, vol. iv, *The Delhi Sultanate*, Bombay, 1960.
Imperial Gazetteer of India, Oxford, 1908.
Punjab State Gazetteers.
Selections from the Sacred Writings of the Sikhs, trans. by Trilochan Singh, Jodh Singh, Kapur Singh, Harkishen Singh, and Khushwant Singh, London, 1960.
The Sikh Religion, a Symposium by M. Macauliffe, H. H. Wilson, Frederic Pincott, John Malcolm, and Sardar Kahan Singh, Calcutta, 1958.
Sikhism and Christianity in the Punjab, special issue of *Religion and Society*, vol. xi, no. 1, Mar. 1964.

Pañjābī and other works in Gurmukhī

Ādi Srī Gurū Granth Sāhib Jī, Srī Damdamī Bīṛ, various printed editions. Standard pagination 1430 pp.

Ādi Granth, BM MS Or. 1125.

DĀN SIṄGH, *Khālsā Tavārīkh dā Pahilā Pattrā*, Amritsar, 1937.

GOPĀL SIṄGH, *Pañjābī Sāhit dā Itihās*, Chandigarh, 1962.

—— *Srī Gurū Granth Sāhib dī sāhitak viśeṣatā*, Delhi, 1958.

GURBAKHSH SIṄGH (G. B. Singh), *Srī Gurū Granth Sāhib diān Prāchīn Bīṛān*, Lahore, 1944.

GURDĀS BHALLĀ (Bhāī Gurdās), *Kabitt Savayye*, Amritsar, 1925.

—— *Vārān Bhāī Gurdās*, ed. Hazārā Siṅgh and Vīr Siṅgh, Amritsar, 1962.

GYĀN SIṄGH, *Panth Prakāś*, Amritsar, 1923.

—— *Tavārīkh Gurū Khālsā*, Amritsar, 1914.

HARBANS SIṄGH, *Japu-niraṇay*, Chandigarh, 1963.

HARINDAR SIṄGH RŪP, *Bhāī Gurdās*, Amritsar, 1952.

JANAM-SĀKHĪ, *Colebrooke Janam-sākhī* (*Valāitvālī Janam-sākhī*), IOL MS Panj. B6, S 1728.

—— Photozincograph Facsimile of the *Colebrooke Janam-sākhī*, Dehra Dun, 1885.

—— Lahore Siṅgh Sabhā lithographed edition of the *Colebrooke Janam-sākhī*, Lahore, 1884.

—— a janam-sākhī published by M. Macauliffe with introduction by Gurmukh Siṅgh, being the *Hāfizābād Janam-sākhī*, Rawalpindi, 1885.

—— *Purātan Janam-sākhī*, edited by Vīr Siṅgh, Amritsar, several editions.

—— a janam-sākhī related to the *Purātan* tradition, IOL MS Panj. B40.

—— *Miharbān Janam-sākhī*, MS no. SHR: 427 of the Sikh History Research Department, Khalsa College, Amritsar, being *Pothī Sach-khaṇḍ, Pothī Harijī*, and *Pothī Chatarbhuj* of the *Miharbān Janam-sākhī*.

—— Miharbān Jī Soḍhī, *Janam-sākhī Srī Gurū Nānak Dev Jī*, being *Pothī Sach-khaṇḍ* of the *Miharbān Janam-sākhī*, edited by Kirpāl Siṅgh and Shamsher Siṅgh Ashok, Amritsar, 1962.

—— A *Bālā* janam-sākhī, IOL MS Panj. B41, S. 2885.

—— A *Bālā* janam-sākhī, BM MS Or. 2754. I.

—— A *Bālā* janam-sākhī, SOAS MS. no. 104975.

—— A *Bālā* janam-sākhī, Hāfaz Qutub-dīn, Lahore, S. 1928 (A.D. 1871).

—— A *Bālā* janam-sākhī, Mālik Dīvān Būṭā Siṅgh, Lahore, S. 1928 (A.D. 1871).

—— A *Bālā* janam-sākhī, Maulvī Maibūb Ahmad, Lahore, A.D. 1890.

—— A *Bālā* janam-sakhi, Munshī Gulāb Siṅgh and Sons, Lahore, several editions.

—— *Gyān-ratanāvalī* (*Manī Siṅgh Janam-sākhī*), Manuscript in the possession of Professor Prītam Siṅgh, Patiala.

—— *Gyān-ratanāvalī* (*Manī Siṅgh Janam-sākhī*), Charāg Dīn and Sarāj Dīn, Lahore, A.D. 1891.

—— *Mahimā Prakāś Vāratak*, Khalsa College, Amritsar, MS SHR: 2308.

—— *Mahimā Prakāś Kavitā*, Khalsa College, Amritsar, MS SHR: 2300A.

—— *Jīvan kathā Srī Gurū Nānak Dev Ji Mahimā Prakāś* (*Vāratak*) *vichon*, ed. Kirpāl Siṅgh, Bedi Printing Press, Dehra Dun, 1959.

JODH SIṄGH, *Bhagat Bāṇī Saṭīk*, Ludhiana, 1957.

—— *Gurū Nānak Simaratī Viākhiān*, Patiala, 1967. (Punjabi University Gurū Nānak Memorial Lectures for 1966–7.)

JODH SIṄGH, *Guramati Niraṇay*, Ludhiana, n.d.
—— *Ṭīkā Japujī Sāhib*, Amritsar, 1911.
KĀHN SIṄGH NĀBHĀ, *Guramat Prabhākar*, Lahore, 1898.
—— *Gurumat Mārtaṇḍ*, Amritsar, 1962.
—— *Guruśabad Ratanākar Mahān Koś*, 1st ed. in four vols., Patiala, 1931; 2nd ed. revised with Addendum, in one vol., Patiala, 1960.
KĀLĀ SIṄGH BEDĪ, *Gurū Nānak Bhāṣā*, New Delhi, 1962.
—— *Gurū Nānak Niraṅkārī*, New Delhi, 1966.
—— *Gurū Nānak Daraśan*, New Delhi, 1965.
KARAM SIṄGH, *Gurapurb Niraṇay*, Amritsar, 1913.
—— *Kattak ki Visākh?*, Amritsar, 1913.
MAHINDAR SIṄGH RANDHĀVĀ, (ed.) *Pañjāb*, Patiala, 1960.
MAHITĀB SIṄGH, *Śrī Gurū Granth Sāhib Jī vich dite nāvān te thāvān dā koś*, Lahore, 1933.
MOHAN SIṄGH UBERĀI, *Pañjābī Bhākhā te Chhandābandī*, Lahore, 1938.
NARAIṆ SIṄGH, *Sikh Dharam dīān Buniādān*, Amritsar, 1966.
PRATĀP SIṄGH, *Bhagat Daraśan*, Amritsar, 1944.
RATTAN SIṄGH BHAṄGŪ, *Prachīn Panth Prakāś*, Amritsar, 1962.
RATTAN SIṄGH JAGGĪ, *Dasam Granth dā Paurāṇik Adhiāin*, Jullundur, 1965.
—— *Vichār-dhārā*, Patiala, 1966.
—— (ed.), *Vārān Bhāī Gurdās: Śabad Anukramaṇikā ate Koś*, Patiala, 1966.
SĀHIB SIṄGH, *Bhagat-bāṇī Saṭīk*, Amritsar, 1959–60.
—— *Śalok Bhagat Kabīr Jī*, Amritsar, 1949.
—— *Srī Gurū Granth Sāhib Darapaṇ*, 10 vols., Jullundur, 1962–4.
SANTOKH SIṄGH, *Nānak Prakāś* and *Sūraj Prakāś*, 13 vols. edited by Vīr Siṅgh and comprising: vol. 1, *Śrī Gur Pratāp Sūraj Granthāvalī dī Prasāvanā*, being Vīr Siṅgh's Introduction; vols. 2–4, *Śrī Gur Nānāk Prakāś*; vols. 5–13, *Śrī Gur Pratāp Sūraj Granth*, Amritsar, 1927–35.
—— *Vāratak Srī Nānak Prakāś*, prose summary of the *Nānak Prakāś* by Naraiṇ Siṅgh, Taran Tāran, 1941.
SARDHĀ RĀM, *Sikhān de Rāj dī Vitthiā*, Lahore, 1892.
SHAMSHER SIṄGH ASHOK, *Pañjābī Hath-likhatān dī Sūchī*, 2 vols., Patiala, 1961 and 1963.
SHER SIṄGH GIĀNĪ, *Guramati Daraśan*, Amritsar, 1962.
—— *Vichār Dhārā*, Ludhiana, n.d.
—— *Vichār Mālā*, Ludhiana, 1951.
TĀRAN SIṄGH, *Gurū Nānak, chintan te kalā*, Amritsar, 1963.
TEJĀ SIṄGH, *Japujī (Saṭīk)*, Patiala, 1952.
——*Sikh Dharam*, Patiala, 1952.
TEJĀ SIṄGH OVERSEER, *Khālsā Rahit Prakāś*, Lahore, 1914.
VĪR SIṄGH, *Pañj Granthī Saṭīk*, Amritsar, 1950.
—— *Santhyā Srī Gurū Granth Sāhib*, 7 vols., Amritsar, 1958–62.
—— *Srī Gurū Nānak Chamatkār*, 2 vols., Amritsar, 1928 and 1933.

Guru Śabad Ratan Prakāś, Line Index of the *Ādi Granth*, Patiala, 1963 (original edition compiled by Kaur Siṅgh Nihaṅg entitled *Srī Gurū Śabad Ratan Prakāś*, Peshawar, 1923).
Mahānkavī Gurū Nānak, Patiala, 1956.
Śabadārath Srī Gurū Granth Sāhib Jī, text and commentary on the *Ādi Granth*, n.p., 1936–41.
Srī Gurū Granth Bāṇī Beurā, Amritsar, 1914.
Śrī Gurū Granth Koś, 3 vols., Amritsar, 1950.

Hindī

Bhagīrath Miśra and Rājnārāyaṇ Maurya, *Sant Nāmdev kī Hindī Padāvalī*, Poona, 1964.
Govind Triguṇāyat, *Kabīr kī vichār-dhārā*, Kanpur, S. 2009, (A.D. 1952).
Hazārī-prasād Dvivedī, *Hindī sāhitya*, Delhi 1955.
—— *Hindī sāhitya kā ādikāl*, Patna, S. 2009 (A.D. 1952).
—— *Hindī sāhitya kī bhūmikā*, Bombay, 1950.
—— *Kabīr*, Bombay, 1950.
—— *Nāth-sampradāy*, Varanasi, 1966.
Jayarām Miśra, *Śrī Gurū Granth Darśan*, Allahabad, 1960.
Kabīr, *Kabīr-granthāvalī*, ed. Śyāmsundardās, Prayag, 1928.
—— *Kabīr-granthāvalī*, ed. with introduction by Pāras-nāth Tivāri, Prayag, 1961.
—— *Kabīr kā pūrā Bījak*, ed. Prem Chand, Calcutta, 1890.
—— See also English etc., bibliography under Ahmad Shah and Vaudeville, Ch.
Paraśu-rām Chaturvedī, *Kabīr-sāhitya kī parakh*, Prayag, S. 2011, (A.D. 1954).
—— *Uttarī Bhārat kī sant-paramparā*, Prayag, 1951.
Prabhākar Māchave, *Hindī aur Marāṭhī kā nirguṇ sant-kāvya*, Varanasi, 1962.
Puruṣottam-lāl Śrīvāstava, *Kabīr sāhitya kā adhyayan*, Varanasi, S. 2007 (A.D. 1950).
Raidās, *Raidās jī kī bānī aur jīvan-charitr*, Belvedere Press, Allahabad, 1908.
Rājnārāyaṇ Maurya, '*Hindī sāhitya men santamat ke ādi pravartak: Sant Nāmdev*', in *Journal of the University of Poona* (Humanities Section), no. 17, 1963, pp. 127–40.
Rām-chandra Śukl, *Hindī-sāhitya kā itihās*, Kaśi, S. 2014, (A.D. 1957).
Rām-kumār Varmā, *Sant Kabīr*, Allahabad, 1947.
Rāṅgey Rāghava, *Gorakhnāth aur unkā yug*, Delhi, 1963.
Vinay-mohan Śarmā, *Hindī ko Marāṭhī santon kī den*, Patna, S. 2014 (A.D. 1957).
—— *Sant Nāmdev*, Delhi, n.d.

GLOSSARY

Ādi: first.
agiān (*ajñāna*): ignorance, nescience.
amar: immortal.
amrit (*amṛta*): the nectar of immortality.
anahad śabad: the mystical 'sound' or 'unstruck music' which is 'heard' at the climax of the *haṭha-yoga* process (q.v.).
antaḥkaraṇa: the collective mind; the seat of collective thought and feeling.
aṣṭapadī: a poem or hymn of eight, or occasionally more, stanzas.
Asū (*Aśvin*): the seventh month of the lunar year.
avatār: a 'descent'; incarnation of a deity, usually Viṣṇu.

Bābā: 'Father', a term of respect applied to sants, faqīrs, etc.
bāṇī (*vāṇī*): speech; the utterances of the Gurūs and *bhagats* (q.v.). recorded in the *Ādi Granth*.
baqā': the Sūfī concept of a continuing existence within the condition of union with God.
bārah-māhā: 'twelve-month' or calendar poem.
Bedī: a khatrī sub-caste.
Bhādon, Bhādron: the sixth month of the lunar year.
bhagat (*bhakta*): an exponent of *bhakti* (q.v.); a devotee.
bhakti: belief in, and adoration of, a personal God.
Bhāī: 'Brother', a title applied to Sikhs of learning and piety.
Bhallā: a khatrī sub-caste.
bhaṭṭ: a caste of bards and genealogists.
buddhi: the mind as the source of wisdom, intelligence.

chamār: an outcaste leather-worker.
chapātī: unleavened wholemeal bread.
chhant (*chhandas*): metre, measure; in the *Ādi Granth* a poem or hymn of variable length.
chitta: mind, intellect, reasoning faculty.
Choṇā: a khatrī sub-caste.

darśan: view, vision; audience with a person of regal or spiritual stature, visit to a holy shrine or object; the six systems of brahmanical philosophy.
darveś: dervish, a Muslim mendicant (esp. Sūfī).
dasam duār (*dasama dvāra*): 'the tenth door' as opposed to the nine physiological orifices of the human body; according to *haṭha-yoga* theory the mystical orifice which gives access to the condition of *sahaj* (q.v.).
deś: country.
dharma, dharam: the appropriate moral and religious obligations attached to any particular status in Hindu society.
Dharamrāj: *Yam* (q.v), the god of the dead in his role as divine arbiter of the fate of each individual.
dharmsālā: a place of worship; an inn (generally a religious foundation) for pilgrims and travellers.

dhikr: the Sūfī discipline of 'remembrance' or thinking on God.
Dhuppaṛ: a khatrī sub-caste.
dil: heart.
dīp (*dvīp*): continent, island.
doāb: area between two rivers.
dohā: couplet.
Ḍūm, Ḍom: a depressed sub-caste of Muslim genealogists and musicians, also called *Mirāsīs*.

fanā': dying to self, the Sūfī concept of the merging of the individual self in the Universal Being.
faqīr: 'poor man', Muslim ascetic; loosely used to designate Sūfīs and also non-Muslim renunciants.

ghaṭ: heart; body.
ghāṭ: landing-place, bathing-place, place where corpses are cremated.
giān (*jñāna*): knowledge, wisdom.
Gopāl: in Vaiṣṇava usage an epithet of Kriṣṇa ('Cow-herd'); in Sant and Sikh usage a name of the non-incarnated God.
goṣṭ: discourse.
guṇa: the three vital 'qualities' or constituents of cosmic substance which by their varying proportions determine the nature of all that exists.
gurdwārā: Sikh temple.
gurmukh: a follower of the Gurū.
gurū: a spiritual preceptor, usually a person but sometimes understood as the divine inner voice.
gurupadeś: the teaching of the Gurū.

Hari: in Vaiṣṇava usage Viṣṇu; in Sant and Sikh usage the non-incarnated God.
haṭha-yoga: 'yoga of force', a variety of yoga requiring physical postures and processes of extreme difficulty. For an account of its physiological theories see p. 191, n. 4. See also *Nāth* (q.v.).
haumai: self, self-centredness.
hiradā (*hṛdaya*): heart.
hukam: order.

janam-sākhī: a traditional biography, esp. of Gurū Nānak.
janeū (*yajñopavīta*): sacred thread.
jaṅgam: a member of a Śaivite sect of itinerant yogīs.
jīv: soul, spirit, psyche.
jñān: see *giān*.
julāhā: weaver caste.

kabitt: a poetic metre.
Kaliyug: 'the era of strife', the fourth and last of the cosmic ages; the age of degeneracy.
Kānphaṭ: 'split ear'; sect of yogīs, followers of Gorakhnāth and practitioners of *haṭha-yoga* (q.v.), so called because of their pierced ears in which rings are worn. Cf. *Nāth*.
karma: the destiny, fate of an individual, generated in accordance with the deeds performed in his present and past existences.
karoṛī: a high-ranking revenue collector of the Mughal period.

Kattak (*Kārtik*): the eighth month of the lunar year.
kavitā: poem.
Khālsā: the Sikh order, brotherhood, instituted by Gurū Gobind Siṅgh.
khaṇḍ: region, realm.
khatrī: a mercantile caste, particularly important in the Pañjāb.
kīrtan: the singing of songs in praise of God, generally by a group and generally to the accompaniment of music.
kos, *koh* (*krośa*): a linear measure varying from one to two miles in different parts of India. In the Pañjāb it has generally been computed as the equivalent of one and a half miles.

lākh: one hundred thousand.
laṅgar: public kitchen or refectory.
loṭā: a small metal vessel.

mahant: chief; superior of a monastery or other religious institution.
man (*manas*): mind, heart, soul, psyche.
mañjī: a small string bed; areas of jurisdiction designated by Gurū Amar Dās.
manmukh: one who follows his own self-centred impulses rather than the guidance of the Gurū. (Cf. *gurmukh* q.v.)
mantra: a verse, phrase or syllable of particular religious import, in some cases believed to possess magical qualities.
maqāmāt: (plural form of *maqām*) the stages of spiritual development in the Sūfī ascent to mystical union.
mātā: mother.
mati: intellect.
maulānā: a title accorded to Muslim judges or other Muslims respected for their learning.
māyā: (in Vedānt) cosmic illusion; (in Sant and Sikh thought) the corruptible and corrupting world, with all its snares, presented to man as permanent and incorruptible and so masquerading as ultimate truth. In Sant and Sikh usage the term has strong moral overtones and is frequently symbolized by lucre and women.
miharāb: the niche in a mosque which indicates the direction of the *Ka'bah* (*qiblah*).
Mirāsī: See *Ḍūm*.
mullah: a teacher of the law and doctrines of Islam.
murāqabat: the Sūfī discipline of meditation.

nadar, *nazar*: sight, glance; grace.
Nām: the divine Name, the expression of the nature and being of God in terms comprehensible to the human understanding.
namāz: Muslim prayer, esp. the prescribed daily prayers.
narak: hell.
Nāth, sect: A yoga sect of considerable influence during the time of Gurū Nānak. The origins of the sect are not wholly clear, but there can be no doubt that its development owed much to Śaivite teachings and to tantric Buddhism (the Vajrayāna or Sahajayāna school). The term *nāth* means 'master' and the *Ādināth*, or 'Original Master' was generally held to have been Śiva. In addition to the *Ādināth* there were believed to have been nine other *Nāths*, master yogīs who had attained immortality through the practice of *haṭha-yoga* (q.v.) and who were

supposed to be living far back in the fastnesses of the Himālayas. According to some traditions Śiva was one of the nine, but the leadership was generally accorded to Gorakhnāth. The idea of the nine immortal *Nāths* probably evolved by analogy with the eighty-four immortal *Siddhs* (q.v.) of tantric Buddhism, also accepted by the Nāth sect. All external ceremonies were rejected as futile, the inward discipline of *haṭha-yoga* being affirmed as the only means of obtaining immortality. Caste distinctions, sacred languages, and scriptures were also rejected as worthless. The yogīs of the Nāth sect exercised little influence upon the educated, but amongst the mass of the population they commanded a certain respect for their extreme austerities and a considerable fear on account of their supposed magical powers. The members of the sect are also called Kānphaṭ yogīs (q.v.).

nawāb: governor, viceroy.

nirguṇa: without 'qualities' or attributes, unconditioned. (Cf. *saguṇa*.)

Paltā: a khatrī sub-caste.

pāṇḍā: brāhmaṇ genealogist.

paṇḍit: an erudite person; a mode of address used for brāhmaṇs.

panth: path; sect; community.

param: supreme, ultimate.

paṭvārī: village land accountant.

pauṛī: lit. staircase; stanza.

pīr: the head of a Sūfī order; a Sūfī saint.

pīṭh-sthān: the fifty-one places where, according to tantric mythology, pieces of Satī's body fell after her dismemberment by Śiva.

potā: son's son; descendant in the male line.

pothī: volume.

prāṇāyām: breath control, a yoga technique.

pūjā: worship, esp. idol worship.

Pūran-māsī: the full-moon day.

qalandar: itinerant Muslim ascetic.

qāzī, *qāḍī*: a Muslim judge, administrator of Islamic law.

rāg: a series of five or more notes upon which a melody is based; melody.

ridā: heart.

Śabad (*Śabda*): Word, the divine self-communication. (The capitalization does not correspond to the Gurmukhī or Devanāgarī forms, but is used in transcription to indicate the distinction expressed in written English by 'Word' as opposed to 'word'. Cf. also *Nām*, *Hukam*.)

śabad (*śabda*): word. In Sikh usage a hymn of the *Ādi Granth*.

sach (*satya*): truth; true.

sādhanā: method of attaining or 'realizing' an ultimate spiritual objective.

sādhū: medicant, renunciant, ascetic. See also *Sant*.

saguṇa: possessing 'qualities', attributes; manifested, usually as an *avatār* (q.v.). Cf. *nirguṇa*.

sahaj: the condition of ultimate, inexpressible beatitude; the ultimate state of mystical union.

sākhī: (1) testimony, witness, evidence; (2) section of a *janam-sākhī* (q.v.); (3) *dohā*, couplet.

śakti: the energy or potency of a god (usually Śiva) expressed in his feminine counterpart. *Śakti* worship, performed by tantric sects (Hindu and Buddhist), commonly included magical *mantras* (q.v.) and symbols, sexual practices, and the consumption of flesh and alcohol. See also *Tantra*.

śālgrām (*śālagrāma*): ammonite found in the bed of the river Gaṇḍakī, prized as sacred stone on account of the spiral patterns in it which are regarded as representations of Viṣṇu.

sampradāya: sect, school, tradition.

saṅgat: a gathering, assembly, congregation.

Sant: In general usage *sant* serves as a synonym for *sādhū* (q.v.). The word has, however, two specific connotations: (1) a member of the Vārakarī sect of Maharashtra; (2) a member of the *Sant* tradition of Northern India, a loose fellowship of believers in a supreme, non-incarnated God. The usage in this study is normally the second of these two specific meanings. Within the tradition itself the term *sant* is used as a synonym for *sādh* or *sādhū* in the original sense of one who controls his senses (*indriya*) as opposed to the common modern and somewhat debased usage which designates an itinerant religious mendicant. In Kabīr's usage it denominates 'a perfected one', or 'one who has triumphed over death' (Ch. Vaudeville, *Kabīr Granthāvalī* (*Dohā*), pp. xiv–xv). The term is not used as a group or sectarian appellation until much later. It is to some extent an unsuitable designation, for it involves the risk of confusion with the Vārakarī sect. The alternative appellation *Nirguṇa Sampradāya*, or *Nirguṇa* tradition, avoids the risk of confusion in this respect, but the term *nirguṇa* ('attributeless', q.v.) is not a wholly accurate description of the Sants' understanding of the nature of God, except insofar as they explicitly rejected its antithesis, the *saguṇa* (q.v.) concept of divine *avatārs* (q.v.).

Satgurū: the True Gurū.

Sati Nām: the True Name.

satsaṅg: the fellowship of true believers, congregation.

savayyā: panegyric.

Siddh: Eighty-four exalted personages believed to have attained immortality through the practice of yoga and to be dwelling deep in the Himālayas. In the janam-sākhīs the term is frequently confused with *Nāth* (q.v.).

ślok: couplet or stanza.

sūbah: province.

sudī: the light half of a lunar month, the period of the waxing moon. Cf. *vadī*.

tahsīl: subdivision of a district.

takht: throne; seat of royal or spiritual authority.

Tantra: texts enunciating the forms of *śakti* worship (q.v.).

ṭhag: thug; strictly, a member of the cult of ritual murderers who strangled and robbed in the name of Kālī, but loosely used for any highwayman or violent robber.

ṭhāṇedār: officer in charge of a police station.

tilak: a sectarian or ornamental mark made upon the forehead.

tīrath: a sacred place, a place of pilgrimage.

tīrath-yātrā: a tour of important places of pilgrimage.

Trehaṇ: a khatrī sub-caste.

trimūrti: 'triple form', the Hindu triad comprising Brahmā, Viṣṇu, and Śiva, representing the creative, sustaining, and destructive principles respectively.

tulsī-mālā: a garland of basil leaves carried by Vaiṣṇavas.

turīā (*turīya*): the condition of ultimate bliss, a term derived from tantric Buddhism.

Udāsī: an order of ascetics who claim as their founder Sirī Chand, one of Gurū Nānak's two sons.

udāsī: lengthy journey, tour.
Uppal: a khatrī sub-caste.
ur: heart.

vadī: the dark half of a lunar month, the period of the waning moon. Cf. *sudī*.
Vāhigurū: 'Wonderful Lord', God.
Vaikunṭh, Baikunṭh: the paradise of Viṣṇu.
Vaisākh, Baisākh: the second month of the lunar year.
vār: an heroic ode of several stanzas; a song of praise; a dirge.
vāratak: prose.
visamād: immense awe; ecstasy engendered by awe.

Yam: the god of the dead.
yug: cosmic era.

BIOGRAPHICAL INDEX

Events and relationships recorded in the janam-sākhīs *and other sources*

DOCTRINAL INDEX

Concepts and Terminology

GENERAL INDEX

Abd al-Qādir Jīlānī, 126, 142.
Abdul Rahmān, 76, 84.
Abhai Pad Pothī, 19.
Abhoj, 105.
Achal (Baṭālā), 29, 35, 49, 64, 65, 75, 93, 120 n., 141.
Ādi Granth:
— compilation, 5, 14, 15, 149.
— Kartārpur MS., 17, 100–1.
— works of the Gurūs, 217.
— works of Gurū Nānak, 5, 6, 10, 11, 31 n., 53 n., 69, 118, 125, 133, 147, 148, *161–2*, 163, 230.
— works of Gurū Aṅgad, 142–3.
— works of the *bhagats*, 81.
— works of Kabīr, 156.
— works of Nāmdev, 154 n., 156 n.
— works of Ravidās, 154 n., 156 n.
— as source for the life of Gurū Nānak, *7–8*, 147, 227, 228.
— scriptural *Gurū*, 2, 163.
— metres, 8 n., 11 n., 135 n.
— containing dates of Gurūs' deaths, 100.
— containing *Hakīkat Rāh*, 115.
— commentaries, 167.
Ādināth (Śiva), 11 n.
Afghanistan, 91.
Ahmad Shāh Abdālī, 2, 23 n.
Āhōm kingdom, 111.
Āīn-i-Akbarī, 133.
Aitcheson, Sir Charles, 16.
Akbar, 138 n.
Alāuddīn Husain of Gaur, 111.
ʿAlī, Sheikh ʿAlī of Kābul, 4.
Allahābād, 56, 66, 74, 88, 89.
Almast, Udāsī *mahant*, 85.
Amar Dās, Gurū, 5, 14, 23 n., 28, 31 n., 32, 42 n., 63, 101 n., 156 n., 162, 163, 210.
Amritsar, 16, 120 n.
Anabhī Jain, 47, 76, 88.
Anand Acharya, Swami, 127, 129–30.
Aṅgad, Gurū, 49, 75, 94, 101 n., *142–3*.
— name bestowed, 50.
— appointed to succeed Gurū Nānak, 35, 36, 50, 64, 65, 76, 143, 146.
— in the *Bālā* tradition, 23, 24 n.
— works, 53 n., 63, 142–3, 202 n.
— reference to Gurū Nānak, 8.
Apabhraṃśa, 153.
Āratī, 51, 57.
Arjan, Gurū:
— compilation of *Ādi Granth*, 1, 2, 5, 81 n., 148, 149, 162.
— references to Gurū Nānak, 8.
— association with Bhāī Gurdās, 14, 29, 100.
— works, 17, 79, 80, 115 n., 141 n., 155 n., 156 n., 163.
— Mīṇā opposition, 18 n., 19, 20.
— date of death, 101.
— doctrine of God, 167, 198.
Āsā, legendary land, 31, 42, 76, 80.
Āsā dī Vār, 219.
Assam, 92, 110–12.
Ayodhyā, 56–57, 66, 74, 81, 84.

Bābar-vāṇī, 7, 87, 135, 137, 138, 163.
Bābur, 4.
— invasions, 3, 5 n.
— Gurū Nānak's descriptions of invasions, 7, 87, 135–8, 146, 162, 163.
— sack of Saidpur, 44, 62, 64, 65, 66, 69, 75, 93, 132–8, 144, 146.
— sack of Ṭillā, 62, 66, 75, 93, 134, 135.
— visit to Dīpālpur, 63.
— discourse with Gurū Nānak, 75, 82, 93, 134, 138.
— reference to Daulat Khān Lodī, 108, 109.
Bābur-nāma, 109.
Badrīnāth, 127.
Baghdad, 17, 18, 35, 64, 65, 67, 69, 75, 93, 125–32, 142 n.
Bahāuddīn, Pīr:
— discourse with Gurū Nānak, 47, 70, 76, 77, 82.
— dying message to Gurū Nānak, 50, 75, 141.
— Gurū Nānak's discourses with *potā* of Bahāuddīn, 31, 60, 65 n., 93, 123 n., 141–2.
Bahikiriā, 63.
Bahilo, Bhāī, 24 n.
Bahlūl Dānā, 127–31.
Bahlūl Lodī, 4, 108.
Baijnāth, 78.
Bairāg, sect of yogīs, 11 n.
Baisākhī festival, 55.
Bajaur, 133.
Bajīd, Sheikh, 39, 73, 88.
Bālā, Bhāī, 18, 23–24, 27, 123 n.
Bālā janam-sākhīs, 13, *21–24*, 25, 28, 69, 116.

PRINTED IN GREAT BRITAIN
AT THE UNIVERSITY PRESS, OXFORD
BY VIVIAN RIDLER
PRINTER TO THE UNIVERSITY